POINT ROBERTS

BACKSTORY

Tales, Trails and Trivia From

An American Exclave

Mark Swenson

ISBN 9780692931684.

LCCN 2017912119.

Printed by Village Books, Bellingham, Washington.

Cover design by Brendan Clark.

Front cover photo by Mark Swenson.

Back cover photo by John Carr.

CONTENTS

ACKNOWLEDGEMENTS

I'd like to recognize and thank the people who sat down with me to validate my understanding of the Point's history and add a human element to all the facts and dates from my research, including Kris Lomedico, Ruby White, Pauline De Haan, Sylvia Schonberg, Joan Thorstenson Linde and Stephen Hedlund. The staff members at the Point Roberts branch of the Whatcom County Library System, the Western Washington University Archives and Records Center, Whatcom Museum Archives, and the members of the Point Roberts Historical Society were all most helpful in sourcing reference materials. I appreciate their willingness to share their favorite stories to help make the story of Point Roberts come to life.

INTRODUCTION

It's easy if you just pop down to the Point to get gas or pick up a parcel to not see much and assume there's nothing at Point Roberts except a bunch of gas stations and parcel depots. The main drag up and down Tyee Drive from the border station to the commercial strip – less than a mile – is mostly trees. You see no houses. You see no parks. You see few stores. Read any travel or trivia blog where Point Roberts is mentioned or somebody has discovered it on the map for the first time, and the comments section invariably includes a post stating "there's nothing there." It's no wonder they come to that conclusion, for at first glance there indeed doesn't seem to be much.

How wrong, this thought! Yes, there isn't much *of* Point Roberts to begin with, less than five square miles in total. But that's not the same thing as there not being much *to* Point Roberts. This book was partially written to dispel that notion there's nothing at Point Roberts. In reality, Point Roberts has had one of the more interesting and full histories of any town in the Salish Sea, a story worth knowing. Hopefully this book will help visitors and outsiders know there is quite a bit to see, where to see it and why it's cool.

I wrote this book to tell the fascinating history of Point Roberts. Few towns of its size have played such a pivotal role in the history of the Salish Sea. It's been over a third of a century since the last comprehensive historical book about Point Roberts was written, Richard Clark's 1980 book *Point Roberts USA: A Canadian Enclave*. The local historical society's well-attended events demonstrate a strong interest in the Point's history. Much is documented about the canneries and Icelandic settlers. This book will dig into the backstory of those familiar events, and also update the Point's history with events and trends from more recent years and the present day.

Every Point Roberts school kid can tell you Point Roberts was named by George Vancouver for his friend Henry Roberts; they've even done holiday pageants about it. This book drills into the backstory of that friendship, describing where they met and what they did together. My mom taught me the history of the Salish Sea that way, always describing the bigger context of a particular event or roadside marker. When asked when a bridge or something was built, she told you not only the date but what was there before, why it was built, who favored and opposed it, how it impacted the native people, working people and the environment. I applied that interdisciplinary thinking at The Evergreen State College where I learned how to think critically about political economics and social change. As a result, this book provides a wider context for the history of Point Roberts, to better appreciate how what happened here was of such significance far beyond the shores of the Point. Knowing the backstory of Point Roberts' history helps one appreciate this tiny town all the more.

The British secretary of state for foreign affairs, Lord Claredon, who was busy negotiating the end of the Crimean War with Russia in 1856, found time to comment on little Point Roberts. He said it "cannot be of the slightest value to the United States," writing it off as an "inconvenient appendage." Inconvenient? Yes, no doubt about that. But inconvenience is not insignificance. Those who take time to explore Point Roberts will come to realize Point Roberts isn't only defined by the border. Its breathtaking vistas and significant location in the middle of the Salish Sea explain more of what makes Point Roberts unique than the fact it is merely yet another border town. Naturally, much is influenced by the border, but some of The Point's stories have nothing to do with the border, and a fair number are compelling simply by its position as a peninsula uniquely jutting into the middle of the Salish Sea. Once you're impressed with its history, Point Roberts then seals the deal with abundant wildlife and gorgeous views of the Salish Sea in all directions.

I was inspired to write this book due to my personal connections with Point Roberts. I am the fourth generation of my family to earn a living at Point Roberts. My great-grandfather, my grandparents and my aunt all fished for salmon at Point Roberts. Our family has had a 107-year presence in Whatcom County, dating back to when my great-grandfather, a Slavonian immigrant, arrived in 1910. In August 1985, I called my grandparents to tell them I would be coming through Bellingham for a few days on my way home from a road trip to Banff. They of course wanted to see me, but they made clear it was the height of sockeye season, and if we were going to get together, it would be working on grandpa's gillnetting boat at Point Roberts. After a long day of fishing on the reef we caught a shipload of salmon; grandpa knew right where to go since he had learned to fish for salmon in the 1920s right off the Point. In the 1930s my grandfather was the backup guy who brought supplies, mail and people to Point Roberts when the main ship, the *Tulip*, was out of service in dry dock. I have lived in Point Roberts for fifteen years and have lived over a third of my life in Whatcom County. Long before it was a public park, like many locals, I was chased out of Lily Point when it was private land. I choose to live here; border and exclave hassles are outweighed by the orcas, bald eagles, herons, beaches and boat traffic I see from my window. Point Roberts is my home and I'm proud to share it with you.

This book tells the story of Point Roberts in both a temporal and spatial way. It describes historical events and lists many historical dates, but connects them to a place in a spatial way using a fifteen-mile self-guided tour around the peninsula. Instead of a chronological timeline, the stories and history are told where they happened in the order they are encountered along this route. A tale about nineteenth century history might be quickly followed by a story from recent history. I like this interdisciplinary approach better that way: the exclave is best understood when the history, economy, natural environment, sociology and community challenges are all approached as a collective entity, not as a border town, not as an exclave, not as an Icelandic community, not as a peninsula or reef, but all of these things. Walking in the footsteps of history is a powerful experience, and this book hopes to connect the Point's rich history to a sense of place.

With this book you can explore it all, or imagine it from afar. Follow along its eight chapters to check out what Point Roberts has to offer.

 This symbol represents navigational instructions for the tour. Let's go.

MAPS

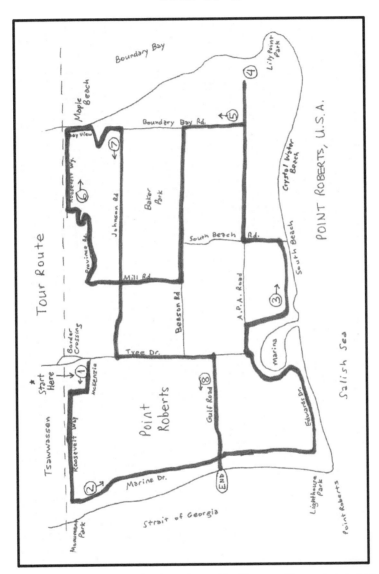

Figure 1: Tour route map of Point Roberts, Washington. The route is bold-faced. The numbers on the map refer to the chapters of this book. Start near the border crossing, at the corner of Tyee Drive and McKenzie Way.

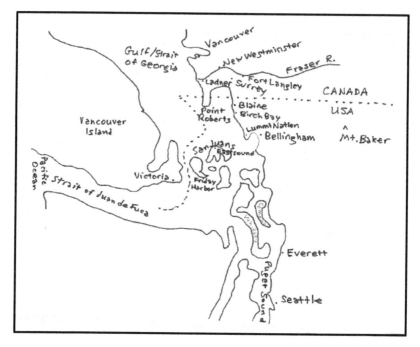

Figure 2: Regional map of the Salish Sea, showing key locations mentioned in this book. Point Roberts commands a central position in this ecosystem.

CHAPTER 1 • BORDERLINE MAD

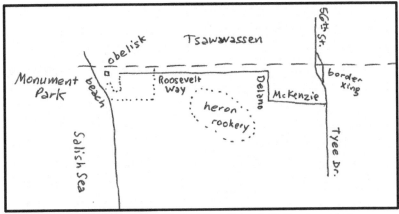

Figure 3: Map of Chapter One. Start at Tyee Drive & McKenzie, end at Monument Park. Distance: 1 mile (1.6km).

There is only one road into Point Roberts, so if you are arriving by land, you will need to clear United States Immigration and Customs to enter the town. The creation of the border across the peninsula in 1846 created the town of Point Roberts because it's surrounded by water on the three sides. Borders by their nature divide things, resulting in geographies next to one another with different and sometimes clashing laws and norms. This means things happen in border towns which just wouldn't happen in Anytown U.S.A. We'll explore how the border defines and makes Point Roberts unique.

As you drive toward the immigration booths, look for the meter-tall concrete border marker on the right curb by the stop sign. It marks the 49th parallel, which is the boundary between Canada and the United States. The Treaty of Washington on June 15, 1846 established this arbitrary line on the map as the boundary, creating

America's oddest town. The border defines Point Roberts; it would not exist in its current form without it. The border is a tangible presence in daily life for its thousand-plus inhabitants.

The marker stands next to roadside barriers blocking access to Roosevelt Way, the northernmost east-west street in Point Roberts, just inside the border. Traffic used to be able to drive along Roosevelt Way across these border lanes. As traffic volumes increased and later, post-9/11 security protocols were introduced, allowing cross-traffic in the zone between border stations became untenable and the street was closed near the border crossing.

BORDER CROSSING

This circle of latitude being the forty-ninth means Point Roberts is a bit closer to the North Pole than it is to the Equator. At the summer solstice, the sun is up for sixteen hours, twelve minutes, whilst at the winter solstice, it rises for only eight hours, fourteen minutes. For Point Roberts workers, it's dark going to work and coming home in the long winter. Less than one eighth of the Earth's landmass is north of this line, which crosses twelve countries: the United States, Canada, France, Germany, the Czech Republic, Austria, Slovakia, Ukraine, Russia, Kazakhstan, China and Mongolia. Paris, France, the largest city between the forty-eighth and forty-ninth parallels, lies nine miles south of the 49th parallel. Its Charles de Gaulle Airport lies precisely on the 49th parallel exactly even with Point Roberts. Interestingly, though this is the border between the United States and Canada for thousands of miles, over seventy-two per cent of Canada's population lives south of the 49th parallel, including the cities of Toronto, Montreal and Ottawa. Seven of Canada's ten provincial capitals are south of Point Roberts; only Edmonton, Regina and Winnipeg lie north. It's another story at the 49th parallel south of the equator. Almost no humans inhabit the lands south of the 49th parallel in the Southern Hemisphere.

Many are surprised to learn tiny Point Roberts is the third-busiest U.S.-Canadian border crossing on the 49th parallel, with around 1.5 million car crossings annually. Blaine's two border crossings, the Peace Arch (Douglas) crossing & the Washington State Highway 543/B.C. Highway 15 crossing are the only busier ones, which together serve nearly five million cars each year. Of the eleven U.S. states sharing a border with Canada, Washington has the third-largest volume of car crossings annually, after only New York and Michigan. One in seven cars entering Washington from Canada at a land crossing does so at Point Roberts.[1] Across the entire Canadian border, as of 2014 Point Roberts is the fifth-busiest city with a border crossing. Only Buffalo, Detroit, Port Huron and Blaine handle more traffic. Though perceived as quite rural, on average a truck crosses the border at Point Roberts every ten minutes.[2]

It was as late as 1919 that a border station was even built for land entry to Point Roberts, when a road was first constructed in Canada to reach the boundary line. Before this, it would take two days to travel over land from the nearest point on the United States mainland at Blaine, so the vast majority of traffic came by boat. Customs officers would make several visits each month to Point Roberts in the early years of the 20th century. With the road reaching Point Roberts in 1919, a border station was needed. A tarp was strung between trees making a tent-like shelter for the customs officers who visited two or three times per month.[3] Traffic volume grew from 8800 in 1923 to 37,000 in 1930.

The tent was probably a bit ripe by the time Point Roberts got its first proper border station building fifteen years later, in 1934, built for $165 in private funds (about $3000 today). The government leased it for seven years as a border station. Occupying the station's two rooms as the first Point Roberts-based customs official was Pa Davis, who served from 1936 to 1957. With a formal border station, crossing volume exploded to 224,000 in 1936. Even then,

Point Roberts was already the third-busiest border crossing west of Detroit.

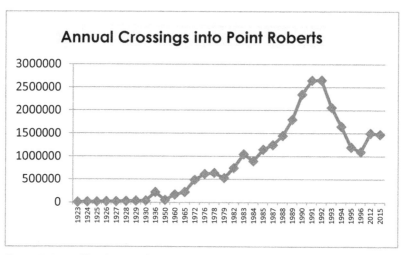

Figure 4: Annual border crossings into Point Roberts, Washington.

In 1942, residents protested the limited operating hours of the border crossing. The Canadian crossing for northbound traffic into Canada was open until midnight, but the U.S. crossing for southbound traffic into Point Roberts closed at 8 P.M. Anybody who arrived after closing time had to park their car at the border and walk to their home in Point Roberts, and then return the next day to clear customs and retrieve their vehicle.[4] The U.S. crossing wouldn't match Canada's midnight closing time until 1949. The 1950s saw "free flowing traffic the rest of the day," which essentially meant the border was unguarded after closing time.

The hours were expanded to sixteen hours a day in 1959, but with a huge increase in Canadians coming to Point Roberts with the opening of the Massey Tunnel, traffic volume demanded twenty-four hour service, which began in 1961.[5] The tunnel was a game changer: Vancouverites could get to Point Roberts in less than a half hour, eliminating the need to wait for a ferry to cross the Fraser

River, or to drive upriver to New Westminster to cross the river upstream. Growth exploded in the 1960s, and Point Roberts outgrew its little two-room border station. A new building was erected in 1968, with a dark wood national park ranger station look. By 1972, annual crossing volumes hit a half million for the first time and leveled off around 600,000 for the rest of the 1970s.

Tsawwassen widened 56th Street to two lanes going up the hill toward the boundary line in 1977, enabling the United States to expand its border facilities. A third booth for visitors coming in to Point Roberts was added in 1979, along with extra rooms added on to the main building and a new covered secondary inspection area. 1987 saw the addition of a lobby, more offices and a private search room. With three lanes coming into Point Roberts, the greater capacity saw increased volumes, with crossings hitting 750,000 in 1982 and surpassing the one million mark in 1983. Reagan administration budget cuts in April 1983 prompted calls to close the Point Roberts border crossing at night or even eliminate it altogether! It never came to that, but it reminded locals just how tenuous their practical existence was, vulnerable to fiscal policy and political whims about border policy made thousands of miles away.

The 1980s were a time of growth in Point Roberts and the border saw steady crossing volume increases, doubling from 1987 to 1991. Volumes hit 1.25 million in 1987, just shy of 1.5 million in 1988, 1.8 million in 1989 and 2.35 million in 1990. The peak years were 1991 and 1992, with 2.65 million crossings annually, including 10,000 cars in one day on August 24th. These years coincided with a strong Loonie and the introduction of the Goods and Services Tax in British Columbia. When 1993 clocked in only two million crossings, there had not in the previous nineteen years been two plus years of declining border traffic, and since 1974 there had only been five years where volumes declined at all.[6]

In February 1995, a proposal in Washington D.C. was raised to introduce a three dollar fee (which would be nearly five dollars in today's money) to cross the border.[7] This caused alarm in Point Roberts and other border towns. At first residents, though concerned, assumed it would quickly die in committee. They started freaking out when the bill advanced in Congress in February 1996.[8] There wasn't final resolution for over two years, all the while hanging over locals' heads as to the effects on their personal comings and goings (a daily commuter to the mainland would have to pay $120 per month), as well as the Point's volatile economy. Local residents breathed a sigh of relief when the fee proposal was finally rejected. The border station you're driving through today opened July 21, 1998.

Figure 5: Point Roberts Border Station in June 2002, just before the NEXUS lane was added. Wbaron at English Wikipedia [GFDL (http://www.gnu.org/copyleft/fdl.html) or CC BY-SA 3.0 (http://creativecommons.org/licenses/by-sa/3.0)], via Wikimedia Commons. https://commons.wikimedia.org/wiki/File%3APoint_Roberts_poe.jpg

The first Canadian border station was located at the bottom of the hill in Tsawwassen on the northwest corner of 56th Street and 12th Avenue where Tim Hortons stands today. This original border station was used from 1922 to 1935, but stood on the property until 1965. In 1935 the Canadians built a border station building at the actual border.[9] The Canadian border station through which you'll leave Point Roberts opened in April 1987.[10]

Today, there are about 1.5 million crossings at Point Roberts annually. On average that's over 4000 per day, nearly triple the Point's population. With all that traffic, both countries conveniently post border wait times for Point Roberts on their websites, though Point Roberts wait times are not listed on digital highway signage or Washington's mobile app.

In the late 1980s, traffic was growing rapidly, and the border was frequently jammed with long lineups. Tiny Point Roberts has few goods and services and residents must frequently cross the border just to get common errands done, things everybody else takes for granted; a day with multiple trips across the border isn't unheard of. More and more, frustration was being voiced at the inconvenience of unpredictable hour-long waits for these errands, sitting in the lineup behind Canadians coming over to fill up the tank with cheap gas. Calls began for a dedicated locals-only lane, outraging Canadians who wondered why they should be relegated to the long lines when they were spending money and generating local gas tax revenue.

In the mid-1980s there were two northbound lanes leading to the Canadian border station. Tensions spiked on July 12, 1985 when border traffic was especially heavy. The backup extended for 3000 feet down Tyee Drive prompting Canadian officials to open both lanes, leading cars to line up in both northbound lanes on Tyee Drive. As a result, emergency vehicles couldn't get through to evacuate an injured person, galvanizing calls for some sort of prioritization or separation of border traffic. Border officials and government representatives received petitions and letters calling for a dedicated lane for residents, which would be signified by a window sticker. A local survey indicated seventy-seven per cent of Point Roberts residents wanted some form of a locals-only lane. It became apparent early on there was not consensus on exactly who constituted a local. Would it only be for U.S. citizens or anybody who owned property in Point Roberts, a majority of whom were Canadian?

In April 1993, the community was shocked to learn the locals-only lane had been rejected. However, in an effort to address long wait times, the federal governments of the U.S. and Canada announced a dedicated lane was going to open, but instead of it being an exclusive lane for locals, it would be a "trusted traveler" lane. The idea was people who cross the border frequently could pay to enroll in the program, undergo a background check and receive an RFID card to use in a dedicated lane. Under this system, the *immigration* portion of the time it takes to clear the border is already done via the background check; no swiping of passports was required. It would also eliminate verbal questions about where the person lives and such. Only *customs* formalities – declaring what was purchased outside the country and what is being brought over the border – would need to be asked of each traveler. News of this was initially not taken well, as not everybody has can pass the required background check and in-person interview. Even a minor infraction from decades ago could result in a rejected application.

It was also around this time officials were concerned about Roosevelt Way crossing the border lanes. There was strong public sentiment to keep Roosevelt Way open, the only street in Point Roberts which spans the entire peninsula west to east. Residents were dismayed to learn the new trusted traveler lane would require Roosevelt Way to be closed, compounding the dissatisfaction with the trusted traveler proposal.[11] Locals floated an idea which would curve Roosevelt Way to the south so it crossed Tyee Drive south of the U.S. border station land, but it was not adopted.

The new trusted traveler program was called PACE, which stood for Peace Arch Crossing Entry because it was piloted at the Peace Arch (Douglas) border crossing at Blaine. One of the three southbound booths became the PACE lane entering Point Roberts, and in 1994 a third northbound lane on Tyee Drive leading into Tsawwassen was added for use as the trusted traveler lane. PACE was designed for what the locals wanted – shorter border wait times – though the means to the end was not what the town had envisaged. The goal of the trusted traveler approach was to get a high enough share of the vehicles crossing the border to be PACE participants, whose cars were processed in less than half the time due to their prescreening. Although locals were initially hesitant about it, PACE got off to a fast start and quickly became a popular and coveted status. It opened at the Peace Arch in June 1991[12] with an immediate backlog of 22,000 applications. Point Roberts had northbound and southbound PACE lanes open by September 1994.[13] At its peak in 2000, 28% of border traffic used the PACE lane.[14] Analysts predicted if they could get enrollment to 45% of cars, wait times would be reduced from an average in those years of sixty minutes to just fifteen. PACE would never reach anywhere close to that number; it ran for seven years before being abruptly shut down in September 2001.

After the terrorist attacks of September 11, 2001, the border was actually closed for several hours – locals could not enter or leave town by land – and then reopened with intense scrutiny of each person. Passports became required where a driver's license had been acceptable before, and a computer check of documents was run, each scan adding latency to the time required to clear each person arriving at the border. Two hour waits to enter Point Roberts were common, with the lineup of cars stretching to 12th Street in Tsawwassen, which is ironic because that was the location of the first Canadian border station years before one was established at the actual border. Television crews from CNN visited Point Roberts November 26, 2001 to report on the security measures and long lineups which were still occurring nearly three months after the terrorist attacks.[15]

With the experience of the PACE program under its belt, a new program emerged in the post-9/11 security state. With tougher criteria and improved computer databases, the NEXUS program, run by U.S. Customs and Border Protection and the Canadian Border Services Agency, was introduced in 2002. The NEXUS program is specific to crossing the border between the United States and Canada. NEXUS represents thirty per cent of traffic at the Peace Arch crossing at Blaine. Today NEXUS has over one million enrollees, and Point Roberts has the highest per-capita enrollment in NEXUS of any town in the United States.[16]

From the government's perspective, being deemed a trusted traveler is a privilege which is granted and can be taken away at the direction of a border official, for which there is no realistic appeals process. For many in Point Roberts, NEXUS feels like a necessity. A study looked at the "buffer" time cross-border travelers factor in to their trips, which is the amount of extra time they must leave their house for a transborder trip to make it to their destination on time. If a non-NEXUS user wants to avoid being late with 95% certainty, they must arrive at the crossing an average of fifty-five minutes early. A NEXUS user gets those same odds with only five minutes of buffer time.[17] If one non-NEXUS member crosses the border just once per week, enrolling in NEXUS means over fifty hours a year in time savings, over an entire work week of time freed up. A daily non-NEXUS crosser loses over five weeks of time per year leaving early to have enough time to endure border waits. The trade-off to live in a beautiful spot like Point Roberts and not have to factor in this buffer time is ten dollars a year, but also allowing the federal government to take photographs, fingerprints and iris scans, undergoing a thorough background check and being tracked in very large databases. It's a trade-off many North Americans don't have to consider as they go about their daily lives.

A tremendous number of people and volume of goods cross the border daily. Border traffic represents a huge portion of the economy, signals patterns in human migration, fosters cultural exchange and provides the lifeblood of communities situated along the boundary. All of this is true in Point Roberts and these important dynamics are watched closely. Indeed, researchers visit border communities to analyze border traffic and conduct surveys about reasons for transborder trips. Such a survey was made in Point Roberts in July 2013 when 1871 people were interviewed. The Whatcom Council of Governments and Western Washington University's Border Policy Research Institute had conducted two previous surveys at the four mainland border portals and the third survey in 2013 included Point Roberts for the first time. It found full-time American residents made up only eight per cent of crossings at Point Roberts. A commanding ninety per cent of travelers were from British Columbia. Another notable insight from the survey was the short duration of trips made to Point Roberts. A full forty-three per cent of trips into Point Roberts are for fifteen minutes or less and fifty-five per cent last less than an hour.[18] This means many B.C. visitors wait longer in the lineup to get into Point Roberts than the time they actually spend in it.

 After clearing immigration and customs at the international border crossing, continue ahead, south on Tyee Drive.

Many speak of a feeling one gets when entering Point Roberts. Take in your surroundings as you emerge from the border station and pull onto Tyee Drive. The scenery immediately changes from Tsawwassen's developed 56th Street, with sidewalks, commercial businesses and large suburban homes. These literally stop at the border. On the Point Roberts side, you are deposited onto a rural road. Despite being the main drag through Point Roberts, Tyee Drive has a thick canopy of firs and cedars towering over it; even on a sunny summer afternoon the road resembles a canyon through the forest. This isn't the only road in Point Roberts which provides this sensation; indeed you'll feel the forest canopy throughout this tour. It's a great metaphor for the difference created by the border. On the north side you're in a wealthy suburb of a great Pacific Rim metropolitan area, and on the south side of the line you're immediately transported to a rural American backwater. Some liken the feeling to being on an island, which isn't so far-fetched. It once was an island, early explorers mapped it as an island, and it's sometimes called a "lost San Juan island." Island or not, it's a psychological evolution; you feel you've entered a different space. Many describe how they start to relax just by entering this space. This intangible feeling, hard to describe, it an essential part of the Point Roberts experience. A thousand lucky locals get to live here, and despite border hassles, most love it. Originally named Boundary Line Road, Tyee (meaning "chief") Drive heads to the heart of Point Roberts, but we will take the first right.

 Take the first right onto McKenzie Way.

BORDER BLASTING

Immediately after turning from Tyee Drive onto McKenzie Way, notice the forested land on your left. It was very nearly clear cut in 2015 by a corporation from outside the community against the wishes of the vast majority of local residents. Border towns have problems which are not immediately evident to outsiders. Minor decisions can have a disproportionate impact on the community and its character, impacting the economy, free passage into and out of town, with environmental, health and safety ramifications. These impacts of the border on Point Roberts are not all nineteenth century history lessons. Modern everyday life in Point Roberts is affected by the border in countless ways, and one of those is in media. In the radio industry, a border blaster is a term for a radio or TV station whose broadcasting towers are in a different country than where the primary audience – and often the studio itself – is located. The term is often used to describe AM radio stations whose signal from towers in Mexico is directed into the United States, often with strong wattage exceeding what is allowed by the Federal Communications Commission in the United States. Some are blasted at 500,000 watts, ten times what is allowed in the United States. Powerful Mexican stations based in Tijuana are heard as far north as the San Francisco Bay area, overpowering stations near it on the radio dial in southern California. Houston, Texas station KDRC had to move its position on the dial because of interference from Mexican border blasters. Because Mexican radio station call letters start with X, these "X stations" have been a nuisance since World War II. In 1975, the rock band ZZ Top recorded a song on their fourth album *Fandango* named "Heard it on the X," which commemorated the famed disc jockey Wolfman Jack, who owned two major AM border blasters, XERB and XERF. George Lucas used border blaster XERB, a border blaster from Rosarito Beach near Tijuana, in *American Graffiti*'s soundtrack in 1973. XERF was a powerful radio station broadcasting from Via Acuña, Mexico, 150 miles west of San Antonio, Texas. Border blasters were also featured in other songs and movies. Wall of Voodoo sang about border blasters in their 1983 song "Mexican Radio" which reached number 18 on the charts in Canada. The band traces their influence for the song to listening to border blasters. It was featured on a season 9 *Seinfeld* episode, "Reversing the Peephole," sung by Kramer. ZZ Top's rise to fame was facilitated by border blasters who sent ZZ Top's signal across the US with their "lots of watts." The band with the big beards went on to play a live set of "Heard it on the X" on XERF.

In "Heard It on the X," ZZ Top sing, "We can all thank Doctor B who stepped across the line. With lots of watts he took control, the first one of its kind." The band refers to the pioneer of border blasting, Doctor John R. Brinkley. John Brinkley, the son of a poor Appalachian doctor who died when John was ten, wanted to be a doctor from an early age. Married at age 22, Brinkley didn't let the lack of a medical degree stop him from jumping into medicine. He and his bride travelled the country in 1907 pretending to be Quaker doctors, selling virility potions and assorted huckster remedies.[19]

Figure 6: Portrait of John Brinkley c1921. Source: Sydney Flower, The Goat-Gland Transplantation (Chicago: New Thought Book Department, 1921) http://www.archive.org/details/goatglandtranspl00flow

He enrolled in an unaccredited medical school, but reached a point where he couldn't make tuition, and they refused to honor his transcripts, prompting Brinkley to buy a medical degree from a diploma mill. With diploma in hand, he set up shop in 1913 in Greenville, South Carolina, placing advertisements promising to cure male virility, pre-dating Viagra by four score.[20] Brinkley's medicine was actually just a shot of colored water for twenty-five dollars, the equivalent of over $600 today. Sixty days later he skipped town with unpaid bills.

He moved around but eventually joined a medical practice, used his earnings to pay his tuition and get an unaccredited medical degree, allowing him to practice medicine in several states.[21] For a time he was married to two women at once, but eventually convinced one woman to divorce him to avoid bigamy charges. With one wife, he settled in Milford, Kansas in 1918. One day, a man came into his office complaining of sexual problems, for which Brinkley's solution was to transplant goat testicles into his ball sac.[22] For the enormous fee of $750, which is $10,000 in today's currency, Brinkley performed this operation on men all over town, some of whom died.[23] Brinkley merely placed the goat balls into the sac, did not connect them to any seminal fluid tubes. As a foreign object, the body merely absorbed the matter, and many men became infected.

Nonetheless, his first patient's wife somehow became pregnant and gave birth to a bouncing baby boy. Brinkley quickly promoted her pregnancy as a testimonial in his advertisements. The old huckster in Brinkley couldn't resist the opportunity to promote his goat balls transplantation surgery as a magical cure for dozens of ailments, even for excessive farting.[24] Of course, in the twenties, one couldn't say goat balls, so Brinkley referred to his miracle cure as goat *glands*, and Brinkley's term is used today in the film industry, referring to a silent film which has a vocal track added after the fact to make it palatable to audiences who had quickly rejected silent films upon the arrival of the talkies.[25] Written up in major newspapers, Brinkley hired an agent to help with promotions. As one of the first practitioners of marketing campaign management in the United States, and launched a direct mail campaign with the slogan, "the ram that am with every lamb."[26] The publicity kept patients streaming in the door, but also put him on the radar screen of the American Medical Association and one Morris Fishbein, a doctor who excelled at exposing medical fraud.[27]

The early twentieth century was a time of all kinds of fantastic medical claims, and the new era of the printed advertisement helped fuel all kinds of snake oil salesmen. As ridiculous as this seems in current times, Brinkley's claims were en vogue in his day; indeed, another doctor, Serge Verenoff, had gained notoriety transplanting monkey testicles into men. Brinkley noticed Verenoff would conduct live demonstrations of his surgery, giving Brinkley the idea of conducting his own public demo. In 1920, the Chicago press watched as Brinkley transplanted goat testicles into 34 men, including a judge, an alderman and the chancellor of the University of Chicago Law School.[28] The resulting press grew his stature to the point *Los Angeles Times* owner Harry Chandler offered Brinkley a challenge in 1922: perform a transplant on one of his editors. If successful, Chandler promised to make Brinkley the most famous surgeon in America, but a botched job would result in career-destroying negative publicity. The resulting operation on one nervous editor was deemed successful, and Brinkley welcomed new patients, including Hollywood celebrities, with all the new media coverage.[29] Whilst hobnobbing in Los Angeles, Brinkley got to see Chandler's radio station, KHJ. Brinkley immediately knew he had to have his own station to harness the power of radio for marketing his goat testicle transplantations.

In 1923, Brinkley established KFKB,[30] and spent hours on the radio every day linking his goat gland operations to improved sexual health, playing on patients' fears, desires and egos. Actual programming of music, storytelling and astrology were mere fillers around Brinkley's own advertorials. It worked; Brinkley's practice grew further, and with the proceeds he endeared himself to the Milford community, buying all manner of infrastructure for the town, including electricity, sewers, sidewalks, and a post office to help process all the mail he was receiving. He sponsored the local baseball team, called the Brinkley Goats.[31] One of his popular bits was called "Medical Question Box," one of the earliest radio advice call-in shows. Brinkley would diagnose the problem with one of his own remedies, which could be conveniently purchased at a participating pharmacy in the "Brinkley Pharmaceutical Association," who sold his potions at exorbitant prices, of course with kickbacks to Brinkley.[32]

After a series of exposés about medical diploma mills in the press, in July 1924 a jury in California indicted issuers of fake medical degrees and some of the doctors who bought them, Brinkley included. Kansas' governor refused to extradite Brinkley because of how much revenue he brought in for the state government.[33] Brinkley used his new radio platform to brag about his win over the medical establishment, and to get back at Fishbein, who was on the lecture circuit and publishing articles about

Brinkley, who he called a quack and responsible for the death of several patients. However, Fishbein was known only within the medical professional community, and with radio's help, Brinkley's goat balls surgery grew more popular than ever among the general public. Essentially an early pioneer of advertorials and infomercials, his profits grew to $14,000 per week. Brinkley was America's richest doctor.

With rising negative publicity and complaints about Brinkley in the newspapers, in 1930 the Kansas Medical Board revoked Brinkley's license citing evidence of 42 known deaths. The Board was harsh in its rebuke of Brinkley, stating he "has performed an organized charlatanism."[34] Brinkley wasn't going to fade off into the sunset quietly. He responded in true Brinkley grandeur by running for governor of Kansas, which would allow him to appoint cronies to the medical board and get his medical license back.[35] He ran on a populist platform, promising free textbooks, pensions, tax cuts and new water works. He used KFKB to champion the common people and small town pride. He reached out to immigrant communities, giving German and Swedish-speaking supporters air time to campaign on his behalf in their native tongue. Although he ran as a write-in candidate, when it came time to count the votes, Brinkley received over 210,000 votes, beating his opponent, Harry Hines Woodring, who would later to go on to become Franklin Roosevelt's secretary of war. However, over 30,000 ballots were disqualified by the Kansas Attorney General, who had prosecuted Brinkley during the medical board hearings. He had changed the election rules three days before the election, requiring write-in votes for Brinkley to be written only as J. R. Brinkley for the vote to count. The election went to Woodring by 319 votes, who admitted Brinkley would have won save for this late panic-induced rule change.[36]

Having taken his medical license, the establishment next went after his radio station. In late 1930, the Federal Radio Commission declined to renew his radio station license on the grounds the content was mostly advertising, which was illegal. The Medical Question Box program was called out specifically as "contrary to the public interest." He lost his appeals, and Brinkley v. FRC has gone down as a landmark case in broadcast law.[37] Without licenses to practice medicine in Kansas or broadcast radio, Brinkley sold KFKB and left Kansas, moving to Del Rio, Texas. A border town like Point Roberts, Del Rio offered Brinkley one important asset: its proximity to land outside the FRC's control.

That land was Mexico. The Mexican government was all too happy to issue Brinkley a license for a 50,000 watt radio station in Ciudad Acuña, just across the newly-built International Bridge over the Rio Grande from Del Rio.[38] This X-station, XER-AM, was the first border blaster and blast it did at 840AM, with twin 300-foot towers.[39] Thumbing his nose at Fishbein, who urgently tried to shut him down, in October 1931 Brinkley signed on to "the sunshine station between the nations." Even U.S. State Department's pressure on the Mexican government made no difference. XER's wattage, upped to 150,000 in 1932, would eventually swell to an amazing one million watts, the most powerful radio station on Earth by some measure. The high wattage of border blasters like XER causes strong interference in local communities near the radio towers. XER caused metal bedsprings to hum and car headlights to magically switch on.[40] Its signal was received through phone lines and even metal fencing and dental appliances.[41] Heard as far away as Canada, it was easily picked up back in Kansas, where Brinkley once again ran for governor in 1932, this time printed on the ballot as an independent. Using XER to campaign for office, he received even more votes than 1930, a sum over 244,000, but lost to Alf Landon, who would later go on to become the Republican candidate for President.[42]

To fill up the broadcast day with content, Brinkley sold air time for third party infomercials, and soon XER was airing ads for life insurance, religious propaganda (think autographed pictures of Jesus Christ), crystals and "genuine simulated" diamonds. A rich man by the mid-1930s, Brinkley lived in a mansion on acreage with a dozen Cadillacs and his own zoo stocked with Galapagos Islands wildlife.[43] Just as ZZ Top gained fame on X-stations forty years later, the music Brinkley aired on XER actually launched the music careers of many well-known musicians including Patsy Montana, Red Foley, Gene Autry, Jimmie Rodgers and the Carter Family, earning Del Rio the nickname Hillbilly Hollywood.[44]

As he had done in Kansas, in Del Rio Brinkley used XER to dish out medical advice to males suffering from an array of perceived sexual problems, using keen senses to sniff out low self-esteem. He wrote prescriptions for his pills, potions, shots and his goat balls transplantation surgeries. During his time in Del Rio, Brinkley introduced his thousand-dollar "prostate rejuvenation" surgery (he "rejuvenated" it by removing it), with post-surgery care requiring Brinkley pharmaceuticals. When one potion failed to help, purchasing another treatment would surely do the trick.[45]

For a time Brinkley commuted back and forth between Del Rio and Milford, Kansas, where protégés were staffing his old medical practice. During this time, Brinkley often phoned it in, literally. His voice on XER was actually him in Kansas where he was not allowed to broadcast or dispense medical advice. He was doing just that: dispensing medical advice over phone lines to a broadcast emanating from Mexico. This prompted the federal government in 1932 to pass the Brinkley Act, banning the practice in the United States. Undeterred, Brinkley pre-taped his content in Kansas and later played it back when he returned to Del Rio, starting this practice widely used in broadcasting today.

Alas, Brinkley's good thing would not survive the decade. It all came crashing down, starting in 1939, when Fishbein published a series of exposés on Brinkley titled *Modern Medical Charlatans*.

Brinkley sued for libel and damages but lost, the jury finding him to be "a charlatan and a quack."[46] The ruling spurred further lawsuits totaling millions of dollars. XER was shut down when radio bandwidths were allocated in a treaty between the United States and Mexican governments and the Internal Revenue Service was sniffing around on claims of tax fraud. Brinkley declared bankruptcy in 1941, which induced three heart attacks and an amputated leg. Awaiting trial on mail fraud investigations by the Post Office, Brinkley died of heart failure in May 1942. Although broke, Brinkley pioneered many techniques used today in advertising, marketing, election campaigning, lack-of-self-esteem exploitation and radio broadcasting standards.

As FM radio's popularity rose, in 1972 Mexico and the United States signed a communications treaty called "Agreement Concerning Frequency Modulation Broadcasting in the 87.5 to 108 MHz Band" to ensure border blasting could not happen on the FM radio dial, but no such agreement has ever been signed for AM radio stations, and Brinkley's invention of the practice of border blasting continues, officially tolerated, to this day.

The United States is not always a victim of border blasters; it has done much border blasting itself around the world, with the U.S. government's Radio Free Europe blasting into eastern Europe during the Cold War and anti-communist propaganda on Radio Martí beamed into Cuba to this very day. Mirroring Mexican border blasting into the United States, similarly United States has border blasters which beam into Canada. This does not include American stations broadcasting for an American audience which happen to be close to the border but whose signals are within allowed maximum strength and unintentionally bleed into a neighboring country due to proximity, as frequently happens in the Seattle, Detroit and Buffalo media markets. Border blasters differ by intent in that their towers are situated in one country but intentionally direct their signal into another.

There have been several border blasters from the United States into Canada. Stations in Burlington, Vermont and Plattsburgh, New York target the Montreal market. Stations in tiny Pembina, North Dakota, with a population half the size of Point Roberts, have beamed into Winnipeg for years. Like Point Roberts, Pembina was settled by Icelandic immigrants.

Border blasting is a good example of the issues facing border towns. One such border blaster near Point Roberts is radio station KRPI, marketed as Sher-E-Punjab at 1550 on the AM dial. Founded in 1984, it previously had Christian programming before switching to a South Asian programming format, broadcasting from Whatcom County into Metro Vancouver's large South Asian community centered in Surrey, British Columbia.

KRPI has studios in Richmond, British Columbia but its tall towers loom over Ferndale, Washington, southeast of Point Roberts on the Whatcom County mainland, airing foreign language music and talk to Surrey, British Columbia. Facing opposition in Ferndale due to interference from the radio towers, in May 2012 KRPI applied to the FCC to increase its power, clarify its intended audience, and quietly went through the motions to move its five 150-feet tall towers from Ferndale to Point Roberts and up the power to 50,000 watts, the highest power authorized to any AM radio station in the United States. It would be one of only 225 radio stations with that much wattage anywhere in the U.S. The site of these towers would have meant clear cutting the lovely forested canopy in the lot at the corner of Tyee Drive and McKenzie Way, marring the wooded entry which has forever been the iconic entrance to Point Roberts, plus many other negative consequences from the high wattage.

Initially getting clearance from the Whatcom County planning department, the Point Roberts community got wind of the deal at the eleventh hour after initial approvals had already been granted to

KRPI. Locals were horrified this had slipped past them in obscure legal notices and unnoticed public hearings. Citizens rallied to form a committee to stop the towers, hired lawyers, held fund raisers, and in a David versus Goliath fight, sued KRPI's owners. A three year legal battle ensued.

During the fight over the towers, many referred to KRPI as a pirate radio station, but this is inaccurate. Pirate radio stations broadcast illegally, akin to the underground radio station in the 1990 movie *Pump Up the Volume*, where Christian Slater plays a high school student who jury rigs a radio station in his basement to broadcast teen angst to his suburban schoolmates. Many pirate radio stations originate offshore. Radio Hauraki was a famous pirate radio station in New Zealand. In the 1960s, New Zealand's government held a monopoly on radio broadcasting, prompting Radio Hauraki set up its transmitters on a ship three miles offshore just outside territorial waters from 1966 to 1970, much to the irritation of New Zealand authorities. It still broadcasts today, though now on shore and legally. In contrast, border blasters are licensed by the government from where the signal originates; they just send excessively-powered signals or provocative content into another territory, or get licensed in a more permissive country than the country into which they want to operate as was the case in Point Roberts.

Despite the fact their studios and advertising are in Metro Vancouver, KRPI claimed their real intended audience was in Whatcom County, and thus the Point Roberts towers were serving local customers. This was exposed as disingenuous when a KRPI PowerPoint presentation was discovered which clearly stated the Point Roberts site was selected due to its proximity to the Canadian border and the market of over 200,000 South Asian listeners in Metro Vancouver. Ironically, the 3,000 Sikhs who do live in Whatcom County, mostly near Lynden, who KRPI claimed was their intended audience, would not have been able to hear very much on KRPI had the station moved to Point Roberts, as the signal would have been pointed north, away from mainland Whatcom County.

KRPI was silent on another important factor in the case, the harmful effects of electromagnetic radiation from the towers. Opponents pointed out the towers would violate the standards used by KRPI's own engineers, which require a tower farm site to be a safe distance from populated areas. The engineers' own standard is one-volt/meter. Following this standard, by comparison Bellingham radio station KGMI has a population of 410 people within the one-volt/meter range. Point Roberts and Tsawwassen would have had 6,189 people within that range.

In October 2014, a Whatcom County hearing examiner ruled the Whatcom County planning department erred in issuing the radio tower permits because they were in violation of structure height ordinances. The height limit in Point Roberts is twenty-five feet, with variances allowed to forty-five feet. The proposed radio towers were three times higher than even the higher variance limit. Thus, the conditional use permit BBC Broadcasting had been granted was revoked.

KRPI hired top legal teams from Washington D.C. and Seattle and appealed to Skagit County Superior Court. The appeal was heard in October 2015. In its effort to boost its corporate profits at the expense of the community's wishes, KRPI used several arguments. They tried to say radio towers under Whatcom County law were "essential public facilities," but the judge ruled radio towers are not essential under state law, and are only deemed essential under county law with a conditional use permit, which had been denied. They then tried claiming Point Roberts was the last site available in Whatcom County for the towers, but this was easily disproven by pointing to over 300,000 acres in Whatcom County where zoning would allow tall towers.

The community won its case in that the towers would far exceed Point Roberts' twenty-five foot height restriction. KRPI countered on appeal that the FCC had given them a waiver for the height restriction, but an Appellate court sided with Point Roberts and said counties have the right to decide where oversized structures can be located. By the skin of their teeth the community won the battle, preventing the towers from marring the entrance to their community, and, perhaps mindful of what Brinkley started with border blasting in Del Rio, stopping the blanketing the peninsula, including Tsawwassen's twenty thousand-plus inhabitants, from harmful interference and health concerns of powerful and unwanted radio signals in their community. KRPI's actions are a good example of an outsider's exploitation of the border and lack of empathy for the community's opposition to its presence. It seems the apple didn't fall far from Brinkley's tree.

 Continue west to the end of McKenzie Way. The street curves to the right and ends at Roosevelt Way, onto which you turn left.

You're on one of the most unique streets in North America. A two-lane road carries cars east and west on the northern edge of Point Roberts. As you drive down Roosevelt Way, you'll spot shiny metal border markers every few hundred meters across the ditch on the right hand side of the street. These current markers were placed in May 2002.[47] They mark the border with Canada. The left hand side of Roosevelt Way is in the United States and the houses on the right hand side are in Canada. No government fencing separates the two nations; most homeowners have fencing around their lot, but not all do. Several Canadian homes have gardens, horseshoe pits and patio chairs placed right up to the line with the United States, in the narrow piece of land between the border line and the ditch. Canadian homeowners must maintain a ten foot vista north of the boundary line. One unfortunate homeowner who had built a deck into the ten foot zone was ordered to remove it in October 1986.[48] As you go along Roosevelt Way, you will pass on the U.S. side the

Point's water reservoir, built in 1989. There will be much more about water in Point Roberts in chapter 7. The land across the street from the reservoir on the Canadian side was a turkey farm before World War II.

Figure 7: Roosevelt Way, looking east from Monument Park. The houses are in Canada, the road in the U.S. Photo by Mark Swenson.

 At the end of Roosevelt Way, pull into Monument County Park.

MONUMENT PARK

Being roughly rectangular in shape, one of Point Roberts' best features is all four of its corners are public parks. Monument Park occupies the northwestern corner of Point Roberts. It's the least-visited of the four corner parks; often you will have this entire park to yourself. And it's a great park, with the most significant historical monument on the Point, clifftop views of the Strait of Georgia, a trail down a forested ravine, and a quiet beach with ribbons of sand bars at low tide.

The eight-and-a-quarter acre Monument Park was opened in 1964. The park has no fees, but no facilities either, other than parking for a few cars. The park offers a grand view of the Strait of

Georgia from high atop a 135 foot cliff. Built in 2009, a 950-foot path winds through the woods and then down a switchback trail to the lovely pebble beach. This beach is the very corner of the United States. The iconic thing to do on this beach is to stand in that corner. Just offshore there is a large navigational border marker made of several pilings and a large letter B on yellow diamond-shape signs. Look further offshore, just to the left of the port facility, and you'll spot two more square concrete navigational border markers. Position yourself so you're lined up with these markers, the waves lapping at your toes. You are standing on the north-northwesternmost piece of land in the lower 48 states. If possible, time your visit to coincide with a low tide, when the receding waters reveal extensive sand bars and tidepools. In summer it's common to see a person sunning themself on the beach just a few meters north from you, but in a different country. Here there is no signage, fence or border wall – you'd never know there was an international boundary here – just a secluded beach much as it has looked for centuries.

The west-facing view across the Salish Sea makes afternoons warm and the sunsets beautiful. All the land you see on the other side of the Strait of Georgia is Canada. The island directly even on the other side is Galiano Island, and then moving south, to your left, is Mayne and then Saturna Islands. The taller mountains behind these islands are on Vancouver Island. Turning your gaze to your right, the Strait of Georgia stretches north between Vancouver Island and the mainland of British Columbia toward Alaska. Alaska is the destination of cruise ships and the Bellingham-to-Alaska ferry, which began service in October 1989.[49] These large ships are brilliantly illuminated at night as they glide past the Point.

ROBERTS BANK

The border makes Point Roberts an isolated corner of the United States, but its central location in the Salish Sea makes it a very busy corner in Canada. Canada is above the 49th parallel for thousands of miles from the Great Lakes all the way out to the Salish Sea, where for the first time you can turn left and access Canadian lands below the 49th parallel on the West Coast. To get from the British Columbia's Lower Mainland to the provincial capital of Victoria on Vancouver Island, you go by Point Roberts.

Whilst Point Roberts can feel like a lonely and remote outpost in an isolated corner of the United States, it is places like Monument Park which shake you back to the reality that if you step just a couple meters north you are instantly in the third largest metropolitan area in Canada, home to 2.4 million people and all the bustling services and infrastructure they require in this very busy metropolis. It is ironic Point Roberts is so remote when it's so close to such huge infrastructure. Indeed, 15,000 people per day – 5.5 million people annually – pass Point Roberts by sea and air. Between the ferries, cruise ships, freighters, fishing crews, pleasure craft by sea, and being directly under the main approach for commercial jet traffic coming into and out of Vancouver International Airport, Canada's third-largest for take-offs and landings, as well as Boundary Bay Airport just five miles north of Point Roberts, millions of people are within close range of Point Roberts each year without even knowing it.

At low tide, the bank becomes partially exposed in a web of sand bars, which are fun to explore. The native Coast Salish people knew where navigable channels through the tideflats allowed their canoes to get all the way up to the beach, which is reflected in their name for Roberts Bank, either sha sum kum, meaning "place where canoes bump in shallow water," or Shesumkun, meaning "a navigable trough through the bank allowing for canoe passage." Either way, Roberts Bank is a bit easier for most of us to pronounce.

Looming in the distance to the northwest from the view at Monument Park, the Canadian government has built major port infrastructural projects which are current forms of a centuries-long tradition of leveraging the Roberts peninsula's unique location in the Salish Sea. Roberts Bank is found on the west coast of the Roberts peninsula. A bank is a shelf of shallow water extending out from the land which then dramatically falls off to very deep water. This bank starts at the southwest tip of Point Roberts, where the water is over 250 feet deep right off the beach, and gradually extends away from the beach out toward and past these port facilities, which had to be built on the edge of the bank, and connected to land by causeways. The water is less than fifty feet deep where these facilities are built on the edge of the bank where the land gives way to water two hundred feet deep. They were also placed on the bank as close to the international boundary as possible, reaching out into the Salish Sea right up to the line with mere meters to spare.

The large coal terminal visible just three miles off shore from the park is the Roberts Bank Superport. The Superport is a major facility of Port Metro Vancouver, Vancouver's port authority. It's a big operation overall, owning over twenty facilities across Metro Vancouver which generate over ten billion dollars annually to Vancouver's economy. It's the largest port in Canada, the fourth-largest in North America and the fifth-largest in the western Hemisphere. Construction of the Superport started in 1968, and the facility opened in 1970. Further expansions in 1983 enlarged the original twenty hectare (49 acre) port to 113 hectares, and 2010 saw another significant expansion. The portion of the facility for container ships is called Deltaport and was added in 1997. Local residents keep track of all the shipping visible from Point Roberts by visiting websites like marinetraffic.com which display data about ships seen offshore, including the ship's name, country of registry, destination, route, speed, photo, recent ports of call and current status. Ferries and their destination can be identified at bcferries.ca.

Calls for fossil fuels to remain in the ground to stop climate change have an impact on the Superport, because the huge facility processes vast amounts of coal. On the standard western approach into Vancouver International Airport, one can get a good aerial view of the facility from the left-hand window seats on commercial airplanes and only then is it apparent how huge the port is. A road and rail causeway connects the port to the mainland, allowing long snakes of trains to deliver coal from the Canadian interior; six hundred individual cars in five trains travel onto Roberts Bank each day to unload coal. Huge mountains of coal are piled up, ready to be loaded onto ships. It is the single busiest coal export terminal in all of North America, with thirty million tons of coal being moved around each year and one million tons piled up at any one time.[50] All this makes residents of Point Roberts uneasy, fearing pollution of the Salish Sea waters teeming with life, the struggling fisheries and the beloved beaches ringing the Point. The sandy bottom of the shallow waters teem with herring, smelt, skates, flounder, surfperch and sardines. Seriously endangered, orcas frequently play nearby. Enormous sturgeons are occasionally seen coming out of the Fraser River and have been known to beach themselves on the causeway. And the worry is not without reason; Roberts Bank suffered its first marine accident in December 2012, when a Japanese bulk carrier crashed into the structure, wrecking one hundred meters of causeway and a coal conveyor. Thirty tons of coal fell into the Salish Sea, threatening the fragile ecosystem.

Figure 8: Roberts Bank Superport's piles of coal are seen at sunset from Point Roberts. Photo by John Carr.

The impact of living next to the Roberts Bank Superport extends beyond the threat of a coal spill into the water. A thin layer of black coal dust coats everything in the exclave. Stuff which should be white – homes, cars, boats, patio furniture – take on a drab grey color. Indeed, a 2001 study found the Superport emits 715 metric tons of coal dust every year, with a University of British Columbia study determined coal dust emissions doubled from 1977 to 1999. Point Roberts is directly in the main wind direction of these massive piles of coal, but lacks a car wash facility.[51] Owners of sleek white boats in the Point Roberts marina are constantly washing off the grey layer of coal dust, especially during the dry summer months. Some even apply a Teflon coating to make cleaning off the coal dust easier. White patio furniture similarly gets coated with grey grime from the Superport. The west sides of homes on Point Roberts are typically grey and need to be pressure washed to eliminate the coal film. The Superport started hosing down the coal piles in the 1980s and has expanded its dust abatement program over the years, but admits it's impossible to eliminate coal dust completely. Today it spends $1.5 million each year to wet down the coal. Five 125-foot high water towers rise above the coal piles. Coal piles are misted down with thirty-eight spray rings, and seventy-nine rain guns sprinkle water onto the coal piles.[52] The port has placed coal dust monitoring stations in Point Roberts and Delta, B.C.[53] Don Miller, senior officer for regulation and enforcement of air quality for Metro Vancouver, said residents assume the dust coating their property is from coal, but studies show it largely consists of road dust, diesel exhaust and only a small amount of coal.[54] Concerns about coal are increasingly in the headlines on both sides of the border; a proposal to construct a coal export facility on the U.S. mainland across from Point Roberts near Cherry Point was recently rejected over impacts it would have on the Coast Salish people's treaty-protected fishing rights.

In front of the Superport from the Monument Park vantage point is the B.C. Ferries Tsawwassen terminal, built on an island next to the Superport, connected to the mainland by a separate causeway. This ferry terminal, built in 1959, serves the Canadian Gulf Islands you see in the distance, and two cities on Vancouver Island,

Nanaimo to the north and its busiest destination, Swartz Bay, the main ferry gateway to the provincial capital at Victoria at the southern tip of Vancouver Island. Ferry service between Metro Vancouver and Vancouver Island has been going as far back as the earliest white settlers. Originally Hudson's Bay Company (HBC) offered passenger and freight service. In 1901, Canadian Pacific Railway assumed responsibility for ferry service, establishing sailings between downtown Vancouver and downtown Victoria. This five hour ordeal was in place as late as the late 1950s, when it was recognized a shorter and more reliable service was needed. In July 1958 British Columbia Premier W. A. C. Bennett created the British Columbia Ferry Authority, the government-owned forerunner of today's privatized B.C. Ferries. The next task was to find a location for a major mainland ferry terminal. Experts wanted to choose Steveston, just north of Roberts Bank across the Fraser River from Ladner. Others favored White Rock as the terminal location. Tsawwassen was deemed a poor choice because, sticking out so far into the Salish Sea to get to the edge of the bank subjected the ferries to rough seas in winter. But the transportation minister Phil Gaglardi chose Tsawwassen to break the tie, and construction began in early 1959 by filling in the island first with 2.3 million cubic meters (3 million cubic yards) of boulders, rocks and gravel fill, and then building the causeway back toward the mainland. In 1959, Tsawwassen was a sleepy beach town along Boundary Bay, the Massey tunnel hadn't opened yet and the ferry terminal had no connection to any existing mainland infrastructure, so Highway 17 had to be built as well, an eleven kilometer highway connecting the ferry terminal to Highway 99 (along the route of today's Highway 17A). The choice of location may have been controversial, but over the years the terminal has thrived and expanded to multiple ferry berths.

The ferries complicate the pronunciation of Tsawwassen. Famous among British Columbians for having two pronunciations of its name, Tsawwassen is pronounced with a silent T among older generations (including my grandparents), on B.C. Ferry announcements and, according to some, by the Tsawwassen First Nation people. These days, most local residents pronounce the T and make the first S silent. In recent times, the cool kids have taken to calling it "T-town," specifically emphasizing the T.

HERON ROOKERY

When a ferry comes in to the Tsawwassen ferry terminal, a long line of cars disembark and make their way along the Highway 17 causeway. Just as the causeway reaches the mainland, the tall Tsawwassen cliffs – English Bluff – loom on the right. Perched in the tree tops are four hundred great blue heron nests, the largest great blue heron rookery, or nesting colony, in all of the Salish Sea, bigger than any other in all of the British Columbia Lower Mainland or the Pacific Northwest. If the passers-by have their car windows open, they can hear the rookery before they can see it; the collective sound of all the heron chicks crying day and night for food is surprisingly loud as it reverberates across Roberts Bank. Found only in the New World, great blue herons stand between three and four-and-a-half feet tall. Soaring overhead drone-like, they make a loud squawking noise as they hunt for fish at this prime location and can be seen in large numbers prowling in the eelgrassy tidelands. The forest canopy of the entire hillside is painted grey with guano. Perched in the trees are large nests where four eggs are hatched each spring.

This rookery has been the site of important research on heron behavior. Occupying an enormous nest higher than all the others on English Bluff is a pair of bald eagles. This is striking because bald eagles are public enemy number one to the great blue heron, yet these herons choose to live here, right below their chief predator. The herons and eagles have formed a symbiotic relationship. This pair of eagles keeps other eagles away – the researchers have determined their radius of patrol is 250 meters – which makes the area safer for the herons. The two eagles who guard the rookery do

Figure 9: Great Blue Heron, one of the symbolic animals of Point Roberts. Photo by Gary Kramer, U.S. Fish & Wildlife Service.

take the occasional heron as a snack, especially the chicks but sometimes an adult. However, since there is safety in numbers, a little predation is tolerated in exchange for the protection of the overall rookery. The research conducted here on Roberts peninsula revealed in 2013 for the first time seven in ten herons choose to nest near a bald eagle nest.[55]

The herons showed up at this spot in Tsawwassen one day in 2004 and began building nests. A week earlier, all of these hundreds of herons lived in Point Roberts. This rookery had their nests in alder and cottonwood trees just off McKenzie Way in Point Roberts, near the reservoir you passed on Roosevelt Way, for nearly a quarter century. The herons had originally lived on English Bluff before that, but as Tsawwassen grew in the 1970s and development encroached on their nesting area, they moved to Point Roberts and set up between 350 and 400 nests in a relatively tiny four acre spot. They thrived in the 1970s and 1980s at this fifty by three hundred meter spot, and Point Roberts became famous for being the home to this largest-in-the-region heron rookery, home to a quarter of all herons living on the Salish Sea.[56] The April-through-August nesting season meant the northwest corner of Point Roberts was alive with the cacophony of these magnificent birds. One reason they did so well was during this time bald eagles had been devastated by DDT, pushed to the brink of extinction. DDT was banned in the United States and Canada in 1972, and by the millennium their numbers had rebounded, especially in Point Roberts with its enormous rookery, a buffet for juvenile bald eagles looking for an easy meal. Now it's the herons which are on Canada's Species At Risk list.

As if the bald eagles weren't enough, the herons' nests in Point Roberts were threatened by development after water became easier to get in the late 1980s. Calls grew for protecting their nesting habitat. Heron benefit concerts were held as early as November 1988, just a few months after Point Roberts secured a water supply, which unleashed development. After some tree cutting near the rookery in 1990, a ban on development in a radius around the site was enacted, and renewed in 1993.[57] In 1995, three parcels of land off McKenzie Road were purchased by private individuals to preserve land for their nests and the Washington Department of Fish and Wildlife bought more acreage on the perimeter of the colony. Despite these conservation efforts, some trees with nests were cut down during construction of the adjacent golf course in 2001. Famous for being skittish and easily disturbed, the rookery struggled in 2002 and 2003, and in the span of mere days in June 2004, the herons had had enough, and hundreds of pairs of heron left, leaving nests, eggs and even chicks behind. Literally no nests were occupied by 2005. When five years had gone by with no occupation of the nesting colony, development of the area was permitted.

TREATY OF WASHINGTON

Monument Park's most notable feature is its twenty-foot obelisk, the westernmost point on the U.S.-Canadian border. This is officially known as Monument Number One on the 49th parallel. Of the 8,000 pillars which mark the entire U.S.-Canada border, this is by far the largest, averaging three feet in width. For years it was dwarfed by an ugly steel frame navigational beacon perched on the cliff edge, but today the obelisk stands alone in all its glory.

It's remarkable the actual physical border markers on the ground were placed from west to east at a time when it wasn't easy to get to the west coast. In April 1861 the heads of the American and British boundary commission agreed a stone obelisk should be built in Point Roberts to mark the western terminus of the U.S.-Canada boundary, proposing, "While a larger mark can give no greater significance to the spot on which it stands unless there were a special agreement to that effect, as the coast of Point Roberts… is undoubtedly the most prominent point it is quite consistent that the most prominent beacon should be placed upon it."[58] The British Commissioner, John Hawkins, lobbied for the obelisk in a letter to the British foreign secretary in October 1861. He explained the isolation of Point Roberts caused him to scale back the grandeur of the monument, citing in the letter its twenty foot height and £1500 budget, "of comparatively small size for the purpose intended, having been so designed solely on the ground of economy," and in a

Figure 10: Boundary Marker #1 obelisk at Monument Park. Photo: Mark Swenson

statement current residents of Point Roberts will appreciate, Hawkins added, "a sum probably representing twice to three times that for which it might be performed in most other parts of the world."[59]

With both countries agreeing to split the cost, the monument was made in New Westminster, British Columbia by E. Brown. Its forty tons are made of solid cut granite, each block weighing between one and two-and-a-half tons. The shaft of the obelisk is made of stone imported from Scotland and floated around Cape Horn. In 1862, the monument's blocks were transported by a British gunboat to the beach below the park, where they were hauled up the cliff using Coast Salish labor on specially-built tracks up the hillside. At one point when it was part way up the bluff it fell back down to the beach. Each side of the obelisk has inscriptions cut into the granite. The north face lists Capt. J. C. Prevost, R.N., Capt. G. H. Richards, R.N., Lt.-Col. J. S. Hawkins, R.E. The east face displays Lat. 49° 0' 0", Long. 123° 3' 53", Erected 1861. The south face reads Archibald Campbell, U.S. Commssr. The west face is inscribed Treaty of Washington, June 15, 1846.

The obelisk contains some secrets. The stonemasons put a coin under each corner and the builders inscribed their names on the inside of the obelisk. It is also a tomb. A British soldier died during the project just as the base was installed, and his body was buried at the base of the monument.

The obelisk has its detractors. Critics complain the obelisk makes no mention of the fact it denotes a boundary, and doesn't even name either country, yet the organizers made sure their names made it onto the monument. Though not the only example of commissioners being named on monuments, it is uncommon and thus has earned the derision of "monumental egotism."[60]

Today the obelisk is in the shadow of a multi-million dollar home built right up to the last Canadian centimeter. In fact, ten feet of Canadian land on the north side of the obelisk was donated by the homeowner in 1958.[61] Had this donation not occurred, the lot would have gone right up to the monument, preventing the ability to walk around it.

The story of how the international boundary at Point Roberts was defined begins with the signing of the Treaty of 1818 between the United States and Britain. The U.S. got quite a bit in that treaty, including fishing rights off Newfoundland and Labrador, a major land concession by Britain which transferred the Red River Basin (large portions of Minnesota and North Dakota including the city of Fargo) to the United States. The treaty set the border at the 49th parallel from the Lake of the Woods between Manitoba and Minnesota west to the Rockies. The Northwest Angle, another exclave like Point Roberts, was created by this treaty. Beyond the Rockies, the treaty called for joint occupation with Britain. The Americans called the area encompassing Oregon, Washington and mainland British Columbia "Oregon Country," whilst the British called it "Columbia District." From 1818 to the mid-1840s, to the west of the Rockies there was no border; it was a veritable no-man's land shared between the United States and Britain's Hudson Bay Company. Both parties wanted the area, but there were practically no settlers yet, only a few trappers, so there did not seem to be a rush to draw lines on the map. How folks then could not see that having inhabitants of two different countries comingling in the same geographic area would be a problem sorting them back out later after they had settled, cleared the land and built settlements is hard to understand now. However, as time wore on and more homesteaders arrived, joint occupation became less tolerable for both parties.

Initially, settlement got off to a slow start. Earlier expeditions by the British and Spanish didn't find the coveted fur mammals they were expecting, so there seemed to be no rush to settle the Salish Sea after 1792. European settlement of the Pacific Northwest began in the form of trading forts. Astoria, Oregon was the first American-owned settlement west of the Rockies, being established in 1811 as Fort Astoria by the John Jacob Astor's Pacific Fur Company, though American ownership would be short-lived. In 1813, Pacific Fur was acquired by a British corporation, North West Company, making Astoria the first British port on the Pacific coast of the Americas. Hudson's Bay Company bought out North West Company in 1821. Fort Astoria would be British for the next quarter-century. Hudson's Bay Company established Fort Vancouver along the Columbia River (site of present-day Vancouver, Washington), one hundred miles upriver from Astoria in 1824, firmly establishing British presence far south of where we think of Canada today. British control was felt closer to Point Roberts with the opening of Fort Langley along the Fraser River in 1827 and Fort Victoria in 1843. The first fort directly on the U.S. side of the Salish Sea was Hudson's Bay Company's Fort Nisqually, at present-day DuPont, Washington near Olympia. Its 1832 opening was prompted by a murder, causing the company to realize they needed a fort between Forts Vancouver and Langley.

The histories of Fort Langley and Point Roberts are interwoven. Located forty miles northeast of the Point, Fort Langley was the closest Hudson's Bay fort to Point Roberts and before canneries opened in the 1890s was a place of trading for the Coast Salish people who lived at and around Point Roberts. During the Fraser River gold rush, Point Roberts was a stopover location for gold miners on their way to Fort Langley. Hudson's Bay officials would go past Point Roberts – and even stop there – on their way between Forts Langley and Victoria. Point Roberts also features frequently in Fort Langley archives.

Like a chain of Howard Johnsons or Starbucks outlets, the Hudson's Bay Company was the first brand-name corporate chain store in North America, with five convenient locations between the Columbia and the Fraser Rivers by the time the border was established, only one of them located north of the 49th parallel. The Americans didn't have much settlement or presence in the area going into the 1846 boundary treaty negotiations. Hudson's Bay Company had the Salish Sea and Columbia River sewn up, and just 360 miles south of Astoria, the southern boundary of Oregon Territory, was not a border with the American state of California in those years, but in fact was the northern border of Mexico until 1848, two years after Point Roberts was created.

James McMillan held the post of Chief Trader for Hudson's Bay from its founding in 1827. He had explored and surveyed the lower Fraser River, including poking around at Point Roberts, as he explored a site for a new fort. Fort Langley was ultimately built in the summer of 1827. A bit of excitement was created on Christmas Eve 1827 by his first surprise audit. The company sent Alexander Mackenzie, Fort Vancouver's Chief Trader, to inspect Fort Langley. Mackenzie was ready for some holiday eggnog – the stiff kind – when he arrived at Fort Langley. He described a harrowing trip just past Point Roberts. After having been trapped in ice flows in the mouth of the Fraser River and harassed by the native Musqueam, Mackenzie was able to get a message to a sympathetic Kwantlen man who rushed it to Fort Langley. McMillan was able to send an armed rescue squad to fetch Mackenzie, who arrived to a smug McMillan, counting the Brownie points he had accumulated for the effort. He ushered Mackenzie into the dining room for a holiday feast. Fort Langley had just received a shipment of liquor and it was put to immediate use.

Mackenzie duly impressed, it was agreed McMillan should return with Mackenzie to Fort Vancouver to share a progress report about Fort Langley's first few months of operation. McMillan packed up 1,200 furs as proof of his fort's trading prowess, and together McMillan and Mackenzie headed out from Fort Langley. They got as far as Point Roberts, but a major storm prevented them from going further; the Strait of Georgia was tossing up huge waves, too much of a match for the Chief Traders' ships. They hunkered down on Point Roberts to wait out the storm, but it continued non-stop for ten days. McMillan hadn't counted on being gone from Fort Langley so long – he thought he'd have been back from Fort Vancouver by now, so he excused himself from the journey and brought his furs back to Fort Langley. After a break in the storm, Mackenzie was able to get off Point Roberts and continue through Haro Strait into the Strait of Juan de Fuca. There, Mackenzie and his entire party were murdered by a party of the Clallam people.

When news of the tragedy reached McMillan, he organized a revenge mission with sixty men to find the killers. Two Clallam families were encountered, eight people including four children, who were summarily executed by McMillan's forces though it would seem likely had nothing to do with Mackenzie's murder. The revenge didn't end there; another group of trappers, the Cadboro party, soon thereafter went to Clallam territory. The Clallams invited them to shore for a council meeting with the real intent to murder the Cadboro party. Instead, the Cadboro troops firebombed the entire Clallam village, every last hut, all forty canoes, and took seventeen more Clallam lives.

The journals of early Fort Langley personnel contain illuminating notes about Point Roberts, including these samples:

Less than a year after it had been launched, the schooner *Cadboro* anchored off Point Roberts July 14, 1827, and log books indicate: "number of Indians in groups on beach and in canoes around our vessel." At Point Roberts, there was "a large camp of about one thousand Indians, inhabitants of Vancouver Islands who periodically cross the gulf to Fraser's River for the purpose of fishing."[62]

McMillan, August 25, 1827: "Families from the Saanich village at Point Roberts have been passing in continued succession during the day all bound for the salmon fishery." (The term Saanich was often used in those years as a general term for all the Northern Straits Coast Salish people, not only those from today's Saanich First Nation.)

McDonald, October 21, 1828: "A few Indians about, one of them the chief from Point Roberts village, traded 20 beaver skins. He and his followers also brought us one hundred of the small salmon and ten or twelve of the very large ones. They now take them in great abundance."

McDonald, October 22, 1828: "Chiche,nooks, the chief of Point Roberts, his young men again brought us two hundred which will make four casks of good salted salmon."

McDonald, August 20, 1829: "By an Indian just arrived from the mouth of the river the assemblage of natives in that quarter is immense. On Point Roberts alone he says that no less than 200 canoes landed the other day."[63]

With all this well-documented activity, we can dispel with the myth officials didn't know Point Roberts existed when they chose the 49th parallel as the border. Point Roberts is not an error or oversight. Detailed maps made from earlier voyages of discovery by George Vancouver in 1792 were still being used by McMillan and the *Cadboro* which clearly showed the Roberts peninsula straddling and extending south of the 49th parallel. The ease and simplicity of using a straight boundary line over the western half of the continent seems to have been a greater benefit than the inconvenience of a resulting exclave. Indeed, instead of dumb bureaucrats back East accidentally creating Point Roberts, the opposite is true: both countries knew of it and wanted it. The U.S. Navy sent Charles Wilkes to explore and map the region as early as 1841, well before the Treaty of Washington. The Navy spent eight days mapping Point Roberts, noting the 49th parallel created an exclave, but viewing it as important to, and included within, the U.S. territorial claim. Wilkes' maps and findings were used by U.S. negotiators in defining the border to include Point Roberts in their negotiations with Britain. The peninsula was considered strategic and valuable largely because it is near the mouth of the Fraser River. It was only twelve years after the treaty, in 1858, when the British engineers arrived to mark the border that they made a mild attempt to ask the U.S. to cede the peninsula, though the British never heavily campaigned to own Point Roberts.[64] Point Roberts is not a surprise or mistake after the treaty; they knew Point Roberts was here.

Figure 11: Map of disupted areas in the Treaty of Washington. Photo: No author provided. Roke~commonswiki assumed. https://goo.gl/images/P7Vnis

By the 1840s, joint occupation with Britain in Oregon Country was becoming a political campaign issue. The United States was in an expansionist mood in the 1844 election. The Whig party wanted to take Texas from Mexico, and James Polk's Democratic Party campaigned for "Fifty-four forty or fight," indicating they wanted to kick out the British all the way up to the Alaska border – almost all of Britain's Columbia District. Polk won the election, and put an offer on the table to Britain: the border would be drawn at the 49th parallel, a major compromise by the U.S. from the 54th parallel demand, but the U.S. wanted to continue the line across Vancouver Island. Britain declined. By April 28, 1846, the U.S. put on the pressure, notifying Britain they were abrogating the treaty of 1827 which provided for joint occupancy. This brought Britain to the table, and they agreed to the border along the 49th parallel, but successfully negotiated to keep all of Vancouver Island. That's why B.C. has significant territory, including its capital Victoria, some forty miles south of the 49th parallel today.

The border – and thus Point Roberts – was established west of the Rockies along the 49th parallel on June 15, 1846 with the Treaty of Washington between the United States and Britain, signed in Washington, D.C. It is also known as the "Oregon Treaty" although Oregon isn't mentioned in the official U.S. name of the treaty: "Treaty with Great Britain, in Regard to Limits Westward of the Rocky Mountains."[65]

If you were a white settler, this part of the world was a lonely place in 1846. There were only a couple of towns and trading forts. The first actual town, not a fort, on the Salish Sea was Olympia, Washington, settled in 1846, the same year as the border treaty. For the next five years, Olympia, at the far southern end of Puget Sound, would be the only town on the Salish Sea besides, of course, the Coast Salish villages and camps. It would take a dozen years before any crews started to physically mark the border on the land.

A British Party under the command of British Commissioner Captain John Hawkins of the Royal Engineers, in co-operation with a similar party from the United States, under the command of U.S. Commissioner Archibald Campbell, were organized to work out the protocol for the survey work to physically mark the 49th parallel, starting in Point Roberts.

Campbell, with General John G. Parke as his chief surveyor, arrived in Victoria on June 22, 1857, but members of the British Commission were not there yet. Campbell discussed the survey in a general way with Capt. James Prevost, Commander of HMS *Satellite*, but decided not to wait longer and got to work on his own, giving him a year's start on Hawkins. Using a map from the 1824 McMillan expedition, Campbell and the Americans started at the extreme western point of the 49th parallel which was here at Monument Park. This is quite remarkable. The intuitive plan would have been to start in the Rocky Mountains where the 1818 border stopped, and then continue westward into the unknown lands all the way to the Pacific, but it went the other way, starting at remote Point Roberts and going east.

When the British surveyors arrived in 1858 they established Camp Semiahmoo on Semiahmoo Bay, just north of the border between present-day Blaine, Washington and White Rock, British Columbia, on what is today the Semiahmoo First Nations Reserve. The site was situated on a little strip of open land near the mouth of the Campbell River, which offered a fresh supply of water and its channel provided water access over the tidal flats at low tide. While at this site the troops constructed about a mile and three-quarters of road along the shore of Semiahmoo Bay between the boundary and Camp Semiahmoo in a time when there were no roads in the area.

It was at Camp Semiahmoo on August 13th, 1858 where Campbell and Hawkins finally met to formally discuss the boundary survey. In the middle of the rugged Northwest, the two groups hosted each other on consecutive evenings with official banquets and formal salutes. Housewarming parties complete, they got busy marking the border. Small work boats were taken from there across Boundary Bay to Point Roberts. The soldiers stayed in the area three autumns and winters from 1857 through 1859, the most active work starting in 1859 once the instruments had determined the right location. The holdup had been from astronomers from the United States and Great Britain each identifying the border's location differently. The British Boundary Survey party consisted of about 100 men, including men of the Royal Engineers and civilian axemen, who had the latest instruments of the day. They looked down on the Americans' crude instruments and even the Americans themselves, who they perceived as uneducated. The result was the British and Americans worked independently, each making their own surveys working from a different camp. In this way they occasionally conferred but neither would get in the way of the other. Americans started cutting a thirty foot wide clearing on the border line through the forest, doing the first 10 miles. The British then did the next ten miles, and they alternated along like this. They placed iron posts periodically which read "Treaty of Washington, June 15th, 1846."

The British and American crews naturally eyed each other up. The Americans were self-conscious the British would look down on them as inexperienced and novice, and with good reason. The British did have good experience and training, but their book smart training and formal, rigid methodologies were amusing to the Americans as they fumbled around and struggled to apply those learned skills in the rough Salish Sea wilderness. The British initially questioned the quality and accuracy of the Americans' work, especially the work of Joseph Harris, but upon inspection Harris had some of the most-accurate readings. Point Roberts is mentioned in the diaries of Harris and others with regards to surveying accuracy. U.S. Assistant Astronomer and Surveyor G. Clinton Gardner wrote in early September 1858 of a situation where the British questioned Harris' line in Point Roberts, but when they double-checked it was the British who were in error by the length of a football field. Gardner writes, "Mr. Harris started back for Tummeahai, but before crossing the Lake an express from Camp Semiahmoo arrived, reporting a discrepancy between his work and that of the English (Commission) in the triangulation extending the line over Point Roberts; consequently Mr. Harris repaired to Camp Semiahmoo leaving his party at Chiloweyuck Depot. Upon a thorough examination of that work, showing it to be without error, 'the slight difference' of one hundred yards in the position of the 49th Parallel on Point Roberts was discovered in the computations of the English Survey."[66] Gardner goes on to write of a similar situation happening later at Sumas. Although the British came to begrudgingly acknowledge the quality of the Americans' work, the Americans couldn't shake their boorish rough-and-tumble reputation. One British surveyor recorded, "The Americans at their garrison celebrated their Xmas party in their usual way. One man stabbed, another shot at, and several heads broken and eyes blackened."[67]

As the British moved inland, east toward present-day Sumas, Campbell occupied Camp Semiahmoo. The Americans' camp was therefore on Canadian soil but there weren't a lot of other options other than taking time and money to create something from scratch on American land. Perhaps due to the unusual arrangement, a visit was made by a government audit inspector from December 10 to 12, 1858. The Colonel and Inspector General Joseph Mansfield conducted a full inspection. Remarkably, Camp Semiahmoo had been built by the British just 100 meters from a village of Semiahmoo Coast Salish. Mansfield described the Semiahmoo as harmless, peaceful and living in longhouses, but noted that there were over one hundred natives living at Point Roberts, who he found to be "a drunken set, disposed to mischief."[68] It seems the Point's reputation with alcohol got off to an early start.

It's a novel feeling to know on this enormous planet, you're standing exactly on the 49th parallel. Or are you? Not to burst your bubble, but the International Boundary Commission was wrong; the border isn't correctly marked. The obelisk is not actually on the 49th parallel. As the British and Americans worked separately, they would sometimes be up to a mile off where they thought the 49th parallel actually was. After the completion of the boundary survey, Hawkins and Campbell convened to compare notes and adjust the border as necessary before publishing their findings. They issued a report May 7, 1866 which was promptly misplaced and incredibly not found and published until thirty-three years later, in 1899. Government officials were dismayed to learn that Hawkins and

Campbell rarely met to compare notes. When they did meet up and found discrepancies in their findings, they did not take the opportunity to adjust the border while they were still there with their instruments. Instead, perhaps to stay on friendly terms, they merely split the difference and drew the official border equidistant between each camp's line, maintaining the error to this day. When Hawkins and Campbell's compromise was discovered years later, the officials were not pleased and ordered a new boundary survey, conducted between 1901 and 1907. This led to an entire new boundary treaty signed in 1908, but with many towns and homesteads already built up around the original boundary line, the idea of sorting out the messy situation of entire towns suddenly being in a different country was daunting and the 1908 treaty gave up. The United States and Britain agreed to keep Hawkins and Campbell's original work, despite the fact in many places it deviates from the actual 49th parallel.

The obelisk is actually 800 feet north of the true 49th parallel.[69] Before you plant a Canadian flag in Monument Park, be aware the border is now considered a settled legal matter. Carl Gustafson, Senior Field Engineer at the International Boundary Commission in Ottawa, in an April 1996 letter to John Cummins, of Delta, member of B.C. legislature, stated the boundary is not determined by today's precise technology showing the actual 49 degrees north latitude, "but by the original monuments that were placed by the joint British and U.S. boundary commission. This means that the monuments themselves, maintained in their original location, define the boundary between the two countries, notwithstanding any discrepancy between the demarcated line and the theoretical lines. The validity of the boundary as marked on the ground as determined by the International Boundary Commission is not a matter of legal dispute and it could not be successfully challenged in any court."[70] Had the actual 49th line been used, most of the Maple Beach neighborhood and Monument Park would be in Canada. But they're not, because this obelisk itself represents the international boundary, not the true 49th parallel line we can scientifically determine today with our GPS devices.

The obelisk itself is not owned by Whatcom County Parks, nor the county, state, U.S. government, Canadian government or private landowners. It is jointly owned by the United States and Canada via representation in the International Boundary Commission. The IBC itself maintains the structure. Special federal legislation protects the obelisk under the International Boundary Commission Act of 1960, which imposes a fine of $500 and/or six months in jail for damaging or disturbing the obelisk.[71]

Figure 12: Signs warn people to only cross at official border crossings. Photo by Makaristos (Own work) [Public domain], via Wikimedia Commons.

The connections made by the crew during the American occupation of Camp Semiahmoo would go on to be the source of some of the earliest people to settle Point Roberts. When the boundary survey work was done, Parke's cook, John Harris (no relation to Joseph Harris), settled in the early 1860s at a place in

Blaine between Dakota and California creeks previously owned by John Elwood. Harris would go on to become Point Roberts' first permanent white settler, and Elwood would eventually move to Point Roberts as well, in 1875; their stories are covered in chapter 3.

SMUGGLING

Even in these early years when the boundary had just been marked and the smoke still smoldered from the slashing of the forest to clear the border line, the border had already caused changes in behavior. The American soldiers, apparently a rough group, were well-supplied with whiskey by Blaine's first settler, a guy named Shaw. Like many business strips just outside of military bases today, Shaw was known for always having the hooch, regularly attracting soldiers looking to come down from Camp Semiahmoo to party. According to early news reports in the *Blaine Journal*, things got out of control one day when the soldiers, led by Parke, showed up when Shaw was away and his wife was home alone. Shaw returned home to find the soldiers had raped his wife, causing him to retaliate by shooting a sergeant, who shot Shaw in the chaos. And all that was with the boss around; imagine if he hadn't been there.

Borders create the conditions for smuggling, where a buck can be made moving and selling goods which are restricted, taxed or more expensive on one side. It creates artificial markets and restricts movement, interrupting the flows shaped by nature. Smuggling and illicit trade, often involving alcohol, are frequently the result of borders, and due to its position on the border, Point Roberts not only saw its share of the resulting activity, it became known for it.

From the parking lot at Monument Park, you'll see a residential street partially blocked by a curb barely a foot high which prevents cars from driving through, but otherwise is completely open without fencing. An old smuggling trail, today the cul de sac just beyond the curb is Tsawwassen's English Bluff Road. That's Canada. The U.S.–Canadian border is often called the world's longest undefended border, and nowhere epitomizes that fact more than where you're now standing. No fence here stops anybody from merely walking across the street into Canada. Of course, you can get in big trouble for crossing the border other than at an official crossing, so resist the urge to sneak across.

This very crossing was the route of much of the Point's rum running. Untold numbers of cases of booze were brought down from Canada and stored in secret caches in Monument Park's hillside, ready for pickup by stealth boats from the U.S. mainland to retrieve the loot. Other goods were smuggled going north. During Prohibition, to make smuggling easier there was a wooden staircase down the bluff to the beach, such was the frequency of smuggling here. In addition to booze, another product was smuggled as well: human trafficking. This is a historical trail used by Chinese workers

Figure 13: The international border is kept clear along Roosevelt Way, at right. A small bright yellow curb separates Monument Park's parking lot in the U.S. in the foreground from a Canadian cul de sac and Tsawwassen home at left. Photo by Mark Swenson.

to get into the United States to work in the canneries.[72] It had been an active smuggling trail for so long, folks in Point Roberts called this original route the Old Road.

Three short blocks north of here at the corner of English Bluff Road and 1 Avenue, a colorful character in the history of Point Roberts, Pansy Mae Stuttard and her husband Rupert ran the Point's brothel, or at least a Prohibition-era roadhouse, or both. Stuttard originally ran a brothel on the northern tip of Vancouver Island. She had a medical degree from New York and although she ran the town's brothel she also delivered the local babies. Moving on, she then spent time running several of Vancouver's brothels before finally settling on twenty-seven acres along the bluff just over the border and down a trail from the Point Roberts obelisk. In late 1925 she received a license to sell beer by the glass under the name The Goat Ranch.[73] I like to think of it as the Point's equivalent of One-Eyed Jack's roadhouse in David Lynch's *Twin Peaks* (set and filmed 125 miles south of Point Roberts at Snoqualmie Falls, Washington). Pansy Mae's tavern was Point Roberts' speakeasy, where thirsty Americans suffering under Prohibition could get a shot of whiskey just north of here. It is widely believed Pansy Mae also ran a brothel in the Goat Ranch. With very few settlers in Tsawwassen this essentially would have been The Point's brothel. Pansy Mae catered to fishermen, cannery workers and the young men of Point Roberts.[74] Recalling at age sixty-four his antics as a young man, one local resident described, "I can also remember seeing quite a lot of local young boys (and just maybe myself included) piling onto a logging truck and driving up the Old Road and along the bluff past the marker to a saloon run by a lady known as Pansey-May (sic). The fathers soon found out about the boys' activities and soon put a stop to it tho – well, almost."[75]

Soon after the closure of the Goat Ranch in 1933, B.C. Hydro forcibly purchased her land, but Pansy Mae insisted on being paid in "real money," that is, U.S. dollars. She was granted this request, but the cash was later stolen in a burglary. Pansy Mae moved up the street to the lot where Fred Gringell Park is today.[76] In the 1950s, Pansy Mae went on to attract more attention. By 1958 Pansy Mae was living across Boundary Bay in White Rock. She made headlines at age eighty-four as the Pistol Packin' Mamma when she unleashed a blast of gunfire from her twelve-gauge shotgun at intruders who broke into her home. In the commotion she was struck in the head and not discovered for four days. The neighbor who found Pansy Mae called an ambulance, a priest and a hearse; Pansy Mae survived and framed the invoice for the hearse, famously saying, "The Lord don't want me and the Devil won't take me." Her entrepreneurship of exploiting laws along the border is a key part of the history of Point Roberts and a prime example of the smuggling which inevitably arises due to borders.

Sometimes people smuggle themselves over the border. This spot is likely where a reality TV personality smuggled himself into Canada in the summer of 2009. Ryan Jenkins was a good-looking guy from Calgary who had resettled in Las Vegas. He'd had some success in a real estate development and investing, amassing a net worth of $2.5 million. He had a confident attitude, a crafty mind and experience with beautiful women. He liked fast cars, and his LinkedIn profile boasted a license to fly commercial airplanes. In short, he was perfect for reality TV, a fact noted by a reality TV producer who spotted Jenkins in a casino in Las Vegas, swaggering around the joint surrounded by women.

In 2009, VH1 created a new reality show called *Megan Wants a Millionaire,* in which seventeen male contestants competed for the love of the show's star, Megan Hauserman. Hauserman was a blonde reality TV veteran who had been a *Playboy Cyber Girl of the Week*, won season three of *Beauty and the Geek* and its $125,000 prize, placed third on season one of *I Love Money*, ended up in tenth place on *Rock of Love: Charm School* and appeared in eight other reality TV shows. The show's twist evident from its name, the contestants in *Megan Wants a Millionaire* were actually millionaires ranging in net worth from one to ten million dollars. Taping finished in February 2009. Taking the nickname Smooth Operator on the show, in one episode Jenkins is shown in a quiet moment with Hauserman where he reveals he needs to marry an American to be able to work in the United States, but that he won't make her sign a pre-nup. Despite this classy introduction, Jenkins won the first episode. He placed fourth in episode two. In the opening of the third installment, aired on August 16, we see Jenkins showing off his moves for picking up women to the other guys. The contestants then formed teams to design a marketing campaign for Megan's Chihuahua, with the winning team's captain earning the show's first solo date with Megan. Jenkins' team developed a line of gourmet dog food. Their detailed cost-benefit analysis predicted annual sales of $68 million and secured the team the win and Jenkins the solo date, dinner at a French restaurant with transportation in an Aston Martin. Confident and poised, he had a knack for reality TV and a real shot at winning the show. Although VH1 had invested a lot of money in the show, aired three episodes and heavily promoted the series all summer, the rest of the taped episodes would never air.

Jenkins met his wife, model Jasmine Fiore, in a Las Vegas casino in March 2009, a month after the filming had wrapped up on *Megan Wants a Millionaire*. They married two days later on March 18 in a wedding chapel on the Las Vegas strip. Fiore originally hailed from Santa Cruz, California, beginning her career as a swimsuit model, and then progressed into body-painting art and appearances in Las Vegas casino shows. She got some work in TV commercials for swimwear and adult phone sex lines. By summer 2009 at age twenty-eight she had acquired a real estate license and hoped to open a gym. From the start, their marriage didn't seem happy. Friends frequently found them feuding; she was a bit flirtatious; he a bit jealous.

Although taping had finished on *Megan Wants a Millionaire* and the episodes wouldn't begin airing until August, producers contacted Jenkins to be a contestant on another reality TV show, season three of *I Love Money*. This show features fan favorites from other reality shows competing in mental and physical challenges, vying for a quarter-million dollar prize. With his marriage shaky, Jenkins jumped at the chance to get away and be sequestered in Manzanillo, Mexico during the taping from late June to early August. For her part, during this rocky time in her marriage whilst Jenkins was in Mexico, Fiore resumed contact with a guy she had been seeing before she married. During taping in Mexico, Jenkins became aware of Fiore's contact with her ex, making him determined to get his bride back. In early August when Jenkins returned from Mexico, friends and family saw them reconcile in August to the point they went to San Diego together for a poker tournament. What changed? Although he was under a non-disclosure agreement from the producers of *I Love Money* because the show wouldn't air until January 2010, Jenkins confided to Fiore he had won the competition and its $250,000 jackpot. Perhaps hoping to open the gym, Fiore agreed to reunite. Jenkins had fame, fortune, and a blonde model as his bride. Things were looking up.

They attended the tournament at the Del Mar Hilton across the bay from San Diego on the evening of August 13th. During the evening, however, they slipped back into their old ways. Whilst Jenkins was playing poker, Fiore was texting with another guy. Fiore was reminded of Jenkins' penchant for pretty girls and his jealous tendency. The couple was captured on video leaving together at 2:30 A.M., and were seen an hour later at a nightclub in downtown San Diego. During this time, Fiore's phone vibrated again from another text. Though it was Fiore's phone, it is likely Jenkins had the device; a return text read "suck it." Their departure after a blowout fight in the club was the last time Fiore would be seen alive.

Jenkins was seen on video at 4:30 A.M. arriving alone back to their hotel in Del Mar. He checked out at 9:00 A.M. Twenty-two hours later, at 7:00 A.M. on August 15, a female body was found in Buena Park, California, inside a suitcase in a dumpster; the victim was nude, beaten and strangled. Identification of the body took three days because the killer had removed the victim's teeth and fingers, presumably to hinder identification. Jenkins reported Fiore missing at 8:55 P.M., telling police they had traveled up to their Los Angeles home after the evening in San Diego, and Fiore went out to run errands but never returned. Her car was found in a parking lot a half mile away with ample evidence of blood and hair.

Jenkins left Los Angeles the next morning on August 16. He drove to Las Vegas to pick up his 21-foot ski boat. He would miss VH1's airing that night of the episode three – the last to air – of *Megan Wants a Millionaire* as he drove north on Interstate 15. Jenkins was in contact with his lawyer and the police on August 17, informing them he was in Utah on his way to Canada to resolve an immigration matter and to see his mother. His next movements suggest he had stopped to pick up his boat because he was headed to Point Roberts.

The next day, August 18, positive identification of Fiore's body in the suitcase was made by tracing serial numbers on the woman's breast implants. For the first time, Fiore's murder was reported in the media. When Jenkins reached the Salish Sea August 19, he stopped in Birch Bay and learned Fiore's body had been identified. VH1 had just announced they were placing *Megan Wants a Millionaire* on hiatus. Jenkins couldn't know that the Whatcom County Sheriff was on his tail after receiving tips of seeing Jenkins' BMW SUV towing a ski boat toward the Canadian border. And they found it: his BMW SUV and an empty boat trailer were discovered at the Blaine marina, its engine still warm. By now over forty federal agents from both countries were patrolling Boundary Bay on a manhunt by land, sea and air. Jenkins made it through the dragnet, bringing his boat into the Point Roberts marina. It was dinnertime on August 19 as he pulled into an empty slip on D dock, where he stopped to help a passer-by carry some stuff. Police were closing in though. Local sheriff's deputies were canvassing the marina with Jenkins' photo as early as 7 P.M., but they didn't find his ski boat until just after midnight. Perhaps Jenkins, thinking he was a suspect, had panicked and headed to Point Roberts so he could get to family members there and in Vancouver.[77] Jenkins had visited family in Point Roberts when he was younger and would have been aware of places where it was possible to get into Canada. This open cul de sac at Monument Park is one of the likely places where he could have crossed.

Film crews arrived in Point Roberts from Vancouver and Seattle. CNN and TMZ beamed footage of the Point Roberts marina around the world showing Jenkins' boat being towed out of the marina entrance by the United States Coast Guard the following morning, August 20, as police in California charged Jenkins with first-degree murder. At the same time, Jenkins was already in Canada on his way up the Fraser River Valley. Turning on the TV in a motel room, Jenkins saw the salacious coverage where the media had already tried and convicted him. The police in pursuit, Jenkins was terrified and alone.[78] On August 23, he was found deceased in the motel in Hope, B.C. Hope had run out for Jenkins; he was thirty-two.

The fourth episode of *Megan Wants a Millionaire* would have aired that day, but on August 24, VH1 cancelled the rest of the season and deleted all video of the series from the Internet. Another contestant from the show later confirmed Jenkins placed third. *I Love Money* season 3 was cancelled the same day and no episodes were ever aired.

Despite being used as a smuggling den, Point Roberts has one of the lowest crime rates in America. Often called the largest gated community in the United States, safety comes from the fact every person and car license plate coming in and out is photographed, citizenship documents scanned and tracked in a massively parallel relational database management system, and criminals denied entry. Of course that safety comes at the cost of foregoing a significant amount of privacy; every time you arrive at or leave from Point Roberts at its land border crossing, you have to tell a federal government official where you're going and why. In that way, the border is felt every day by residents of Point Roberts.

VANCOUVER EXPEDITION

The boundary surveyors were not the first white people to see or set foot on Point Roberts; that happened sixty-seven years earlier. Much of the history of Point Roberts has happened at sea level, down by the water's edge, but because the modern-day visitor's vantage point is often from the beach looking out to the sea, it's important to realize the first Europeans to notice Point Roberts saw it from the sea due to its elevation; they thought it was yet another San Juan or Gulf island. The land north of the peninsula looked like a swampy tidal flat, so it took a couple of tries before they realized it's a peninsula. This 135-foot tall vista at Monument Park is a good place to comment on those early explorers.

It's important to put the European discovery of Point Roberts into historical context of the eighteenth century. It was a time when the last major bits of large, unexplored parts of the globe were surveyed in high-risk, high-reward expeditions funded by the imperialist powers of the day. Global travel was already common and growing exponentially, fueled by the first global corporation, the Dutch East India Company, a global trading firm which even extended into closed societies of the day like Japan. Despite this global network, there were parts of the globe which were still uncharted. As recently as 225 years ago, maps had a large blank spot for the Salish Sea; nobody knew a major inland sea existed. The race was on by the major European powers to fill in the map, document and name it, and claim it for the crown. Point Roberts was discovered as part of these vast global expeditions.

Figure 14: As late as the 1790s, no Europeans knew the Salish Sea existed. World maps like this 1625 Dutch map simply showed a gap with nothing north of California. The Salish Sea was the last spot on the globe to be filled in thanks to the Vancouver Expedition. Image by http://www.geographicus.com/mm5/cartographers/bormeester.txt [Public domain], via Wikimedia Commons

The first Europeans on the scene in the Salish Sea were the Spanish. This surprises many people because the Spanish aren't thought of as having a major influence today in the Salish Sea, until names like San Juan Island, Lopez Island, Rosario Strait, Gabriola Island remind us of Spain's early presence. Spain at the time owned the vast majority of the New World. Their empire included most of Latin America save Brazil and a few small British, French, Danish and Dutch backwaters. It extended up into much of what is today the western United States. Today's capital of New Mexico, Santa Fe was the capital of New Spain as early as 1608. Spain owned Texas, New Mexico, Arizona, Colorado, Utah, Nevada and California. California was still part of Mexico as late as 1848, two years after Point Roberts was created. The Spanish weren't going to stop there. In 1774, Spain first visited Nootka Sound on Vancouver Island, a bit north of the entrance to the Salish Sea. By the 1780s, they were exerting control all the way up the coast to Alaska, with a trade monopoly between North America and Asia. Spain soon became busy challenging Russia's fur trading in Alaska, launching multiple missions to establish presence and survey *their* lands. Alaska place names such as Valdez result today.

The Spanish explorers under the command of Don Francisco de Eliza were the first Europeans to see Point Roberts during their exploration of the Salish Sea. Thinking it detached from the mainland, it was named Cepeda Island[79] in June 1791. Eliza's name for the Strait of Georgia was El Gran Canel de Nuestra Senora del Rosario la Marinera, which means The Grand Canal of Our Lady of the Rosary. The southern arm of the Strait of Georgia between Bellingham and Anacortes, Washington, is Rosario Strait, which comes from Eliza's original name for the Strait of Georgia. The Eliza expedition noted natives at Point Roberts: "At Cepeda Island there is an incredible quantity of rich salmon and numerous Indians, much more docile and tractable than those at the entrance [to the Strait of Juan de Fuca]."[80]

The Spanish were soon joined by the British. Captain Cook found Nootka Sound thirteen years earlier in 1778 on his third global voyage, but somehow missed the wide entrance to the Strait of Juan de Fuca. Ironically, the last-on-the-scene Americans ended up with half of today's Salish Sea, including Point Roberts. American Robert Gray reached Nootka Sound as late as 1788, but the Americans were the earliest to actually get its people into the area as settlers, helped by the Lewis and Clark expedition in 1804. Corporations established trading forts to monopolize trade in the surrounding region, and the Salish Sea was up for grabs. Spain, Britain and the United States were all vying for ownership. Unlike earlier voyages, it wasn't enough to get there first, plant a flag and say it's yours; with little unexplored land left in the world, by the 1780s it had become more important to have boots on the ground, with proof of settlers, commerce and improvements in order to defend ownership. The *Edinburgh Review* declared Oregon Country "the last corner of the earth left free for the occupation of a civilized race. When Oregon shall be colonised, the map of the world may be considered as filled up."[81] The corporations were competing with each other for business from trappers and native people. Corporate forts represented proof of the establishment of imperialist power in the region.

Britain sent Captain James Cook on three major global voyages over a twelve year period, starting with a 1768 expedition which saw European discovery of New Zealand and major parts of Australia. Cook began his second voyage four years later in 1772, sailing on the HMS *Resolution*. The southern half of the globe at the time had huge gaps, and Cook's second voyage set out to determine if there was a large southern continent, the fabled Terra Australis. The voyage would become the first to cross the Antarctic Circle. Aboard the 111 foot ship was a crew of 112, including two young officers, George Vancouver and Henry Roberts. The two of them would spend a three year, round-the-world journey on a ship barely as long as three school buses. Vancouver later boasted when the ship reached its furthest-south point in the Antarctic ice flows, and he shimmied out on the bowsprit, he had been further south than any person ever.[82] It was a time of adventure and optimism for the two, Roberts at age sixteen and Vancouver just fifteen. As an able seamen rank Vancouver was fortunate for a boy his age to be a captain's servant. After two years of service, Vancouver would achieve midshipman rank, earning priceless lessons and fatherly mentoring by a great captain, especially one as famous as Cook.[83]

That professional and personal tutelage came at a price. Living conditions on naval ships for midshipmen and master's mates were pretty rough, and chief among the raw conditions was the stench. Vancouver's quarters were in the ship's "cockpit," the lowest deck over the ship's hold. Depending on the size of the ship, the cockpit would house twenty to thirty-six men in a space from five hundred to a thousand square feet. There they would eat, sleep and spend free time below deck. The flavorless meals included salted meat, hardtack, cheese, pease porridge (a hummus-like legume and ham pudding), soup and maybe a vegetable. Potable water in short supply, the daily dinnertime beverage for these teenagers was a gallon of beer or a pint of rum grog. Being far below the water line, the space was pitch-black save for stinky tallow candles. Further stench came from rancid slime oozing from food casks, excrement buckets and putrid bilge water. Dangerous toxic gases could kill a crew member but were no match for the vermin in this lowest part of the ship; sometimes a thousand rodents were found at the end of voyages.[84]

Conditions on the ship were the downside; as on any naval voyage, R&R in the tropics was the upside. As teenagers, Roberts and Vancouver and their fellow shipmates were in their sexual prime. "At nightfall, women would swim out to the anchored ships, selling sex for a handful of nails. Iron, in any form, was the usual pay for a prostitute. Tender tropical nights in the arms of an obliging girl were an expected perk on any South Sea expedition."[85]

Apparently not wanting the fun to end, both Roberts and Vancouver re-upped for another tour of duty on Cook's third voyage which would take them to Nootka Sound. The focus of all the world powers on Nootka Sound was because in the 1770s it was the key to finding something many people believed existed, but ended up being a fool's errand: the Northwest Passage.

Starting in 1776, the third voyage used two ships, HMS *Resolution* again, and HMS *Discovery*. This time, Vancouver was a midshipman on the HMS *Discovery*, and Roberts was the master's mate on the HMS *Resolution*, Roberts' master being none other than

Figure 15: Henry Roberts. Photo by Thomas Gainsborough [Public domain], via Wikimedia Commons.

William Bligh of later 1789 HMS *Bounty* fame. Roberts' contribution extended beyond the usual duties of a master's mate, for Roberts held special talents as a cartographer. Considered works of art, Roberts' beautiful and accurate charts are mostly attributed to Cook. Roberts liked working with his hands, which showed not only in his maps, but also in his detailed paintings, including a famous rendition of HMS *Resolution*.

Cook's third voyage would mean the European discovery of Hawaii, after which the expedition went on to the west coast of North America. They missed the entrance to the Salish Sea, somehow not seeing the ten-mile-wide entrance to Strait of Juan de Fuca. They were headed for Nootka Sound, where they spent two months in the spring of 1778.

A young man aboard the ship wrote in his journal of how the young men on the ship met their sexual needs during their spring at Nootka. The sailors approached the native men and made it clear they would make it worth their while if they would arrange young women to visit the ship. Three fathers thereafter brought their own daughters to the ship. The sailors found the young women "exceedingly dirty," thus they devised a "ceremony of purification" whereby the young men bathed the girls in warm water and soap. The negotiated payment for renting out their daughters for the night was a polished and gleaming pewter plate. Soon more fathers were bringing their daughters to the ship. After all the pewter plates were depleted (the diary notes "many of us after leaving this harbor not being able to muster a plate to eat our salt beef from"), the still-horny sailors then traded the kitchen furniture for more sex.[86] Roberts was twenty-two that spring at Nootka, confident and popular among the crew; he would have had no problem attracting the attention of a pretty woman. Vancouver was twenty, but much more introverted. He was reserved, rigid in his thinking and sweated heavily from a bad case of hyperhidrosis. He lacked confidence when around others, and probably wasn't what we'd call a babe magnet. My theory is the older and more outgoing Roberts, who had grown up together with Vancouver as teenagers, was a big brother to George. Roberts may have ensured Vancouver was able to negotiate a night of fun. As Vancouver led the girl to a quiet part of the ship after the purification ritual, Roberts may have flashed him an atta-boy grin. Vancouver would no doubt remember this boost of confidence later.

Leaving Nootka Sound, the expedition continued north to Alaska and made an unsuccessful attempt at navigating a frozen Bering Strait. The ships returned to Hawaii in January 1779, arriving during a feast. Debate rages as to whether the Hawaiians thought Cook was the god of their festival, or if the generosity the crew received was merely part of the festive celebrations. Regardless, the crew set out in February for another major voyage only to suffer damage soon after leaving Hawaii, forcing them to turn back. When the men returned to where they had been staying before, the party vibe was gone. This time the Hawaiians committed petty thefts and expressed an air of hostility. On February 13, entrusted as a young officer with a small boat, Vancouver's quick thinking and bravery saved the life of *Discovery's* master Edgar, by stepping in to take a blow from an oar on his own body and then rescuing Edgar from the water.[87] On Valentine's Day, a small lifeboat was stolen. As he had in Tahiti and other places, Cook tried to grab a hostage to hold in order to get the boat back, and in a decision which would principally cause his death, Cook personally kidnapped the ruling chief of the island of Hawaii, but this failed. Roberts and Vancouver were standing together on the beach when the king's attendant stabbed Cook to death on the beach. The natives carried off Cook's body where they embalmed it and set it on fire. Vancouver was selected to lead a mission to retrieve Cook's remains, in no small part due to his knowledge of the Hawaiian people's culture and language, though his attempt was unsuccessful.

For the next decade after Cook's third voyage, Vancouver and Roberts stayed busy in the Royal Navy. During this time in the 1780s, Roberts created large, highly-detailed world maps. They were designed to visualize the voyages of Captain Cook, depicting routes, dates, sites of landfall and historical notes. In 1784 an official atlas of Cook's voyages, *A Voyage to the Pacific Ocean*, was posthumously published in London, with maps created by Roberts. Roberts' maps started a stampede to get to the Northwest for the fur trade. The furs brought from Cook's third voyage to China turned out to be in huge demand; the Chinese went nuts over them, paying over $100 per pelt, about $2200 in today's dollars.[88]

In addition to that official map, Roberts also created another especially elaborate version of the map containing much more detail than the official atlas. Using different wash colors to shade areas of British and Russian control it had annotated notes in the side panels and explicitly stated there was no Northwest Passage from the Pacific to Hudson's Bay. Hudson's Bay Company was furious Roberts included certain geographical features like the Coppermine River which they wanted to keep secret to maintain their monopoly. Roberts sold this feature-packed secret version to William Faden in London, who published it one month after the official atlas, marketing it as the lost chart of Captain Cook. The maps from some of Roberts' secret copper plates are highly prized and trade at a premium today in antique map auctions.

Vancouver busied himself during the 1780s with several naval commissions, including one at Port Royal, Jamaica where his skills in astronomy, hydrography and navigation were put to use. He was paired with Master Joseph Whidbey to perform a thorough survey of the reefs at the harbors of Port Royal and Kingston. Charts published years later bore their names and were used later for buoy placement.[89] Vancouver rose to rank of First Lieutenant, under Captain James Vashon. During this time he met a number of men who would factor in to Vancouver's next mission, including Joseph Baker and a young midshipman named Peter Puget.[90]

By 1789, Britain was gearing up for another expedition to the southern oceans (whale lovers will cringe at what was then called the "Southern Whale Fisheries") to explore the potential for whaling. A new ship was commissioned for the British Navy for this purpose, delivered in 1790. Henry Roberts, now recognized as one of the Navy's most-experienced hydrographers, was named as Captain.[91] Roberts was looking forward to getting back to exploring on the high seas. He was one of the most popular commanders in the Royal Navy under whom to serve, and sailors were anxious to serve under a commander who had a reputation for treating his men well. Roberts selected Vancouver as his second-in-command, the First Lieutenant, and named Joseph Whidbey as Master. The newly-built ship was named HMS *Discovery* after Cook's ship on which Vancouver had served as midshipmen for three years.

As *Discovery* preparations were under way, tensions were spiking at Nootka Sound. Spain and Britain, and toward the end of the decade, the Americans, amped up aggressive moves against each other, with Nootka Sound becoming the proxy battleground for control of the north coast and the Salish Sea. Roberts received instructions in March 1790 to not provoke the Spanish, who wanted to reinforce their presence in the northern Pacific coast region from their base at Nootka as a way of stopping Russian encroachment in their fur trade.[92] The Spanish had arrived in May 1789, to find ships sent from China by a British entrepreneur by the name of John Meares to bring fur back to the Far East. The Spanish felt their lands were being encroached on, so they briefly seized the ships, including one the British trader had built with Chinese labor in Nootka. When the British crews were released they sent word back to Meares in China of the scuffles. Meares rushed to London to raise the alarm of aggressive Spanish behavior in lands the British considered theirs, arriving in Britain in May 1790. Suddenly the

Figure 16: George Vancouver. [Public domain], via Wikimedia Commons

Nootka crisis whipped Britain into a frenzy of jingoistic clamor, the citizens urging the government to act to defend British interests.[93] They needed to send a mediator to settle things with the Spanish, and then to establish a British presence in the region by conducting a formal expedition of discovery to map and stake claim to the region. Britain prepared for war with Spain and began readying a naval fleet named the Spanish Armament. When the navy looked around for a proper ship with which to lead the expedition, the best choice was to cancel Henry Roberts' southern whaling expedition and use the *Discovery* to meet the Spanish at Nootka and explore the region. With the escalating Nootka crisis, British sovereignty in the Northwest and the fortunes to be made in sea otter fur had eclipsed the priority of the whaling industry.[94]

The British military build-up spooked war-weary Spain, who came to the bargaining table.[95] In an attempt to prevent the dispute from opening a new war front, Spain signed the Nootka Sound Convention in Madrid on October 28, 1790. The first of several treaties in the Conventions, it called for any buildings and land which Spain had seized at Nootka Sound would be given back to Britain. Britain cancelled Roberts' expedition, and Vancouver received the Commander assignment on December 15, 1790 to go to the Pacific Northwest on the *Discovery* to ensure the Nootka Sound

Convention was being followed on the ground, get the Crown's stuff back, and to conduct a geographic survey and get a good look at this region over which Britain almost went to war. The expedition was also to determine once and for all if the fabled Northwest Passage existed. Vancouver later stated his expedition removed "every doubt, and set aside every opinion of a Northwest Passage."[96] Lastly, Vancouver was to determine the native people's temperament and the potential for trading and settlement.

In 1791 at age thirty-three Vancouver and his crew of 152 left Britain. Vancouver had been able to select his own officers, many still available from the cancelled Roberts expedition.[97] Not as popular as Roberts, Vancouver had very high standards and a short temper, but with Britain at peace there weren't a lot of commissions available, and the crew was happy to sign on to an anthropological naval adventure where they would face danger and encounter natives in their wild undiscovered habitat. Vancouver led the ships with just the power of his naval rank. Fifteen among the crew were "young gentlemen," on board as midshipmen, able seamen and master's mates. They were snobby young men from well-to-do families. Despite his knowledge of the Pacific Ocean, his capable astronavigation skills and impeccable record as a midshipman and lieutenant,[98] they hated Vancouver, seeing him as short, fat, balding, bug-eyed, and, suffering from a bad case of hyperhidrosis, as sweating all the time. His fits of temper were initially seen as eccentric but as the journey progressed, many became convinced Vancouver was insane.[99] Zachary Mudge, 20, was first Lieutenant. Peter Puget, 26, was second Lieutenant and had learned navigation from Vancouver. Baker, 24, was third Lieutenant, collated data and drew charts. Vancouver selected Whidbey, 34, who had served under him in Jamaica. They would certainly earn promotions to commands of their own after such an expedition, and with their family connections. Archibald Menzies, 37, came along as botanist.[100] After Cook's murder, security measures required big expeditions to have a second ship. Accompanying *Discovery* was the *Chatham*, commanded by William Broughton, 29.

Figure 17: The *Discovery*. Photo: [Public domain], via Wikimedia Commons

As they were sailing south in the Atlantic toward Cape Town, Eliza's Spanish expedition had found Point Roberts, giving it the name Cepeda Island. After resupplying at Cape Town, Vancouver sailed to and wintered in Hawaii after stops in Australia, New Zealand and Tahiti. Worrying about infections among the crew, he forbade his sexually-frustrated young men below lieutenant rank from shore leave in Hawaii, a decision sharply at odds with naval custom then and now.[101] Mindful of witnessing Cook's murder thirteen years earlier, Vancouver declined to come ashore at Kealakekua Bay.[102] Civil war was raging in Hawaii, and Vancouver was repeatedly asked for guns, but he declined to get involved.

They left Hawaii and sailed for the North American mainland, reaching a point a hundred miles north of San Francisco on April 16, 1792. Heading north, they ran across American Captain Gray and his *Columbia Rediviva* on April 28. Vancouver sent Puget to exchange information. Gray told them of a large inlet which went inland at least fifty miles.[103]   Armed with this tip, Vancouver pressed on, trying to get as far north as fast as possible in order to have the daylight needed to navigate. The next day they entered the Strait of Juan de Fuca. Sailing up the strait on April 30, Baker was the first to spot a snow-capped volcano in the distance; Vancouver named the mountain for him. They reached Discovery Bay near Gardiner, Washington, and used it as a base to start charting every inlet and outlet in small sail and row boats; the larger *Discovery* and *Chatham* were far too large to safely explore around the submerged reefs. On May 7 they spent several days exploring Hood Canal. They took the *Discovery* down to Bainbridge Island, staying there from May 18 to the 29th. Vancouver named an island in the southern sound for his former Captain in the Caribbean, Vashon. Mount Saint Helens was named May 19th for Alleyne Fitzherbert, the first Baron Saint Helens.

On May 20th, Vancouver sent Whidbey, Puget and Menzies on a one-week trip to explore the far southern end of the sound. They spotted Mount Rainier that day as they sailed around Vashon Island. Menzies catalogued plants and Puget wrote of the natives and their customs, including the Nisqually Indians they visited May 21st.[104] Puget described the Nisqually as wearing deer skins, though some warriors had fancier moose hides. They wore black and ochre glimmer, giving them a fierce appearance, but Puget found them friendly and traded trinkets with them. They returned to the *Discovery* on the 27th and took a few days to organize their data and create charts. Suitably impressed with his work, Vancouver named the waters south of the Tacoma Narrows Puget's Sound on June 2.

Whilst Puget was down south, on the *Chatham* Broughton was busy exploring the San Juan Islands and Possession Sound at present-day Everett, Washington. On May 29th, everybody met up at Tulalip Bay. Whidbey checked out the largest island in Puget

Sound, a long skinny island for whom it would be named by Vancouver on June 4th. Whidbey was met by over two hundred natives at Saratoga Passage who wanted to trade. He was surprised to find they had items of European origin from having traded with other inland tribes.[105] As they all pressed north, Vancouver described a rough tide, not realizing he was crossing the Skagit River delta. Vancouver named the mainland New Georgia for King George III. That name didn't stick once it ended up in American hands but it did stick to the other geographical feature they named for George III: the Strait of Georgia, the northern arm of the Salish Sea, into which they would soon sail.

On June 11 they continued north, entering the Strait of Georgia and anchoring in Birch Bay.[106] They would make it a base for exploring the next part of the Salish Sea. Vancouver went ashore to look for a good spot for a camp, finding the Terrell Creek estuary an ideal spot, shaded by a thick black birch forest. Menzies would name the bay for these trees. The crew quickly settled in; on a warm summer day, the very first order of business was to set up a brewery.[107]

Vancouver got Puget and Manby up early at 5 A.M. on Tuesday, June 12 and set out in two small sailing yawls loaded up with a week's worth of supplies to explore the Strait of Georgia. Broughton was left behind to conduct local surveys from Birch Bay in the *Chatham*. As they crossed Boundary Bay, a forested peninsula with tall cliffs loomed closer. Vancouver wrote in his journal about seeing Point Roberts as he sailed from Semiahmoo Bay: "The point constituting the west extremity of these bays, is that which was seen from the ship, and considered as the western part of the mainland, of which it is a small portion, much elevated at the south extremity of a very low narrow peninsula; its highest part is to the southeast, formed by high white sand cliffs falling perpendicularly into the sea: from whence a shoal extends to the distance of half a mile round it joining those of the larger bay. From this point, situated in latitude 48 degrees 57 minutes, longitude 237 degrees 21 minutes (which I distinguished by the name of Point Roberts, after my esteemed friend and predecessor in the *Discovery*) the coast takes a direction N. 28W."[108] The white cliffs are Lily Point and the shoal is the Point Roberts reef. We'll visit these places in chapter 4 of this book. Basically, Vancouver named three entities after Henry Roberts: Point Roberts, the Roberts peninsula and Roberts Bank, all on June 12. Significantly, these names were used by the McMillan expedition thirty-two years later in 1824, which is likely the next time Europeans came near Point Roberts. Their maps in turn were used in subsequent history, such as the 1846 Treaty of Washington and the 1858 gold rush and boundary survey, helping the Roberts name stick to all these geographic features.

Captain Vancouver saw the Northern Straits Coast Salish summer home at Lily Point. They saw the frames of the longhouses and the long lines of tall salmon drying racks along the beach. Visiting on June 12 Vancouver was a little too early to see Lily Point in action. Had he visited just a few weeks later he would have seen hundreds of Coast Salish people living at Lily Point, its lowlands seething with activity.

Landing at Point Roberts, Vancouver thought the village at Lily Point was deserted, and would think the same of other empty camps he would come across, not realizing the Coast Salish people travelled seasonally. After a couple of weeks he would later conclude these camps weren't abandoned, but rather lived in seasonally when food sources were abundant. Vancouver's journal described what Lily Point looked like in the offseason – essentially how the Coast Salish left their homes at the end of the salmon season. He writes of many framed longhouses with huge timber beams supported by fourteen foot tall uprights carved with symbolic figures. The enormous ceiling beams fit into notched cuts in the upright beams, leaving Vancouver to wonder how they were able to lift them into place.[109]

Vancouver wanted to press on. It was slow going up the west coast of Point Roberts as the men rowed in a hot day with no wind for the sails. They constantly got caught on the sandbars of the coastal bank, which were littered with logs. Vancouver somehow failed to realize the slow drag was because he was crossing the delta at the mouth of the largest river by volume on the west coast of Canada, the Fraser River. Vancouver was trying to get to Point Grey, visible in the distance, but wasn't making sufficient process, his men were exhausted from rowing, so giving up on Point Grey, Vancouver had them instead row all the way across the Strait of Georgia to anchor in the Gulf Islands for the night, which probably didn't seem like much of a relief to the crew. The evening of the day Point Roberts was named was no picnic. After eleven hours of rowing, they got to the Gulf Islands after midnight. After some quick rations, and unable to find a beach on which to sleep, the men had to sleep in the row boat for a few hours before having to get up early to fulfill the mission of getting to Point Grey on the opposite side of the wide strait.

Back at base camp, Broughton's team had explored Bellingham Bay. On a survey trip, Whidbey had spotted the Spanish in the Gulf Islands heading toward Point Roberts. A Spanish exploration led by Dionisio Alcalá Galiano sailing in the *Sutil* and the *Mexicana* explored in the northern waters of Boundary Bay, arriving after dark. When dawn came, Galiano saw the land connected all the way to Point Roberts. It was a peninsula, not an island as Eliza had mapped. Cepeda wasn't an island, so Galiano renamed it Point Cepeda.[110] It was a useless move. Vancouver's name for what the Coast Salish called Cheltenem would stick, and it is named for his longtime buddy Henry to this day.

Having confirmed Point Roberts a peninsula, it was still morning when Galiano sailed down from the top of Boundary Bay toward Lily Point and encountered Broughton. Whidbey had raced back to Birch Bay to inform Broughton of the Spanish presence, prompting Broughton to take out the *Chatham* to meet up with the Spanish. Broughton found Galiano just off Lily Point where they traded intelligence on their respective missions. Galiano rounded Point Roberts and headed north toward the upper part of the Strait of Georgia, in the direction of where Vancouver was exploring. At the same time, running low on food, Vancouver was making his way back south toward base camp at Birch Bay. They were bound to eventually run into each other, and they did on June 21 at Point Grey, below today's University of British Columbia. Vancouver went aboard the Spanish ship and would later write in his journal he was "mortified" to see they were following an existing map of the Salish Sea. Vancouver realized he wasn't the first European to be here. Galiano was using the map of José María Narváez's expedition the year before, under command of Francisco de Eliza, when Point Roberts had initially been named Cepeda Island. They were on identical missions to find the Northwest Passage and defend their interests in the Nootka Conventions. Vancouver and Galiano established rapport, made easier by the fact Galiano knew a little English, and agreed to collaborate by divvying up the work to finish the world map in the Salish Sea. Low on supplies, Vancouver needed to get back to the *Discovery* at Birch Bay, but rowing across the Fraser River delta again wore out the crew, and on June 22 Vancouver and his crew again stopped at Point Roberts, coming ashore this time to spend the night.

After their visits to Point Roberts, the Vancouver Expedition continued up the Salish Sea toward the north end of Vancouver Island. They encountered many Coast Salish people who wanted to trade. Unlike his rich underlings, Vancouver had no family fortune and his pension would be just half pay, so he made trades himself. Soon his cabin sported a huge pile of otter pelts, each one equivalent to two months' pay.[111] By parallel processing for three weeks, the British and Spanish finished the maps for the last parts of the Salish Sea by July 13. After that they split up and separately went to check out whether Vancouver Island was attached to the mainland or if it could be circumnavigated. Beating Galiano around the island, Vancouver became the first to determine Vancouver Island is indeed an island. They stopped at Nootka Sound to wait for and meet with the Spanish, after which they sailed down the Pacific coast. The exploration of the Salish Sea was finished.

They poked into Grays Harbor July 18 and finally found the Columbia River, with the *Chatham* able to cross the dangerous Columbia River Bar at the river's mouth and anchor at Cape Disappointment at present-day Ilwaco, Washington. It lost a small boat in the process. The *Discovery* failed to cross the bar and so pushed on south because the men were coming down with scurvy and they needed to get to tropical areas for fruit. They named Mount Hood on October 29, and reached San Francisco on November 14. The *Chatham* caught up on November 26. They continued down to Baja California and then back to Hawaii for the winter. The next two years of the expedition would be spent exploring in Alaska. Vancouver arrived back in England October 15, 1795.

Arriving home there was no welcome for one of the longest world expeditions ever conducted.[112] The timing of the Vancouver Expedition coincided with Britons back home focused on the threat from Revolutionary France and Napoleon Bonaparte. Tensions with France had started boiling over in 1792, the year after Vancouver started his expedition, and escalated whilst Vancouver was at Point Roberts. The otter pelts didn't add much to his pension; within a year of returning he was in debt.[113]

The Vancouver Expedition named thousands of places and plants, and impacted history in the Hawaiian Islands and solidified

British control of Australasia. Navigation in the Salish Sea used Vancouver's highly accurate maps for decades after the voyage. Detractors point to the fact that whilst Vancouver mapped dozens of insignificant bays and islets he astonishingly missed the four of the biggest rivers on the west coast of North America, failing to spot the Columbia, Skagit, Fraser and Skeena Rivers.[114] Vancouver was pretty sure if the Northwest Passage existed it wasn't at lower latitudes, so he quickly pushed north, wanting to get as far north as early as possible so as not to squander the summer months. Stephen R. Bown wrote in *Mercator's World*, "How Vancouver could have missed these rivers while accurately charting hundreds of comparatively insignificant inlets, islands, and streams is hard to fathom. What is certain is that his failure to spot the Columbia had great implications for the future political development of the Pacific Northwest."[115] Vancouver made no geographic entries between Point Roberts north to Point Grey, when in fact one of the largest rivers on the west coast of North America spills into the Salish Sea right where he traveled. The Fraser River delta's multiple arms are small as they flow into the Strait of Georgia and admittedly can be hard to see during flooding and high tides against the low marshy tidelands. The year before Eliza's expedition missed it as well, though the Spanish knew they were close to a big river because of the muddy water; Vancouver made no such note.

Visiting five continents in four-and-a-half years, having lost only six men, an unheard of feat, Vancouver had accomplished the mission. In doing so, he changed the history of colonial era rule in this last-explored part of the world. The Nootka Conventions established the paradigm that sovereignty was not claimable merely by spotting the land first, but must be backed up with actual occupation.[116] Nootka did not establish a northern boundary for Spanish America, but it did tilt the balance of power in the region toward the British. Spanish lands would be passed to the United States by a treaty in 1819; the Americans would claim that treaty with Spain granted it exclusive sovereignty of the Oregon Territory, setting the stage for the Americans' negotiating position in the Treaty of Washington in 1846 which created Point Roberts. But back in 1792, the goal of the Vancouver Expedition was to walk the talk of Nootka and actually get its people there, draw charts, name geographic features, and pave the way for future settlement in order to back up British claims of sovereignty. It is ironic the British gave Point Roberts its name in a quest for British sovereignty, but it ended up becoming a U.S. territory fifty-four years later.

No sooner had Vancouver arrived back in England, when Henry Roberts departed on a mission of his own against the French threat. Roberts left February 9, 1796 to attack Dutch possessions which were now owned by France after the French invasion of the Netherlands. He would never return. Leaving England four months after Vancouver's return to England, Roberts became Captain of the frigate HMS *Undaunted*. He sailed to Guiana, on the north coast of South America. The Dutch had licensed sugar plantations to corporations, getting rich on taking a cut of profits for over 125 years. Of Guiana's three western colonies, Demerara and Essequibo were owned by the Dutch West India Company, and Berbice was controlled by the Society of Berbice. Colonists from Barbados had begun settling in these Guiana colonies, and Roberts was joining other British ships to take the three western colonies from the Dutch. Meeting up with Captain Thomas Parr in charge of HMS *Malabar* along the way, the two led a 1200-man squadron. By April 22 they had captured the three colonies for Britain with little resistance, along with its 400 sugar cane plantations. Possession actually flipped back and forth between Britain and the Netherlands a few times until 1814, when it was finally settled for Britain. As a result of Roberts' mission to take the colonies for Britain, the three colonies eventually merged to become British Guiana, and in 1966 became independent Guyana. The colonial capital's Dutch name of Stabroek was renamed Georgetown in 1812. The Netherlands retained possession of Guiana east of these three colonies, which is the present-day Dutch-speaking country of Suriname.

Neither Vancouver nor Roberts enjoyed a long life. Four months after capturing British Guiana for the British, Roberts was in the Caribbean when he contracted yellow fever. He died August 25, 1796 at age forty. Two days later the HMS *Undaunted* was shipwrecked off the east point of Jamaica. His son Henry was also on board as midshipman, and also died of yellow fever on the same voyage.[117] Henry Roberts gave his life for Demerara to be British. In a twist of history, we will see later a boy would be born in Demerara to a Scottish family who would later factor in Point Roberts's history. As for Vancouver, enduring a chronic illness, he died on May 12, 1798 at Petersham, England, also at age forty, probably of Graves' disease or myxoedema. He spent the last two years of his life writing his autobiography of his expedition, clocking in at a half million words. Vancouver had spent virtually his entire adult life at sea and never married, but his legacy is secure. He filled in the last big gap on the globe and gave Point Roberts its name.

 Exit Monument Park by going south on Marine Drive.

MARINE DRIVE

On the left is the Bald Eagle Golf Club, which in its early years ranked sixth in the United States for unique golf courses.[118] There had been several attempts to build a golf resort previously, and a five-acre, twenty-tee driving range opened for a few years at the southeast corner of Tyee Drive and Benson Road in 1977.[119] The current country club was initially proposed in August 1988, approved in late 1989, and construction began in January 1993.[120] Immediately in February 1993 the developers were forced to hire a heron biologist due to concerns about the rookery adjacent to the course.[121] Three holes were re-routed to preserve enormous nests. The L-shaped course leaves a heron buffer on the northeast quarter of the property. It finally opened as Point Roberts Golf and Country

Club in September 2001, over eight years after construction began.[122] Occupying the northwestern corner of Point Roberts, the golf course is so close to the border, a slice on the fifth hole can send your ball into another country; the border essentially serves as out-of-bounds.

Figure 18: Point Roberts Golf and Country Club in 2015. Photo by Mark Swenson.

Over 25,000 rounds of golf are played on the 18-hole par-72 course each year. Golfers share the grounds with deer, coyotes, turtles and eagles. *Golf Digest* ranked it number eight on its 2004 list of Best New Affordable Public Golf Courses in the United States. A panel of seven hundred golfers evaluate new courses, grading them on shot values, design variety, memorability, aesthetics and playability, though only fifteen on the ratings panel made it to Point Roberts to check out the course in person.[123] The original plans called for a large number of homes along the fairways. Aside for a handful of townhomes, the residential plans never materialized, leaving several empty paved cul de sacs. The golf club's name is a bit ironic given it is the eagles which in large part drove away the great blue herons which locals were trying to protect from the development of this golf course.

The land on both sides of Marine Drive used to be a farm owned by a colorful resident named Reno Reno Reno. That's Reno as his first name, Reno as his middle name and Reno as his last name.

Reno's farm was the Triple R Ranch, locally called Reno's Farm. The farm had several manmade lakes which Reno stocked with bullfrogs to provide a food source for the nearby heron rookery. In the winter, Canadian boys would sneak over the border to play hockey on the frozen ponds.[124] Today, they're water traps on the golf course. Situated on the farm was Sunset Café. Reno owned a beauty school and invented a haircut, the Reno Curly Cut. Capitalizing on its popularity, Reno secured a patent on the mathematical equation used to get the style's angles just right.[125]

A bit further down Marine Drive on the left is an A-frame building built in 1958 which used to be the home of The Roof House, a coffee shop known for their delicious pastries. For a while in the early 1990s it was of all things a Scandinavian restaurant.[126] Across the street in the early 1970s a small café called Drift Inn served sandwiches, ice cream and gifts until closing in 1972.

With such beautiful views and lots of rural architecture, Hollywood has found Point Roberts a good place to shoot; two movies and one TV series have been filmed in Point Roberts. In addition, another movie has been made from a book written in Point Roberts. We'll learn about each of these in turn during the tour, starting in this area. Here on Marine Drive, a science fiction movie was filmed in Point Roberts between September 24 and December 22, 1987.[127] *Beyond the Stars* was released in March 1989 and stars Martin Sheen and a young Christian Slater. Slater plays Eric, the teen son of an Apollo program computer scientist. Aspiring to be an astronaut someday, Eric contacts Paul Andrews, the thirteenth man on the moon, played by Martin Sheen, in fictitious Cedar Bay, Oregon. Andrews is a black sheep in the astronaut community, but Eric is about to learn Paul's secret. Robert Foxworth, F. Murray Abraham and Sharon Stone also star in the film written and directed by David Saperstein. It was filmed in Alabama, Vancouver and Point Roberts.

Continue south on Marine Drive. At Gulf Road continue straight on Marine Drive.

CHAPTER 2 • THE TULE

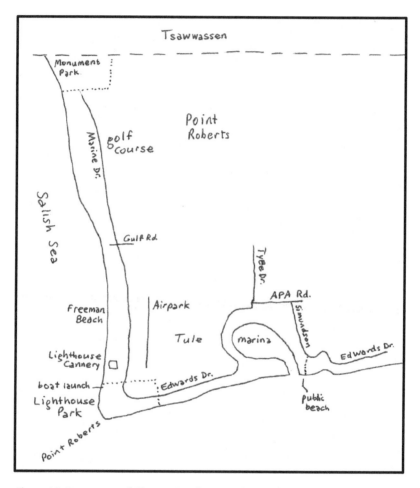

Figure 19: Route map of Chapter 2. After crossing Gulf Road, continue to drive south down Marine Drive, stop at Lighthouse Park, then end at the marina. Distance: 3.9 miles (6.3km)

Although Point Roberts is defined by the border, there are other border towns. Point Roberts is special not only due to the border. Point Roberts ups the ante and stands out because it's surrounded by water on three sides with maritime views in all directions. Visitors can access the waterfront at several points, and so Point Roberts makes it easy to connect with the sea. Point Roberts' novelty comes not only from the fact you had to show a passport to get in, but once you're in this geopolitical exclave you are immediately touched by its physical beauty and the connection you have to nature.

This is not just any peninsula. This particular peninsula is significant because it extends for miles into the middle of the Salish Sea's deep waters. The peninsula was created when ice a mile thick came down from the Canadian mountains, quarrying and scooping out deep troughs which became the Salish Sea, but leaving the Roberts peninsula as a headland. The Point has been sloughing off and gradually eroding ever since. Point Roberts protrudes into the path of millions of salmon heading for the Fraser River. Its seven-and-a-half mile coastline makes it home to iconic wildlife. Point Roberts has both shallow sand banks but also beaches which precipitously give way to extremely deep water immediately offshore, meaning you can get up close and personal with large marine mammals. This proximity to deep water also provides mainland British Columbia with its major port infrastructure on the Roberts peninsula. Ships headed to Vancouver's extensive port facilities all pass by Point Roberts. Its central location in the Salish Sea puts it physically between British Columbia's largest city and its provincial capital. It has capitalized on its position at the junction of people, government, commerce, animals, culture and language. These make Point Roberts significant regardless of the border cutting across the peninsula.

The southwestern quadrant of Point Roberts is low-lying flat land. With a no-bank waterfront access, much of the history of Point Roberts has happened here. It is a great place to connect with the sea, but also where the sea sometimes bites back. This chapter will explore these flat lowlands.

Geographically, Point Roberts is a roughly rectangular 4.9 square miles, about the size of three of Vancouver's Stanley Park. It's approximately one-and-a-half miles north to south and two-and-a-half miles east to west. The international boundary with Canada forms its northern and only land-based border along the 49th parallel. Its western shore is the Strait of Georgia, a broad, twelve-mile wide inland sea, dividing the west coast of the North American mainland from Vancouver Island, easily seen offshore to the west from Point Roberts. The 16,000-foot south coast offers a unique southward perspective of the United States and Canada from the north. The idyllic San Juan Islands and Gulf Islands archipelago are scattered eleven miles offshore. The east coast of Point Roberts is Boundary Bay, a large shallow sandy bay which extends north from United States waters into Canadian waters. Leaving Canada by boat in Boundary Bay requires entry into United States waters to get to the rest of Canada; as Point Roberts is a land exclave to the United States, Boundary Bay is a water exclave to Canada.

Point Roberts' topography ranges from beaches to cliffs; meadow to forest. A ridge runs from the northwest to the southeast, averaging 160 to 200 feet above sea level. The northeast and southwest corners of Point Roberts are low-lying flatlands at sea level. Tyee Drive bisects Point Roberts north to south, from the border crossing gradually downhill to the large marina on Point Roberts' south coast. The higher elevations have a thick cover of second growth evergreen and deciduous forest, whilst the low-lying flatlands are covered in meadows and tidal wetlands, now diked into polders. Tucked behind mountainous Vancouver Island, Point Roberts lies in a rain shadow, so it has a drier climate than Vancouver and Seattle.

Point Roberts is a peninsula today but thousands of years ago it was an island. The Salish Sea used to flow all the way in to the North Delta headland above today's Alex Fraser Bridge on B.C. Highway 91. Below that, there were boggy marine marshes and sand bars which eventually joined with river sediment building up from the Fraser River. This mix is how Burns Bog's brackish water formed peat, slowly connecting the Roberts peninsula to the mainland, at least seasonally in the beginning. When white settlers arrived it was basically a series of sandbars, muddy mounds and early diked polders which enabled travel between Ladner and Point Roberts. Dikes built in the 1930s truly made the Delta lowlands solid ground year round.

SALISH SEA

The waters off Point Roberts have two official names, the Strait of Georgia and the Salish Sea. The Roberts peninsula juts into the center of the deep waters of the Strait of Georgia, one of the bodies of water which make up the Salish Sea. The term Salish Sea is a relatively recent invention, coined in the 1990s at Western Washington University. It is a single term used to refer to the Strait of Georgia, Puget Sound, the Strait of Juan de Fuca and the smaller bodies of water, passes, channels and such which connect them. It's not uncommon to read or hear people refer to Point Roberts as being on Puget Sound. Point Roberts is nowhere near Puget Sound. The official northern end of Puget Sound is Admiralty Inlet, roughly where the Port Townsend-to-Coupeville state ferry route to Whidbey Island is. This northern extent of Puget Sound is a full fifty-six miles south of Point Roberts.

The need for a name to more conveniently and accurately refer to these bodies of water as a single connected and interdependent ecosystem arose in the mid-1970s because of the discovery of oil in Alaska's arctic. The Alaska Pipeline brings oil from the North Slope to Valdez to be loaded onto oil tankers and brought to refineries at Whatcom County's Cherry Point and at Anacortes. The resulting boom in tanker traffic in Washington waters, and the risk of oil spills, brought attention at state and federal levels. And not without reason: 120 barrels of Persian Gulf crude oil spilled at Atlantic Richfield's refinery at Cherry Point June 4, 1972, coating the beaches with oil from Cherry Point to White Rock and Crescent Beach in Boundary Bay. Whilst no oil was seen at Point Roberts, this was far too close for comfort.[128] It was clumsy and awkward to refer to Washington's inland marine waters, and in the case of the 1972 spill impacting the beach at White Rock, there was a need to use a single term which could also refer to Canadian waters. The waters encompassed by the term Puget Sound had grown over time. Legislation was passed to refer to waters as far north as Point Roberts as Puget Sound. Even laws on the books in Washington refer to Puget Sound when the intent is clearly all Washington state waters. The confusion is used by both plaintiffs and defendants in lawsuits. Terms like "northern Puget Sound" began being used for the Washington portion of the Strait of Georgia in the 1980s. Residents of Whatcom County and the San Juan Islands did not appreciate this inaccurate blanket reference, but many liked the convenience of having a single term for Washington's inland marine waters.

Folks began arguing about which name was appropriate for Washington's waters north of Puget Sound. This would have clarified the name of the water into which Point Roberts extends, but all of these missed the bigger point that all of these waters are, as put by the Salish Sea Studies Institute, "a single integrated estuarine ecosystem."[129] Goals like reducing pollution and restoration of salmon runs and marine mammals could only be accomplished if all of these bodies were managed as an ecosystem spanning two countries, and that became the driver for a new term. The name would primarily further the goal of viewing these bodies of water as one. Using names like Puget Sound, with a strong connection to only one part of the larger estuarine ecosystem, could not accomplish this goal.

The term Salish Sea borrowed inspiration from the native Coast Salish people who lived on these inland bodies of water. The use of the term Salish encompassed the inland waters for which a name was sought and acknowledged their original ownership of these waterways. The first attempt to officially get the name Salish Sea adopted was raised in 1989, but it was rejected for not having sufficient popular usage. Supporters of the name were encouraged to use it. It was popular in the San Juan and Southern Gulf Islands. Orca watching excursions and researchers appreciated one term for waters which are home to the Southern resident orcas. Educators, land planners and researchers all found the term useful and effective at furthering their work.

Eventually managers of natural resources which span the international boundary came to realize the Salish Sea term helped them view and understand their resources as belonging to a larger ecosystem, which opened avenues for resource management when viewed more holistically. A 1994 study of what we now call the Salish Sea awkwardly used "Strait of Georgia, Puget Sound and the Juan de Fuca Strait" over and over, and conferences at the time tried clumsy names like the "Georgia Basin Puget Sound Ecosystem."

Ultimately, the name Salish Sea stuck, helped by its appearance on maps. Dedicated maps of the Salish Sea have been created, often without the international boundary drawn, to emphasize the unity of the ecosystem. By 2005 conferences were using the Salish Sea term, with names like "Science for the Salish Sea," "Knowledge for the Salish Sea," and "the Future of the Salish Sea." The Coast Salish people were early adopters of the term, using it in their 2008 mission statement about fisheries sustainability: "To conserve and restore the Salish Sea ecosystem to a level that ensures the sustainability of the Coast Salish People and our cultural life ways." The term's originator re-applied for formal recognition of the name as a geographic term. Washington approved the name as a formal geographic place in October 2009 and British Columbia followed suit in February 2010.[130]

The name has proven useful. It has helped the Coast Salish people get a seat at the table at many critical local and federal decision-making entities for natural resource management, especially salmon runs. It has also influenced plans for regulating the increase in oil tanker traffic from oil pipelines and refineries, an appropriate closed-loop outcome from a term whose birth was born from concern about the early years of oil development a third of a century ago. New pipelines to bring Alberta oil sands to the Superport and expansion proposals for the facilities at Cherry Point bring this issue close to home at Point Roberts. With some predicting it's a matter of when, not if, an oil spill mars the Salish Sea, quite likely affecting Point Roberts in a major way, the Salish Sea term is used to bring government agencies on both sides of the border to collaborate to try to mitigate the risks of oil spills in this delicate ecosystem.

The population of Point Roberts is among the eight million people living on the shores of the Salish Sea, and all share an interest in maintaining the environment. In researching and writing this book I have found the name Salish Sea to be very helpful in understanding the Point's past and how we can view the future. Recent progress in managing the inland waters around Point Roberts as a singular entity across borders, government entities, non-governmental organizations, tribes and First Nations is proof the adoption of the term Salish Sea is fulfilling its promise and was well worth the effort in establishing this name.

Marine Drive comes down onto the flat, sea-level plain with easy access to water, which for eighty years was the only practical way to get here. This meant a lot of Point Roberts history has occurred in this southwestern quadrant of the exclave. It's the locale of its first European settlement, its airport, marina, dikes, a major park, campground and former cannery sites. This low-lying area served, and continues to serve, as a key link to the outside world.

ROBERTS TOWN

There were reports as early as 1853 that white people were fishing at Point Roberts. The next whites to visit were the Boundary Joint Commission engineers who marked the border between 1857 and 1859. It was during that time that a settlement formed on Point Roberts. In November 1857, a man named Macaulay, or something similar based on various news reports of the era, was arrested in Point Roberts for selling smuggled booze to the Boundary Commission surveyors. The *Victoria Gazette* reported the arresting officers found gold dust on him, which he explained had come from the headwaters of the Fraser River.[131] He was conveyed to Victoria, and eventually news spread down to San Francisco. The Fraser Gold Rush was the result, born here in Point Roberts. In the spring of 1858 all boats in the Salish Sea were going north, with many men deserting their jobs to join the rush; between twenty and thirty thousand men would head for the Fraser River goldfields. Entrepreneurs weren't going to pass up an opportunity to make a buck supplying these miners and a small settlement popped up in this area of Point Roberts, a convenient stop on the way up to the goldfields. Roberts Town was born.

Nothing remains of Roberts Town today. First mentioned in May 1858, not much is known about the settlement, but it was substantial enough to handle hundreds of people. The steamship *Commodore* anchored off Roberts Town with 450 miners from California on their way to the gold fields,[132] a number Point Roberts wouldn't match in its own population until the 1960s. Roberts Town was ready to outfit them. There were some half-dozen buildings and some wagons selling supplies the miners would need in the mining camps. There were two hotels to house the miners who needed to spend the night before heading up the river.

In an early nod to the role alcohol would play on Point Roberts, the stores and saloons of Roberts Town sold copious quantities of whiskey. Saloons were packed with gold miners, British soldiers from the boundary commission, and fishermen. In its two years of existence, vast amounts of whiskey were smuggled, bought, sold, fought over and stolen. Smuggling of rotgut whiskey and other contraband would continue in the early years of Point Roberts, whose bad reputation was frequently mentioned in newspapers with reports of wild brawls, smuggling, piracy and other nefarious pastimes.[133] Even the boundary soldiers in the area to map the border were in on the smuggling. American soldiers had whiskey to trade to the British, who offered beef and other hard-to-get goods. There was also trading with the Coast Salish, who still outnumbered white settlers by the thousands. The Hudson's Bay Company had already outfitted the native people with guns, pots and their signature blankets. The market was saturated; the Coast Salish weren't interested in those goods anymore. Initially the Coast Salish had rejected alcohol, but as that was about all the Americans had left to offer, more and more natives made trades for alcohol.[134]

Roberts Town was significant enough to be a stop in the Mosquito Fleet, a loosely-connected group of independently-owned steamships who provided transportation between towns on the Salish Sea decades before road were built. With a population of maybe several dozen or more, including overnight visitors, on any given night, it doesn't sound like much, but when compared to what else existed at the time, Roberts Town was one of the only settlements around. Thirteen miles east, Camp Semiahmoo had 200 people, flush with all the border surveyors. Fort Langley housed only fifty people thirty-five miles to the northeast. The big metropolis of the area was Victoria, fifty-five miles south, home to just four hundred.

It's not known exactly how long Roberts Town was in existence but it was probably about eighteen months. On the night of July 18, 1859, over a year since the earliest known reports of its founding, news reports cite a major fire which burned the store of William Fitzpatrick with a loss of $5,000 ($145,000 in today's money), and

$700 ($20,000 today) in damage to a building formerly occupied by Captain McLean. McLean owned one of the hotels; the Wiley Brothers owned another.[135]

At the time, control of Vancouver Island had transferred from the Hudson's Bay Company to become a formal Crown Colony in 1851. The Governor of the Colony of Vancouver Island was Sir James Douglas. Mainland British Columbia was still under the control of Hudson's Bay Company. Douglas watched the streams of prospectors heading up the Fraser River to the gold fields, and saw opportunity for the Crown. Seeing Roberts Town as competition, Douglas decreed in May 1858 all miners going up to the goldfields must come all the way over to Victoria to get a mining permit and pay taxes. These mining licenses were a much-needed revenue source for the young colony. By the end of June, over 2200 licenses had been sold in Victoria, whose population swelled to five thousand. The miners were also searched and handguns were confiscated, as Douglas did not want large numbers of armed Americans in his colony, a policy which hasn't really changed to this day. Inspectors also searched miners for goods miners had brought for trading with Indians, because HBC held a monopoly on all trading.

A nonstop procession of boats of all sizes, from canoes to steamships, made their way across the Salish Sea to Victoria. *The Victoria Gazette* issued daily reports of the "flotilla." One such report read: "Our bay presented a fine sight on the occasion of the departure of about fifty skiffs, canoes and boats for Fraser River. Not less than 400 miners left our town yesterday in this manner."[136] Sadly, many of these boats were not sufficiently seaworthy, and many ships were wrecked and miners drowned before they even made it to Fraser River, let alone the goldfields. Many of the lost were unknown, alone and far from their families.

Despite thousands of miners obeying orders and going out of their way to get permits in Victoria, many did not. As early as May 21, 1858, Douglas himself parked on the HBC steamer *Otter* at Point Roberts to ensure miners didn't leave Roberts Town and head directly north for the mouth of the Fraser River. To help him, Douglas had Captain James Prevost of the *Satellite* sail over to Point Roberts to meet him. They set their anchors and collected taxes from miners who were not following the rules to go to Victoria. Captain Prevost foresaw the problem of the HBC monopoly. Since HBC was unable to keep up with demand for mining supplies, it was only natural miners would seek out alternatives like Roberts Town to provision themselves for the hard work up in the goldfields. Prevost knew this was a cause of Roberts Town's famous smuggling, and urged Douglas to keep the *Satellite* positioned just off Point Roberts in British waters to intercept American miners trying to sneak into the Fraser River, handling customs and enforcement of permits and taxes. Miners tried to get around paying, but the blockade was effective. The *Satellite* was nothing to mess around with; its firepower proved an effective deterrent and the *Satellite* issued 358 mining licenses at its anchor off Roberts Town in just the first few days of its presence there. A newspaper story from the time reported, "Mr. Purser Welch, of the steamer *Surprise*, informs us that on his last trip up, some fifty of the passengers – mostly Irishmen – refused to buy licenses, and expressed their determination to disregard the law in this respect. When off Point Roberts, just at the mouth of the Fraser River, the *Surprise* was ordered alongside of the *Satellite*, boarded by her officers, and … each passenger obliged to show his license, under penalty of being put ashore. These prompt measures brought the rebellious to terms, and they were very glad to be allowed to purchase their licenses and proceed on their way." Prevost would patrol Point Roberts until June 26, 1858.[137]

And even if they somehow made it past the *Satellite*, there were additional patrols and checkpoints upriver at Fort Langley. Any miner found at Fort Langley without permits issued by the *Satellite* or in Victoria were fined five dollars (equivalent to $150 today). Americans viewed the Victoria permit and tax rule as a way to maintain the HBC monopoly. After all, many of the tax collectors weren't British personnel, but HBC personnel. Even United States officials protested the permits. Diplomatic communications were exchanged between the Governor of Washington Territory, the U.S. State Department in Washington, D.C., and the British Foreign Office to complain about the legality of what the U.S. Secretary of State deemed "the blockade of the mouth of the Fraser River by order of the Hudson's Bay Company."[138]

The folks back in London started to take notice of the gold rush commotion in the Salish Sea. It was finally time for the crown to take control of the west coast mainland of British North America from Hudson's Bay Company. As more became known of this area, and as more settlers reached the area, Britain wanted to establish itself as owning the jurisdiction, and to stake ownership of the natural resource wealth on the mainland, making clear the Crown owned the land, not HBC. Hudson's Bay Company had been increasingly staking claims to resources like salmon, which was becoming a bigger share of their trading. Most of the salmon the Crown and HBC wanted would swim by Point Roberts. On August 2, 1858 the British Parliament converted HBC's mainland territory into the Crown Colony of British Columbia. Douglas was named Governor, meaning he would govern both the British Columbia and Vancouver Island colonies, on the condition he was to sever all ties with HBC. On August 1, 1858, Douglas departed from his home in Victoria to travel to the mainland for his inauguration, but the tides were such he couldn't get all the way to Fort Langley that night, so he overnighted in Roberts Town on the eve of his swearing in as Governor. Salmon, the gold rush and British nationalism all caused settlement in Point Roberts but in an example of the tail wagging the dog, tiny Point Roberts played a role in triggering the creation of the Colony of British Columbia.

Figure 20: James Douglas. Photo: Author unknown [Public domain], via Wikimedia Commons.

Once inaugurated, Douglas got busy with governing the colony. Douglas' second-in-command, Lieutenant-Governor Richard Moody selected New Westminster as capital of British Columbia, but he called it Queenborough. It took no less than Queen Victoria to rename Queenborough to New Westminster a year later on July 20, 1859. As a result, Douglas would often go back and forth between Victoria, New Westminster and Fort Langley. The accommodations and brawls in Roberts Town couldn't have been too bad as just a few weeks after inauguration Douglas again overnighted at Roberts Town. On the evening of August 30, 1858 Douglas and twenty-two Royal Marines and fourteen Royal Engineers stopped for the night at Roberts Town before continuing on the next day on the *Satellite* (yes, the same ship which had been blockading the Point) to meet up with the *Recovery* anchored in the Fraser River.

Three months later, on the occasion of the installation of the new British Columbia colonial government, an elite group of government bigwigs came to Roberts Town. An entourage of no less than Rear Admiral Robert Lambert Baynes, Commander of British naval forces in the Pacific, Colony of Vancouver Island Chief Justice David Cameron, the "Hanging Judge" Matthew Begbie and Governor Douglas all climbed aboard the *Satellite* in Victoria and headed up Haro Strait on their way to Fort Langley for the ceremonies. They all spent the night November 18, 1858 in Roberts Town, with the *Satellite* returning to Victoria. The dignitaries were picked up the next morning at Roberts Town by the

Otter, which took them to the *Beaver* which was moored and waiting at Ladner to head up river to Fort Langley. The *Otter* was a side-wheeler and the second HBC steamship to operate in the area, after its more famous sister ship the *Beaver*. Before being drafted for service in the Fraser River gold rush, the *Otter* had been busy running between HBC forts around the Salish Sea. After its service in the gold rush, the *Beaver* continued to ferry officials between Victoria and New Westminster, right past Point Roberts, until she was wrecked in 1888 at Prospect Point in Vancouver's Stanley Park. Despite using Roberts Town for its convenient location in the Salish Sea midway between Victoria and Fort Langley, and maybe because of having spent time there, the young colonial governments were wary of Roberts Town's reputation and the powerful economic influence it had in the Salish Sea despite its small size. Soon after arriving in British Columbia, Moody took a tour of the area, since his job was defense and control of the young colony. Moody said Point Roberts was "a serious thorn in our side. A smuggling town is being built on the American portion and by and bye there will be a Citadel of the First Class."[139]

These nights when Douglas slept in Roberts Town, one wonders if he realized the significance of its namesake. The Henry Roberts for whom Roberts Town and Point Roberts is named is the same Henry Roberts who captured Demerara in Guiana for Britain from the Dutch. In doing so, colonists were needed to populate the newly captured lands. A Scottish couple moved to Demerara from Barbados. John Douglas was a merchant from Glasgow who had married a mixed-race Creole woman, Martha Ann Telfer. They had three children; Jimmy was the middle child, born in 1803 in Demerara just seven years after Henry Roberts captured it from the Netherlands. He would grow up to become Sir James Douglas, who would blockade, but also thrice sleep in Point Roberts, named for the liberator of the colony in which he was born. In a twist of irony, Henry Roberts gave his life for Demerara to be British so Douglas could be born, yet Douglas would grow up to compete with the town named for the same man.

Most miners went bust in the gold rush, and though they were not supposed to visit Roberts Town on the way *to* the goldfields, nothing prevented them stopping there on the way back, and as a convenient first-port-of-call in the United States, many did. Also active in Roberts Town were the Coast Salish people. They were often hired as guides, packers and canoeists for those heading north, and many were hired to take miners back home in canoes on their way south.

Soon, the gold rush was over, the miners stopped coming, and Roberts Town declined. As Roberts Town was fizzling out, the U.S. Department of the Interior engineers surveyed Point Roberts section by section from June through October 1859. At that point, Point Roberts became a military reservation, from September 13, 1859. During its military reservation status, Point Roberts fell into a slumber as the rest of the Salish Sea boomed.

Evidence of whites at the Point as early as 1853 and a town as early as 1857 makes it one of the earliest settlements on the Salish Sea, which demonstrates how lucrative the fishing at Point Roberts was. To put it into context, consider that as late as 1849, Olympia, which had been established in 1846, was the only white non-fort settlement on Puget Sound. The only Hudson's Bay Company forts on the Salish Sea were established in 1832 at Fort Nisqually (at present-day Dupont, Washington), and Victoria, established in 1843. Seattle was only settled in 1851. The towns around Bellingham Bay got started in 1854. Roberts Town was one of only five towns in all of Whatcom County at the time, together with New Whatcom, Sehome, Fairhaven and Semiahmoo (the first three of which would merge to become Bellingham in 1903). Roberts Town was one of the earliest towns in Whatcom County; Lynden wouldn't be settled until 1871, Ferndale until 1872, and downtown Blaine was not established until 1884. Ladner was not established until 1868. The city of Vancouver wasn't founded until 1862, five years after Roberts Town and sixty-six years after its namesake George Vancouver died. When Roberts Town thrived Vancouver Island was still its own British colony. As late as 1848, all of California was still owned by Mexico. Alaska was still Russian; the United States wouldn't buy it for ten more years.

In the same summer as Roberts Town was booming and the engineers were busy marking the border at Point Roberts, on June 15, 1859 an American shot a British pig found in his garden on San Juan Island, just fifteen miles south of Point Roberts. The dead pig sparked the Pig War, a fifteen year conflict between the United States and Great Britain. The 1846 Treaty of Washington stated the

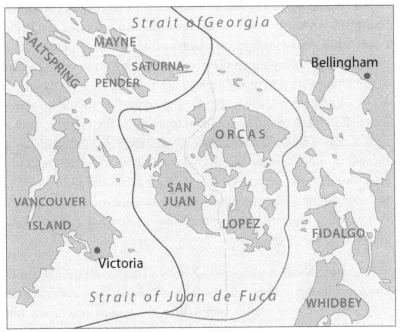

Figure 21: Map showing the lands 10 miles south of Point Roberts disputed in the Pig War. The U.S. and Britain both wanted the San Juan Islands. By Pfly [CC BY-SA 3.0 (http://creativecommons.org/licenses/by-sa/3.0) or GFDL (http://www.gnu.org/copyleft/fdl.html)], via Wikimedia Commons.

border between the United States and Britain was "along the forty-ninth parallel of north latitude to the middle of the channel which separates the continent from Vancouver Island, and thence southerly through the middle of the said channel, and of the Strait of Juan de Fuca, to the Pacific Ocean."

The trouble was there is an island archipelago in that channel – the San Juan and Southern Gulf islands – and there were actually two major straits which could be interpreted as being the one in the middle: Haro Strait, between Vancouver Island and San Juan Island, and Rosario Strait, on the east side of the San Juan Islands separating them from the Washington mainland. The intended route was not clear.

The boundary survey began when U.S. Commissioner Archibald Campbell arrived in Victoria on June 22, 1857 to meet his British counterpart, John Hawkins. Hawkins wasn't there, so Campbell had his team start surveying on their own. Five days later Campbell left Point Roberts to return to Victoria to meet Prevost on board the HMS *Satellite* to discuss where the boundary line should go after it leaves Point Roberts. The events leading up to the Pig War were so urgent that Campbell and Hawkins wouldn't finally sit down to discuss the boundary survey for over a year, even though both men were in the same general vicinity of each other and the Americans were already marking the border during those thirteen months. The British were distracted during that time blockading Roberts Town during the Fraser gold rush.

The British and Americans had been trying to work on where the boundary line should go after it leaves Point Roberts for two years before the pig was shot. James Prevost, a year before his duty blockading Roberts Town, led the British team and Archibald Campbell, in the middle of his duties marking the border at Point Roberts, took on the Pig War post for the Americans. Campbell appointed Parke his Second Commissioner. On June 27, 1857,

Prevost and Campbell met for the first time on board the HMS *Satellite* at Victoria (just five days after Campbell had tried to meet Hawkins in Victoria before giving up and going to Point Roberts to start the boundary survey). In their negotiations, Prevost and Campbell discussed the Treaty of Washington's meaning of how the border should proceed from Point Roberts "in a southerly direction." Campbell argued for the boundary to be drawn down Haro Strait, as the Americans were interested in the agricultural opportunities in the San Juan Islands. Prevost wanted the border drawn through Rosario Strait, giving the San Juan Islands to Britain as a buffer zone so the American boundary wouldn't be right off Victoria's eastern beaches. He feared American control of all the straits connecting the Strait of Georgia and the Pacific Ocean. Campbell argued Rosario Strait is not southerly from Point Roberts; it is far to the southeast. If the map was drawn that way, the boundary would extend far west into the Salish Sea only to accommodate Point Roberts, and then return back far to the east toward Lummi Island. A compromise line down the middle of the San Juan Islands was quickly rejected. A stalemate was declared in December 1857; they reported back to their governments without a solution, doubtlessly eager to pay attention to the Fraser Gold Rush and the troubles at Roberts Town which was ramping up at the time.

Meanwhile, as the situation was up in the air, both countries tried to establish a firmer presence on San Juan Island. Hudson's Bay Company opened a sheep ranch, and over twenty-five Americans had settled on the island by mid-1857, including Lyman Cutlar, who shot the pig in his garden on June 15, 1859. The pig belonged to a worker on the British sheep ranch, who rejected Cutlar's offer of ten dollars compensation ($280 today), demanding $100. Cutlar requested U.S. military assistance after British officials tried to arrest him. Roberts Town was still booming when 461 American troops and 2140 British troops were quickly stationed in camps on either end of San Juan Island. Today these camps are preserved as the San Juan Island National Historical Park, the closest U.S.

National Park to Point Roberts. The Pig War helped many of the crew from the boundary survey at Point Roberts and Fort Bellingham to be able to continue working by going to San Juan Island and likely contributed to the decline of Roberts Town.

Less than three months after the pig was shot, on September 13, 1859 Point Roberts became a military reservation as a potential resource for the looming war in the San Juan Islands. Tensions were high as Prevost called for Britain to forcibly invade and take back all of the Salish Sea – essentially the state of Washington – whilst the Americans were distracted by the Civil War in the U.S. South. The Point Roberts Military Reservation would have been a major staging ground for the defense of the San Juan Islands and American territory in the Salish Sea if the British did escalate the war, but no military personnel or equipment was ever stationed at the Point Roberts Military Reserve. Kaiser Wilhelm I of Germany was chosen to serve as arbitrator to resolve the Pig War. His arbitration commission met in Geneva for nearly a year. On October 21, 1872, the commission decided in favor of the United States, selecting the American-preferred boundary of Haro Strait. The British withdrew from San Juan Island in November 1872. American troops left San Juan Island in July 1874, fifteen years after the pig was shot, one of the longest "wars" in U.S. history, in the backyard of Point Roberts.

AIRPARK

On the right is Freeman Beach, a neighborhood of cottages named for Harry Freeman. He built the original row of small cottages here in the early 1930s. Freeman moved to Point Roberts in 1911 and with the profits from selling his New Westminster hotel bought this area from its original owner, Edward Tinkham, a wealthy wool merchant. The area had been known as Tinkham's Grove from the turn of the century, and was often used for town picnics and ball games. In 1931 Freeman rebuilt his own home and, following the trend we'll see in other neighborhoods on this tour, subdivided the land to construct a dense neighborhood of cottages. Back then the road through the west side of Point Roberts was the lane inside the Freeman Beach neighborhood; the road ran along the beach in front of the cottages.[140] The road we've been traveling on, Marine Drive, wasn't built until 1934 after the flood of 1932 devastated this low-lying area prompting the street to be rebuilt a bit more inland.

Across the street from Freeman Beach, you can get a glimpse of the green grassy strip of the local airport, the Point Roberts Airpark. Arriving by air is certainly the most scenic way to get to the Point, and save having a boat, this is the only way to get to Point Roberts for those who cannot cross the Canadian land border due to criminal convictions and the like.

The Point Roberts Airpark, with coordinates of 48°58'47.0"N 123°04'44.0"W, has a single 2265-foot north-south grass air strip. The Airpark was originally called Ray Young Field after its founder, a cartoonist at Disney's Buena Vista Studios in Hollywood. Young drew Bugs Bunny at his day job, and had a penchant for flying in his off hours.[141] He bought the land for the airport in 1967, and air service was inaugurated in August 1972, and immediately it was clear there was demand for the service to transport goods from the mainland. "The problem of buying goods in the U.S. and getting them home to Point Roberts led the Youngs to initiate their flying service," explained the local newspaper.[142] Soon after its opening, five airplanes began regularly bringing goods from Blaine by air. In 1982, the Airpark hosted its first fly-in. Planes from six air clubs landed at Point Roberts.[143] After his death in 1985, Young's wife closed the airport. During the time it was closed, it was not being maintained. Seven years later the Airpark was still closed when a World War I double wing plane landed on the grass strip. Young might have recognized the airplane; it belonged to Disney Corporation. They were filming a movie on July 4, 1989 but a paperwork problem prevented it from landing at Canada's Boundary Bay Airport, and the Airpark was the plan B.[144]

Young's wife sold it in September 1996[145] to Robin Lamb, who spent three years improving the field so it could reopen to aviation. Eight acres of trees & brush were cleared, the strip was re-graded, and facilities were added in 2000. Today, over half a dozen pilots are based at the Airpark. Commercial air service on started in 2009. San Juan Airlines provides scheduled commercial flights to their hub in Bellingham for $120 or so each way. There are two flights a day to Bellingham on Tuesdays and on Thursdays, one in the morning and one in the afternoon. Direct flights can be arranged to Eastsound and Friday Harbor and even Seattle. If you fly out from Point Roberts, have a friend drop you off; the Airpark is so small there's no parking lot.

Point Roberts is in a busy air corridor, with planes from Vancouver International, Boundary Bay, Victoria and its own Airpark all crowding the sky. With all that traffic, there have been some incidents at Point Roberts. In aviation's early history, a plane taking off from Port Dix Airport in Victoria crashed into the town pier in the 1930s. In the World War II years, the flat lowlands along Boundary Bay's northern shore brought the arrival of an air force base just north of Point Roberts. Opening April 10, 1941 the Royal Canadian Air Force Station Boundary Bay opened. Eventually becoming Canadian Forces Station Ladner, it closed in 1971, reopening in 1983 as Boundary Bay Airport. Several defense aircraft had crashes during World War II near Point Roberts. On July 27, 1943, just a few feet off Lighthouse Park but in 540 feet of water, P/O M. A. Foster's P-40 aircraft was recovered. On December 15, 1944, three air force servicemen were killed during a bombing exercise in waters just off Point Roberts, including the base's most-experienced pilot. Three more crewmembers were able to bail out and were rescued. After a normal takeoff, suddenly all four engines stopped at once, forcing the plane into a shallow dive from which it never recovered. A problem in the electrical system was likely, but the survivors weren't sure and the cause was never revealed. The men stationed at the air force base were in shock for days.

Boundary Bay Air Force Base lost two Liberators in two days on January 9th and 10th, 1945. Three of the seven passengers were killed in one of the crashes which happened in Point Roberts during a bombing practice run. Four crew members parachuted to safety. The crash was caused by an explosion in the bomb bay. A leak in a heater was blamed, and following this Point Roberts crash, heaters were banned in all five Liberators, which wasn't popular that winter. The waters just off Point Roberts were referred to as the Point Roberts Bombing Range. On June 26, 1945, the crew of a Liberator plane ran into difficulties at 1:45 A.M. The B24 was on its second run on the bombing range. The first bomb had dropped all right. On the second run, a control panel light indicated the bomb had gone and the bomb doors were closed. The plane crashed shortly thereafter.

Kept secret for years, the Japanese launched ten thousand fire balloons to North America during World War II. These balloons carried 300 pounds of explosives each and were carried by air currents to North America where they were intended to crash into the forests, sparking forest fires, which would drain resources from the Allied war effort. One landed on a beach at Point Roberts and failed to explode.[146]

In the decades after the war, more aviation incidents occurred. In August 1950, Robert MacPherson, owner of a B.C. industrial bearings distribution firm launched during World War II, was flying from Vancouver to a summer home in the Sunshine Coast. A Royal Canadian Air Force pilot during the war, he tried to make an emergency landing at Point Roberts after his plane's engine stalled and the plane went into a tailspin. MacPherson was instantly killed.

Figure 22: Japanese Fire Balloon which landed on the beach at Point Roberts. Photo by Canadian Department of National Defense/Library and Archives Canada.

Civilians reported to the RCAF station they saw a plane crash and explode off Point Roberts on October 22, 1956, but after searches by the RCAF and the U.S. Border Patrol the plane was never found.

More recently, a Bellingham float plane crashed on takeoff at South Beach on October 9, 1978, when its pontoon strut snapped causing the left wing to strike the water. Fishermen toed it to shore in rough seas.[147] In May 1994, a plane collided with a deer at the Point Roberts Airpark.[148] Being so close to the border means some mix-ups occur. A Canadian plane accidentally landed in the U.S. at the Airpark in May 1988.[149]

LIGHTHOUSE CANNERY

Further down on the right, the large yellow building played a major role in Point Roberts history, as a former cannery and later a ballroom and nightclub. The Lighthouse Packing Company was founded in 1934 by Archie McMillan, who had been a fish trap operator since his youth. Just after founding the cannery, fish traps were outlawed, but individual fishermen still supplied salmon for the cannery. (Fish traps and fishing in general is covered in chapter 4.) After six years, the cannery was sold to the Iwersen family. After initially operating it as a salmon cannery, the economic conditions of the Great Depression prompted the Iwersens to refit it as a clam cannery. The operation canned native littleneck clams collected in the Gulf Islands and brought to the cannery by dump truck, where they were dumped in huge piles in front of the cannery. One day, border inspector Pa Davis was in a mood to go by the book, and stopped a truckload of clams because they were supposed to be in boxes. Tempers rose as the delay put the highly-perishable clams, loose in the truck bed, at risk of spoilage.[150]

Whilst other shellfish get most of the attention, the humble clam has played a major role in the history of the Salish Sea and doesn't get the attention it deserves. Oysters were popular in the San Francisco Bay area, and when the industry there had depleted their local stocks, they came to the Salish Sea to harvest oysters. Clams were caught in the process, and sent to market, creating demand for clams. The Coast Salish people dug for littleneck clams with sharpened sticks, cooking them between layers of seaweed on hot rocks in pits for a soup of clams and tubers – essentially today's clam chowder without the cream.

In the commercial clam industry, baby clams with shells just a quarter inch across are planted into a groomed tidal flat an inch apart, as one plants seeds in a garden. Some growers use mesh cubes anchored to the sea floor at low tide. Clams burrow three inches, filtering plankton for three years before they're harvested by workers walking along with a clam rig, a tool with prongs which dig up and collect clams as the worker walks in a line, done today the way it has been done for over a century in the Salish Sea.

Nobody in the Salish Sea is more closely identified with clams than Ivar Haglund, a Seattle politician, radio personality and restaurateur. In 1938, Haglund opened Seattle's first aquarium at Pier 54 and a fish and chips shop on the Seattle waterfront, followed by the famous Ivar's Acres of Clams restaurant in 1946. For the next forty years, Haglund would be a Seattle institution, famous for his publicity stunts, radio shows and local folk music.

From one of the founding families of Seattle, Haglund was born in 1905. His maternal grandparents had bought Alki Point from Doc Maynard, one of Seattle's original settlers, and Ivar was very much aware of and had respect for Salish Sea history. He was a natural ham and came to be an expert in Northwest folk music; he could sing over 200 songs by heart. He would continue to sing throughout his life, on stage, around town, as he grew his business empire and on radio. Ivar got into radio by chance in 1940, filling in as a guest for a local radio personality who needed a last minute replacement. He sang some of his folk songs intermixed with stories about the Pacific Northwest. Before long, Ivar's presence on the radio propelled him to be the Salish Sea's greatest folk musician. This attracted national folk singers of the 1940s. When Woody Guthrie and Pete Seeger visited Seattle, they stayed with Ivar and his wife. During a visit, they taught Ivar an 1877 Northwest folk song called *Old Settler's Song*, whose last line goes, *"No longer a slave of ambition, I laugh at the world and its shams, and I think of my happy condition, surrounded by acres of clams."* This song became the inspiration and catch phrase for his restaurant. Ivar the restaurateur would go on to become a media celebrity, starting with a 15-minute radio show each Sunday called "Around the Sound with Ivar Haglund." He had a regular role on a local TV station's children's program in the 1950s, playing the role of First Mate Salty, a sidekick to Captain Puget.

On a trip to Oregon, Haglund visited the aquarium at Seaside, which features seals visitors can feed. He studied how the operation worked. Back in Seattle, he built a tank at Pier 54, circulated in salt water from Elliott Bay and fed seals, sea lions and other northwest sea life. Ivar could be found in a captain's hat on the sidewalk out front singing folk songs to draw in customers. He found it an easy way to make a dime during the Depression. He had an innate sense of how to generate free publicity, like taking a baby seal dressed up in doll clothes in a pram to see Santa Claus in a downtown department store in 1940. Ivar liked corny puns and used them in all kinds of memes and campaigns, and even in the motto of his restaurants, "keep clam." School kids were enraptured by his stories and songs about Barney Barnacle, Herman the Hermit Crab and Oscar and Olivia Octopus.

The aquarium would close in 1956 due to pollutants in the bay killing off his zoo animals. The aquarium may not have lasted, but the Acres of Clams restaurant did. Time and again, Ivar was clever enough to capitalize on events near his restaurant, with his signature corny style. In 1947, a tanker truck spilled a thousand gallons of syrup across the street from the Acres of Clams. With a rushed order of pancakes from the kitchen, Ivar grabbed a huge spoon and ran over to the spill, happily posing for the press who had arrived on the scene. The photo was carried by the wires globally with the headline "Crown Prince of Corn." Ivar also started an annual littleneck clam-eating contest, with the 1948 winner eating 131 clams in ten minutes.

After Maine Senator Margaret Chase Smith lobbied for a postage stamp commemorating sardines, Ivar approached Washington's Senators for a clam stamp. A friend printed several thousand stamps in sheets, which Ivar sent with a bag of clams to Washington Senator Warren Magnuson. Ivar basked in the press, including a widely distributed photo of both of Washington's Senators enjoying Ivar's clams with Smith. When Ivar began selling the realistic stamps in his gift shop in 1960 the Postal Service confiscated & incinerated the stamps.

In 1965, Ivar started sponsoring Seattle's annual fireworks display on the Fourth of July, which was touted as the Fourth of Julivars; the sponsorship by Ivar's Restaurants lasted for forty-three years. By the early 1970s, waves of Seattleites had grown up at Ivar's on Seattle's waterfront. The ordering counter is open to the sidewalk, with patrons walking up to order their clams or fish and chips, and then sitting on outdoor picnic tables on the pier. Children delighted in feeding French fries to the seagulls. Not everybody appreciated the daily feeding frenzy, especially Harbor Tours next door at Pier 56, who in 1971 hung a "do not feed the seagulls" sign, citing health regulations. They should have known with whom they were dealing. Ivar countered with a sign facing Harbor Tours' pier welcoming seagulls and inviting his customers to feed them, saying, "I don't want to embarrass my neighbors, they do what they want to on their pier and I'll do what I want to on mine. I consider sea gulls the unpaid guardians of public health. They keep the waterfront free of garbage. They are beautiful useful scavengers," defended Ivar, delighting in the resulting tsunami of free publicity, and lots of French fry sales.

A few blocks from his Elliott Bay restaurant stands Seattle's iconic Smith Tower, named for its builder, Lyman Smith, the Smith of Smith-Corona typewriter fame. Built in 1914, it was one of America's earliest skyscrapers, and was the tallest building on the west coast for forty-eight years until Seattle's Space Needle was constructed in 1962 for its world's fair. Haglund bought the thirty-eight-story, 489 foot (149m) tower in 1976. Coincidentally, Gustav Iwersen had been the building's elevator operator decades earlier.[151] Haglund topped the Smith Tower with a sixteen foot windsock he had bought on a trip to China. By now, one would think it was clear what Ivar was capable of when provoked, yet a city official cited Ivar for violating city ordinance. Ivar did what he did best; he harnessed the power of a media campaign portraying himself as the victim of a nanny state. Ivar won, and the city granted a variance for salmon-shaped windsocks.

In one of his last publicity stunts, Ivar wanted to try to get boxcars moved from the railroad tracks across the street from his restaurant, so in 1983 merely as a stunt, he joked about running for a seat on the port commission. Ivar rode the publicity for a while, but then missed the deadline to withdraw from the race, and his name stayed on the ballot. As a beloved Seattle institution, he attracted voters and won a six-year term to public office by over thirty thousand votes. The bureaucracy was tedious and he missed many meetings, offering to make amends to his unamused fellow commissioners with free clam chowder. He wouldn't survive his term; Ivar would succumb to a heart attack in January 1985 at age seventy-nine.

For a time Ivar Haglund was one of the Iwersens' best customers for canned clams and clam nectar. Point Roberts was the source of the canned clams upon which Ivar built his fame.

Figure 23: The Breakers brand of seafood packed in the Lighthouse Cannery. Photo: Outdoor display at Point Roberts Community Center.

The Iwersens were busy as owners of the Breakers tavern, so they closed the cannery in 1961. For the rest of the 1960s, the property served as a boat launch and even a small trailer park. In 1972, it reopened as a restaurant and nightclub known as The

Cannery. The old boiler room was now the kitchen. Pete Hoeruegel and Company led the band Saturday nights, drawing crowds of ballroom dancing Canadian couples. After tweaking the name in 1982 to Cannery Row, in 1984 it changed to Boondocks for the rest of the 1980s. Nationally-famous big band leader Woody Herman played at the Cannery to the Lawrence Welk crowd in the 1980s, working well into his seventies to pay off millions in IRS debt due to bad bookkeeping in the 1960s.[152] A younger crowd was in attendance in 1988 when Boondocks hosted REO Speedwagon and Sarah McLachlan concerts. A restaurant named Petticoat Lane Café opened inside Cannery Row in 1982. The name swung back to Cannery Restaurant and Lounge in 1990. It was known for its clam nectar. Incredibly, in January 1992, the Cannery was renamed Boondocks again, and then in the mid-1990s back to the Cannery! It became Pier Point Restaurant in 1998, but after a couple of years it closed and today sits empty yet promising along Marine Drive. Few locals or visitors can drive by and not see an attractive, large, beachfront building with so much history and potential.

Figure 24: Lighthouse Cannery sits empty on Marine Drive. Photo by Mark Swenson.

Every so often the local newspaper reports plans to develop the property into a conference center, hotel and/or resort but lack of sewers, financing and permits continue to limit development on the Point. Locals invariably take an "I'll believe it when I see it" attitude to these announcements.

The large yellow cannery serves as a handy Point Roberts landmark for watercraft in the Strait of Georgia. George Vancouver found Point Roberts without a big yellow cannery, but one of the most famous explorers of our time couldn't find Point Roberts despite the fact he was actually looking for a big yellow cannery. Sir Ranulph Fiennes, third cousin to actor Ralph Fiennes, has earned the title World's Greatest Living Explorer by the *Guinness Book of World Records*, has explored the entire globe from pole to pole but failed to find Point Roberts, though in his defense it was a bit foggy that day.[153] In 1972, Fiennes led the Headless Valley expedition through the Nahanni Valley in the Northwest Territories and northern British Columbia. The expedition was the first crossing of Canada north to south, inland but going by water. Even today, much of the rugged interior of that part of Canada is unexplored. Fiennes and his team, including a BBC TV camera crew, traveled in small rubber boats through the valley's famous four canyons, with mammoth waterfalls twice as high as Niagara Falls, narrow canyons and hungry wildlife. Coming down into the Lower Mainland, the expedition needed to reach the U.S. border by water to achieve its goal. As the closest point of the United States to the mouth of the Fraser River, Point Roberts was the finish line of this herculean trek. But Fiennes couldn't find it. He had emerged into the Salish Sea in a thick fog. He was helplessly lost in pea soup when he heard the locals, and a Delta police launch, calling out to him in the fog. Fiennes writes in his autobiography of the expedition, "A sea mist crept over the Delta marshes and we nosed cautiously west into Pacific waters until, clear of hidden shoals, our route lay south to Point Roberts. A fog horn sounded through the murk; a dead, clammy sound and many times we lost each other and all sense of direction in the fog."[154] At four o'clock, Fiennes heard a Delta officer calling out, "This is it, folks, you done it. We're in in Yank territory now." The explorers cracked open champagne as they were guided by the launch to the beach in front of the Lighthouse Cannery for what would have been a photo finish in better weather.

Fiennes continues, "The sea slapped softly on a gentle beach. There were many people with flashing lights and cameras, a U.S. ranger with a drooping Stars 'n Stripes and a Mountie with a Maple Leaf. Ginnie and Sarah were there and a host of well-wishers. We had crossed the 49th Parallel; many cold green leagues from the Nahanni and the Arctic Circle."[155]

Fiennes would go on seven years later to his most famous expedition, the 1979 to 1982 Transglobe, which made Fiennes the first man to reach both North and South Poles overland. He led six unsuccessful attempts to reach the North Pole unaided between 1986 and 1996, and led the longest unsupported polar journey across the Antarctic in 1993 until Fiennes had to call it off due to crotch rot after wearing the same pair of underwear for fifty days. Fiennes retired in 2000.[156]

LIGHTHOUSE MARINE PARK

At the southern end of Marine Drive is Lighthouse Marine Park, situated on the southwest tip of Point Roberts and one of the Point's must-see sights. The federal government had kept this land for a light, but they never got around to building a proper lighthouse. Ownership passed to the township where it remained undeveloped land for decades. There was no fence; anybody could drive in. It was mostly gravel, dirt and lots of trash. As one of its final acts as it was being dissolved by the state, the township deeded the land to the Parks District, which became official in February 1971.[157] Plans were drawn up, survey work was completed in record time and cleanup started quickly thereafter. It took two years to clear the land and create the park. A 1972 real estate ad in the local paper chortled, "Point Roberts is 'on the move'!! Have you seen what is happening at Lighthouse Park? Drive by and take a look!! No longer is it a repository for assorted garbage and broken bottles. Its very contours have changed beyond all recognition."[158] Opened June 16, 1973 as part of the Whatcom County Parks system, Lighthouse Marine Park offers twenty-one acres of windswept

Figure 25: The southwest corner of Point Roberts was undeveloped land for decades until it became a park in 1973. Photo by Whatcom Museum #1995.1.20986; Bellingham, WA.

grounds, trails and beaches on both the west and south side of the Point. A gravel trail runs along the shore offering an amazing 270 degree view of the Strait of Georgia. Standing at the tip of the southwest point, the viewshed extends from the North Shore mountains of Burrard Inlet, the Canadian Gulf Islands, the U.S. San Juan Islands, most of Whatcom County's shoreline on the mainland and Mount Baker. The park offers a wooden boardwalk, funky 1970s-era picnic shelters, trails, a boat launch and seasonally-placed dock, but despite its name, no lighthouse. On summer days, over three thousand people visit the park each day. A thirty-site campground is open April through October with fire rings, water, flush toilets and showers in the main campground across Marine Drive.

Much has changed over its four decades as a park. From the beginning, there was a toll booth guarding the entrance to the park. Whatcom County residents and property owners could enter for free but all others had to pay an entry fee even to briefly check out the view. The fee was one dollar when the park opened in 1973.[159] That doesn't sound like much but it is the equivalent of $5.87 in today's money. By the 2000s it had risen to four dollars. On average a full half of drivers refused and drove away. Canadians make up 94% of license plates in the park.[160] The fee was finally eliminated in 2006.[161] In the early 1980s the park was closed on Wednesdays and Thursdays due to budget cuts; [162] today it's open seven days a week. The original 60,000 square foot boardwalk is considerably smaller now after major portions rotted. A cool thirty-five-foot lookout tower constructed from surplus power poles found on the site was demolished. Over the years there has been an orca museum, gift shop, concession stand serving hot dogs, soft drinks and snacks in season. The park even had an espresso stand in 1993.[163] No concessions operate today.

The park architect's original design called for a few features which never materialized. Just off the boardwalk was to be a giant sandbox for children. The large field and group camp were to have been kept as swampy wetlands. Cut into berms built near shore were to have been niches containing picnic facilities and fire pits. The campground across the street was originally for overflow parking (the park's plans called for parking for 300 cars), reached by car over a bridge crossing the ditch, but by foot via an underground pedestrian tunnel under Marine Drive. (An alternative plan would have reshaped Marine Drive behind the campground before joining Edwards Drive so the road wouldn't cut through the park.) There would have been a lighthouse, of course. The vision was described by the first park manager, "We hope to encase it [the present light] in some sort of material which would make it look more like an old fashioned lighthouse."[164] None of that ever got built, but Lighthouse Park is still a wonderful park. Let's explore it now by walking from the parking lot along the shoreline trail.

EXCLAVES

The expansive views from the path help you to see you're in an exclave, a part of a country's territory only reachable by land by traversing a foreign country. With a border 5525 miles long, the boundary between Canada and the United States is the longest in the world. Much of this border is a long isolated straight line, either between Alaska and the Yukon, or the very long, very straight 49th parallel. However, nature does not come in straight lines, and along the U.S.–Canadian border there are six populated exclaves. Alaska, of course, is the big one, the largest exclave in the world. Point Roberts is the closest piece of American territory to Alaska, five hundred miles up the coast to the north.

Curiously, each end of the boundary on the 49th parallel and each end of the U.S.-Canadian border are bookended by exclaves. Heading east from Point Roberts, the next exclave is on the Manitoba – Minnesota border at the eastern end of the portion of border which follows the 49th parallel. The northernmost place in the contiguous United States and the only place in the lower 48 north of the 49th Parallel is the Northwest Angle. It's a piece of U.S. land on the north shore of Lake of the Woods which can only be reached by land by driving sixty-three miles through Manitoba. Several islands in the lake are also U.S. territory. One needn't reach it by land, however. Many fly in by private aircraft or arrive by boat. In winter, driving by ice road from mainland Minnesota is possible. Only one hundred or so live in this exclave which they call The Angle. Immigration and customs is handled by a roadside kiosk with videophone to a remote official. The big draw which makes travel to this exclave worth the hassle is top notch walleye fishing.[165] Off the north coast of Northwest Angle is Magnusons Island, and on the north coast of Magnusons Island is American Point Island, home to Penasse, the northernmost town in the lower

48. Reachable only by boat, it is the northernmost tip of the little hump in the top of Minnesota.

The Northwest Angle ended up as an exclave because of Benjamin Franklin. Franklin negotiated hard with Britain at the end the Revolutionary War in the 1783 Treaty of Paris to draw the boundary of the newly-independent United States from the boundary waters in the Great Lakes to the "most northwesternmost point" of the Lake of the Woods, and from that point due west to the Mississippi River. But the maps they were using were wrong, and the Mississippi didn't come up far north enough to have the line drawn to it from the Northwest Angle. So, when the boundary was drawn to the west on the 49th parallel in 1818, the line was drawn from Franklin's northwestern point mentioned in the 1783 treaty due south to the 49th parallel, creating the Northwest Angle.

The easternmost U.S. exclave is the Alburgh Tongue, a Quebec peninsula which extends over the boundary line into Lake Champlain. Because it has the town of Alburgh, Vermont on it, population two thousand, there is a bridge to it from the rest of Vermont, so unlike the other exclaves you don't have to go through Canada to reach it by car. Canada has two exclaves in the United States as well. One is on First Nations land. Akwesasne Reserve is a small Quebec community which can only be reached by land from the rest of Canada by going through New York.

The other Canadian exclave is Campobello Island, an island of New Brunswick in the Bay of Fundy which can only be reached by land by crossing the Franklin Delano Roosevelt Bridge from Lubec, Maine. Just like Point Roberts' superlative is that it is the north-northwesternmost town in the lower forty-eight, Lubec has its own superlative; it's the easternmost tip of the continental United States. Campobello Island is home to FDR's summer home, today the showpiece of the Roosevelt-Campobello International Park.

Campobello Island has so much in common with Point Roberts they officially became sister cities in May 2017. (Outside North America, the term "twin towns" is more common.) Over 2000 towns in the United States are in sister city relationships with other cities in 136 countries, beginning in 1931 when Toledo, Ohio became sister cities with Toledo, Spain. The similarities between the Point and Campobello are numerous. The far western and eastern ends of the U.S.-Canadian boundary are bookended by pene-exclaves, meaning the exclaves are not land-locked. Both exclaves have extensive salt water coastlines. Both are busy during summer season and dead in the winter. Both the Salish Sea and the Bay of Fundy are known for their very high tidal swings, over ten feet difference between low and high tide. The population is very similar, 1300 in Point Roberts and 1200 on Campobello Island. During a visit to Campobello, I was struck by how both exclaves have a very similar feel. Each has a rural feel since neither exclave has a real town center or dense business strip. Both towns have a long history of smuggling. They both allocate of a significant portion of their limited area to a sprawling golf course. Each has one large main supermarket to serve the exclave. Even the border experience is familiar: leaving Campobello Island and returning over the bridge to the United States at the Lubec port of entry, I was pulled in to secondary inspection. Sister cities, indeed!

Despite all of these similarities, there are differences. Aside from the obvious difference each exclave is in the opposite country, Campobello Island has ferry service to Deer Island, New Brunswick, providing a link with the rest of Canada in the summer season, eliminating the need to go through the United States when traveling by car. At fifteen square miles, Campobello Island is three times larger than Point Roberts in area. Point Roberts is growing, whilst Campobello Island is not. Campobello used to have a population of 1305 like Point Roberts, but it lost over eight per cent of its people since the mid-1990s. With more area, Campobello Islands is also less dense than Point Roberts, 80 people per square mile versus 300 on the Point. Campobello Island has a main provincial highway running across its length with an eighty kilometer per hour speed limit, compared to Point Roberts who has no numbered county highways, let alone state-level highways, and a maximum speed limit of fifty kilometers per hour. With Point Roberts being relatively rectangular, its beaches are fairly straight and its roads are in a grid; it has few curvy roads. Campobello Island by contrast has few straight roads; most curve around its jagged coastline. The New Brunswick island feels more like a tourist destination than Point Roberts; in addition to having several motels, the town has an icon which is used as a consistent theme throughout the community. Head Harbour Lighthouse on Passamaquoddy Bay at the northern tip of the island is something of a town mascot. The white tapered octagonal 51-foot tower is made of wood and sports a large red cross on its exterior. The lighthouse is prominently featured on business signs and billboards all over the island. Miniature versions are seen everywhere, from a ten-foot version advertising whale watching tours to many one-foot versions in residential gardens.

For the record, there are three additional unpopulated U.S. exclaves on the U.S.-Canadian border, and we've come this far, we might as well list them all. There is a tiny unnamed Manitoba peninsula which extends below the 49th Parallel in a lake which straddles the border near Saint John, North Dakota. There is another exclave on Lake of the Woods named Elm Point, 3400 feet of land located off the Manitoba mainland just south of the Northwest Angle. Province Point is a tiny Quebec peninsula which extends across the boundary line into Lake Champlain just each of the Alburgh Tongue.

Stroll along the seaside trail and pause at *Sunsweep*, an international art project specifically for U.S.–Canadian exclaves. *Sunsweep* is a continent-wide, three-part international art project created by renowned Michigan artist David Barr. It was given to the people of Point Roberts as a symbol of international friendship, unveiled November 2, 1985, ironically a cold and drizzly day.[166] It was originally to have been placed at Monument Park, but tree cover blocked the setting sun rays from the sculpture, so the Lighthouse Park site was used instead.[167] As an international art project, two other exclaves have the rest of *Sunsweep*: American Point Island in Lake of the Woods, lying offshore from the Northwest Angle, and at Ragged Point on Campobello Island within the International Park. Intended as a gesture of international goodwill, all of the *Sunsweep* sites require land travel through another country. They were all carved from a single slab of polished Canadian black granite inscribed on the base with these words: "Aligned to the north star, solstices and equinoxes, portrays the path of the sun from east to west." The six hundred pound, five foot high stones are etched with an image of a woman's hand traced by concentric rings that fan out resembling a topographical chart,

Figure 26: *Sunsweep* at Lighthouse Marine Park. Photo by Mark Swenson.

each ring becoming more circular to form a perfect circle with the last ring. Point Roberts and Campobello Island have an identical arch-shaped shape, whereas the Minnesota installment contains two wedge-shaped pieces which complete the arch.

LIGHTHOUSE

The trail continues to the navigation beacon at the very southwestern tip of the peninsula. This point is the geographical feature called Point Roberts. Overlooking the Strait of Georgia, the Point Roberts Light is a square metal skeletal tower holding a diamond-shaped red and white checkerboard patterned symbol. The beacon emits two white flashes every fifteen seconds in coordination with the lights at East Point on Saturna Island and Active Pass.[168] It is the northernmost light along the coast of the contiguous forty-eight states. The Point Roberts Lighthouse Society was founded in 2000 to campaign for a proper lighthouse to be built on this spot.

Figure 27: Point Roberts Lighthouse. Author collection.

The U.S. government kept this land for a lighthouse in 1908 when they vacated the Point and opened it to settlement. They erected a wooden framed lighthouse in the 1920s and it stood here into the 1960s. In the early years it was manually tended to by Sarah Olson, then by Jeff Martin who staffed it for thirty-seven years. The light slid on a track into the housing at the top of the tower. In a nightly ritual, the light keeper would walk from their home to the lighthouse regardless of the weather, climb the tower, clean off soot and fill with lamp with fuel. The light keeper knew just how much fuel to add for the light to last the night but no more, as supplies were only received every three to four months.[169] The light was electrified in 1931. By the 1960s the twenty-five foot tall frame structure was completely covered in carved initials. It was damaged during Typhoon Freda. This equivalent of a Category 3 storm struck Point Roberts and much of the Salish Sea and Pacific coast in October 1962.[170] Freda knocked out many of the power lines across the peninsula; Point Roberts was plunged into darkness for four days.[171] Typhoon Freda killed 53 people around the Salish Sea – more than any other Salish Sea weather event – with gusts up to 160 miles per hour (260 km/h). Freda, also known as the Columbus Day Storm, caused $2.7 billion in damage, part of which was from the 35 million cubic meters of timber blown down, a United States national record.

USCGC *POINT ROBERTS*

When people ponder the name of the exclave – Point Roberts – most attention goes to the word "Roberts," and any Point Roberts school kid can tell you Point Roberts is named after Henry Roberts, the "esteemed friend" of George Vancouver. But what about the other word in the name? What is a point, actually? Wikipedia redirects the geographic word "point" to "promontory." Another online dictionary defined a point merely as a peninsula. Yet another suggested it was a cape, but with shorter cliffs. Whilst there are quite a few geographical features beginning with the word Point, such as Kitsap County's odd Point No Point, Point Roberts is the only actual town in Washington which begins with the word Point, although there are towns which end with the word Point, such as Hunts Point and Yarrow Point near Seattle. No localities in British Columbia begin with the word. Given this, it was interesting that in 1964 the U.S. Coast Guard began naming their cutters between sixty-five and ninety-nine feet in length, which hadn't previously been given names. All of these cutters are named after places beginning with the word Point. These cutters became known as the Point-class cutters. One such ship, built in 1962 at Curtis Bay,

Figure 28: United States Coast Guard Point Class Cutter. Photo by United States Coast Guard Historian's Office.

Maryland and previously known as WPB-82332, was christened as the USCGC *Point Roberts* in January 1964. Named for our very own Point Roberts, Washington, it was operated by four men, but allowing for shift changes, it carried a crew of eight.

The Point-class cutters replaced the aging wooden hull patrol boats in use at the time, and sported a steel hull and aluminum superstructure to save weight. Engine exhaust was expelled through a transom rather than the normal stack, allowing an unobstructed 360-degree view from the ship's bridge, a vital feature in search and rescue and combat work.

The USCGC *Point Roberts* never came to its namesake in the Salish Sea. It was used by the Coast Guard almost entirely in Florida, where it performed law enforcement and search and rescue missions for thirty years until it was decommissioned in 1992. In those thirty years of service, it was a workhorse. Throughout the 1960s and 1970s, it rescued divers and crews from sinking or disabled fishing vessels. It evacuated from large ships injured seamen needing medical help on shore. In the 1980s, much of the work turned to fighting drug smuggling, a fitting job for a ship named for Point Roberts. On November 28, 1982, she seized the *Lago Izabel* and *Gigi* 120 miles off the coast of Georgia carrying twenty-five tons of cannabis. In August 1988 she escorted the Honduran vessel *Unicorn Express* into Mayport where one thousand

Figure 29: Two covers postmarked on board the USCGC Point Roberts with special franking to commemorate the cutter's use in recovering debris from the space shuttle Challenger.

pounds of cocaine was discovered in a hidden compartment. Its fifteen minutes of fame arrived in 1986 when it was close to the scene where the space shuttle *Challenger* blew up. USCGC *Point Roberts* was used throughout January and February to find and recover debris from the explosion to aid investigators in determining a cause.[172]

After decommissioning in February 1992, the ship was transferred to the Environmental Protection Agency as research vessel *Lake Explorer* stationed at Duluth, Minnesota. Today it is kitted with state-of-the-art research equipment to monitor and assess the health of the Great Lakes. It does important work determining the effect of pollution, climate change and other human-caused disturbances to the watershed.

TRAILS

The location of Point Roberts at the tip of a peninsula means many think of it as being a dead end of Tsawwassen's 56th Street. Thus it's counterintuitive to think of Point Roberts being on the route of major regional trails, but it is. In the last couple decades, the concept of water trails has emerged. Water trails are defined by the U.S. National Park Service as "recreational routes on waterways with a network of public access points supported by broad-based

Figure 30: Picnic shelters and boardwalk at Lighthouse Park. Photo by Mark Swenson.

community partnerships." These marked trails traverse rivers, lakes, canals and coastlines and are intended for kayaks, paddleboards, canoes, rowboats and rafts; some include motorized use. Camping and picnic sites are available at regular points.

Point Roberts is the starting point of one of the most significant of America's national system of trails. The Salish Sea is home to the Cascadia Marine Trail (CMT), a water trail stretching over 160 miles from the northernmost point at Point Roberts all the way to the southern end of Puget Sound. The CMT retraces Coast Salish trading routes and the Vancouver Expedition's voyage through the Salish Sea. Users of the trail get a feel for how the Coast Salish glided their beachable canoes across the Salish Sea's inlets, bays, islands and reefs for thousands of years. Just as the native people stopped along the way at camps they maintained in order to fish and gather food in line with seasonal abundance, the CMT offers paddlers and rowers sixty-six campsites and 160 day-use sites with non-motorized boat access points. Following its creation in 1993, its success led it a year later to be named a National Recreation Trail (NRT). There are over 1100 NRTs in the United States, which contribute to health, conservation and recreation goals of the nation. CMT's designation was important, only a few NRTs are water trails; most are hiking trails and bike paths. Jointly administered by the National Park Service and the United States Forest Service, NRTs were authorized in 1968 by the National Trails System Act. New trails can only be named by the Secretary of Interior or the Secretary of Agriculture. The CMT was named one of just sixteen long-distance National Millennium Trails. Selected by the White House Millennium Council in June 2000 from fifty-eight nominees, they are "visionary trails that reflect defining aspects of America's history and culture."[173] Lighthouse Marine Park is the campsite for this station on the CMT, with four campsites available to non-motorized craft. It's a tricky approach over the open water of the Strait of Georgia, with strong riptides at the tip of the point, and a large cobble rock beach approach. The navigational beacon is a useful landmark for trail users.

ORCAS

This is the best place on Point Roberts to watch for marine mammals. The Salish Sea is home to three pods of orcas, and whilst they may be seen any time of year, your best chance to see these majestic creatures is in July and August when they occasionally breach right offshore. Other whales, porpoise, harbor seals, sea lions and otters may be seen too.

The frequency with which orcas are seen from Lighthouse Park has resulted in Point Roberts being added to another trail: the Whale Trail, a network of viewing sites around the Salish Sea and the Pacific where visitors may view orcas and other marine mammals from shore. The mission of the Whale Trail is to inspire appreciation and stewardship of whales and the marine environment. It is a non-profit organization in partnership with the National Oceanographic and Atmosphere Administration, the Whale Museum of Friday Harbor, the Washington Department of Fish and Wildlife, the Seattle Aquarium, Whatcom County Parks and Recreation and National Marine Sanctuaries. Sites can only get on the list if they offer a reasonably good chance of seeing orcas at some point in the year, in a publicly-accessible viewpoint. Forty-nine viewing sites meet the criteria, and number one on the list is Point Roberts' Lighthouse Marine Park. It is the northernmost point on the trail, and the only one north of Port Townsend reachable from the mainland not requiring a ferry ride. From 1984 to 2014 there was a mini orca museum located on the boardwalk, providing three decades of visitors information and photos about the local orcas.

People have come to Lighthouse Park for years to see orcas. In the late 1960s a young orca in particular was delighting visitors. Named Lolita, she loved playing at Point Roberts, breaching and tail slapping the waters right off the beach. Lolita was an expert spy-hopper, sticking her head above the water to look around with her excellent eyesight. She was twelve feet long and three, maybe four years old. The mortality rate for calves ranges from forty to 100 per cent, so she was lucky to have made it this far as a juvenile. She belonged to a group of orcas called a pod, and her pod was one of several pods who make up a clan. Within the clan, her pod had its own culture, diet, social structure and vocalizations, averaging twelve known calls.[174] Whales born into the pod remain with the pod for life. Orca pods are hierarchical, with power handed down through maternal lines. Sons stay with their mothers; daughters may branch off to form new matrilineal lines. Life is communal; all adults care for the young. Although many orcas around the world eat seals, the three pods making up this clan of "Southern Resident" orcas in the Salish Sea uniquely eat salmon, and lots of it: 145 pounds a day. Lolita would spend summers at Point Roberts and the San Juan Islands. Autumns are spent in Puget Sound hunting for chum salmon, and in winter the orcas travel extensively in the Pacific Ocean from Alaska to Monterey Bay, California. There are three pods of resident orcas whose home is the Salish Sea, who exhibit a behavior unique to all other orcas. All three pods will gather together and put on a group show of breaching, spy-hopping, rolling, slapping and lunging.

On August 8, 1970, Lolita was swimming with her pod, heading north along Whidbey Island about to enter Rosario Strait toward their favorite fishing spot at Point Roberts. Orca hunters, including one Ted Griffin who owned an aquarium on Seattle's waterfront, quickly got in front of the animals, blocking their path with explosives in the water. The orcas knew they were in danger; over sixteen members of their family had been captured recently to be sent to the marine park industry to perform for their captors' profit; more had died trying to escape capture. They quickly turned around, and headed south, down around the southern tip of Whidbey Island, and back up the east side of the island. The hunters pursued in motor craft, trying to get them into the first inlet, Holmes Harbor, but the mothers and calves split off at the last minute and headed further north. The hunters had to scramble to get back in front of them, and were able to herd them into Penn Cove, where the orcas were trapped. The hunters used nets to separate the whales, manipulating the females between two to five years old into floating pens. These smaller ones were taken to keep shipping costs down so profits would be higher.[175] Lolita was exactly the kind of whale the hunters wanted, and they ensnared her and six other orcas that day. The air was pierced by shrill vocalizations, and it's not hard to understand what they were saying, calves calling for their mothers; mothers shrieking back. The calls were hauntingly heard all around central Whidbey Island. More orcas arrived, swimming right up to the nets, trying to get close to their trapped family. Over one hundred orcas were in a major commotion in Penn Cove; more than the current number of Southern Resident orcas living today. The waters of the cove chopped as the orcas flapped their fins. They were breaching and spy-hopping to get a good view of their trapped family. Lolita and the other trapped orcas were hoisted out of the water and loaded onto flatbed trucks, all in full display in front of the historic Captain Whidbey Inn and downtown Coupeville. The last orca taken from the Salish Sea that day, Lolita disappeared as the trucks lumbered away, headed for the Mukilteo Ferry en route to the Seattle Marine Aquarium, and ultimately sent to corporate aquatic theme parks like SeaWorld. And all of this was legal at the time, with no permits, fees or reparations required. At Seattle Marine Aquarium, including another orca captured that day at Bainbridge Island, eight orcas were herded into two tanks. They were waiting to be sold to marine parks for up to $25,000 each.[176]

During the commotion in Penn Cove, in addition to the orcas captured alive, an adult female outside the nets drowned trying to get to the calves, a fact noted by local media stories. Additionally, four more calves drowned. To prevent the public from knowing about the collateral damage, their bellies were slit open and filled with rocks. Chains and anchors were added, sinking the evidence from view. But on November 18, three of the dead orcas washed up on a Whidbey Island beach, to public outcry. The harvesting of orcas for profit had attracted the attention of the general public who were increasingly seeing orcas not as killer whales with a ferocious reputation, but as an intelligent endangered species worthy of protection. Protesters picketed the aquarium, especially angered by the needless death of the orca mother and calves. Losing so many females that day, including the older female, cruelly ripped apart the matrilineal social fabric of the Salish Sea orcas from which they have never recovered.

The orcas captured that day in Penn Cove did not fare well. They were sold to marine parks all over the world. They didn't do well in captivity; all except Lolita were dead within five years. A month and a half after arriving in Seattle, Lolita was sold to the Miami Seaquarium on September 24, 1970 in order to be a girlfriend for a previously-captured orca, Hugo. Coincidentally, Lolita and Hugo were from the same Southern Resident clan, meaning they could communicate with each other. In the initial weeks they were kept in separate tanks, over 100 meters apart. Park staff were amazed they were making shrill calls to each other across the park. The staff did not realize they were related. Lolita and Hugo would live and perform together for a decade. When Hugo reached adolescence, he started ramming his head against the wall, yearning to return to freedom in the Salish Sea. It wouldn't happen. In March 1980, he forcefully rammed his head into the tank wall and died of an aneurysm. All told, in the 1970s, the Salish Sea lost over a third to perhaps a half of its orcas due to capture by for-profit corporations, the majority bought by SeaWorld. Listed as an endangered species since 2005, the resident orcas of the Salish Sea have been devastated by their ruthless and indiscriminate capture in the 1970s. A National Marine Fisheries Service report issued November 18, 2005 upon the listing of the Southern Resident orcas as endangered stated, "The capture of killer whales for public display during the 1970s likely depressed their population size and altered the population characteristics sufficiently to severely affect their reproduction and persistence."[177]

The harvesting of orcas for profit had begun nine years before Lolita's capture. The first orca to be captured and exhibited in a marine park was Wanda, displayed in 1961 at Marineland of the Pacific in Los Angeles, but tragically Wanda died after three days. The second orca ever captured and put on display, and the first Southern Resident orca captured in the Salish Sea and put on display, was Moby Doll. He was captured in July 1964 eleven miles south and within view of Point Roberts, near Saturna Island. That wasn't how it was supposed to go. Moby Doll was supposed to be killed and used as a life-size taxidermy model for the Vancouver Aquarium. When he didn't die when shot, he was towed for twelve hours in heavy seas to Vancouver and exhibited in a pen on the waterfront and later at Jericho Beach. He didn't eat for two months as his novice captors offered him all the wrong food. A chance lingcod was snatched by Moby Doll in his pen, and soon he was eating two hundred pounds a day. Although he died after three months in captivity, the episode marked a turning point in attitudes about orcas. In its obituary for Moby Doll *The Times* of London wrote, "the widespread publicity – some of it the first positive press ever about killer whales – marked the beginning of an important change in the public attitude toward the species."[178] Visitors included the Duke and Duchess of Winsor, and a young Ted Griffin.[179]

Next to lose his freedom was Namu, captured near the north end of Vancouver Island in June 1965. It took eighteen days to tow Namu south past Point Roberts to Seattle via Deception Pass, where thousands of people looked on from the 160-foot tall bridge. He was heavily promoted at Ted Griffin's aquarium at Pier 56 on Seattle's waterfront where Namu developed a working relationship with a human. For the first time, a trainer performed routines with an orca, Griffin holding on to Namu's dorsal fins as he was pulled through the water.[180] The image of a killer was crumbling as the public saw a new perspective of orcas. The changing attitudes were noticed by *National Geographic*, who featured Namu in its March 1966 issue. Crowds came to see a "killer whale," and discovered they were gentle and entertaining to watch. A business was born; people would pay to see orcas, so more orcas were needed.

A female Southern Resident was swimming in Puget Sound with her calf in early 1966 when she was harpooned by Griffin from a helicopter. The goal was to capture the calf as a girlfriend for Namu. The calf's mother died from the harpooning, as intended. Griffin weighed down her body with an anchor and sunk the evidence. Given the name Shamu, the calf was netted and brought to Seattle. It didn't go well. Devastated by the death of her mother, Griffin sold her to the then-new SeaWorld San Diego theme park for $75,000.[181] Shamu was flown by airplane to San Diego, the first orca to be transported by air. With slick corporate marketing, SeaWorld elevated Griffin's early attempts at using confined wild orcas to a new level. When SeaWorld bought a marine park in Ohio in May 1970, Shamu was flown back and forth between California and Ohio, adding to the stress of captivity. Shamu died in August 1971 after earning millions for SeaWorld in the six years she was their captive. More orcas soon followed, but they were all called Shamu to the public, to profit from the heritage of the calf ripped away from her murdered mother in the Salish Sea.

In 1967, a pod was stunned with bombs and herded into a bay in Puget Sound and five were captured, with another three being drowned. One was trucked to the Vancouver Boat Trailer and Sports Show, where it was put in a small tank as a trade show exhibit hall prop for ten days, after which it was moved to the Vancouver Aquarium in Stanley Park. In February 1968, another pod of over twelve orcas was corralled in Carr Inlet. This time, two more were captured, including a three-year-old male named Hugo who in May was sent to Miami's Seaquarium. Over time, the Salish Sea's orcas developed defensive techniques against their hunters. They learned the noise of the hunters' engines and would separate when being chased, the calves going with the mothers one way, the males luring the captors as decoys in another direction.

Canada banned the capture of orcas in 1970, the same year of Lolita's capture, but orca hunting continued legally in U.S. waters into the mid-1970s. Eight more orcas were taken in 1971. In 1972, hearings were conducted for hunters who were applying for permits to capture twelve more orcas. The hunters stated they believed there were 500 orcas in the Salish Sea; the actual number was only twenty per cent of that number. It was beginning to dawn on some people just how much of the local orca population had been taken and how few might remain. Nobody knew there were in reality less than one hundred left. Carl Crouse of the Washington Game Commission said at the time, "We are somewhat concerned that the same pod of whales is being worked on."[182] Eight permits were issued in 1972. At the end of that year, the federal government took over management of the capture of orcas with the Marine Mammal Act. The last Southern Resident orcas were taken in 1973. Transient orcas who visit the Salish Sea from other areas continued to be harvested in the Salish Sea until 1976. That year in Budd Inlet near Olympia, an assistant to Washington's Governor happened to witness SeaWorld capturing orcas from his sailboat. He saw SeaWorld use aircraft and explosives to herd the orcas into nets in violation of their permit terms. Washington sued SeaWorld, and a district court ordered SeaWorld to permanently give up its permit to capture orcas in Washington. SeaWorld moved on to capture orcas in Iceland.

Despite widespread awareness of the impact capture was having on the numbers of orcas remaining in the wild, as late as 1983 corporations were trying to capture orcas. Victoria's Sealand applied in 1982 to conduct an orca hunt. In 1983, seven years after having been banned from Washington, SeaWorld tried again to capture more orcas in the Salish Sea to perform tricks in front of spectators for a new generation of profits, as many of their orcas were dying off several decades earlier than they would have in the wild. A federal hearing was heard in Seattle on August 16, 1983 on a SeaWorld proposal to capture one hundred orcas "for public display and research purposes." SeaWorld openly asked the National Marine Fisheries Service for approval to capture *all* the remaining resident orcas in the Salish Sea for their sole profit. This public hearing was only held because Washington Senator Slade Gorton had asked the fisheries agency to postpone action on the request until public comments could be heard. Before that, SeaWorld had lobbied hard against any public hearings on their secret scheme. Gorton, a member of the Senate Commerce Committee, had to threaten SeaWorld with going before a full Congressional hearing in order to force them to back down and agree to a public agency hearing.[183]

By 1987, the only Southern Resident orca captured from the Salish Sea still alive was Lolita, still performing her routine shows at the Miami Seaquarium, her dorsal fin flopped down at her side. One hundred per cent of captive orcas have dorsal fin collapse because of the weight of gravity on their tall dorsal fin as they spend their life on the surface of the water in their shallow concrete pools. Dorsal fin collapse occurs in the wild in only one per cent of orcas, since they spend most of their time under the surface in deep waters.[184] When she's not performing during the day, and all night long she is kept in an eighty foot tank where she lies limply still. Lolita's tank is the smallest orca tank in the United States, and does not meet Animal Welfare Act standards which call for a tank forty-eight feet wide compared to Lolita's thirty-five feet width. The tank is only twenty feet deep at its deepest point.[185] Miami Seaquarium has broken promises to build Lolita a new tank for thirty-eight years. The aquarium has refused many proposals to play to Lolita recordings of the vocalizations from the Southern Resident pods

Figure 31: Lolita performs at the Miami Seaquarium, her home of four decades.
Photo by Averette at English Wikipedia [CC BY 3.0
(http://creativecommons.org/licenses/by/3.0)], via Wikimedia Commons.

from the Salish Sea, or to lease her out for a return visit, or to purchase her. Lolita remains at the Miami Seaquarium to this day, the longest-held Southern Resident orca. From her Salish Sea home around Point Roberts in a tight social network, Lolita has spent more than forty years confined to a tiny cement tank, the last three decades all alone.

SeaWorld contends it holds orcas in captivity to help conservation efforts, but for every one thousand dollars of SeaWorld revenue, it's believed only sixty cents goes to conservation. That's about one nickel of the admission price. Despite some token conservation efforts, many orcas have died in SeaWorld parks. After three orca-related deaths at SeaWorld in California, the public saw SeaWorld's treatment of orcas, and the resulting orca behavior, in the 2013 CNN documentary *Blackfish*. Since the film's release attendance sank at SeaWorld San Diego, profits plunged by eight-four per cent, its CEO was forced out and it lost over half its market value as a multinational corporation.[186] Jared Goodman, director of animal law for the People for the Ethical Treatment of Animals said, "Families just don't want to buy tickets to see orcas going insane inside tiny tanks, and SeaWorld's profits, like the orcas, won't recover until the abusement park empties its tanks."[187] SeaWorld revealed a bit of its corporate culture when in the summer of 2015 a SeaWorld employee was caught having infiltrated animal rights groups who are working to stop the exploitation of captive orcas. In the resulting backlash, the people of California voted in 2016 to ban SeaWorld from breeding orcas, to stop them from forcing orcas to perform tricks and to force them to end its theatrical shows. The law only covers SeaWorld California; SeaWorld will continue using orcas to perform tricks for profit in Orlando and San Antonio until 2019. In its anti-animal rights marketing campaign, SeaWorld said it would replace the theatrical shows with "educational programs" in a more "naturalistic setting," though it admits these programs will be held in the same tiny concrete tanks they use today. SeaWorld continues to reject any alternative options including coastal sanctuaries, penned ocean cages or release of its profit-driving orcas.

In the fifteen years during which the Salish Sea's orcas were plundered, over 275 whales were caught in nets. Fifty-five ended up in aquariums and theme parks. At least twelve died during capture. Worldwide, 150 wild orcas were taken into captivity, with 127 of these now dead. Worldwide today there are fifty-six orcas held in captivity, twenty-three of which were wild-caught and thirty-three captive-born. Twelve marine parks currently hold orcas in captivity in eight countries; SeaWorld currently holds twenty-three orcas in captivity. At least forty-five orcas have perished in SeaWorld tanks. SeaWorld still holds for profit in San Diego the oldest living wild-caught orca in captivity, Corky, a Northern Resident captured in 1969 from Vancouver Island.[188] Sadly, the plundering of orcas did not end in the 1970s; it continues today.

Since 2002, at least thirteen orcas have been captured from the wild, mostly in Russia. Today the Southern Resident orcas of the Salish Sea are an endangered species. They visit Point Roberts frequently each summer. They are often seen April through September; July and August being peak months, and Lighthouse Park is the best spot to see these majestic creatures – for free – as they play right off shore. If you see Southern Resident orcas during your trip to Point Roberts, appreciate the fact you're witnessing something special; today, there are just seventy-six of them left in the wild.

DAO

In Point Roberts, there's a very real connection one feels between the land and the sea. The land and sea at Point Roberts both define and isolate the space. Point Roberts owes its existence to a symbiotic equilibrium between these forces; you feel the yin/yang balance when here. Lighthouse Park presents a fun dichotomy with its manufactured straight lines of the slant-cut wood and angled roofs of the picnic shelters contrasting with the wild, twisted windswept trees and beaches surrounding it. It is this yin/yang balance which inspired a park ranger in 1999.

Movies have Oscars. Plays have Tonies. Board games have Mensa Selects. The Mensa Select award has been given to the five best board games each year since 1990. The award commemorates games which are "original, challenging and well-designed." At the twelfth Mensa Mind Games competition in 2001, a game called Dao won. Dao was invented here in the wedge-shaped house in Lighthouse Park's parking lot. The park manager during those years, Ben van Buskirk, was ideating with a friend, Jeff Pickering, during the lax winter 1999 season. Observing that games seemed popular, they invented a board game, naming it after their interest in Taoism, a Chinese religion based on the doctrines of Lao Tzu, a sixth century philosopher. Taoism promotes simplicity and selflessness with a concept of wu wei, meaning non-doing. It means to limply go with the flow like a leaf floating down a babbling brook, undulating quickly in rapids, then briefly getting trapped in an eddy or behind a rock. Dao mirrors wu wei. Van Buskirk and Pickering noted in their patent application, "While (board) games fulfill their respective particular cultural objectives and requirements, none of the prior art describe a competitive game that includes significant elements of Daoist philosophy. The Daoist philosophy includes order and harmony, rejection of unnecessary violence, simplicity, inclusion, meditation, lack of concern with interim rewards, and the fine balance between defense and offense. Further, none of the prior art describe a board game that readily includes players who have sight, hand or motor difficulties... (and do) not involve personal aggression against an opponent by jumping, capture, or scoring."

Played on a four-by-four playing square, two players each have four game pieces made of smooth stones, like those lining the beaches of Lighthouse Marine Park. On each player's turn, a stone is moved in any direction as far as it can until it reaches the edge or runs into another stone. Symbiotic yin-yang elements uniquely blend natural flow with the strategy of facing 110,000 valid positions, with power techniques, as you try to get your four pieces in certain formations, like a line of four in a row, or in a two-by-two block, or four corners.

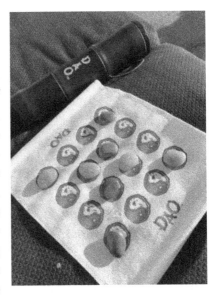

Figure 32: The Dao playing square. Photo by Mark Swenson.

Taoism's selflessness is incorporated by a rule in Dao under which passive behavior is rewarded. If one of your pieces gets boxed in by your opponent's pieces, you win.

Dao is what's called in gaming circles an "abstract strategy" game, like checkers, and Connect Four. After playing a few rounds of Dao, one realizes games can degenerate into a stalemate situation. Equally-skilled players can prevent the other from winning indefinitely, one triumphing only when the other makes a mistake. With only sixteen spaces on the board, one often finds itself playing the only move available which won't let your opponent win, resulting in a confining feeling one doesn't get with chess, for instance. These limitations are common in abstract strategy games, though Dao's simplicity makes these more conspicuous. Cynics would suggest Dao's multiple ways to win were needed by its designers after they realized the game often ends in a draw. A thinking person's game, in some ways Dao isn't so much a game you try to win as much as it helps you focus your mind analytically. One can imagine the dark, dreary winter night when van Buskirk and Pickering invented a game which was fun to play with a friend whilst chatting, with the game being played during the conversation. Deceivingly simple, if one focuses too much on what you're saying to your friend, you might miss an obvious move to your opponent who was paying closer attention during your chat. Many rounds are over in a couple of minutes, but if skilled players focus on the game, it can last for over ten minutes; one player even played a single game for over nine hours.

Dao started shipping in January 2000. A hit here on the Point, more have been sold to Point Roberts addresses than people who live here. An international Dao tournament was held in Point Roberts in May 2000. Easy to learn for players of any age, Dao is a great analogy for Point Roberts itself. Dao's yin/yang vibe with its elements of passiveness followed by power plays is analogous to techniques the residents of Point Roberts have had to use to survive as an isolated exclave.

The home where Dao was invented in Lighthouse Park is a fine example of Pacific Northwest contemporary architecture.

Northwest contemporaries have a mod look noted for their extensive use of unpainted wood inside and out. Shingles are sometimes used on walls, and often wood planks are installed on a diagonal, sometimes aligning the angle of the siding to wide overhanging eaves. These homes are easily spotted by their asymmetrical floor plans, floor-to-ceiling glass, a minimum of decoration, and flat or low-pitched roofs. The rest of this chapter travels along Edwards Drive, passing several great Northwest contemporaries, especially on a side loop at Harbor Seal Drive.

 Leave Lighthouse Marine Park and turn right on Marine Drive, which bends through the park to become Edwards Drive.

DIKES, POLDERS & TSUNAMIS

Edwards Drive follows the Point's southern shore. Before the 1914, this area of Point Roberts was a large swampy area – part of it an actual lagoon – called the Tule. That word has two meanings. "Tules," pronounced TOO-lees, are grass-like sedges which grow in the American west. "Tulies" are also a term to describe the boondocks or someplace far away. Both meanings seem to apply to the area called the Tule in Point Roberts. The marshy land when this was still a tidal basin grew the ten-foot tule grasses. From the vantage point of most homesteads on higher land, this area was a barren part of the Point, its own boondocks. Indeed, through the 1980s the Lighthouse Cannery was a nightclub called The Boondocks, located in the Point's tulies.

The Salish Sea would surge in to the Tule at high tide, filling the lagoon right up to the edge of the forest canopy, covering 160 acres and stranding large logs and miscellaneous flotsam and jetsam. There was a cut in the beach through which salt water filled and emptied the lagoon twice daily. When the tide was ebbing, the rush of water out of the lagoon made the opening fifteen feet deep and thirty feet across, making passage along the beach impossible. But locals describe occasions when it would get plugged up with large amounts of driftwood such that it was possible to scamper across the debris to the other side of the opening. To give an idea of size, when clear, forty-foot sloops could enter the lagoon at high tide, make turns and generally move about in the lagoon.[189] The Tule lagoon made the beach on the southwestern corner of the peninsula seem like a sand spit at high tide rather than the straight diked shoreline of today. In her seminal *History of Whatcom County*, Lottie Roeder Roth described the marshy nature of the Tule east of Lighthouse Park in 1926: "Approaching Point Roberts from the water, one can see the low lying Lighthouse Point with its sea marshes and fields of gently swaying grasses."[190]

As you travel along Edwards Drive, you'll notice the low-lying land below you on the left-hand side of the street. Making up the southwestern quadrant of the peninsula, these are the Point Roberts polders. Created from the dike on which you're traveling, today these polders stretch from the western shore all the way to South Beach Road, and make possible many features of Point Roberts: the airport, modern housing subdivisions, a marina, agricultural fields and cabins. The process of creating the polders out of the Tule began over a century ago. After some flooding in the winter of 1913-1914, the opening to the lagoon was filled. The George and Barker Cannery filled the inlet with webbing from used fish traps. Homesteader Joseph Largaud, who owned a farm to the east of the Tule, created a sluice. The lagoon was drained, turning it into arable, if still swampy, farmland. An original dike was built here in the late 1910s, but it was not strong enough to stop tidal surges from Pineapple Express storms. Winter storms continued to feed the Tule's wet, marshy land as they easily breached the shore.

At 10:00 A.M. on December 23, 1932 a major windstorm with eighty mile-per-hour winds combined with a king tide caused a major flood on Point Roberts. The entire southwestern quadrant of the peninsula, six hundred acres in all, was flooded when a four hundred foot section of the old dike broke, the water reaching as far north as Peltier Road and as far east as Tyee Drive. Six homes were swept off their foundation. Entire chicken coops were washed away, killing 700 of a flock of 1500 birds. Fifteen cows were rescued but required men to wade shoulder-deep to help them swim to safety in an all-day effort. Endless rows of fence posts and barbed wire fencing popped out of the ground. The flood was so devastating the water stayed inland, ebbing and flowing with the tides, for three years. When the waters receded the farmers found the land inoperable from the reentry of sea water into the soil. The community urgently needed to fix the dike, but their requests for funds or assistance for the remote exclave were ignored. Finally a state legislator heard their cries for help. Albert Edwards, a Democrat from Bellingham, had just been elected as a legislator, but quickly learned how to use the state government processes to secure funding for local projects. The Point Roberts residents had been asking for dike funding, but Edwards knew he could get Works Progress Administration money if the project was classified as roads works. The road would be built on top of a dike, killing two birds

Figure 33: The new Dike Road in 1934 (today's Edwards Drive). Photo by Corbett, Whatcom Museum #868; Bellingham, WA.

with one stone. Construction was completed in 1935. Originally named Dike Road, the locals showed their appreciation to Edwards, who would stay in state government until 1963, by renaming the road Edwards Drive, upon which you're now traveling.[191]

The dike and the natural upper tidal zone forms a berm stacked high with driftwood on the south shore of Point Roberts, holding back the Salish Sea. But the seaside residential homes along Edwards Drive do get flooded from once-a-decade winter storms. On December 16, 1982, Edwards Drive suffered three million dollars in damage. Southwesterly gales on the Strait of Georgia battered the Point's south shore. Twenty-five foot surf swept a home off its foundations, and heaved a thirty-five foot deadhead way past the high water mark. The 1400 block of Edwards Drive bore the brunt of the storm. Dozens of homes on the sea side of the dike were flooded, their lots flooded with seawater, mud, logs and debris. Some lots had over twenty feet of salt water which had washed over the driftwood, then trapped between the driftwood berm and the dike in their lots. Homeowners returned to find they needed to swim from the Edwards Drive blacktop to their home, some of which had inches-deep mud in the living room. The parking lot at Lighthouse Park was a lagoon with seawater deep enough to cover hubcaps on parked cars. Altogether, roads suffered $1.2 million in damage, with another $1.8 million in damaged private property. The next decade a similar storm in December 1996 caused similar damage to the south shore as well as breaching the seawall at Maple Beach and Tsawwassen's Centennial Beach and Beach Grove neighborhoods. Fifteen homes were destroyed in mudslides, and many families were unable to enter their home for over two weeks. To top it off, three feet of snow fell right after the flood.[192]

 Edwards Drive becomes Marina Drive as it bends around the Point Roberts Marina, meeting the bottom of Tyee Drive.

Looking up Tyee Drive, you can see the Canadian border station nestled among evergreens at the top of the road. At the intersection of Tyee Drive and APA Road, the former site of an iconic red barn torn down in the summer of 1977,[193] there is atop a pole an unusual looking tower, with seven bulbous white plastic nodes stacked atop each other. This northernmost tsunami warning siren in Washington was installed in September 2009.[194] Protected by dikes and with sea level land at high risk, tsunami evacuation route signs were installed all over Point Roberts in March 2008.[195] When the siren is heard, people are to get to higher ground, as indicated by the route markers.

Many towns throughout Washington, Oregon and northern California have tsunami warning systems. Many communities, including Point Roberts, participate in the Great Shakeout each October, an annual earthquake and tsunami drill, where businesses, first responders and students practice safety measures stemming from a natural disaster. Purchased with federal grants, the sirens are easily heard in the outdoors, which is the intended audience. Following some blasts of the siren, a voice message urges people to get to higher ground. However, those in homes or cars could miss the warning if playing loud music. Washington is a big believer in the reassurance and early warning tsunami warning sirens give a community, yet Oregon and northern California are decommissioning many of theirs.

Oregon officials are reconsidering tsunami warning sirens. Tillamook County and the city of Waldport have removed dozens of sirens. The city of Coos Bay, Oregon and Del Norte County, California are rethinking their systems. Battered by salt air, parts are hard to find to maintain the 1950s-era sirens which once were used for civil defense warnings. California and Oregon are planning to switch to reverse 911 alerts sent to phones instead. These systems generally work by automatically opting in all local landline phones, with smart-phone users opting in. Anybody can register to receive texts and emails. There are pros and cons to each approach. To reach locals at home, mobile phones are becoming ubiquitous. However, tourists and those outdoors may not be within mobile phone range in the rugged West Coast, or be registered to receive alerts. Newer tsunami warning systems can convey specific instructions and recommended escape routes.

Amazingly, in all of the three West Coast states, the tsunami warning system only works for tsunamis generated by far-away earthquakes. Though the West Coast is at high risk for severe earthquakes, tsunamis generated from American or Canadian earthquakes won't trigger this system, which is why it's important to move to higher ground in the event of an earthquake even if the sirens are silent. For situations where the tsunami is still many hours away from hitting the coast, Oregon and California officials suggest people have a chance to be warned through a variety of media, including online alerts, social media and broadcast media.

Figure 34: Tsunami evacuation route signs in Point Roberts. Photo by Mark Swenson.

Therein is the difference between Washington and its southern neighbors' tsunami systems. In Oregon and California, maintenance of the sirens is the responsibility of municipalities and counties. The state of Washington pays the cost of upkeep for sirens, and installs a standardized system activated by satellites.

Going east on APA Road, turn right on Simundson Road.

MARINA

There had probably been calls for a marina at Point Roberts for as long as people have been living here, but with the town pier (see chapter 8) failing in the 1950s – it would permanently close in 1959 – and no way for boats to land at Point Roberts, in November 1958 folks organized the Point Roberts Harbor Committee to lobby to get a harbor built. Since few general-interest community organizations existed in those years, the committee's scope was defined more broadly than just the harbor, with an additional task to "generally educate county, state and federal authorities of the economic plight of the Point and its growing dependence on Canada."[196] The committee advocated for a broad, stable economic base to ensure Point Roberts would grow and, in their minds, even survive. With representation of many community groups, including the Grange Society, Businessman's Association, Commercial Fish Packers and Commercial Fisheries Association, the committee quickly drew up its plans. It approached the U.S. Army Corps of Engineers to do a feasibility study and economic survey of not only a harbor but the residual economic benefit to the community of having one. The Army Corp came back with its findings which recommended a $3 million marina for commercial fishing boats be dredged just north of Lighthouse Park, and that yes, it would spur the economy of the exclave. That was all well and good, but $3 million was well beyond the means of the tiny community, with barely 175 full-time American citizens living here at the time. Officials at every level of government ignored the people of Point Roberts. Federal officials would only provide some of the monies if the local community could find local matching funds. The Port of Bellingham had been a sponsor, but withdrew when it couldn't come up with its $1.2 million share.[197] The County Board of Commissioners also claimed poverty. Down in Olympia, state-level government officials would not even consider using their budget, citing tiny Point Roberts as not being a priority for the state.[198] Meanwhile, the lack of a harbor contributed to maritime deaths. A major storm hit Point Roberts in late February 1972. The tug *Haro Straits* hit a submerged log and sank. It was located just off shore but in 400 feet of water. The crew of five was lost.[199]

The harbor idea sat on the shelf for nearly two more decades. Finally built in 1977 as a private development, the Point Roberts Marina is one of the largest manmade marinas in Washington. Built where the Tule lagoon once was, the polder was excavated to form a comma-shaped basin, and then a cut was made through Edwards Drive to the sea. The breakwater jetty was added last.[200] There was confusion during the development phase, so typical of bureaucratic nature of projects in Point Roberts, when it was exposed during the Shoreline Substantial Permit hearing that the shoreline development permit was issued before the county's shoreline management program was completed, apparently a big no-no.[201]

Figure 35: The dredging of the marina in 1977. Photo by Whatcom Museum #1995.1.42303; Bellingham, WA.

After the marina basin opened, the finishing touches on the project came a bit later. The marina building was added in 1982.[202] The land by the marina building was filled in with dirt excavated from the marina basin, which required time to settle before it could support the weight of heavy vehicles. Simundson Drive was added only after the land stabilized. Originally plans called for a resort development around the marina basin, including a residential village of condominiums, a social center, community recreational facilities and retail shops ringing the marina basin. Serious proposals were advanced in February 1991 to begin construction but things fell through, though a restaurant has been located at the marina since July 1992. Various owners have used different strategies for the marina. Some positioned it as inexpensive moorage for Canadians; indeed, some 95% of the vessels are registered to British Columbians or Albertans.[203] Others saw it as a mega-yacht destination to rival Roche Harbor,[204] since the marina has slips for yachts up to 120 feet. News stations from Seattle sent camera crews to cover a fire on October 6, 2007 which destroyed five boats.[205]

Figure 36: Edwards Drive ran along the southern shore until the marina entrance sliced through it in 1977. Photo by Mark Swenson.

In early 1995 there was serious talk of starting passenger ferry service from the Point Roberts marina to Friday Harbor and Bellingham. An April survey that year of Point Roberts voters indicated 77% wanted a community pier and the creation of ferry service, the number one answer in the poll.[206] Studies were ready by September, estimating ridership as high as 18,000. The plan had an amazing amount of detail. Two ship sizes were evaluated: one which had a capacity of 120, and a smaller one which could carry sixty-five. The fare was going to be $38, with the ferry dock being located at the marina.[207] That effort died, but new efforts arose again in 1998 about ferry service to Blaine with continuing service to Bellingham. The easier access to Point Roberts enabled by ferry service would be a financial boon but would change the nature of the exclave. Point Roberts would still be an exclave, but the removal of the Canadian travel necessity would change much about vibe of an exclave. It would alleviate some of the burdens and sometimes serious challenges of living in Point Roberts when one's ability to cross the Canadian border is an issue. It would also change the psychological feeling one gets from the Point's isolation.

The 1995 ferry discussions were for a private ferry, but the state of Washington runs the world's largest public ferry system. Washington views its ferry system as part of the state highway system. All ferry routes in Washington allow the continuation of a state highway. The promising news for Point Roberts is that Blaine harbor, just across the bay from the Point, is the northern terminus of Washington State Highway 548. This highway was designated in 1991 and is fourteen miles long. It starts near Ferndale, heads west to the big refineries, then turns north and skirts Birch Bay and comes into downtown Blaine on Peace Portal Drive, the original Pacific Highway. It ends at the roundabout at the Blaine Marina and Interstate 5, Point Roberts visible in the distance. It would be natural to extend Highway 548 by ferry from the Blaine harbor to Point Roberts to provide a reliable and vital link to an underserved community in Washington and an alternative access to Vancouver. Another plan could be to upgrade a park in Point Roberts to a state park, which would also necessitate ferry service, as all Washington state parks must be served by a state highway.[208]

A good example of how Point Roberts' unique position in the middle of the Salish Sea plays an oversized role despite its small size is the presence of the Royal Canadian Marine Search and Rescue Section 8. This unit provides search and rescue services 24 hours per day, 365 days per year across 600 square miles of the Salish Sea. Section 8 was formed in 1976 in response to the sinking of a pleasure craft which resulted in the loss of a fishing boat aiding in its rescue. Once encompassing the Steveston, British Columbia area at the mouth of the Fraser River, in 1988 the section was split. Steveston became section 7 and Point Roberts became home to section 8, perfectly suited for rapid response to situations in both Boundary Bay to the east as well as in the Strait of Georgia and the Gulf Islands to the southwest, covering a thirty mile radius from Point Roberts.[209] It is the only Canadian marine search and rescue resource based in United States waters, and takes full advantage of the facilities at the Point Roberts marina, including fuel, parking, office, not to mention public visibility. It offers boating safety resources to yacht clubs, schools and the public. A local non-profit society helps with fundraisers for equipment, vessels, maintenance and training. The Point Roberts Marina donates the moorage slip for the section's boat.

The brick path around the marina is public, and the south side of the marina building has a large field with picnic tables, some forlorn-looking basketball hoops and parking lot. An undeveloped field leads to a public beach, part of a small park given by the marina to the public in exchange for cutting an opening in Edwards Drive. The park was created from a 1975 agreement between the marina and the Whatcom County Board of Commissioners, with advice from the county parks board, which specifies the size, location, ownership, development responsibilities and liabilities of the park. There are two ways to reach it: walking through the field south of the marina building, or via a public path from Edwards Drive. There was supposed to be development of this park, including a public fishing pier, parking lot, washrooms, picnic tables and a trail to the marina but these were never developed, caught in a political game of hot potato as to which of the joint parties to the agreement is responsible for taking action and footing the bill.[210] The promised parking lot was solved by sharing the marina's parking lot, and the promised restrooms were solved by sharing the washrooms in the main marina building.[211] The public beach is a narrow shore of sand and pebbles between the marina channel jetty and the townhomes.

Figure 37: A lazy afternoon quayside at the Point Roberts Marina. Photo by Mark Swenson.

This flat southwestern part of Point Roberts was and is the site of much of what keeps Point Roberts going. The flat land offers space for the airport, a boat launch, its marina. It offers a vantage point for marine mammals, including the iconic orca. It has been flooded, and the ultimate flood, an earthquake-triggered tsunami could devastate this part of the exclave. The border defines Point Roberts, but Point Roberts gets much of its significance from its geographic position, a bit of land sticking out into the center of deep waters of the Strait of Georgia.

 Simundson Road starts to squiggle around townhouses and then resumes as Edwards Drive.

This connection to Edwards Drive was built in August 1987[212]. Between 1977 and 1987 there was no road between the marina offices and this next portion of Edwards Drive.

The neighborhood turns denser with residential cul de sacs chock full of cabins and cottages. We'll explore who occupies the Point's homes next.

CHAPTER 3 • WHO WOULD LIVE HERE?

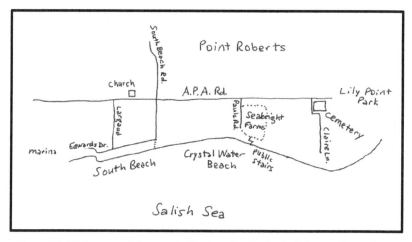

Figure 38: Route map of Chapter 3. Start at the Marina building on Simundson Road and travel east on Edwards Drive to South Beach Road and east on A.P.A. Road to Lily Point. Distance: 2 miles (3.2km)

It's not easy to live in Point Roberts. It's isolated from the rest of the country, and daily life can be a big hassle. Who would want to live here? There have been several eras of peoples who have inhabited Point Roberts. We'll cover the first era, the thousands of years of inhabitation of Point Roberts by the Coast Salish people, in Chapter 4. Since European contact, there have been four distinct eras of settlement.

1	Pre-Contact Coast Salish	Until 1791
2	Initial Settlers	1792 – 1892
3	Development Era	1893 – 1952
4	Canadian Era	1953 – 1987
5	Current Era	1988 – present

From European contact until the twentieth century the Point was used by the initial settlers, smugglers and transients, including the first settlement at Roberts Town. Next, the third era saw the arrival of the Icelandic settlers and the height of the salmon industry with its salmon traps and canneries. Much of the Point's development and existing infrastructure was created then. This was followed by the fourth era, during which Canadians dominated the Point, buying property and focusing on recreation. The current era began in 1988, marked by rapid growth enabled by the provisioning of utilities and the growth of the Internet and parcel services.

ERA 2 – INITIAL SETTLERS

The first white people to spend time on Point Roberts were transient: the merchants and miners of Roberts Town, the surveyors and engineers marking the border and plotting the land, smugglers, pirates and early whites who fished sporadically at Point Roberts. The low-lying lands of Point Roberts we explored in the last chapter provided the access for this transient usage of the peninsula. This opportunistic era of Point Roberts spanned a century from 1791 to 1893.

Point Roberts was one of the very first places to see white newcomers in the Salish Sea. The first known report of a white person at Point Roberts was the mysterious figure Portuguese Joe, a fisherman from the Azores. Working on a Portuguese whaling vessel, Joe and five other crew jumped ship and rowed ashore at Point Roberts around 1850. In 1861 Portuguese Joe joined the Cariboo Gold Rush, overcame aggression to befriend the Musqueam people and in doing so married a Coast Salish princess. Instrumental in the founding of Vancouver, he was the second proprietor on Burrard Inlet, giving pioneer John Deighton, better known as Gassy Jack, competition for the first time. Joe, whose real name was Joseph Silvey, opened a saloon and grocery store combo in 1868. Silvey's store and saloon doubled the available goods to buy and alcohol to drink, making early Vancouver a rough place.

Gregorio Fernandez arrived and opened a store between Gassy Jack and Portuguese Joe, and also became known as Portuguese Joe. When Fernandez's nephew came on to the scene, he was a third Portuguese Joe. When records were uncovered showing one Portuguese Joe was stabbed in a drunken brawl and another Portuguese Joe was shot in the leg in a different fight, historians aren't sure which Joes were injured and if one of them was the Point Roberts Portuguese Joe.[213]

After Roberts Town fizzled out in 1859, and despite Point Roberts being a military reservation, the first permanent white person to settle on the Point was John Harris in 1873. Born in Texas, Harris was raised by Indians in New Mexico after having been taken captive as a boy. He served as a scout with General Scott's army in the Indian & Mexican Wars and had many adventures and escapes. Harris joined the Boundary Commission, working as the cook for Lieutenant Parke. When the commission ended in the early 1860s, Harris settled in Blaine at what was known as the Elwood place, in the narrow land between California and Dakota Creeks.[214] He saw opportunity to squat on a nice piece of land in the Point Roberts Military Reservation, and moved there to raise stock. He was called "Long-haired Harris," and was married to a Coast Salish woman, with whom he had two daughters.[215]

Harris had a farm but also fished around Point Roberts to the anger of the Coast Salish, who came to Point Roberts and threatened him in July 1873. The situation was serious enough to be written about in the Bellingham newspapers, like this July 12, 1873 article in *The Bellingham Bay Mail*: "Indian Intimidation at Point Roberts – Mr. John Harris was in town last Friday, and complained of the threatening attitude of certain Indians from beyond the British line who came to the above named Point and ordered him off the fishing ground, stating that they were sent there by the agent and representing themselves as belonging to the United States Reservation. Mr. Harris was too sharp for them, however, and told them they had no rights there that he was bound to respect and refused to leave; that they didn't belong to the reservation, and even if they did the place was outside the limits. This made the Indians very insolent, and nothing but the coolness of Mr. Harris, and the close proximity of his trusty rifles, prevented a collision with serious results. It is hoped that Mr. McGlynn, the agent, will guard against a repetition of these proceedings." Apparently squatting on a military reservation wasn't too considered too serious a crime or a hush-hush matter if the local media openly reported on squatting at the Point, calling Harris a "settler" and "pioneer" in articles. It is as though the military didn't care or perhaps even expected it. No doubt had the Pig War escalated, the squatters would have been evicted but with the conflict on a low simmer for years, squatters on Point Roberts could be ignored.

The next two settlers were also named John. John Elwood moved to Point Roberts in 1875 from Blaine. John Waller arrived in 1877 to set up a fish trap at Lily Point. Roth mentions two of the three Johns in her book: "Harris and Waller were the only settlers at Point Roberts; Harris, who had been engaged in the cattle business for a number of years, and Waller, a newcomer, engaged in fishing."[216]

Though the Johns were the first settlers on Point Roberts, they weren't alone. Reports from the time cite several murders from the 1860s through the 1880s by smugglers who used Point Roberts as a hiding place. By 1883 more squatters had arrived and occasionally fought, sometimes with dire consequences, something the Point would become known for. For several months, Harris and a Greek settler, Charles Mitchell, had been bickering. When Harris was out for a stroll with his gun, he ran across Mitchell and the two got back into their feud. The younger Mitchell wrestled the gun from Harris and beat him with it. Harris' daughter and her husband came along and drove off Mitchell but it was too late, Harris died at home. A Semiahmoo judge acquitted Mitchell for self-defense.[217] Point

Roberts' reputation as a rough and tumble place, crawling with smugglers and murderers is not hyperbole, and contrasted greatly with a relatively low crime rate on Whatcom County's mainland. Roth writes, "As a rule the rural districts were well-behaved and orderly, and crime was very exceptional. The whole northern part of the county, therefore, was greatly stirred by the report that John Harris, the pioneer of Point Roberts, had been murdered."[218]

 Continue along Edwards Drive, pausing at Largaud Drive.

Largaud Drive is named for Joseph Largaud, who owned a farm and mill on this street in the early 20th century. The Point was logged of its old growth forest quite early; many of Whatcom County's mills were used to provide the lumber to rebuild San Francisco after its devastating 1906 earthquake. Today, the Point is mostly blanketed by second-growth forest, giving it its rural forested feel. These forests now cover a third of the land.[219]

On the south side of the intersection with Largaud Drive, an easement path leads to the beach. This is an historical smuggling trail. Canadian rum runners would bring loot down this trail to the beach and bury it in the sand, covered with driftwood, whilst an agent stood guard. On a moonless night, American smugglers would land on the beach, dig up the contraband, and smuggle it south.[220]

Another colorful early resident, William Pollard, lived on the Point in 1886. Pollard was already a convicted murderer by the time he arrived in Point Roberts. He had served a year-and-a-half sentence in the state penitentiary for murder. After killing a guy's dog, Pollard got into a knife fight, killing the dog's owner in a Sehome saloon. During his time in Point Roberts after getting out of prison, Pollard got into a quarrel with a fellow fisherman, John McSweeney, who ended up being stabbed to death. This time, Pollard was acquitted, and Point Roberts chalked up another murder. Pollard left Point Roberts to live on Clark Island near

Lummi Island, given to him by Captain Eldridge of Bellingham. After his handyman drowned Pollard went mad, believing his island was haunted. He died in June 1908.[221]

Amid the early settlers, the remote exclave became a favorite hideout for a cast of nefarious characters. Historylink.org states, "Point Roberts evolved into almost a no-man's land, a dangerous haven for smugglers and otherwise lawless men, where you could find trouble easily if you wanted. During the 1870s, despite the risks, a few homesteaders moved to the point."[222] These early settlers were all squatting on a military reservation. In July 1884 the military reservation status ended, but the federal government retained ownership of the Point. The U.S. Interior Department decided to vacate from Point Roberts in 1890, keeping only a section on the southwest corner for an intended lighthouse, today's Lighthouse Marine Park. Point Roberts was divvied up into forty acre parcels. Speculators from British Columbia crowded in the land office to get and flip a chunk of land, prompting the government to give priority to squatters who settled before 1884, during the military reservation era. If you squatted on military land, you got to keep it; if you squatted on federal land after it was no longer military property, you couldn't. The only settlers who qualified as pre-1884 residents were Kate Waller and Horace Brewster, causing the government to cancel the sale. With the speculators gone, seventeen legitimate settler households who had homesteads but had arrived after 1884 were left in limbo. The community created a school with twenty-seven kids, built roads, planted orchards and constructed buildings, but the weight of knowing they didn't have title to their land and could be moved off at any moment hampered life and long-term planning. The status of the Point's federal ownership was up in the air, and everybody was waiting for the Interior Department to decide what was going to happen to Point Roberts. Normal homesteading processes like the Homestead Act didn't fit the legal situation in Point Roberts, so the local squatters banded together to organize the squatting population and other important decisions.[223]

Thus, Point Roberts was in some ways an anarchist community. Though many people associate the word anarchy with chaos, the political science theory of anarchism is actually a philosophy of common people self-organizing and directly administering a society, without a separate class of capital-owning bosses and layers of government. A good example of how this worked for over a year in a major metropolitan area is Barcelona from 1936 to 1937 during the Spanish Civil War. Anarchists ran almost all functions of society in Barcelona, collectivizing most sectors of the economy, as George Orwell described, "It was the first time I had ever been in a town where the working class was in the saddle... Every shop and café had an inscription saying that it had been collectivized; even the bootblacks had been collectivized and their boxes painted red and black. Waiters and shop-walkers looked you in the face and treated you as an equal."[224] The staff kept showing up to work and took over running the business, including bakers, milkmen, grocery store staff, tram drivers, energy plant workers, hairdressers, brewers, printers, pharmacists, bank tellers, factory workers, miners and carpenters. Central teams made the rounds to coordinate affairs and make exchanges across industries. By managing the food supply chain, surplus food was routed to new communal dining halls so nobody went hungry.[225] Hours were cut to provide work for the unemployed; more people began spending money in the economy. Economic and societal functions actually performed better, with the workers having practical operating experience. Workers streamlined processes and cut bureaucratic red tape based on their expertise in their trade.[226]

Though the Point Roberts economy was not collectivized, the Point was federal land with no local federal caretakers. It had no local government and many of the big community decisions were made by the people coming together. In this accidental anarchist community, let's call it anarchistic rather than anarchist, over one hundred residents on the Point mutually self-organized their society, mutually organized the community's affairs, public improvements, community buildings, schools and roads. Each family had their own profession, earned their own income and had personal property, but much of the major community decisions were discussed in a self-organized society with basically no functioning local government until the introduction of the township in 1911. Popular institutions like the Grange society and the Lutheran congregation were utilized to bring the community together to facilitate dialogue and decision-making.[227]   There was some governmental presence on the surrounding waters as authorities patrolled for smuggling and fish piracy (there were no roads to Point Roberts then), and the canneries had security staff, but these in no way constituted a local government.   Despite the lack of local government protection, businesses thrived, a post office was established, ships brought people and supplies, a school educated children, all essentially self-organized.   Though the residents certainly did not consider themselves anarchists politically – indeed, they were *hoping for* governmental rule and recognition – this cooperatively-run town went on, not for one year like Barcelona, but for an incredible thirty-eight years, from 1873 to 1911. For all intents and purposes, Point Roberts was perhaps the longest-running anarchistic society in the western world.

Point Roberts was anarchistic in another way.   Australia was settled by convicts, Pitcairn Island by *Bounty* mutineers and Point Roberts by squatters. Whenever discussion of the Point's squatters comes up in present-day conversation, there is an awkward chuckle. For many, squatting is trespassing and theft.   Others take a more progressive view of squatting. There are over one billion squatters living on planet Earth today, occupying abandoned or unoccupied land or buildings they do not have legal permission to use.[228] In the developing world, vast slums encircling major metropolitan areas are home to squatters. People squat to get access to limited housing, to conserve buildings from demolition or as political expression, frequently anarchist in nature. Many current European squats feature social centers with give-away shops, pirate radio stations, bookstores and cafés. Squats were legal in the Netherlands until 2010: a building could be used legally by somebody who needed to squat if it was empty and not in use for twelve months. When a Dutch building was squatted, it was customary to send the owner a letter letting him know his property was now legally squatted, and inviting the local police to make an inspection. Copenhagen, Denmark is home to the famous Christiania squat, population 900, of a former military base, just like Point Roberts. Even in the Point Roberts' squatters' homeland in Iceland, a squat popped up in Reykjavik in 2009 during the country's banking crisis. These Icelandic squatters set up a store where all the goods were free for those who lost their jobs or homes, and a publishing house, but the police raided it five days later. Despite squatting's prevalence, squatting remains a taboo subject for many, and as a result it is omitted from serious policy and academic debate, either as a problem or movement.[229]

As you travel down Edwards Drive, the area becomes dense and thick with cabins and cottages. Many of the original homesteaders' large farms were eventually further subdivided into small residential lots. This area of Point Roberts is known as South Beach. Today, we think of Point Roberts as one entity, but far into the last century Point Roberts was a peninsula which held distinct communities: the town of Point Roberts was at the end of Gulf Road, where our tour will end; Maple Beach on Boundary Bay, which we visit in chapter six, and this South Beach area. South Beach is the ideal place to transition to the next era of settlement in the history of Point Roberts.

📍 Continue along Edwards Drive to the end where it curves to become South Beach Road. There's room to park to explore this area.

ERA 3 – DEVELOPMENT OF POINT ROBERTS

A small handful of very early settlers put down the first roots, but the arrival of a specific ethnic group, Icelanders, propelled the population and development of Point Roberts, basically filling its available land area in farm plots. This largely agricultural era lasted six decades but has faded from visibility in recent years.

Over forty thousand Americans and ninety thousand Canadians (together, nearly half of the current population of Iceland) tell the census they're of Icelandic heritage, descendants of a time in the late nineteenth century when one-fifth of Iceland's population emigrated to North America. An Icelandic colony was established in Wisconsin in the 1860s, and a large group of Icelandic Mormons trekked to Utah, but things really picked up in the 1870s. Large groups and even entire families left famine and miserable living conditions in Iceland. They initially settled in the Great Lakes region and Minnesota, but many ended up in the Dakotas. In a couple of places there were sufficient majorities to warrant Icelandic schools. Icelandic-Americans joined in the general westward migration of pioneers, eventually reaching the Salish Sea. North of the border, the government paid immigrants to move from Iceland and settle in Canada. Many stayed in Manitoba, and a group eventually settled in Victoria.

The first Icelander to settle at Point Roberts arrived on March 7, 1893 from Bellingham. Kristjan Benson encouraged a large group of Icelanders in Victoria, which was in a recession, to join him to squat Point Roberts as an Icelandic community. He told of a cannery about to open which would have lots of jobs as well as several squatters looking to sell out, so affordable homes were available. It was tax-free living, on the condition each man would cooperatively help to build roads for two-and-a-half days without pay in spring and summer.[230] Many agreed and a large group arrived to join Benson. They entered a Point Roberts still in limbo as the federal government, who owned the land, decided what to do with the Point. Homesteading was not yet opened up, and now a huge group of Icelanders were compounding the need for a resolution. With these new arrivals, Point Roberts took on a decidedly Icelandic feel. By 1904, half the settler population (in other words, excluding transient and temporary cannery workers seasonally housed in cannery dormitories) was Icelandic. Daily life was filled with uncertainty as newly-arriving Icelanders wondered whether they would be able to stay, or if the homes they worked hard to build and improve would be put up for auction. Some considered returning to Victoria as the Point was deemed too risky. Letters and petitions were sent to the state legislature in Olympia as well as to President Theodore Roosevelt pleading for a chance to make their homesteads official.[231]

Although there were other nationalities among the population, including English, Irish, German and French Canadian, to some degree Point Roberts was an Icelandic colony. The Icelanders had their own library, church services were in Icelandic and key personnel including the postmaster and grocery store staff all spoke Icelandic. Many Icelandic children only learned English when they got to school. Despite living in a de facto Icelandic colony, the first generations in Point Roberts would often refer to Iceland as "home."

By 1904 fifty-four households with 186 people were squatting at Point Roberts. Their noisy campaign was finally noticed in Washington D.C., and a Special Agent Ed Ellett from the United States Land Office in Seattle was dispatched to Point Roberts in 1904. Arriving by mail boat, he said, "I came to Point Roberts armed to the teeth, thinking the settlers were outlaws and renegades, but I soon found out I was mistaken." The squatters warmly greeted the man they hoped was going to help them. This was their best chance yet to plead their case to somebody official, and they were ready. They met Ellett on the dock and took him on a tour of everybody's house, pointing out land they had cleared, homes which had been built and tidied up with flowers, gainful employment secured, and a stated desire to lawfully own their property.[232]

The Icelanders tended to stick together, often out of expediency due to language. The English-speaking residents reached out to their Icelandic neighbors to help them fill out paperwork about their homestead claim. It would take another four years of anxiety, but in May 1908 President Roosevelt was finally ready to make a decision about Point Roberts. Roosevelt ruled Point Roberts' shoreline was too shallow for large ships and thus was of no use to the government for any future military purpose. Homesteading would be allowed. Ellett's report convinced him the squatters' improvements were significant enough they deserved to be given their properties. Had the squatters had to raise the value of the property, even scraping together a down payment would have forced many off their land.[233]

All the men of the community gathered and traveled to the land office in Seattle to file affidavits of settlement. When the men returned to Point Roberts, the women were all waiting on the shore for their return. As soon as they got to shore, the men leaped off the boat and ran up to their families, showing off the deed to their property. The community put on a big picnic at Tinkham's Grove and sacrificed the largest sheep on the Point, a prized ram. Locals tanned the hide into a luxurious sheepskin rug as a gift of thanks. Teddy Roosevelt sent a thank you note indicating he had placed it in his bedroom in the White House.

Canadian speculators had been eyeing the Icelanders' land, hoping they would be evicted and their property put up for auction. With the news the squatters would be allowed to stay on their land, the speculators moved on. The community began to put down roots and make a living. Knowing their homes were safe, many established farms on their land.

Point Roberts had been divided up into homestead lots. To get a feel for this, all of the land along the east side of South Beach Road from the beach up to APA Road was one homestead and farm, that of the Waters family. Fishing was the largest industry in Point Roberts from the time the Icelandic settlers arrived until the 1930s. Many residents fished during salmon season and made ends meet with agriculture; others were full-time farmers. Fruit, including apples, pears, plums, quince, berries and walnuts were grown. Some fruit trees from the pioneer era still bear fruit on the Point today, easily seen on the side of the road. During the Great Depression, Point Roberts had to fall back on its agricultural roots. The fish traps were closed in 1934, and many people left Point Roberts. Those who stayed, mostly the original homesteaders, doubled down on agriculture to get by. Residents would row out to the fishing boats to trade potatoes and apples for salmon in the 1940s.[234] Others supplied the canneries food for their mess halls. The former fishermen built poultry houses, growing chickens and producing eggs. The upper portion of the Waters land was a series of long chicken coops housing thousands of chickens. Evergreen Lane was originally a service corridor between the coops.

In 1915, a cooperative had been formed on the mainland, the Whatcom County Egg Producers. Prior to this, eggs had been imported from outside the county. Even egg imports from as far away as China were common, but quality varied greatly. The new cooperative implemented an egg grading system, so buyers could expect a consistent product. They chose to differentiate their higher-quality eggs in the Seattle market with a brand called Kulshan. Kulshan is the Coast Salish people's name for Mount Baker, which towers over Point Robert's eastern horizon. Egg producers eventually grew large and merged with poultry feed organizations to create the powerful cooperative, the Washington Egg and Poultry Cooperative Association in the mid-1920s. By 1926, Whatcom County led the entire state in poultry, and would go on to dominate Washington's poultry industry through the 1960s. Farmers in Point Roberts jumped on board, with many joining the cooperative in 1934 and shipping their eggs to Bellingham. Eggert

Burns had the top yield in the entire cooperative with three thousand chickens producing enough to ship four cases of eggs per day.[235] Others belonged to the Whatcom County Dairyman's Association, shipping cream to a Bellingham processing facility on a daily ferry between Point Roberts and Bellingham. Many family farms made money by selling milk to the families staying in cabins.

The farmers also produced potatoes. Point Roberts potatoes were unique. Varieties of potato included White Rose and Epicures which grew very early in the growing season, the earliest potatoes available in all of Washington and in the Vancouver, B.C. area. Potatoes exported to Canada were subject to duty after June 15 each year, so the farmers scrambled to get the potatoes harvested and exported before that whilst they were duty free. The Floury Epicures grown on the Point have creamy white flesh and a white skin with deep eyes. They are known for growing in cold regions and their ability to recover from frostburn. They were grown in Point Roberts from 1934 to 1953.

A unique potato-planting machine was invented here by Laugi Thorstenson. Tin cans were nailed to the spokes of an old wagon wheel. The farmer would place a potato in each can. As the wheel turned, the can turned upside-down, dropping the potato into the furrow. As empty cans rotated upright, another potato was placed in the empty can.[236] Mirroring the success they had in cooperative agriculture with dairy and poultry, the Point Roberts Potato Growers association was organized in the 1930s to help develop a potato market, ship a uniform grade of product, and have branded packaging.[237] The potatoes were supplied to hotels in Vancouver. Many on the Point sold their potatoes to the cannery cookhouses, which fetched $20 per 100 pounds in 1932 ($330 today). Eventually Canada banned the importation of potatoes to protect its own early potato crop, and the expense of sending the Point Roberts crop to the U.S. mainland made growing potatoes unprofitable.[238]

It's not only potatoes which grow early in Point Roberts. Often eight degrees Fahrenheit warmer than Bellingham, tulips bloom three to six weeks earlier than in the tulip-growing towns on the mainland. Lynden farmers formerly planted tulips in Point Roberts in order to extend their selling season.[239]

Agriculture would remain the Point's most-significant economic activity through the Second World War and into the mid-1950s, but the high cost of transportation made goods from Point Roberts expensive and limited the potential to earn a viable income.[240] Without income being augmented from fishing or work on the fish traps, and with smaller farm sizes and little mechanization, the Point's farmers couldn't compete with farmers on the mainland.

The foot of South Beach road had originally been the site of a fish camp operated by Pacific American Fisheries.[241] The fish camp had six buildings including a small store and eatery for the men who worked the fish traps just offshore. The southern shore of Point Roberts had five fish traps to catch salmon headed for the Fraser

Figure 39: The White House, built in 1933, still stands at the center of South Beach, today as a private residence. Photo by Whatcom Museum, 2005.97.1378; Bellingham, WA.

River. The first of the Point's four canneries was built here in the 1880s. The only cannery on the Point to never can salmon, this crab meat cannery's pilings are still visible at the South Beach Road beach access. The cannery's warehouse once stood next to the beach access, storing cannery equipment and the netting for the South Beach fish traps.

In 1933, the white home at the foot of South Beach Road, locally called the White House, was built on the site of the former warehouse.[242] It is a striking example of the Bauhaus architecture popular in the day, with its clean lines and façade, lack of eaves, white wash and circular porthole windows. The west side of the house has always been a private residence. The east side with the round windows was originally a warehouse, and later a store, providing a small market for the South Beach community. The dairy items and eggs in the store were from the surrounding farms. Groceries were brought in by the steamers *Welcome* and *Tulip* from Bellingham. Over the years, the White House has been a Point Roberts landmark and has long been used by fishermen as a beacon and reference point to describe their location.[243]

After the store in the White House closed, a small neighborhood market was built next door in the late 1950s. South Beach Store served the South Beach community through the 1970s, promoting that it was the exclusive store in Point Roberts to sell products from the Darigold cooperative, continuing the dairy cooperative tradition. In July 1980, the store became a restaurant, changing hands, names and menus over the years, including a stint in the 1990s when it tried the Mongolian grill trend.[244] In nice weather, dinner and a glass of wine at a table on the lawn overlooking the beach is one of the Point's finer pleasures.

The recreational potential of Point Roberts was recognized early. Entrepreneurs built camps and small cabins in the 1930s just above the beach to rent out to visitors in the summers.

Figure 40: Today a restaurant, South Beach Store was one of the Point's neighborhood markets, as shown in this 1970 ad.

Adjacent to the White House, at the foot of South Beach Road, is a beach access. This is an access point to the beach and tidelands on Point Roberts. At low tides in the summer, South Beach is one of the finest sandy beaches in Washington, stretching for two miles from the marina to Lily Point. Perhaps no state has made public beach and tidelands access as complicated of an issue as has Washington. There are conflicting laws, modified laws, road abutments, public property, private property, beach property, tidelands property, and a whole lot of misinformation among both the general public and property owners. In most coastal states, beaches and tidelands are in public ownership entirely or at least up to the high tide line, effectively offering near unlimited beach access, but not in Washington.

South Beach's crab cannery was built on the tidelands because when it achieved statehood in 1889, Washington delineated tidelands as separate lots from the lots on shore just above them.

The salmon, clam, oyster and crab industries drove this trend, and it allowed Washington to sell more property and collect more taxes for industries who were only interested in being in the tidal zone. Washington sold tidelands separately from beach lots for eighty years until the state legislature ended the practice in 1971. The result is over sixty per cent of Washington tidelands are in private hands.[245] If that were it, it would be a relatively black and white situation of determining where the tideland boundaries are, but it gets more complicated. Tideland ownership is determined by when the property was purchased, exactly how the language is worded in the deed, ancient common law and nineteen-year tidal averages of invisible high and low tide lines which vary at each beach.[246] Tideland parcels purchased between 1889 and 1911 go down to the mean low tide line. There are two high tides and two low tides most days, depending on the moon. To calculate the mean low tide line, you average the two low tides every day for the last nineteen years. This line is different on every beach in Washington depending on tidal flows in the Salish Sea basin, and indeed can be different for

Figure 41: 1930s-era cabins were rented to campers at South Beach. These cabins overlooked the grassy parking lot at the corner of South Beach Road and Edwards Drive. Photo by Whatcom Museum, 2005.97.1379; Bellingham, WA.

every property owner, including side-by-side neighbors.[247] Tidelands purchased between 1911 and 1971 or so extend lower, to what's called the mean lower low water line. Point Roberts does get minus tides lower than that, so on those rare events it is technically possible to walk on the beach at South Beach during these extremely low tides occur and be on public land, below the private tidelands line. Essentially, private ownership of tidelands means even walking in shallow water, not technically on the exposed sand per se, doesn't get you in the clear. Nonetheless, there is a wide variation of private beaches on the same strip of sand, the actual lines for each lot buried in legalese on deeds most people don't have readily available, which would be needed for any enforcement action. This makes it very confusing to walk on the beach around the Salish Sea.

Besides the actual property lines, there are the attitudes of property owners and the beach walkers. Some property owners post signs, others frantically run around the beach with clipboards confronting beach walkers. Most I talked to actually wished more people could experience the magic of the beaches on Point Roberts and don't mind people walking across the few-dozen feet of beach they own, though they do want to remind people who owns and pays taxes on the beach. I own beach property on Point Roberts and have seen boaters pull up to my beach and spread out blankets, eat picnics, mount sun umbrellas and stay the whole afternoon. Of course, troublemakers spoil the fun for everybody. Even the most permissive property owners draw the line at loud parties, big bonfires, trash and even hanky-panky on their beaches. Some trespassers don't stay down on the tidelands and actually come up on shore past the driftwood and hang out on benches and lawns of private residences without any apparent realization they're on somebody's private property. If you're Native American another set of rules come in to play. Depending on whether a given beach is determined to be a "customary fishing ground" as delineated in treaties from 1855, Native Americans can walk on and even gather shellfish from private beaches and tidelands. Under national policy a 1905 Supreme Court decision in a case involving Yakama tribal fishing it was determined Indians possessing treaty-assured fishing rights must be allowed access across private property to traditional fishing locations.[248]

Many law enforcement officers are reluctant to get involved, preferring parties communicate with each other and try to work things out. In Point Roberts, some neighborhoods dense with cabins all share one beach right, so a relatively small patch of beach can have dozens of homeowners with beach rights. Property owners in these communities with beach rights often let family and friends stay in the cottage, or rent them out, so it's challenging to know who the trespassers are. The Washington State Department of Natural Resources won't take an action on a beach and tideland access dispute until a formal survey of the property is conducted.[249] Officers are loathe to get out tape measures to see if somebody is trespassing, so it's up to property owners to prove there has been a violation. There would also have to be physical evidence of where the suspect was walking, but this gets erased as the tide comes in.[250] Prosecutors say it would be difficult to prove a case of trespassing against somebody for simply walking across a beach. To take action, officers would need to see a deed proving ownership and property line diagrams. Action would only make sense if a jury would find somebody guilty beyond a reasonable doubt, and given Washington's complex laws regarding beaches and tidelands, the entire affair is highly doubtful. A defendant would have an excellent defense because there is another law regarding beach rights which conflicts with everything we've discussed so far.

This law is called the Public Trust Doctrine which can be traced back to the time of Roman Emperor Justinian. It states certain resources are for public use, and the government is required to maintain the public's interest and reasonable use of these resources.[251] The original Roman law states "by the law of nature these things are common to mankind: the air, running water, the sea and consequently the shores of the sea. All rivers and ports are public, hence the right of fishing in a port or in rivers is common to all men."[252] The doctrine is a part of English Common Law and was imported by the original thirteen American colonies and later to every state in the United States. It has been upheld by the U.S. Supreme Court in principle, but they punted interpretation of the law to the states.[253] Essentially, this doctrine means property owners cannot legally keep people from walking on private tidelands. Under this interpretation many of the signs in Point Roberts which read "private beach and tidelands" overstep their authority.[254]

The Public Trust Doctrine is used by most states in the United States. Although most tidelands in Oregon are public, Oregon uses the Public Trust Doctrine to allow the public to walk on the few private tidelands which do exist as long as they don't cause damage; California uses the doctrine in a similar way.[255] Despite the private tidelands laws and the Public Trust Doctrine being in conflict, the Washington State Supreme Court has never affirmed nor denied beachwalking on private land.[256] However, courts have upheld the Public Trust Doctrine many times in non-beachwalking cases, such as the right to take a boat wherever water goes even if it's floating over private property.

The Public Trust Doctrine was used in Washington in the benchmark 1969 Wilbour v. Gallagher case. A Lake Chelan property owner was dumping large amounts of fill dirt into the lake. The Washington State Supreme Court found the property owner did not have the right to block navigation as this was a public right protected by the government, citing the doctrine. It clarified these public rights cover "fishing, boating, swimming, water skiing and other recreational purposes."[257] Three years later, Washington's Shorelines Management Act was approved. This 1972 law attempted to balance shoreline development between public rights and private interests whilst encouraging public use of shorelines.

In the major 1987 Caminiti v. Boyle case, the court found "the [Public Trust] doctrine has always existed in the State of Washington." Furthermore, another 1987 case, the landmark Orion Corp v. State, the court found the Shorelines Management Act supports but does not replace the Public Trust Doctrine, with the public holding intrinsic rights to use shorelines.[258] The ruling stated, "Historically, the trust developed out of the public's need for access to navigable waters and shorelands." The catch is the limits of those rights have not been defined or ruled on.

Just south of Point Roberts in the San Juan Islands, in the Jet Ski Case of 1998 a court found, "The doctrine protects 'public ownership interests in certain uses of navigable waters and underlying lands, including navigation, commerce, fisheries, recreation, and environmental quality.' The doctrine reserves a public property interest, the jus publicum, in tidelands and the waters flowing over them, despite the sale of these lands into private ownership."

One aspect of beach access not in question is where road-ends abut beaches. Point Roberts has several of these, including right here where South Beach Road directly ends at the beach where the crab cannery pier used to be. Under a 1969 Washington state law, any public road which abuts a shoreline is considered legal public access to the water, with public access having top preference, stating, "No county shall vacate a county road or part thereof which abuts on a body of salt or fresh water."[259] It describes these access points as typically "narrow rights-of-way and easements extend across tidelands down to the water. Users should be aware and respect that most tidelands on either side of these sites are privately owned."[260] These road ends may not be vacated by state or local government unless it is deeded to a parks district which will enhance public access. Local governments are supposed to identify these "road ends" as public access points, but ombudsmen have found many access points have been left off of inventory lists, and some even sport private beach signs which mislead the public about the water access. Recent efforts to catalog these sites have resulted in the doubling of identified public beach access points in Washington.

The question of public beach access on private land using the Public Trust Doctrine was almost settled in a court case. The Washington State Court of Appeals found a Bainbridge Island road end at Fletcher's Landing, formerly a ferry landing, could not be blocked by property owners who had purchased the tidelands and were attempting to stop public access.[261] The ruling states the public has a right to cross private tidelands from a road end to get to the water. The Fletcher's Landing ruling did not grant the public the right to turn right or left from that public road end and start walking down the beach. However, the case was not published by the Court of Appeals into the official record, so it cannot be cited or even mentioned in any other lawsuit, and the state Supreme Court declined to hear the hot potato case in an election year, leaving Fletcher's Landing a limited decision. The Public Trust Doctrine's supporters didn't get the definitive ruling for which they had hoped, but it seems the mainstream position to many. Indeed, when Lily Point developers announced in 1984 they were going to enforce private property lines at Lily Point and prevent the Point Roberts general public from walking on the beach from South Beach to Lily Point, Doddi Iwersen testified at a hearing with a simple statement which sums up the relationship between the community of Point Roberts and its beaches, saying, "People have walked that beach for over one hundred years. It would be wrong for that to stop."[262]

These laws contradict one another, and each has been upheld in Washington state courts. The Washington State Supreme Court has never heard a case to resolve this contradiction, leaving each side to have its proponents truly believing walking on certain beaches is or is not allowed to this day. Given Washington's population now exceeds seven million and more and more pressures are on public access points and on property rights, it's surprising this hasn't come to the fore before now, but most agree it will need to be addressed soon. The problem is intensifying with stronger demand on public access and tourism from a limited supply of beachfront property whose cost is out of reach of most Washingtonians. The Point Roberts Community Association in 1969 resolved the "acquisition of beachfront property should be continued by the Parks and Recreation District until 20% of all shoreline property is in public hands."[263] The county ended up meeting that goal, and both local and county parks agencies should clarify and prioritize public access points to water, especially outside the county parks.

 Travel up South Beach Road to APA Road. Make a brief detour half a block to the left to the Lutheran church.

Just to the left is the only house of worship structure ever to exist on Point Roberts, Trinity Lutheran Church, built in 1921 to largely serve the Point's Icelandic Lutheran settlers. The congregation was formed in 1915 with fifty-five members and originally met in the grange hall until this structure was built. A pastor named H. Leo was sent by the Icelandic Lutheran Synod to the west coast and given instructions to organize congregations in Vancouver, B.C., Seattle, Blaine and Point Roberts. The first pastor to serve the Point was S. Olafson, but he served all four Icelandic churches on the Salish Sea, so he divided his time and wasn't in Point Roberts every Sunday; services were in the evenings to allow the pastor to come from another city. The lumber for the church came from a local sawmill. Logs were pushed down to the sawmill on a skid road with corduroy log chutes. The members fund-raised for years to generate the money needed to build the church. Settlers donated wool and the ladies' society sewed quilts to be raffled at fund-raising bazaars. Concerts and other entertainment were performed to raise funds. A local family donated the land from their homestead for the lot in 1916 where the church stands today. The church opened in 1921 with services and Sunday school conducted in Icelandic. By 1934, the services were mostly in English, with an Icelandic service twice a month.

Figure 42: Trinity Community Lutheran Church. Photo by Mark Swenson.

As the share of Icelanders fell as more people moved to Point Roberts over the decades, the Lutheran affiliation was deemed too constraining. In the early 1970s the synod announced the Point Roberts congregation was too small and would be merged with a Lutheran congregation in Tsawwassen.[264] The members decided they didn't want to lose their history and Point Roberts-based church, so they formed a new charter in 1972, changing its name to Trinity Community Church to appeal to all of Point Roberts. In recent years it has returned to a Lutheran affiliation; it is now known as Trinity Community Lutheran Church.

The church building has been steadily improved over the years. The porch was added in the 1950s. A steeple, which houses a speaker system, was added in August 1977.[265] The parking lot on the south side of APA Road was purchased in 1979. It received its current crowning steeple in 1984. The rear wing of the building was added in spring 1996. The church is known in the community for its concerts, made possible by the current Schlicker pipe organ. Its 425 pipes were inaugurated in 2012.[266]

The noted Icelandic-born sculptor Magnus Arnesen lived in Point Roberts in the 1930s. Arnesen was born in Iceland in 1879 and moved to California in the 1920s where he taught at the Berkeley League of Fine Arts. After living in Point Roberts in the 1930s, he moved to Claremont, New Hampshire where he lived until he died in 1970. Arnesen was friends with Halldór Laxness. Laxness was awarded the 1955 Nobel Prize in Literature, the only Icelandic Nobel laureate. Laxness visited Arnesen in

Figure 43: Halldór Laxness. Photo by Nobel Foundation [Public domain], via Wikimedia Commons

Point Roberts in the 1930s during a time Laxness was influenced by the writings of Upton Sinclair. In 1931 he began publishing *Salka Valka*, a series of sociological novels about socialist society. One reviewer stated Laxness "had become the apostle of the younger generation."[267] Laxness also sharply attacked Spiritualist Church leader Einar Hjörleifsson Kvaran. Kvaran, editor of Iceland's largest newspaper, was also the president of the Icelandic Society for Psychical Research whose influential writings in the 1920s had rumors swirling of a possible Nobel Prize of his own.

With such a large block of residents from one ethnic group, the hegemonic feel of Point Roberts lasted for many decades. In 1969, a full thirty per cent of the people in Point Roberts had been on the voter registration roll in 1932. Nine per cent had lived on the Point all their life.[268] It eventually diluted as Point Roberts grew. These days, the census bureau tabulates Icelandic-Americans make up fourteen per cent of Point Roberts. As a result, despite the prominent role Icelanders played in the settling of Point Roberts and their continued proud contributions to the current community, there is little evidence remaining today of this Icelandic history. There are no Icelandic gift shops or imported Icelandic specialty foods and just a few Icelandic flags. The only monument to Icelandic settlement is a small marker in the cemetery. Few people in Point Roberts today can speak Icelandic and it is not taught in Blaine Public Schools. Links to Iceland are maintained through annual exchange programs which bring people from Iceland to Point Roberts for cultural visits. The historical society sponsors events where photos of Iceland are shared by recent visitors. Perhaps the best example of the Point's Icelandic heritage is the names of many of the roads on Point Roberts. Descendants of the original Icelandic settlers still reside in Point Roberts, their names a tangible and present manifestation of a proud Icelandic tradition. In the summer of 1994, over three hundred people attended a celebration of the centennial of Icelandic settlement of Point Roberts. Today, several descendants of original Icelandic settlers – some cousins – still live on the Point. They're in touch with each other daily via speed dial as they have been since childhood. They often bring Icelandic treats like *skyr*, Icelandic yogurt; *pannekoeken*, Icelandic pancakes; and *vínarterta*, a multi-layered cake (always with a minimum five layers, often more) filled with prunes, to community events, providing a link to the Point's Icelandic past, great-grandmothers and grandfathers of an Icelandic presence at Point Roberts which now spans seven generations.[269]

The Development Era achieved significant milestones and established many of the community pillars and infrastructure upon which it still depends today. During this era, the Point got property lines, roads, a border station, post office, school, church, dikes, electricity, retail stores, large canneries, fish traps, homesteads and agriculture. More than all of that, this era tamed Point Roberts from a nefarious outlaw smuggling den to a decidedly American community oriented to the southeast; its economic links were mostly to Blaine and Bellingham. The people had been given their homes, literally, by the U.S. government, and the residents turned to American sources for solving their needs. Ironically, compared to the mainland where the post-war years were a boom time of growth and development, on Point Roberts the late 1940s and early 1950s were a time of uncertainty as people moved away and the economy declined. The last cattle herd was gone by 1953. In the 1950s, the established order was about to be displaced by another force which would reorient the Point's focus to the north.

ERA 4 – CANADIAN ERA

The next era in Point Roberts was the Canadian Era, which saw the Point become a recreationally-oriented town. This resulted in a transformative shift in Point Roberts' economy and culture. New infrastructure in Canada opened a floodgate of visitors and soon a new type of resident settled in Point Roberts. Within a decade, these newcomers would own three quarters of the Point.

Back in 1886, a mob of angry whites ran Seattle's Chinese community out of town, prompting the territorial legislature to ban non-residents who were ineligible for citizenship from owning property. When Washington became a state three years later this law was actually written into the state constitution. The law remained on the books until 1953, when it was changed, allowing Canadians to own land in Washington if they were from a province which allowed Washingtonians to own land. This included British Columbia.

At the time, there had only been a road over the border to Canada for a scant thirty years. A few Canadians had owned property on Point Roberts before 1953, but the change in the law unleashed a flood Canadians buying property, building cabins on the Point and staying all summer. As more Canadians moved in and became the majority of property owners, the focus and dependence of the Point swung from the U.S. to Canada. In the process, the importance of the border, and traversing it, and laws on either side became paramount concerns in the community.

The postwar emphasis on the automobile caused British Columbia to build several major road works in the late 1950s which made it far easier to get to Point Roberts from both Vancouver and the United States mainland. Six years after Canadians were allowed to buy property in Point Roberts, the Massey Tunnel was built under the Fraser River, connecting Richmond and Delta. It was originally called the Deas Island Tunnel, but was renamed in 1967 for George Massey, the Delta legislator who campaigned for the crossing throughout the late 1950s. The tunnel is one of only seven fixed crossings of the Fraser River south of Hope, British Columbia. The first Fraser River crossing was the Pattullo Bridge between New Westminster and Surrey, built in 1937. It was the only bridge spanning the Fraser River in Metro Vancouver for nearly twenty years until a second crossing over the Fraser River was added in 1956, far upriver in the Fraser Valley between Agassiz and

Rosedale, today's B.C. highway 9. The Massey Tunnel was only the second river crossing in the Vancouver area, and would be so for five more years until the original Port Mann bridge between Surrey and Coquitlam opened in 1964. The tunnel caused the cessation of the Ladner ferry, which had run for forty-five years from 1913 to 1959. The tunnel, opened in 1959 by Queen Elizabeth II, is the lowest elevation on a public road in all of Canada. When you drive at the lowest point in the tunnel, you are sixty-five feet below sea level. Setting all kinds of architectural records and firsts, the opening of the Massey Tunnel was a game-changer for Point Roberts, making it an easy sub-hour drive from Vancouver.

With the Massey Tunnel open, traffic patterns changed, bringing B.C.'s main highway a mere seven miles from Point Roberts. In 1962, British Columbia rerouted the main highway from the United States border to Vancouver. It had previously followed the King George Highway due north from the border at Blaine through Surrey and over the Pattullo Bridge to New Westminster and into Vancouver on Kingsway Avenue. Kingsway was the original wagon road between Vancouver's Gastown district and the original provincial capital in New Westminster. The Pattullo Bridge opened in 1937 and the King George Highway was completed to the border in 1940, becoming designated as highway 99 in 1942. In 1934, realtor Edgar Burns built a billboard on this highway near New Westminster, promoting Point Roberts as Little America,[270] the inspiration for the current Little America sign greeting visitors to the exclave at the top of Tyee Drive. When the Massey Tunnel opened, a new highway was built in 1962 veering west from the old northbound King George Highway just north of the Nicomecl River, and hugging the north shore of Boundary Bay, alongside B.C. Route 10, and then through the Massey tunnel and north through Richmond. It completed its entrance into Vancouver over the Oak Street Bridge, which had opened in 1957. With the ease of access, border crossings at Point Roberts quadrupled from 50,000 cars in 1950 to 220,000 in 1965.[271]

At the same time, homesteaders were struggling after the closure of the canneries and fish traps, and the decline of agriculture. As a result, property lines changed. The owners of the homesteads and farms subdivided their land into tiny parcels just big enough for a beach cabin. Many of the homesteaders wanted to attract young families to enjoy the beaches and relaxing summer lifestyle in Point Roberts which they had enjoyed as children. They wanted these summer cabins to be affordable for middle class families and so lots were made very small and friendly financial terms were offered with low down payments and repayments spread out over time. Those small lot sizes are very much on display in South Beach with over twenty narrow lanes of dense beach cabins, some charming, some needing a bit of repair. Vacant most of the year, South Beach bursts at the seams in July and August when Canadians come down for the entire summer and relax. Yesterday's young families are retired couples today, the homes often passed down through generations, neighbors greeting each other every summer. For many current residents, their summer childhood memories were made at the Point Roberts cabin. They fondly recall bingo tournaments and the Darigold-sponsored summertime picnic. It all gives Point Roberts its current clubby retirement community vibe.

All aspects of life were dramatically different by the time the 1950s closed. No longer was the majority a permanent year round population supporting retail stores, infrastructure and services. In a generation, Point Roberts went from being half Icelandic to three-quarters Canadian. The local full-time year-round population fell dramatically, impacting the economy, goods and services, transportation, education and tax base. The need for supply ships from Bellingham dwindled and steamer runs stopped, as Canadians brought the goods they needed from their permanent homes in Canada, and they only stuck around for a few weeks. Today, Point Roberts is still very much a seasonal town. The Canadians drive the Point Roberts economy. By the close of the 1950s, the revenue produced from Canadians in two summer months dwarfed the entire town's receipts it previously needed all year to earn.[272]

Point Roberts had all the makings of a summer resort, including a sunny, dry climate, ringed by beaches, crisscrossed by forest trails and this rural feeling could be yours in a half-hour drive from the largest city in western Canada. Property tax and homeowners association (or strata) assessments were a fraction of those in Vancouver, making the Point a bargain compared to the high cost of living in Canada.

The American residents had reservations about the influx of Canadians but knew market economic forces were at work.[273] Decisions made in the state capitol in Olympia were outside its control. Adapting to the changes, many former farmers became real estate agents. Resentment built in Point Roberts as port, county and state officials refused to cooperate in the harbor affair and the provisioning of utilities. How could these officials offer nothing to Point Roberts when the residents had been sending lots of tax revenue to the mainland? As early as 1952, the salmon catch at Point Roberts alone generated $3 million in the U.S.[274] Much of the taxes assessed in Point Roberts go to the Port of Bellingham, yet they offered no help with the harbor. Whatcom County rubbed salt in the wound in 1961 by reclassifying the farms in Point Roberts from agricultural lands to residential property. Taxes soared, leading to more farmsteads being subdivided into hundreds of residential lots all across the Point. Tax revenues paid to the county soared even more. Yet Point Roberts saw no direct aid or infrastructure projects in return. State-level government was the same story. Taxes were collected in Point Roberts and sent to Olympia, but when Point Roberts asked for resolution to its problems, the state shrugged, suggesting the locals work harder within existing legislation and programs.[275]

The fact these newcomers were not American was acutely felt by the local American population. Many infrastructure and large development proposals were rejected because they would help a largely Canadian community, with too few Americans to make it worth it. Not only did they feel isolated from the mainland U.S., soon there were so many Canadians the Point felt Canadian. Locals struggled to hold on to their American identity. By the end of the 1960s, eighty-five per cent of property lots on Point Roberts were owned by Canadians.[276] The locals ironically depended on revenues from Canadians to keep its economy strong enough to control their future as an American town and not be swallowed up by Canada. That fear of being swallowed up wasn't just in the locals' heads, either. The 1940s and 1950s saw the Canadian press more than once in their editorials call for Point Roberts to be ceded to Canada. The locals on the Point bristled at this affront to their proud nationality; mainland newspapers in Washington took offense at these Canadian editorials.[277]

The Point is empty much of the year because it has to be: especially for frequent day trippers from Delta, Canadians have to be careful not to be in Point Roberts too many days out of the year, as even a quick trip down to the Point for gas counts as a day in the U.S. Going over certain thresholds over a three year average – the actual number of days varies over a multi-year period but in broad terms averages to 182 days a year – can mean having a tax liability and residency issues with the U.S. government. This sets a limit on how much Canadians can get invested in Point Roberts. In a vicious circle, it permanently creates a visitor class who own empty homes dominating the pool of available housing, stifling the growth potential of the Americans in the exclave. Development options are limited as there are not enough people to create a year-round market for more products and services. Empty homes fill most residential lots. Surrounded by water, more newcomers can't fit. Many of the remaining lots are unbuildable due to unsuitable locations for a septic tank or water availability. It perfectly shows how the border impacts, changes and limits local life in an exclave.

For such a small town, with just a few hundred residents for most of the twentieth century, there have been quite a few famous residents. Many of these famous residents were Canadians who maintained a home in Point Roberts. Notably, writers love the silence and rural peacefulness and the inspiration of nature which helps the words flow as they scribe their masterpieces.

Evelyn Caldwell was known to Vancouver women in the 1950s as Penny Wise, the author of a popular and iconic column in the *Vancouver Sun*. The Martha Stewart of her generation, Caldwell's column contained tips for making a stylish home and introduced British Columbians to many foods deemed exotic in the 1950s, that there is Caesar salad in British Columbia is due to Penny Wise introducing the strange salad with its then-bizarre creamy anchovy dressing. Caldwell wanted to be a serious journalist, and worked in journalism from 1928 to 1974, joining the *Vancouver Sun* in 1945. She was the first woman to cross Vancouver's iconic Lions Gate Bridge when it opened in 1938. Although women reporters struggled for acceptance and respect, Caldwell was in her element if there were murders on which to report, until she was eventually banished by a male editor to the society and consumer affairs section. Making lemonade out of lemons, she took on ownership of the role, becoming the first full time consumer advocate writing for a major Canadian newspaper. Her readership loved her consumer affairs but also her early feminist stances, and they eagerly joined letter-writing campaigns she instigated in her column to change consumer laws. She called her fans the Feminine Fighting Force, who were responsible for changing B.C.'s law banning margarine. Her popularity led the *Sun* to send her around the world, even to the Soviet Union during the Cold War to report from behind the Iron Curtain. She visited Canadian troops in 1951 during the Korean War, famously washing her hair in one soldier's helmet, as told in a

July 1951 *Time* magazine article about Caldwell. Modern consumer reporting owes a great deal to the Penny Wise legacy. Her news-you-can-use style to women's interests changed how newspapers across North America approached this content. Caldwell spent retirement in Point Roberts. In 1980 Caldwell continued her Penny Wise column in the Point's local paper of the time, *The Ocean Star*.[278] She died in Point Roberts in 1998 at age 89.

Another notable resident was one of Canada's most beloved authors, novelist and short story writer Margaret Laurence. During the time she and her husband lived in Vancouver, from 1957 to 1962, they bought a small cabin for $1450 on Park Lane in Point Roberts. Kept cool by the shade of the largest Sitka spruce on Point Roberts, the relaxation and quaint setting of the Point inspired Laurence to write most of *The Stone Angel* here, the book for which she is best known. Required reading in many North American schools, the 1964 novel's protagonist and voice is Hagar Shipley, a ninety-year-old Manitoba woman living with her eldest son in Vancouver. The story follows the entire life of Shipley as she chooses love over inheritance and marries against her parents' wishes. Facing family estrangement and economic hardship, the marriage ends when Shipley moves to a new city to start a new independent life, but one in which she must work below her social class to get by. The old canneries in Point Roberts, one still in operation during Laurence's time on the Point, provided the inspiration for the cannery in the book, though the novel is not set in Point Roberts.[279] Laurence died in 1989, but *The Stone Angel* has stayed current. In 2007, the book was made into a feature film, directed by Kari Skogland and starring Ellen Burstyn. Laurence's literary works over the course of her career feature a female perspective on life and the struggles and choices women face in society. In 2016, Canada named her a National Historic Person.

The screenplay for the 1980 Canadian film *Out of the Blue* was originally written in Point Roberts by Leonard Yakir.[280] The story follows a young girl whose father is an ex-convict and whose mother is a junkie. She finds it difficult to conform and finds comfort in a quirky combination of Elvis and punk rock. Yakir was initially to be the director, but in the end, it was directed by and starred Dennis Hopper. Hopper's big comeback, this was the first film he had directed since 1971's *The Last Movie*. It also starred a film comeback for New Westminster-native Raymond Burr. The movie was shot in South Delta in the spring, and later that year it competed for the Palme d'Or at the Cannes Film Festival. In Canada it was released under the title *No Looking Back*.

Just across the border in Delta, British Columbia, there is a famous bird sanctuary on Westham Island in the Fraser River delta named the George C. Reifel Migratory Bird Sanctuary. George C. Reifel was a famous British Columbian with a long and colorful history. Reifel came from a prominent family of brewers who had been making beer in British Columbia since 1888. He became a beer baron himself, but also an entertainment magnate, clever business man, philanthropist and conservationist.[281]

Reifel opened his own brewery in Vancouver in 1910. Under British Columbia's Prohibition in 1917, sale and consumption of alcohol was banned, but not the manufacture of it. He and his father purchased breweries across British Columbia at bargain-basement prices, increasing production for thirsty Americans just across the border. He bought a distillery in New Westminster so he could control the entire liquor supply chain, maximizing his profits and power as a major rum-runner. He owned a fleet of cargo ships feeding most of the western United States with booze. His prize ship, the legendary *Malahat*, was a five-masted World War I naval ship 225 feet long. It transported sixty thousand cases of liquor off the U.S. west coast, just outside American territorial waters. Smugglers would zoom out in speed boats to get the loot. Though frowned upon, rum-running was highly profitable and actually legal in Canada. Reifel stayed in the beer and liquor industry until 1945.[282]

In the 1920s, Reifel bought large tracts of property. He owned the largest home in Vancouver at the time. He built the Commodore Ballroom in 1929 and the Vogue Theatre. He owned Sunset Beach in Vancouver before donating it to the city to create today's shoreline park. He bought and diked land on Westham Island in Delta to create a hunting ground and wildlife reserve which became today's bird sanctuary. He constructed six dikes on his two hundred hectares which created three lagoons to attract waterfowl, feeding the birds grain from his distilleries. Today the sanctuary is the largest migratory bird wintering area in Canada and the largest estuarine habitat on the Pacific coast of Canada. It became a Wetland of International Significance in 1987.[283]

Reifel died in 1958, and his son, George H. Reifel, donated the family land for the sanctuary in 1963, naming it after his father. It became an official sanctuary in 1973. George H. Reifel went on to become a major force in Point Roberts. From his "special home" on the Point, Reifel played a major role in revitalizing the Point Roberts chamber of commerce in 1986. Reifel loved the international flavor of the Point's Fourth of July parade. When the Point Roberts Golf Club was proposed, Reifel was a principal in the development corporation, and his experience in the care for birds helped bridge concerns about the impact the golf course would have on the heron rookery.[284] George H. Reifel died at age sixty-five on March 7, 1992.[285] His wife Norma, also active in the Point Roberts community, died in Point Roberts October 20, 1995 at age sixty-nine.[286]

Many people in Point Roberts are familiar with the Winskill family name because they pass the Winskill Park and Recreation Centre on 56th Street in Tsawwassen on the drive to the Point Roberts border. Molly Winskill was a teacher in Point Roberts and her daughter was born on the Point. Her husband Chris was a member of the Delta Council and the South Delta Taxpayers Society and owned a farm where the park is today. Like the Point Roberts farmers, Winskill was a potato farmer; his potato patch was on today's sports fields and the professional building to the north. Winskill was the founder of the South Delta Early Potato Growers Association which boasted forty members. They competed with the Point Roberts farmers to get their potatoes to market earlier than the other.[287] They sold the farm to create the park in 1968. The swimming pool and recreation facility opened in February 1977.[288]

The Canadian Era would last three decades. It brought Point Roberts out of its agricultural and fishing past, diluted the Icelandic dominance of the population and broke up the large original homesteads into dense residential lots and subdivisions of cottages. In 1988, this chapter of life in Point Roberts ended, and the current era began.

ERA 5 – PRESENT DAY

During the Canadian orientation in the 1960s and 1970s it was difficult for Americans to live on Point Roberts as permanent year-round residents. With a sharply seasonal economy, there weren't enough people to support a large number of businesses. This led to few job opportunities, which meant few new incoming residents. In a classic game of chicken and egg, more businesses didn't come because there was a lack of reliable water and few people, and few people came because there were few jobs. Point Roberts was locked in this kind of stifling environment for decades. Three things shook Point Roberts out of its slumber: a source for water was secured, the growth of Vancouver as a major Pacific Rim metropolis, and digital disruption caused by the Internet. A reliable water supply brought development. The rise of Vancouver's population and its strong economy led to more job opportunities for Americans who lived within Vancouver's orbit.

The arrival of the World Wide Web in the 1990s meant Americans could live here without being tied to the local economy. Today's residents are increasingly Americans who want to be close to and part of the Vancouver metro area and economy, but don't want to or can't live in Canada. More and more people can live anywhere they want because they work virtually online, not having to go into a physical office. Point Roberts' small lots and diminutive homes attract Americans from the cities who want to downshift to an idyllic setting, and the rise of the tiny home movement coincided just in time. Self-employed professionals can be based on Point Roberts and travel occasionally to clients on the mainland. Accountants, lawyers, architects, consultants, sales reps, financial advisors and pilots base themselves in Point Roberts, and drive down to Seattle or Bellingham a few times a month to meet clients or transact business, or fly out of nearby Vancouver International Airport to points across North America and beyond. Mirroring a major trend in the digital economy, today a full seventeen per cent of Point Roberts residents work at home.[289] The Point has evolved from destination to bedroom community.

When Richard Clark wrote his 1980 book about Point Roberts, *Point Roberts, USA: The History of a Canadian Enclave*, he later explained his deliberate selection of the book's subtitle. Point Roberts was heavily dependent upon Canada and Canadians owned most of the Point, prompting Clark to orient the book as a Canadian enclave rather than an American exclave. When the current era began in the early 1990s and the share of Canadian residents fell slightly as more Americans could be based in Point Roberts without needing a local job, the orientation of Point Roberts swung back to that of an American exclave.

The close proximity of Point Roberts to Vancouver has enabled a few stars of major league Vancouver sports teams to choose to base their household for residency purposes in Point Roberts. Players and coaches for the Vancouver Canucks hockey team and the

Vancouver Whitecaps Football Club have chosen to be based in Point Roberts. When an American citizen is traded to a Vancouver team, many look for a way to stay a resident of the United States whilst playing for Vancouver. Since American citizens pay taxes to the U.S. based on their worldwide income, living in Canada can mean higher taxes. Some foreign players live in Point Roberts whilst playing for a Vancouver team in order to keep a U.S. visa until they are traded back to a U.S. team. Point Roberts is the closest American territory to Vancouver, enabling these American team members to get to the stadium in less than an hour through a less-congested border crossing with shorter waits than if these players were based in Blaine. Living at Point Roberts provides a sense of a normal life without being mobbed by fans in Vancouver.

Figure 44: The view from Seabright Farms, looking west along Crystal Water Beach and South Beach to Lighthouse Park. Photo by Mark Swenson.

Examples of former athletes and coaches who have lived in Point Roberts include Alexander Mogilny, Pavel Bure, Dave Nonis and former Canucks coach John Tortorella, whose residency in Point Roberts was frequently commented on in the media and online, usually not positively. There are professional hockey and soccer players currently living at Point Roberts.

DEMOGRAPHICS

The census shows Point Roberts' population grew slowly throughout most of the twentieth century, but has grown rapidly since the late-1980s. In 1904, as the canneries were getting established, Point Roberts had a population of one hundred. In a sense, Point Roberts was more of a bustling town then as it is today; in that year, it had two general stores (compared to only one today), a hotel (none today), a post office, a saloon, a school, and twenty-three homes. A count in 1978 recorded just 422 people after having peaked over 600 in 1970. Of that, nearly half were foreign green card holders. Only 191 were U.S. citizens.[290] The lack of a reliable water source was severely hampering any future for growth. The availability of water, established in 1988, opened up growth on the Point, reversing a decline in population in the 1970s and early 1980s. The 2000 census showed the most growth, a forty-three per cent increase over the 1990 census. The 2010 census counted 1,314 people in Point Roberts today.

Despite the recent trend of very large waterfront homes, Point Roberts is well below state average in affluence. Its median income of $59,000 per household and $39,700 per person trails the state; indeed, less than 11% of Washington state residents are in poverty, whilst over 15% of Point Roberts residents are officially that poor. Poverty is directly tied to education, and just 28% per cent of Point Roberts residents have a college degree, over ten per cent lower than the national average. However, a full 86% of its kids graduate from high school, not an easy feat given the closest high school is on the mainland.

Demographically, the census reports Point Roberts being overwhelmingly white. Ninety-two per cent of residents are Caucasian as of the 2010 census, down from ninety-five per cent in 2000 and ninety-nine per cent as recently as 1990.[291] Whereas African-Americans make up twelve per cent of the United States population, they make up only 0.8% of people in Point Roberts. Six per cent of Americans are Asian-American; in Point Roberts they are only 4.5% of the populace. Just 2.4% on the Point are of Hispanic ethnicity compared to seventeen per cent of Americans. The only race represented in Point Roberts at a level equivalent to national proportions is Native Americans; they make up 0.8% of people on the Point, the same as their national share.

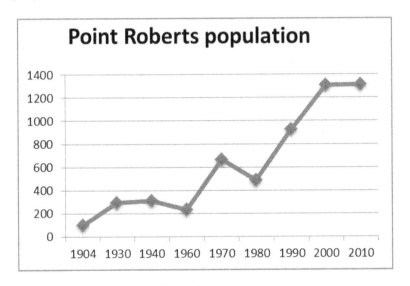

Figure 45: Point Roberts population since 1904

Point Roberts is often described as a retirement community, and this shows in the age breakdown in census data. The median age on the Point is a ripe fifty-three, far above the Washington state average. Two-thirds are over age forty-five. Less than one-fifth of residents are under twenty-five, whereas a quarter is aged sixty-five or older. As late as 1990, only nine per cent of residents were under twenty-five, but the share of young people has grown as year-round families settle on Point Roberts.[292]

In business, marketing departments seek to deliver relevant and personalized content and offers to consumers. The data used to target personalized messages come from data captured from consumers; the data breadcrumbs consumers leave behind as they shop in stores or browse online and use social media. This is possible because of digital transformation in business, massively-scalable databases which can cheaply store every click. Not so many years ago, this was not nearly as easy as it is today. Back then, data storage was very expensive, and databases could not scale to the extent to which they could store vast quantities of information, including individual transactions, online browsing clicks and social media likes. In those days, marketers couldn't personalize a message directly to a specific consumer; marketing messages were the same for everybody based on aggregated data, like a segment, media market or ZIP code. The U.S. Census Bureau sells census data by ZIP code, and before individualized marketing was possible, marketing teams would build statistical models of the types of consumers who lived in each of the United States' forty thousand ZIP codes, creating geodemographically-based segments of consumers. Marketers use these segments to craft messaging at a ZIP code level, figuring most people who live in a community are, based on national averages, relatively similar. A company called Claritas, now owned by Nielsen, the TV ratings people, created a widely-used market segmentation model called PRIZM. Every ZIP code in the United States is scored against their model, and the top consumer segments per ZIP code are identified.

The top five PRIZM segments in Point Roberts reveal an interesting lens through which marketers view people living at the Point. Claritas' public web site features an ability to query a specific U.S. ZIP code and see the top five PRIZM segments.[293] For instance, one PRIZM segment to which many Point Roberts residents belong is called "Back Country Folks," which Claritas describes as remote, far from centers of economic strength. They tend to be older, poorer and live in small houses and mobile homes, "a throwback to an earlier era" of farming. Driving around the Point, one can picture many of the residential lots in Point Roberts fitting this profile.

Another PRIZM segment found in Point Roberts is called "Greenbelt Sports." This segment is upper-middle class and older empty-nesters. They are active in outdoor recreation and tend to be upscale couples who have fled the exurbs to settle in an idyllic place like Point Roberts because they can. One can picture some of the newly-constructed beachfront homes with recently-arrived full-time residents from Seattle and California fitting this description.

Maybe somebody you know in Point Roberts is a member of "Heartlanders," another top five Point Roberts segment. Claritas tells us Heartlanders are unassuming middle class couples with no kids living in small towns. This segment evokes a John Cougar Mellancamp music video, with middle-America interests like fishing, boating and sewing.

There is also the "Simple Pleasures" cohort, another segment of lower-middle class 65+ retirees. These folks worked blue-collar jobs before they retired, and tend to be members of community organizations. There's probably a mail order catalog and *Reader's Digest* in their mailbox, Claritas notes.

Geodemographic ZIP code-based segmentation fell out of favor in the late 1990s. Marketers no longer had to view consumers based on ZIP code averages; it became possible to target individual customers based on their actual behavioral data like what they click on and purchase. Claritas created more segmentation models to stay relevant in the marketing industry. Claritas introduced the ConneXions model, which measures the willingness of a household to adopt new technology. The folks of Point Roberts sound like

Luddites in some of these segments. The Point's top ConneXions segments include "Bucolic Basics," who listen to a lot of radio and limit their tech spend to satellite TV and basic phone service; "Internet Hinterlands," a segment of work-from-home exurban professionals; "Rural Transmissions," who rely on satellite dishes in their isolated communities and have outdated PCs; "Satellite Seniors," who watch TV over six hours a day on average, much of it religious programming; and "Tech-Free Frontier," stragglers who have yet to get their first computer, Internet connection and MP3 player. Many of these tech-centric segments paint a dismal view of Point Roberts as an aging, underdeveloped, technology-averse backwater, where a mildewed satellite dish is regarded as cutting edge. This is an overly harsh and inaccurate portrayal of a Point Roberts which is very much digitally connected.

Segmentation is a useful tool to understand clusters of similar people in a given place. Together, the different segments of Point Roberts paint an increasingly-diverse mosaic of people, each having come to the Point in one of the five eras of settlement and living together today in a special place.

POINT ROBERTS ACCENT

If you get a chance to hear the locals speak you may pick up on the local accent. Point Roberts' exclave position on the border gives it a unique variation of English, borrowing a little in accent from both countries.

In past decades, the entire western United States was grouped into one general accent. Linguists have recently identified a regional variation of North American English called Pacific Northwest English, spoken in many parts of Washington, Oregon and a bit of northern California. It's not as obvious as a New York, New England or Southern accent, but it does technically exist, which surprises many in the Salish Sea region who describe themselves as speaking a generic happy medium variety of English, essentially not having a dialect.

One of the most distinguishing pronunciations in Pacific Northwest English is when there is an "a" or "e" followed by a hard "g." Bag and beg sound the same. Cake and keg are pronounced the same, resulting in some humorous mix-ups. Egg, leg, peg all have a long "a" sound, what is known to linguists as "prevelar raising," and whilst other regional American accents use it, the Pacific Northwest uses it more iconicly than anywhere else. The accent comes from the tongue being a bit more raised. Northwesterners also pronounce soft "o" sounds similarly. Word pairs like "don" and "dawn," as well as "cot" and "caught" sound the same in Pacific Northwest English (both sound like "cot"), where those two words sound very different on the East Coast. Various accents merge sounds like that and what makes each region's accent unique is the particular combinations of merged sounds. By the way, Pacific Northwest English has contributed several words and phrases to English, including cougar, sasquatch, cabin fever, black ice and geoduck.[294]

The Point's isolation afforded a unique opportunity to study competing linguistics in an isolated area, and drew the respected linguist from the University of Victoria, Marjorie Mann. She came to Point Roberts in the autumn of 1987 to conduct a language survey. She recorded the speech patterns of many residents and analyzed the results. What Mann found was remarkable: linguistically speaking, this tiny exclave actually has its own dialect. Canadian residents have assimilated into the community and a steady flow of visitors from Canada all influence speech patterns in the exclave. The Point Roberts dialect is significant in linguistics because along the U.S.-Canadian border, most of the time American English bleeds north, encroaching on Canadian English. In Point Roberts, the influence uniquely travels south. Many features of Canadian English are used by the Point's American population.

"Canadian dialect features have entered and are entering the idiolects of the speakers of American English" in Point Roberts, found Mann.[295]

Basically, the Point Roberts dialect is a mashup of Pacific Northwest English and Canadian English. In Point Roberts, Americans use more Canadian English and less Pacific Northwest English than other Washingtonians. Conversely, Canadians in Point Roberts, living amongst Americans, don't pick up Pacific Northwest English; they keep their Canadian accent. Mann's research concluded that Point Roberts "is tending away from the Puget Sound patterns of thirty years ago and toward the established B.C. Lower Mainland patterns of Canadian English."[296]

For instance, Pacific Northwest English uses words like flapjacks, griddlecakes, baby carriage, sawbuck, string beans, curtains, skillet, faucet, frosting and the word real as a flat adverb, as in "real good," but Mann found usage of these words, common in Seattle, much less frequently used and are in decline by Americans in Point Roberts. Mann noted Americans in Point Roberts had "the subjective impression that the absence of this usage sets them apart from Lower Whatcom County, the neighboring U.S.A. mainland area."[297]

Conversely, Canadians don't pick up a Pacific Northwest accent by living in Point Roberts. They keep pronouncing the word schedule as in Canada rather than adopting the "sk" sound of American English, whilst many Americans in Point Roberts adopt the Canadian pronunciation /'ʃɛdʒuːl/.[298] Further examples include using raised diphthongs in words like "out." Of the word "out," Mann said, "This, more than anything else, points to a tendency on the part of the American informants to acquire Canadian speech patterns."[299]

Many Canadian words are used in the Point Roberts dialect, like teeter-totter instead of seesaw, tap instead of faucet, chesterfield instead of couch and quarter-to instead of quarter-till or quarter-of. As in the English-speaking world outside the United States, a significant share of Americans in Point Roberts say they wipe crumbs from their mouth with a serviette, never a napkin, which refers to a feminine product. The Point Roberts accent means students going to university should wear a touque or else they could end up in hospital, whereas on the mainland students going to the university should wear a knit cap or else they could end up in the hospital.[300] This does not mean a majority or even plurality of the Americans in Point Roberts uses these words and pronunciations, but the usage is prevalent enough for Mann to identify significant linguistic tendencies.

One word adoption in particular which Mann observed in Point Roberts led her to create a new linguistic rule. What's known at curtains in the United States is known as blinds in Canada and often in Point Roberts. And what's known as blinds in the United States is known as shades in Canada and frequently in Point Roberts. This uniquely Point Roberts observation led Mann to define a linguistic rule regarding the word which ultimately prevails when dialects collide in border communities.[301]

It's not just being along the border which makes the Point Roberts dialect special. Arbitrary lines on the map create separation of linguistic practices which are reinforced by media and education. Exclaves provide opportunities to study linguistic use cases available nowhere else. Surrounded by or only accessible from a foreign country, linguistic practices intermingle in uncommon and unpredictable ways as the home country accent and surrounding foreign country accent mix. Mann explained, "Exclave communities are ideal for dialect contact studies."[302] The Point Roberts case shows how the isolation of an exclave creates a self-contained test bed where linguistic changes rapidly develop without a moderating impact from the mainland United States. For instance, Mann found the exclavists used two different pronunciations concurrently, like the Pacific Northwest and Canadian pronunciations of out. This is "particularly common in transition areas, where a single informant may use competing sounds interchangeably in the same word."[303]

The mashup of accents and isolation of the exclave means there is a constant borrowing and mixing of sounds with bi-national interaction, including the many local children who go to private school in Tsawwassen. Point Roberts offers the perfect case study to show what happens when two accents comingle. Mann concluded, "Two dialects in contact retain their essential identity but may borrow features from each other, thus remaining, in a sense, 'co-dominant.' This is the situation in Point Roberts."[304] This whirlpool of pronunciation and word variations results in the occasional new word, the ultimate proof of a unique dialect. Exclaves are significant in linguistics because of the ability to observe instances where concurrently-used accents generate hybridized new words. Mann discovered such a new word coined in Point Roberts. Locals were documented calling a couch which folds out into a bed a "chesterbed," a hybridization of "sofa bed" and the Canadian word for sofa, "chesterfield."[305]

HOUSING

Perhaps no town in Washington is as unoccupied as Point Roberts. The census reports an astounding two-thirds of the Point's housing units were vacant when census workers canvassed the Point. Canadians were not visiting their cottages in the off season when the census was taken. By comparison, Washington's rate of unoccupied homes is only twelve per cent. Of its 3200 acres (1270 hectares), Canadians own ninety per cent of the land and almost seventy per cent of the housing units. Point Roberts' American population is housed in just 678 households, barely one-third of the 2000 homes on the Point. This vacancy constrains opportunities for growth in shrinking the year-round customer and tax base, thus curtailing retail sales and related jobs.

Since Point Roberts' population spiked after 1990 when a reliable water source was secured, housing construction increased rapidly in the last twenty years. As a result, the average age of the housing stock in Point Roberts is significantly below state average. With very few apartment buildings or condos, the Point's rate of rental units is well below state average. Point Roberts grew as a cabin community, with dense neighborhoods of tiny cottages. For nearly a half-century, most housing units were second homes for Canadians, so tended to be small in size. As a result, Point Roberts has a median home value and average number of rooms per house significantly below Washington state average. The popular tiny home movement is well entrenched in Point Roberts; it was a tiny home community long before the craze. With two-room cabins and cottages as well as the modern style of tiny homes on wheels found all over the exclave, today Point Roberts has one of the highest per capita rates of tiny houses in Washington.

 Continue uphill eastbound along APA Road through the South Beach cottage community.

As you travel up APA Road, the cabins give way to larger lots. Newer suburban-style homes are seen, evidence of year-round residents. The original settlers' history is still evident by some of the old homesteads which were never subdivided.

One of the last remaining large cliff-side properties, Seabright Farms was an Icelandic pioneer's homestead. In the 1980s it was leased for use as retreat center for community activities. After a long community discussion, the current residential development was approved. Half of the sixty-eight acre site will remain undeveloped and the property features public walking and horse trails.

Stop at the top of Pauls Road just off APA Road. Pauls Road is named for Paul Thorsteinson, an Icelandic settler who came to Point Roberts in 1894. From the top of Pauls Road, a public trail meanders through a 100-foot forested buffer between APA Road and the Seabright Farms residential development. The preserved buffer was the subject of a long campaign by local residents and serves as a wildlife corridor, so keep a look out for animals. It preserves a cathedral-like canopy of tall trees along APA Road. Enter the gravel trail through the woods. It comes out onto a gravel road, then heads downhill past a barn-like common building, jogs to the left near a community garden and meanders down toward the cliff. It follows the cliff edge back toward Pauls Road, completing the loop.

Take a moment to take the impressive public stairs down to the beach, built in January 2015. The various landings on the wooden

Figure 46: The Seabright Farms Staircase winds its way down the cliffside, descending through the tree canopy to emerge at a public beach. Photo by Mark Swenson.

staircase provide excellent views of the beaches to the west and the marina entrance, and vistas of the Salish Sea in all directions.

ANIMALS

Of course, it's not only humans who live in Point Roberts. The rural land makes an attractive home to many kinds of animals and viewing wildlife is one of the popular things to do on Point Roberts.

As you descend the Seabright Farms staircase, you may come eye to eye with a soaring bald eagle. Point Roberts is home to dozens of bald eagles, and is one of the most important bald eagle habitats in North America. There are ten significant eagle nesting territories on the Point, and nine more day or night roosting areas.[306] One bald eagle family lives near the top of the staircase. Once near extinction, they rebounded and by 1989 the US Department of

Figure 47: Beach-level cabins at Crystal Water Beach with wooden stairs to the street at the top of the cliff. Source: Mark Swenson

Wildlife found a dozen bald eagles living at Point Roberts. Today over 100 bald eagles hang out at the Point year-round. Bald eagles have found Point Roberts to be an ideal home with excellent fishing near their nests in tall trees near the shore. It's not uncommon to see dozens of bald eagles from one vantage point in the spring. Though they are so common they are still fascinating to watch, easily identified by the white heads they get at five years of age.

The Seabright Farms staircase empties directly onto the shoreline, named Crystal Water Beach. This beach got its name from the original settlers, many from sturdy Icelandic stock, who would actually swim in the cold water. Night swimming in the summer was a popular pastime when movement in the water stirs up bioluminescence. Nature's underwater fireworks show, bioluminescence is caused by single-celled plankton which emit light when disturbed, as their defense mechanism. The natural phenomenon is created by over sixty million plankton per liter of water which glow in the water from July to September. On nights with total darkness when there is no moon, stroke the water with your arm or a paddle, looking for sparkly blue lights in the water like, well, crystals.

Running along the base of the cliff on Crystal Water Beach, a row of cabins sit dangerously close to the high-tide line at the base of the cliff. Winter storms have destroyed some of these homes, including five which were taken out in 1997. A complex maze of staircases and cargo elevator rails climb the steep cliff to the street far above. These homes were originally built to rent to Canadians who wanted a summer camp on the beach.[307]

Marine life abounds all around Point Roberts. Oysters, mussels, limpets, sea anemone and marine snails inhabit the shore. Purple sea stars are slowly returning after sea star wasting disease devastated this keystone species across Point Roberts' beaches. The Point's inter-tidal beaches support a wide range of bivalves, including butter clam, littleneck clam, bentnose clam, razor clam, horse clam and basket cockle. There are geoduck clam beds visible on very low minus tides, home to the world's largest burrowing clam. This clam is so huge it cannot withdraw into its shell – most geoducks are a full two to four times larger than the shell. You can't miss them on the beach; their wrinkled siphons poke out of the sand one to four inches like a lawn of uncircumcised phalluses, occasionally squirting streams of water like those urban fountains embedded in sidewalks. Typically weighing in over two pounds, giant eight pound monsters exist; they can live to 168 years. The geoduck is the mascot of my alma mater, The Evergreen State College in Olympia, whose motto is *Omnia Extares*, "let it all hang out."

This beach is home to a large sand dollar colony with hundreds of sand dollars, which appeared in the 1990s. In some places the beach is so thick with sand dollars you can't avoid stepping on them, their brittle bodies crunching under your feet. Sand dollars are widespread from shallow tidal zones to the deep ocean and from both temperate shorelines to tropical beaches. The dry, bleached sand dollars we think of are the skeletons of a fascinating animal common across the Salish Sea, actually a member of the sea urchin family. These whitish dead shells resemble early large American silver dollars. When living, sand dollars' spines are fuzzy and short, covering their soft shells. These spines can be various colors though the ones at Point Roberts are dark purple. The hair-like spines are themselves covered in hairs, aiding in eating and mobility. These spines double as gills, allowing the sand dollar to breathe. Calibrated movement of these velvety spines allows the sand dollar to move. These hairs move food to the mouth, which is at the center of the underside of a sand dollar. Sand dollars are also thought of as resting flat on the beach, but in reality, when the tide is in and they are covered with water, sand dollars often stand on end to anchor themselves. Sometimes they swallow sand to give themselves extra weight and cling to the sandy floor; they can also burrow in the sand to hide from predators or cling to the bottom in strong currents. Sand dollars are found grouped together on the ocean floor in muddy dense beds of up to 625 animals and live six to ten years. The age of a sand dollar can be determined by, as one does with a tree, counting the rings in the shell. Sand dollars have radial symmetry on their bodies with a petal pattern, actually five paired rows of tiny pores, through which they fart. The eat slowly with five teeth-like chewers, which chew food for up to fifteen minutes before swallowing. Food takes two days to process through its small digestive system. Unlike humans, for sand dollars overeating doesn't inhibit sex. Sand dollars reproduce by spraying sperm and eggs into the water and letting the larvae come together on their own, Dao-style.

Figure 48: Sand dollars stand on end in the water. Photo by Chan siuman at English Wikipedia [CC BY-SA 3.0 (http://creativecommons.org/licenses/by-sa/3.0) or GFDL (http://www.gnu.org/copyleft/fdl.html)], via Wikimedia Commons.

Dungeness crabs have long been mentioned in accounts of life in Point Roberts. From the turn of the century, especially at Maple

Beach (covered in chapter 6), boys would wade in the water between sand bars and literally pick them up by the hundred while huge cauldrons boiled water atop beach bonfires. Around 1910 Dungies were eighteen cents a dozen. By the end of the 1920s the price was up to fifty cents a dozen plus an extra one gratis to snack on during the walk home. By the 1950s, they were a quarter a piece. Expect to pay ten bucks for one today (though, despite the fact Point Roberts is literally crawling with them, they're rarely seen for sale in the Point). Though they can sometimes be seen scurrying sideways in shallow water, you will walk by dozens upon dozens of dead Dungeness crabs along the beach at low tide, each a gourmet dinner for a lucky seagull. Today, Point Roberts is still an active Dungeness crab fishery; with the big salmon runs a thing of the past due to overfishing, today Dungeness crabs are the top revenue-grossing fishery in Washington and Oregon. In 2014, nearly $200 million worth of crabs were harvested along the West Coast.[308] More could be caught but thousands of crab pots are lost in the Salish Sea each year. After the state did a gear-removal effort in 2015, thirty-six per cent of the lost or abandoned crab pots retrieved in Whatcom County came from the waters around Point Roberts. Divers using sonar have found 102,212 dead or entangled animals in the abandoned 5400 nets and 3700 crab pots retrieved since the state began the program in 2002. Cormorants, loons, grebes, rockfish, salmon, seals and porpoise have been found in abandoned crab pots and nets. An additional 12,000 lost crab pots lurk in state waters deeper than 105 feet. Bellingham's Northwest Straits Foundation fears a recreational diver could eventually be trapped and drowned by derelict gear.[309] Point Roberts is the center of Washington's Dungeness crab fishery, which harvests 2.3 million pounds of crab per year. The Washington Department of Fish and Wildlife reports "the bulk of the harvest (is) in the Blaine / Point Roberts area." There are only 250 commercial Dungeness crab licenses issued each year by the state, which manages the fishery with pre-season quotas.[310] Most license-holders will head to shallow Boundary Bay off Point Roberts, teeming with Dungeness crab in its eelgrass-choked waters.

Some very large sea creatures make Point Roberts their home. The waters off Point Roberts are home to several superlatively-large animals. Elwood caught a thousand-pound "monster shark" in his fish trap August 15, 1897.[311] The world's largest octopus, the Giant Pacific, can weigh 150 pounds (most weigh around thirty-five) and have a radial arm span of twenty feet. In 1987 a huge Giant Pacific octopus was beached at Maple Beach.[312] There's also the world's largest chiton, also named the Giant Pacific, a sea cradle which can grow to a foot across. Look for the world's largest barnacle; it lives here too. The Giant Barnacle is a foot high and six inches across. The world's largest anemone, the plumrose, grows twenty inches long in waters at Point Roberts. The world's largest jellyfish, the Lion's Mane jellyfish, float off Point Roberts and are often seen on the beach on minus tides. They're the world's longest animal, with some having tentacles 120 feet long, longer than a blue whale; a single Lion's Mane jellyfish stung 150 people in New Hampshire in 2010. The cabezon is the world's largest sculpin, a bottom-dwelling fish. The ones off Point Roberts grow over three feet long. Several whale species are encountered at Point Roberts. A dead gray whale washed up at Lily Point May 7, 1988. The forty-two foot female weighed twenty tons and lying on its side was over six feet tall. It first got snagged on the reef and on the next high tide washed up on the beach. It took an international team of federal, state and provincial agencies to dispose of the whale.[313] In the summer of 1999, the Canadian Coast Guard had disposed of three dead whales by sinking them in Boundary Bay. One was a fin whale which had been struck by a cruise ship, and two were gray whales which washed up at White Rock. Apparently one of them wasn't weighed down properly as it drifted free and washed up at Lily Point.[314] Another gray whale washed up at Point Roberts in April 2000. Inanimate objects also wash up on shore. In March 1984 a mine washed ashore at Lily Point.[315]

To the other extreme in size, take a look at the water. If you see a milky-white cloud in the water, it may be a mass of herring spawning. Each year the location and size of the annual herring spawn changes. It was common at Point Roberts from the 1960s through the 1970s, but dissipated in the 1980s as the spawning location went farther north in the Salish Sea. A large herring spawn returned to Point Roberts in 2015, attracting thousands of birds, including herons, ducks, loons and grebes.[316]

Ironically, although Point Roberts was put on the map by George Vancouver's expedition which was driven in no small part due to the sea otter fur trade, today there are no sea otters at Point Roberts. Otters seen at Point Roberts today (including a meter-long monster seen scampering across South Beach Road quite a ways up from the beach they day I wrote this), despite swimming in an open saltwater sea, are river otters.

Head back up the staircase to Seabright Farms. As you walk on the cliffside trail, don't be startled if you see something slithering on the path or in the grass. Point Roberts has a healthy population of garter snakes. The Point's serpents were noted during early visits by Europeans. In August 1825 British botanist John Scouler stopped at Point Roberts and poked around the marshy peat in tidal berm between the beach and the Tule. In his journal Scouler describes spiky Tule grasses six to seven feet high poking up between large piles of driftwood. Trying to get a good look at the grasses' root system he kicked a piece of driftwood out of the way and was startled by a swarm of what he called coluber snakes, undoubtedly what we know as garter snakes. Scouler had second thoughts about exploring Point Roberts as every single piece of driftwood he dislodged revealed eighteen to twenty snakes. His journal states, "Ground seemed a mass of serpents." He wasn't alone that day. Scouler mentions seeing a large party of Indians and three very large canoes. He ended up hiring a young Coast Salish man to help with his expedition. The snakes are found throughout

Point Roberts, but often encountered in the grassy fields near the water towers behind Baker Field, at Lighthouse Park, as well as throughout Lily Point Park. Longtime residents tell of frequently finding snakes in their gardens.[317]

In spring 2015, workers shoring up the dike in Tsawwassen not far from the Point Roberts border found a den holding five hundred hibernating garter snakes. When disturbed they started waking up, and they were taken away in baskets and brought to a wildlife rescue association to live whilst the dike was repaired. They were then returned to their den still in their hibernating state. In addition to being often seen in Point Roberts and all around Boundary Bay where they like to sun on the dikes, they are also frequently encountered throughout the San Juan Islands. Sucia Island, just south of Point Roberts, is particularly infested with them. Despite being commonly seen, most people know little about them. An important predator in the Salish Sea ecosystem, the species found in Point Roberts is the western garter snake. They are dark grey with

Figure 49: Western Garter Snake, commonly found at Point Roberts. Photo by James Bettaso [Public domain], via Wikimedia Commons.

three colored stripes on their back and can vary considerably in size. Garter snakes are typically found on land, where they eat slugs, worms, baby birds and small mammals. They also can swim and can be seen in fresh water hunting for fish and frogs. When attacking, they both coil around their prey, constricting it, and bite it with mildly toxic saliva. They hibernate in the winter in dens like the Boundary Bay dike and live young are born in the summer.[318]

Larger animals also live on Point Roberts. Mammals include coyote, skunk, raccoons and innumerable rabbits which scatter as you pass. A population of Columbian black-tailed deer lives on the edge of the Point's forests where they can quickly hide, though many of the deer on Point Roberts seem used to seeing cars and are sometimes seen nonchalantly standing on the side of road as cars whiz past; drivers should look for fawns born in May and June. They're sometimes seen prancing on the beach. Throughout the 1970s and 1980s there was a problem with local dogs eating deer.[319] The deer population was estimated in 1971 at 300 deer, "including up to 100 fawns," but there were concerns the deer population was headed for extinction from the dog attacks.[320] Among the odder wildlife sightings in Point Roberts was a rash of bear sightings in 1971[321] and cougar sightings in the autumn of 2005,[322] but none were ever caught or photographed. A beaver dam – complete with beaver – was inexplicably built in the large ditch in front of the Sunny Point Resort RV Park on Gulf Road in November 1999.[323]

Figure 50: A black-tailed deer prances along South Beach in 2009. Photo by Mark Swenson.

Domestic animals of all kinds are also kept at Point Roberts, including cows, sheep, chickens and a llama named Lily. There are also about twenty Icelandic horses on Point Roberts. The first Icelandic horses were imported from Iceland in 1994 and have adapted well to Point Roberts. The good-natured horses are a bit shorter than most horses, twelve hands high instead of a typical fourteen.

 Continue uphill eastbound along A.P.A. Road past Claire Lane to the town cemetery.

CEMETERY

I suppose it's fitting to end a chapter entitled "Who Would Live Here?" by discussing the Point's quaint cemetery. It contains many tombstones of the original settlers, with many Icelandic names. Land for the cemetery was bought in 1914, and the cemetery opened in November 1915, with its first burial a fifteen-year-old boy named Oliver Johannson. Once open, many settlers moved remains from family burial plots on their own land and reinterred them in this community cemetery.

Only two Washington Governors have ever visited Point Roberts. In 1961, seventy-two years after statehood, Governor Albert Rosellini was the first Governor to make it to the exclave, and apparently he only took a few steps on the Point for the centennial celebration of the Monument Park obelisk. Governor Gary Locke visited May 15, 2002, meeting at the community center with locals and with local kids at the school.[324] In March 1993 there were rumors President Bill Clinton would visit Point Roberts in early April. Clinton was in Vancouver for a summit with Boris Yeltsin, and locals had written to him inviting him to visit the exclave during his visit. In the end, no presidential visit would materialize.[325]

The only visit to Point Roberts by a head of state had happened five years earlier on October 22, 1988, when the president of Iceland, Vigdis Finnbogadottir, visited the exclave. She walked in the cemetery, strolling among the tombstones of original Icelandic settlers,[326] impressed the settlers hadn't changed their names in the New World and had kept their original Icelandic names.[327] Finnbogadottir was the first woman directly elected head of state in the world. She was reelected four times, twice unopposed, and earlier in the year before her 1988 visit to Point Roberts she had been reelected with an incredible ninety-two per cent of the vote. She served sixteen years, making her the longest-serving elected female head of government in history. Two years prior to her visit she hosted Ronald Reagan and Mikhail Gorbachev in their famous Reykjavik summit on eliminating nuclear weapons. Today, a plaque in the center of the cemetery commemorates Finnbogadottir's visit, placed there in October 1998 on the tenth

Figure 51: Point Roberts Cemetery. Photo by Mark Swenson.

anniversary of her visit.[328]

The cemetery guards the entrance to Lily Point Park, the crown jewel of Point Roberts. We'll explore it in the next chapter.

CHAPTER 4 • SALMON CENTRAL

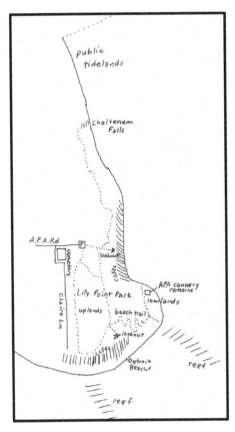

Figure 52: Route map of Chapter 4. This chapter is spent at Lily Point Marine Park.

Very nearly lost to a gated McMansion development, Lily Point Marine Park was brought into the commons in 2008 due to heroic efforts by locals and conservancy groups to buy the land for the public from private owners. Lily Point Park defies superlatives and though merely a county park stands out among parks anywhere in the Salish Sea. It's significant on many levels: aboriginally, culturally, historically, ecologically and recreationally. There is native Coast Salish heritage, it played a pivotal role in Washington's salmon fishing industry, provides a home to countless bald eagles and many other animals, and is simply beautiful.

A critical piece of the Boundary Bay ecosystem, Lily Point offers temperate coastal forests, sandstone cliffs, miles of beaches, exposed reefs at low tide, and views across the Salish Sea in virtually all directions. The park's most notable feature is its 200-

foot tall orange sandstone cliffs which erode to produce sand and gravel for small fish and shoring up the beach. The forested hillside offers shade and perches for many birds including many bald eagles. It has a large reef and tidelands which attract many maritime animals including the iconic sockeye salmon. Lowlands along the beach were the scene of historical events of the center of the region's salmon fishery. Lily Point is simply the jewel in Point Roberts' crown; if you can only see one thing in Point Roberts, this must be it.

LILY POINT PARK

The initial thought for the park was to officially designate it as a preserve, which would have brought along many regulations and restrictions on how visitors could enjoy the park. In the end, it ended up being classified a marine park, which allows for a more laissez-faire attitude, requiring responsibility and sensitivity of visitors to the park's culturally and ecologically significant status. The parking lot and washrooms were added in December 2011.

The Thorsteinson sisters, children of early Icelandic settlers in Point Roberts, used to play in the Lily Point forest at the beginning of the twentieth century. Hidden in the forest were lovely trilliums, a variety of lily. The sisters named the southeastern quadrant of Point Roberts Lily Point because of these trillium lilies.[329] They still grow at Lily Point. Trilliums grow perennially from rhizomes and are hard to spot as just a small stem rises above ground; a single flower with three petals grows on the forest floor. Simply picking a leaf or a part of the plant, even if the rhizome isn't touched, kills the trillium for seven years. Deer can wipe out a grove quickly and it's illegal to pick them in Michigan, Minnesota, New York and Ontario; indeed, it's the official flower of Ontario and official wildflower of Ohio. Because they both use it as official flower, the major league soccer teams in Toronto and Columbus face each other in the Trillium Cup. Native peoples used them for controlling bleeding and diarrhea.

Figure 53: A trillium flower growing alongside a path in Lily Point Park in 2017. Photo by Mark Swenson.

From the parking lot, take the trail at the back of the lot heading to the east (not the trail by the washrooms). At the first junction continue straight ahead to the park's main viewpoint. This viewpoint is perched atop a cliff looking out over Boundary Bay. Looking due east across the bay to the mainland, the high-rise apartment blocks of White Rock and the low-lying buildings of Semiahmoo Spit and Blaine are visible if the weather is clear. Trace the border across the bay to the mainland. Use field glasses to try to spot the border cutout on the forested Vedder and Black mountains and a white monument at the shoreline, Blaine's Peace Arch.

Nestled around well-protected Drayton Harbor on the U.S. mainland, Blaine, population five thousand, is the closest town in the United States to Point Roberts. Its original town site was not in present-day downtown Blaine, but rather out on Semiahmoo Spit, an incredibly thin sandspit which protects Drayton Harbor from the

Strait of Georgia. The town center of Blaine moved across Drayton Harbor to the present site of downtown Blaine in 1884, followed by a post office in 1885, prompted by the construction of the first road from the county seat in Whatcom (later renamed Bellingham). Prior to that, the only way to get to Blaine was by boat. With land access, Blaine's economy diversified from fishing to logging with the construction of the first sawmill in 1885. By 1889, there were four sawmills and two shingle mills.

Dominating the view forty-seven miles to the east of Point Roberts is Mount Baker, or Koma Kulshan as the Coast Salish people call it. The third-tallest mountain in Washington at 10,781 feet, Mount Baker is known for receiving enormous amounts of snow. In the winter of 1998–1999, Mount Baker set, and currently holds, the world record for most snow in one year, an amazing 29 meters (95 feet). Much of this snow ends up in its twelve glaciers, making Baker the best glacier climbing site in the U.S. outside Alaska. Baker is also one of only two mountains in the Lower 48 to boast ice caves (the other being Mount Rainier, Washington's tallest mountain). Although it is an ice-covered volcano, its summit is a relatively flat thirty-five acres. Under all that snow and ice, an active volcano slumbers. Baker erupted eight times in the nineteenth century. Its last eruption was in 1880 though it has ominously spewed steam as recently as 1979.

The Mount Baker Ski Area is the closest skiing to Point Roberts and renowned for being one of the best snowboarding resorts in the world. When snowboarding first came on the scene, many ski resorts banned them, but Mount Baker rolled out the welcome mat, earning it respect in the snowboarding community. Compared to world-famous megaresorts like Whistler with crowds and heated sidewalks, the down-home feel and isolated slopes of Mount Baker is symbolic of the lack of pretention snowboarders crave. It is home to nine chairlifts, the annual Banked Slalom race and snowboard legend Craig Kelly, who liked it so much he moved there. Despite world records for snowfall, the Banked Slalom was cancelled in 2015 for lack of snow, during an El Niño year when the weather acts strangely.

Where there are cliffs, things fall off of them. On December 29, 1978 a hang glider hit the cliff at Lily Point. The injured man was eased down the cliff face to the shore using ropes and a human chain of thirteen rescuers.[330] On March 21, 1982, a 29-year-old Vancouver man fell 150 feet from the sandstone cliffs near the viewpoint, breaking both of his ankles, his hip, and several internal injuries, but surviving.[331] It took thirteen first responders to rescue a seventeen-year-old man who fell off the cliff May 10, 1988.[332] In 2000 a fourteen-year-old fell thirty-eight feet and survived. On June 5, 2001, two twelve-year-olds fell forty feet after climbing up from the bottom.[333] A dog fell forty-five feet, landing on a ledge saving it from a further eighty-foot drop, in October 2007. Three-hour rescue operations are typical; with no roads into Lily Point Park, rescues are challenging to execute.[334]

Near the viewpoint, a spur trail leads north. Running along the cliff edge, it offers peekaboo views of the beach far below. Lily Point Park is a great example of the Pacific Northwest forest, dense with cedars, Douglas fir, western hemlock and Sitka spruce. Nurse logs are covered with moss and lichen and enormous swordferns litter the forest floor. The forests of the Salish Sea have the densest biomass (the total mass of organisms living within a given area) in the United States, and the Salish Sea has the tallest trees in North America, *averaging* 130 feet in height.[335] At the start of the trail, visible from the main viewpoint, an enormous old growth cedar tree stands ten feet (three meters) in diameter. At one time, trees like this covered Point Roberts. At the north end of the trail is a large ravine cutting into the hillside, created by the Point's most majestic waterfall, Cheltenem Falls.

Figure 54: Cheltenem Falls has created a massive ravine on the east side of Point Roberts. Photo by Mark Swenson.

Return to the trail junction and follow the wide main trail to the southern viewpoint. This viewpoint was the site of a major landslide in March 1999 when ten acres of land slid down to the beach. This sloughing actually pushed up the beach over ten feet.[336] The cliffs erode a bit more year after year, and the unstable cliffs could give way in an earthquake. Situated on the ring of fire, the big one is always possible, so resist the urge to lean over the undercut cliff. Local homes hug the cliffs all around Point Roberts, and the risk of landslides becomes relevant when one realizes the Point has been shaken by some strong earthquakes, including one measuring between 8.7 and 9.2 on the Richter scale on January 26, 1700. It is possible some of the current topography of Point Roberts was shaped by this quake. It is sobering to know this scale of disaster is possible here.

Point Roberts is vulnerable to earthquakes originating from three sources: the subducting slab, the overriding plate, and between the colliding plates. Historically, the most damaging events occur at depths of fifteen to sixty miles in the subducting plate.

Since European settlement of Point Roberts there have been three earthquakes over 7.0 on the Richter scale. The two most-recent 7+ quakes caused damage on Point Roberts and nearby areas. One was a 7.1 magnitude earthquake centered at Olympia, 120 miles south of Point Roberts, on April 13, 1949. Eight died around the Salish Sea and in Olympia all large buildings and its water and gas mains were damaged. Most railroad bridges south of Tacoma were destroyed, and it caused a long sandy spit at Olympia to disappear. The other quake was just three years earlier, centered much closer to the Point. A 7.3 quake struck, centered in the Strait of Georgia at Deep Bay, causing the bottom of its bay to sink eighty-four feet; a resulting tsunami killed one. The quake was felt strongly on Point Roberts and nearby areas like Bellingham. Chimneys fell at Eastsound on Orcas Island, just south of Point Roberts. A Port Angeles concrete mill was destroyed, and damage extended as far south as Seattle.

Shallow crustal earthquakes occur in the overriding continental plate within twenty miles of the surface, and strike more frequently. These are usually between 5.0 and 5.5 on the Richter scale, but stronger shallow quakes do occur, such as the other 7+ quake felt in Point Roberts. On December 15, 1872, a 7.4 quake struck near Entiat, triggering a huge mudslide which completely blocked the Columbia River. Many aftershocks were reported, a telling sign of a shallow crustal earthquake.

Other notable Point Roberts earthquakes include a 6.0 tremor centered just twelve miles away at Blaine on January 11, 1909. There was heavy damage in Whatcom and Skagit Counties, where plaster fell and piers and sidewalks were cracked. The earthquake whose epicenter was closest to the Point was a 5.5 quake on January 23, 1920, centered pretty much right at Point Roberts. Damage included many broken windows and cracked walls. On April 29, 1965, a strong 6.5 earthquake centered at Olympia killed seven. In 188 blocks in the capital, one-third of the chimneys were damaged, and brick buildings were damaged across Seattle. Another quake centered in Whatcom County at Deming, just thirty-five miles east of Point Roberts measured 5.2 on April 14, 1990.

Recent quakes felt on the Point include a 5.5 trembler on May 3, 1996 centered 100 miles south of Point Roberts, a 5.8 on July 3, 1999 centered 134 miles south of Point Roberts, several small tremblers in August 1999 centered just five miles south, and a 6.8 on February 28, 2001 centered 133 miles south of Point Roberts, again at Olympia, called the Nisqually Earthquake. It caused two billion dollars damage, killed one and injured over 700 people.

This lookout point is the southeastern corner of Point Roberts. The expansive view extends across the Salish Sea to the Whatcom County mainland. The idyllic San Juan Islands dot the horizon to the south. To the east Birch Bay is visible, from where the Vancouver Expedition launched their trip to "discover" Point Roberts. A bit further south the bright lights of the Cherry Point

Figure 55: The Point Roberts reef exposed during a minus 4 foot tide. Photo by Mark Swenson.

petroleum refineries and an aluminum smelter are reminders of the industrial presence in this natural environment.

Even though you're at the southeast tip of the peninsula – Lily Point – Point Roberts keeps going underwater. At the viewpoint, use the informational marker to locate Lummi Island, if weather conditions permit. Then look midway between the Point Roberts shore and Lummi Island to locate a navigational buoy marking the end of the Point Roberts reef, a shallow underwater ridge. The buoy is far offshore but the water is only four fathoms deep along the reef. One of the largest salmon migration routes in the Salish Sea goes right over the reef which concentrates the schools of fish into dense throngs. For thousands of years this reef was the usual and customary location where the native people of the region fished for salmon. They became known in the region as the salmon people.

The fence wasn't put up until 2011; until then you could stand right at the precipice. Until the 1970s, you could actually drive right up to this southern viewpoint. In the 1960s it was the Point's lovers' lane, with a beautiful view of the Salish Sea as a backdrop to the necking. For years, the beach directly below this viewpoint – the cliff was much taller and closer to the water before the 1999 landslide – was known as Detroit Beach. Young men would, James Dean style, drive old jalopies off the cliff, bailing out at the last minute. For years, kids – mostly Canadian, I'm assured – sent cars off the cliff in a testosterone-fueled laugh. This continued well into the 1990s. One customs officer who had been especially hard on the young folks found his Jeep pushed over this cliff. In the 1940s residents often threw their garbage off this cliff, the tin cans clinking as the garbage bounced down the cliff.[337] The 1999 landslide covered most of this debris, though several rusting chassis and car parts are still on the beach below.

 Walk back to the main trail junction, this time turning right and following the beach trail. Descend the stairs and switchback trail from the upper lands to the beach-level lowlands of Lily Point Park. After a wooden boardwalk over a swampy area, the trail forks in two. Take the trail to the right through a grassy meadow and onto the beach.

Figure 56: Remnants of Detroit Beach. Photo by Mark Swenson.

This southeast point of Point Roberts is Lily Point. The beach here offers a unique 325-degree view from Delta and Burnaby to the north, White Rock and the U.S. mainland to the east, the Strait of Georgia, San Juan Islands and Canadian Southern Gulf Islands to the south and southwest.

COAST SALISH PEOPLE

The summer season cabin culture of today's Point Roberts did not start in the 1950s. The Coast Salish people who called Point Roberts home were the first to use The Point that way. Cabin culture is all about having two homes at which one splits their time, based on seasons, like snowbirds flying to sunny Florida for the winter and living in New York City or Toronto in the summer. In Point Roberts' case, it is Vancouverites spending most of the summer near the beach in Point Roberts, returning to a main home for the rest of the year. The Coast Salish people used Point Roberts in the same way. They had a winter home and several summer homes. The winter home was typically near a river's mouth to the Salish Sea. The territory boundaries typically lined up with food resources, and certain important pieces of land, like the reef at Lily Point, were denoted as shared locations. Several Coast Salish nations shared Lily Point as their summer home, living at Point Roberts July through September, fishing and trading.

In August 1829, while exploring the lower Fraser River, Hudson's Bay Company men from Fort Langley heard about Point Roberts. "Joe," a Coast Salish, told them of enormous numbers of salmon at Point Roberts, where the tribes of the Coast Salish lived together at Lily Point.[338] Within the Salish Sea First Nations, Point Roberts was part of a section known as the Northern Straits Coast Salish, home to the Lummi, Semiahmoo, Cowichan and Saanich peoples. The former two had their winter home on the mainland to the east, and the latter two on the east coast of Vancouver Island to the west of Point Roberts across the Strait of Georgia. Point Roberts was the northern extent of their range; the people just to the north, the Tsawwassen and the Snokomish were the southern extent of the Halkomelem-speaking Coast Salish group, whose language differed to the point it wasn't mutually understandable to the Northern Straits group. The Tsawwassen would also fish at Point

Roberts, typically on the west side of the peninsula, but fished in the Fraser River more often.

The Northern Straits Coast Salish travelled seasonally between homes at resource-gathering areas. They had fishing sites, like Point Roberts, as well as shellfish- and plant-gathering sites. The Lummi wintered at the mouth of the Nooksack River and Whatcom Creek in today's Bellingham Bay, and at Sandy and Cherry Points. This should not be confused with the Nooksack tribe, who lived up river and were a river-centric hunting people who didn't generally fish in salt water. The Lummi were also the primary people who inhabited the San Juan Islands and maintained seasonal homes there too. The Semiahmoo's winter home was at the mouths of California and Dakota Creeks in Drayton Harbor at Blaine, at Birch Bay and at the Campbell River north of today's border. When the Snokomish people were decimated in the 1840s by smallpox, the few survivors joined the Semiahmoo. As the Semiahmoo had not received reservation land in treaties with the U.S. government, the Semiahmoo moved north of the border and took over the Snokomish territory at the mouths of the Serpentine and Nicomekl Rivers which flow into Mud Bay at the north end of Boundary Bay. The Semiahmoo themselves suffered smallpox epidemics in 1862 and 1888 which wiped out large numbers of their people. The Saanich lived on Vancouver Island's Saanich peninsula and the Southern Gulf Islands. The Cowichan lived on the east coast of Vancouver Island near today's town of the same name. Other Coast Salish tribes from further afield, including the Songhees, Sooke, Klallam and Samish, fished at Point Roberts in a complex ritual of etiquette of obtaining permission from the regular site caretakers. Point Roberts is often described as merely a native fishing site, but with the salmon season lasting several months as various species of salmon migrating past, it really could be described as their home for nearly a quarter of the year.

In the off-season Lily Point would look a bit dilapidated. At the end of the season, the Coast Salish disassembled the cedar roofing and siding from their longhouses for the season, leaving just the frame of the house. Lily Point was the first piece of land on Point Roberts upon which Captain Vancouver set foot that day in June 1792. Coming ashore June 12, 1792, Vancouver walked among the naked frames of longhouses and a few battered fish drying racks. His guess was he was exploring ruins, but it was merely a winter-beaten off-season summer home waiting for its occupant to arrive for the summer to move in and spruce things up, just as happens on the Point today. Menzies' journal about landing at Lily Point describes landing "to dine near a large deserted Village capable of containing at least 400 or 500 Inhabitants, tho it was now in perfect ruins — nothing but the skeletons of the houses remained, these however were sufficient to show their general form structure and position. Each house appeared distinct and capacious of the form of an oblong square, and they were arranged in three separate rows of considerable length; the Beams consisted of huge long pieces of Timber placed in Notches on the top of supporters 14 feet from the ground, but by what mechanical power the Natives had raised these bulky beams to that height they could not conjecture. Three supporters stood at each end for the longitudinal beams, and an equal number were arranged on each side for the support of smaller cross beams in each house."[339]

Had Vancouver visited Point Roberts just a month later, he would have seen the homes re-clad with siding and very much occupied, abuzz in activity. Walking down the streets between longhouses in the flat grassy area on Lily Point, Vancouver would have encountered the Coast Salish wearing only deerskin and dog hair blankets and without weapons of any kind. They wore rolls of copper in their perforated noses and ears. Faces were painted with streaks of red ocher and black.[340] Lily Point was a village made up of long houses, each housing several related families. A house group defended the territory and shared care duties of their multifamily community but was independent politically and economically from other houses in the village. The cedar plank-sided long houses were arranged in rows, called streets. Puget wrote in his journal of walking with Vancouver through narrow lanes between the six longhouses at Lily Point. Each house faced the sea and had its own crest which was proudly incorporated onto door frames. There seemed to be a basic tenet of sharing and the common good. Whilst each house obtained, stored and cooked its own food, cross-house groups came together on occasion for labor-intensive tasks,[341] and those with a surplus of food were expected to share.[342]

Walk in the footsteps of history along the beach around the point toward the west. If it's low tide you can see the Point Roberts reef. Down the beach you can explore the rusting car parts of Detroit Beach. Further down a large boulder sports several geometric

Figure 57: "Petroglyphs" at Lily Point Park. The reef is visible in the background. Photo by Mark Swenson.

designs, thought by some to be petroglyphs, though others claim to have seen them carved no earlier than the Nixon administration.

Had Vancouver's visit brought him in contact with the Coast Salish at Point Roberts, as we walked among the longhouses he would have heard the unique sound of the local language. All of the Northern Straits Coast Salish groups speak, with some minor differences, the same language; to the extent they differ they are all mutually-understandable. This language, spoken at Point Roberts for thousands of years, is known for not having a lot of vowels; indeed, some individual consonants are their own syllables. Some words have as many as thirteen consonants in a row with not a vowel in sight. Viewing it, one thinks it impossible to imagine how to pronounce it. With strong agglutination, new words are formed in the Northern Straits Coast Salish language by combining simple words. There is also a unique concept of word taboo, where certain words are so powerful they cannot be used. Indeed, a person's name becomes taboo right after their death and continues to be off-limits until the name is bestowed upon a new family member. To refer to a deceased family member, one must use descriptions rather than the person's name; these descriptions permanently replace the taboo name, thus changing the language. All the Coast Salish dialects are endangered; several are already extinct. Some have just a handful of elderly native speakers left. The Lummi language is currently taught at three schools in Whatcom County.

The mutually-understandable language was a key component which facilitated the Northern Straits regional network of trading groups. They had dried salmon and clams to offer which were in high demand from groups who lacked reliable protein sources. Bonded by language, the Northern Straits Salish frequently traveled to each other to facilitate family links, resource usage and trading opportunities.[343] Their canoes plied the Salish Sea offering salmon and bringing in goods to fill their own pantries. The region was a busy interdependent web of the Coast Salish people, marine mammals and most-importantly, salmon. The native people had drawn boundaries to protect fishing rights to prevent the common salmon resource from being exploited. When the United States and Britain drew an invisible manmade line across the middle of the Salish Sea at Point Roberts they introduced a foreign dimension cutting across a natural ecosystem.[344] The impact of this arbitrary line on the huge salmon fishery and the Coast Salish people would be felt at Point Roberts more than anywhere else.

The Coast Salish people lived at their various sites on the narrow strip of beach between the water and the forest. For them, the water was a sense of place and the land was dense forests full of danger, darkness, loneliness and even death. Going into the forest, with its wild animals and disorienting evergreen canopy was far more dangerous than going out on the water. The sea was where daily life took place.[345] For them, the sea and its shoreline was safety, brightness, their home and habitat, the essence of life. Europeans saw the opposite. The Vancouver Expedition was fixated on the land. They saw ports, timber, locations for settlements and agriculture. Vancouver writes repeatedly in his journals of envisaging the forested land of this region without its trees, replaced by fields, buildings and hedges demarcating property ownership. For him, the sea was merely a method of access to valuable plots of land.[346]

Near the shore long rows of racks were erected upon which the native people would dry salmon as they caught them. The fish were filleted and spread across a wooden rack made of splints. The racks were leaned against long rows of frames for the salmon to cure in the sun. Small smoky fires were lit below the racks to shoo away flies. When dried, the salmon were taken off the splints and prepared for storage to be used as a protein source during the winter. As soon as the racks were free, another batch of salmon was quickly prepared. Indeed, the Coast Salish people's name for the Point was Cheltenem, which meant "place for drying racks of salmon."[347]

The importance of salmon to the Northern Straits Coast Salish cannot be overstated. It was the major protein in their diet and the most important symbol in their culture. The local people also gathered clams at Maple Beach in addition to other sites around the Salish Sea. Plants were gathered and other kinds of fish like sturgeon supplemented the diet. The methods of food gathering by the Northern Straits Coast Salish were, in order of importance, reef net fishing for salmon, salmon fishing at river mouths, shellfish gathering, other forms of salmon fishing, fishing for other fish species, gathering plants, growing root vegetables, waterfowl hunting, sea mammal hunting and lastly land mammal hunting.[348] From the famous potlatch feasts to daily protein needs, salmon was of top importance to the Coast Salish and Point Roberts was their most important place to get it.

Sockeye salmon in the Salish Sea almost all spawn in the Fraser River and run in four year cycles, one very large run followed by three very small annual runs. The ratio between the small runs to the large run can be several thousand to one, and the big runs can be utterly enormous. In peak years the runs were so heavy they seemed to completely fill the rivers; people could actually pitchfork them out of the river. There were so many salmon in the early years they were a nuisance. Farmers tossed them into the fields as fertilizer, fed them to pigs and used their oil as fuel to start fires. With millions of sockeye trying to get into the Fraser en masse they bunched up outside the river mouth, and Point Roberts is where this huge congregation of salmon led to massive investment from white commercial fishing operators. It seemed the unending runs of sockeye could never be exhausted.

Point Roberts' geography and location is perfect for catching salmon. Sockeye salmon enter the Salish Sea from the Pacific Ocean through the Strait of Juan de Fuca, all headed for the Fraser River. To get to the mouth of the Fraser, there are a few routes they can take. When they get to Victoria at the southern tip of

Vancouver Island, they can take the first left and go up Haro Strait between Vancouver Island and San Juan Island. The problem with this route is orcas hang out in Haro Strait off Lime Kiln Park and gobble up salmon like crazy. The other salmon keep swimming east in the Strait of Juan de Fuca until they get to Whidbey Island on the eastern shore of the Salish Sea. They then swim north up through Rosario Strait, past Lummi Island and then up into Boundary Bay. They sense they have to get around Lily Point, which entails swimming over the Point Roberts reef.

REEF NET FISHING

Although many Coast Salish groups fished, none were more associated with salmon than the Northern Straits people. The traditional fishing grounds of the Northern Straits people, centered at Point Roberts, were the most-productive fishing grounds in the Salish Sea. As a result, a unique form of salmon fishing was invented at Point Roberts a thousand years ago, a technique still used to this day. The reef provided the perfect conditions for anchoring nets in a particular manner to intercept the throngs of sockeye salmon.

In the beginning, the Coast Salish people caught salmon by throwing nets into the water and pulling them in. From this method they learned how to catch spawning sockeye and pink salmon during incoming tides. A thousand years ago at Point Roberts, the Coast Salish people invented reef netting as a specialized method of fishing at a shallow reef to trap massive runs of fish during certain tides. Reef netting meant for the first time the Coast Salish could catch not dozens but thousands of salmon per day. At the time the white settlers entered the commercial salmon fishing industry at the end of the nineteenth century, the Northern Straits peoples' most-important economic activity was reef netting.

A reef net is a large net traditionally made of willow bark, some fifty feet by fifty feet. Large stones are used to anchor it to the reef, and cedar floats keep the sides vertically erect. It works like a funnel: placed during specific tides to take advantage of the natural current in the water, it channels the fish up and over the reef into another net suspended between two canoes which is then drawn up to pull the fish into the canoes. New nets were made each year by the women from willow bark and nettles. One net required a huge amount of labor to create. Highly coveted and always in short supply, only a few of the elders owned a reef net and had great status as a result.[349] Much in contrast to the approach of white fishermen as we'll soon see, the Coast Salish created customs and equipment which helped to conserve the sockeye salmon runs. Nets were made with holes in the bottom to allow some fish to escape.[350]

Before European contact, there were complex rules surrounding locations where reef nets were used. A good reef netting site like Lily Point would be held in trust by a specific individual, often the village leader, for use by people in his kin group. Men could get access to a site if the owner of the location was in his wife's family network, enabling visits to multiple sites throughout the Northern Straits territory.[351] When the owner wasn't using the site, after the owner's family had taken their capacity, others in the community outside of the owner's kinship group could use the site if they asked permission from the owner.[352] After dividing the catch, the owner of the site kept any remainder, and thus built enhanced status by amassing extra food which could be used to trade for luxury goods or as a charitable donation to those in need.[353]

When not fishing, the family would make baskets and carvings, which, with the salmon, made up the goods they had to trade in order to diversify their diet. As the groups gathered at Lily Point awaiting the arrival of the sockeye salmon at the start of each summer season, anticipation would grow for the annual first salmon ceremony. The first sockeye salmon caught in a reef net each year would be brought to shore and blessed by a chief in a special ceremony practiced at Point Roberts for centuries.

POST-CONTACT SALMON FISHERY

The Coast Salish people had known Cheltenem was a great place at which to fish for thousands of years. White settlers would discover that fact in the 1850s. Before the white population of Washington Territory had even reached two thousand people, settlers were already recognizing the importance of Point Roberts for fishing. The earliest report of whites fishing at Point Roberts was in a September 10, 1853 article in the *Columbian* of Vancouver, Washington, which noted several men salmon fishing at Point Roberts. It took a while for whites to understand salmon were of value, as they initially focused on timber and fur. Hudson's Bay Company had been trading with the natives to obtain salmon for food, but did not want to be dependent on them for their nutrition.

One of those men fishing at Point Roberts in 1853 was Henry Roeder. He was one of the first two white settlers in Whatcom County, and is most-known for influencing settlement of the towns that would become the present-day city of Bellingham. Born in Herstadt, Germany in 1824, he immigrated to the United States in 1830, settling in Ohio, where he was a sailor and early pioneer in the development of fish traps on Lake Erie. Roeder moved to California in 1850 where he joined up with a partner, Russell Peabody, and together they opened a fish trap operation on the Sacramento River. As competition and overfishing rapidly intensified, they moved north to open a sawmill on Puget Sound. In Olympia, he and Peabody learned of the existence of a large waterfall emptying into a natural deep water bay. Roeder arrived at Whatcom Creek and Bellingham Bay on December 15, 1852. Roeder's relatives claim a Lummi chief gave them the falls and the land surrounding it, and donated the labor of his men to build the mill; there are no sources from a Coast Salish point of view to validate this. With native labor and machinery from San Francisco, the mill opened the following spring. However, by this time, lumber prices in San Francisco had fallen, a drought lowered the water level of the falls, and a constant need to ship in supplies reduced profits. However Roeder's Whatcom Milling Company survived until 1873. Roeder was also instrumental in the history of Point Roberts. In 1853 despite operating several Bellingham Bay business ventures he somehow found time to fish at Point Roberts. When he saw the enormous runs of salmon at Lily Point, he began to think about his old fish traps.

As more and more white settlers poured into the newly-created Washington Territory, the new governor Isaac Stevens knew he had to address land ownership with the Coast Salish. He held a series of treaty negotiations between 1854 and 1857, under which the Coast Salish gave up sixty-four million acres of their territory between Olympia and Point Roberts and were relegated to a few reservations. In exchange for the land, the treaties provided for access to resources deemed important for their sustenance. The Northern Straits Coast Salish people who lived at Point Roberts each summer, along with eighteen other tribes, were signatories to the Point Elliott treaty in 1855 at Mukilteo.

The treaty contained fifteen articles:

Article	Subject
1	Described the lands ceded by natives
2	Described the lands kept for exclusive use by natives
3	Provided for schools
4	Coast Salish must move to reservations within one year
5	Reserved hunting, fishing, shellfish gathering rights
6	Described annuities
7	President has right to remove Coast Salish from reservations
8	Forbid use of annuities for payment of debts
9	Forbid Coast Salish from any "depredations" against whites
10	Banned alcohol from reservations
11	Forbid slavery
12	Prohibited trade in Canada including Vancouver Island

13	Created funds for agriculture on reservations
14	Provided an agency, school, medical facilities
15	Goes into effect when signed by President and Senate

Article 5 provided the tribes with fishing rights, in general and at specific locations, called "usual and accustomed places," which by being called out suggested these places were apart from the reservations.[354]   The Lummi Chief told Governor Stevens "Cheltenem was their best fishing ground" they wanted to ensure they could keep fishing specifically at Point Roberts if they signed the treaty. Promised they could, the Northern Straits Coast Salish signed the treaty and continued to fish at Point Roberts. Indeed, initially the Coast Salish people were encouraged by the government to fish at Point Roberts. Natives were given food aid, but the rations weren't sufficient for their full nutritional needs, so despite the fact the Northern Straits people were fishermen, not farmers, and their reservation land was barely arable, the government in their wisdom instructed the natives to farm.[355] The results were meager, so when the Lummis left the reservation to head up to Lily Point to fish, their government minders didn't really mind. Agent Nathan Hill said, "As they lived on their old hunting and fishing grounds they ought not to expect the Department to feed them regularly."[356]

Meanwhile, the British were handling the same issue a bit differently. James Douglas' approach to the Coast Salish is marked by, if not sympathy, at least a desire to come to an amicable arrangement so as not to have conflicts. He proactively commenced negotiations with fourteen Coast Salish nations immediately after the 1846 boundary treaty, arranging to purchase their lands. These treaties included the Northern Straits Coast Salish people who ended up on the Canadian side of the 1846 boundary, the Saanich and Cowichan nations who had summered at Point Roberts. Under their treaty they were to live on reservations based around their winter villages on Vancouver Island. The Saanich and Cowichan were granted, as in Stevens' treaties, rights to hunt and fish in traditional grounds, but their prime fishing ground at Lily Point, the primary site of their means of sustenance and acquisition of goods for trading, was now across an invisible line in a different country. Douglas was mindful the Americans' stingier policy toward the Coast Salish could result in uprisings, migration or unauthorized trading, so he closely monitored how things unfolded in Washington Territory. Where Stevens had grouped many distinct tribes together on fewer but larger reservations to lower administrative and supervisory costs, Douglas wanted to limit collaboration among Coast Salish nations so he created a larger number of smaller reserves and allowed them to buy land off the reservation.[357]

Whatever the size of the reservation, the 1850s marked a profound change in the geography of the Salish Sea. The Coast Salish saw the Salish Sea as one entity in which they traded, traveled and intermarried. Their sense of the geography held a shared understanding of definitions based on resource availability and family lineage. The adage "fish where the fish are" sums it up. Suddenly European notions of latitude and longitude created an artificial line cutting through the heart of their territory, and nowhere was this felt more greatly than at Point Roberts. Home to Coast Salish from both sides of the line for a quarter of the year, Stevens included Article 12 in the Point Elliott treaty banning the Coast Salish who ended up on the American side of the line from crossing the Salish Sea to Vancouver Island or the B.C. mainland to trade with their cousins. Initially the natives ignored this rule and there were few Americans to police it, but the reservations and treaty rules marked a profound change toward the white people's perspective of the region.[358]

The 1870s would see the white population of Washington Territory explode and overrun the area. As late as 1870 in present-day Whatcom, Skagit, San Juan and Island counties, there were just

534 whites and six hundred Coast Salish. By 1880 the white population numbered 3100 versus just 275 Coast Salish as whites moved in and smallpox continued to decimate natives.[359]

In chapter three we discussed the initial white settlers. John Waller arrived at least by 1877, but possibly either lived or sporadically fished at Point Roberts earlier. Waller's squat was on the lowlands at Lily Point with a homestead and saltery. The naked wood frames of the native longhouses and their rows of salmon drying racks Vancouver had seen in 1792 were still there when Waller arrived. One day he disassembled the natives' structures as the Coast Salish people looked on from the beach. Old Polen, a Lummi, said in a sworn statement, "John Waller… tore down all our shacks. I was there when John Waller tore them down."[360] Old Polen spoke in the Northern Straits Coast Salish language and John Elwood translated into English.

Waller used the wood from the Coast Salish village to build a fence to prevent the natives from camping at Lily Point. The wood from the Coast Salish's own houses were used to keep them from their home, a home they believed was guaranteed to them in the treaty. Although the Coast Salish were promised they could fish at their usual and customary locations, Waller said he now owned the fishing rights and the land at Lily Point. The Coast Salish moved a

INDIAN FISHERMEN'S VILLAGE, PT. ROBERTS.

Figure 58: Coast Salish moved their camp north of Lily Point after being chased off their traditional fishing grounds. Wadhams cannery at Lily Point is visible in background. Photo by Freshwater and Marine Image Bank, Pacific Fisherman annual review 1907, Seattle, WA, 1907, p. 71 [Public domain], via Wikimedia Commons.

bit up the beach and set up camp just north of Lily Point Park at a place later called Goodfellow's Point, but bigger changes would soon come. What Waller would do next would revolutionize the commercial salmon fishery and change the lives of the Coast Salish forever.

FISH TRAPS

Point Roberts was the birthplace of the reef net centuries ago, and in the 1870s was also the birthplace of the most important innovation in the Salish Sea commercial salmon fishery, the local version of the sockeye salmon fish trap. Waller placed the first fish trap in the Salish Sea, indeed, the first trap in Washington north of the Columbia River, at Lily Point in 1878. Thus began a fifty-six year era of fish trapping in the Salish Sea.

A fish trap is a fixed structure of wire, webbing and nets strung between many wooden pilings pounded into the sea floor just off the shore, arranged in such a way as to optimize the way fish swim with tidal flows. A long line of two-inch netting strung across a row of pilings called a lead extends out into the water to funnel the fish toward the trap. The lead's pilings can be over a kilometer long and were wrapped in seaweed so it looked to salmon like a place on the reef to rest. The kelp forest in front of the fourteen feet-wide entrance was cut back to guide the fish in. Once in the entrance to the trap, a wall of trap wire would drop in behind them, forcing the fish to swim further into the trap's maze of a series of pens, each smaller than the last to create density and thus prevent the fish from turning around to escape. As the fish crowded into each chamber, they began thrashing around in the small space; many salmon struggled to the point they had few scales left along their body. The last enclosure was the spiller. Its entrance just four inches wide, it trapped up to 35,000 live fish until lifted out with a dip net into boats and taken away for processing. Called "pound nets" in Lake Erie where Roeder had first used them, the term fish trap stuck in the Salish Sea.

Waller fiddled with a few designs, but his traps weren't catching many salmon. Roeder visited Waller and shared his fish trap experience from Ohio, pointing out Waller hadn't properly aligned the lead to the incoming tide. Taking Roeder's advice, Waller's trap was soon filled to the brim with sockeye salmon. Waller wanted to expand his business but was cognizant of the fact he was squatting, on a military reservation no less, and the government could kick him off Point Roberts at any time. The level of risk was not tenable for the amount he would need to invest. He approached the government in April 1878 with a plan. He would make improvements at Lily Point, including a community wharf, if the government would open the land for a dozen families to homestead and farm.[361] When the government didn't accept the proposal, Waller sold his trap location in summer 1879 for the immense sum of $25,000 (that's a half-million dollars today) to the Pacific Fishing Company, who opened

Figure 59: Sockeye salmon lifted from a Point Roberts fish trap spiller. Photo credit: Whatcom Museum, X.2930; Bellingham, WA.

a trading post.[362]   Six years later, Waller drowned in September 1885 but his body wasn't found until June 1886 when a fisherman found the corpse south of Bellingham in Chuckanut Bay.[363]

Joseph Goodfellow arrived in the 1870s and lived in a log cabin north of Lily Point near the huge boiler still rusting on the beach today. He had a small saltery and was the second fish trap pioneer at Point Roberts. He also experimented with various trap designs, tweaking the configuration of the trap as he learned what worked. Goodfellow would take the fish caught in his traps to a salmon cannery across the border on the Fraser River. When the U.S. Customs Service seized two of his boats in the process of heading to the Fraser, Goodfellow protested by saying the customs officer changed the rules without notice. His case was viewed sympathetically and charges were dismissed.[364]

Another early trap owner was Leonard Pike, son of the Pikes of Pike Place Market fame in Seattle. By 1897 he owned five fish traps at Point Roberts and lived on Point Roberts each year during the summer salmon season. It was hard to get more trap sites because big corporations had bought up most of them so he later built a cannery.

As Waller, Goodfellow and Pike had success with trap fishing, it didn't take long for others to notice and move in. By 1892, fish traps already crowded the reef, even extending beyond it. The two-mile-long reef was completely jammed with over fourteen fish traps side by side. Each trap's gear abutted the next trap's gear. Many more fish traps were placed east of the reef in the shallow waters of Boundary Bay. Each location was named, owned, sold, traded and inherited.

Things exploded after that. Depending how you count (the Point Roberts fish traps bled into the Blaine area fish traps all the way across Boundary Bay) by 1895 there were between twenty-eight to thirty-three fish traps at Point Roberts. To put that into perspective, there were ten traps in all of the San Juans and at Lummi Island, and just a few more at Samish Bay and along Cherry Point. Roughly two-thirds of all Washington fish traps in 1895 were at Point Roberts. And two-thirds of the fish traps at Point Roberts were on the east and southeast side, off Lily Point. There were four that year along South Beach and six on the west shore of the Roberts peninsula which were typically used for the autumn runs of chum, or dog, salmon. Locals recall they used the catch phrase, "the traps stay up til the last dog caught."[365] The statewide count of fish traps surpassed one hundred in 1899, and of the 112 traps in Washington that year, 82 were in Whatcom County.[366] The count varied from year to year, spiking to 163 in 1900 and 194 in 1913, but totaled less than seventy-six in 1905 and 1909. The four-year cycle of the sockeye runs impacted those who wanted to invest in the cost of setting the traps each year. On average, Point Roberts was the site

Figure 60: A large crew works on a well-constructed fish trap at Point Roberts. Photo by Richard Rathbun, Review of the fisheries in the contiguous waters of the state of Washington and British Columbia, Report of the United States Commissioner of Fisheries, 1899, Washington, DC: Government Printing Office, Freshwater and Marine Image Bank [Public domain], via Wikimedia Commons.

of roughly half the state's fish traps for the first decade of the twentieth century. Its share would decline in the 1910s as more traps were set throughout the Salish Sea.

The large number of fish traps at Point Roberts is the all the more remarkable given how huge these structures were. The leads were often built to the 2500-foot maximum length allowed by law. In her book *Among the People of British Columbia*, Frances E. Herring recalled witnessing the fish traps, "To look at the Gulf as we went along, it seemed impossible that any salmon could make its way to the Fraser, so thickly were the traps set."[367] Fish traps were particularly successful because sockeye followed known routes, and the leads were placed in such a way as to intercept those routes.

Such huge structures were labor-intensive to build. Each fish trap required 200 pilings driven into the sea floor starting as early as March each spring, and most were removed in the autumn due to the hazard to navigation and worm infestation.[368] They were re-driven the following year. Two pile drivers performed the lion's share of pile driving at Point Roberts. One was named Tyee, a Coast Salish word for chief; the other, King. The rhythmic sound of the piles being hammered into the sea floor reverberated all over the Point.[369] These workhorses could drive the pilings needed to build one trap in two fifteen-hour days.[370] Pile driving soon became a major source of jobs for the residents of Point Roberts. Starting in spring to get ready for the summer season, fish traps required the skills of pile-drivers, webbers, steam boat operators, tenders and their crews. During fishing season, it would take ten men to lift the salmon out of the trap. It's no surprise fish traps provided more jobs than the famed canneries which only operated in summer season.[371] These jobs were dangerous, especially in bad weather. A resident reminisces, "Len and I can both remember the terrible storm of 1934 – the last year of the fish traps, on which he worked each season from 1927. Len was out in the shack on the traps – three miles out into the Bay – I watched him and his partner through high-powered binoculars out on the platform, until the wind-driven spray cut off my view. Three hours before high water, the swells were hitting the platform around the shack. What I didn't know until later is that Len and his friend had lashed themselves to piles three feet higher than the shack and were still being hit by swells – and there they stayed, for between five to six hours, until they were taken off by the *Karluck* and brought ashore exhausted."[372] Boys played at grown-up professions of the local economy, driving miniature fish traps with small pile drivers in the grass in their back yard or on the beach. They would use pocket knives to carve names in wood to represent the boats loading up on fish.[373]

The Coast Salish were still trying to reef net along the Point Roberts reef, but by 1894 twenty fish traps were squeezed onto the front of the reef, blocking most salmon from getting through. The fish traps provided jobs to the whites but cost jobs from the Coast Salish. Placed in front of the reef nets and intercepting almost all of the salmon, they essentially automated the harvest of salmon. The effect was immense to the Coast Salish as their treaty-protected means of sustenance dwindled. By 1895 the reef netters were only taking a small share of the commercial catch at Point Roberts. Over five million pounds of salmon were harvested at Point Roberts in 1900, but reef nets accounted for only 184,000 pounds.[374]

The Coast Salish watched the whites encroach on their most-productive fishing ground and summer home. As early as the 1870s the Lummis petitioned the commissioner of Indian affairs to intervene on their behalf. It did no good, but they kept trying. An 1894 petition stated: "Living as we do on the shores of Puget Sound (sic) our principal means of subsistence, especially during certain seasons of the year, is fishing our best grounds situated near the reef of Point Roberts of this State. Several years ago white men began to encroach on our ground. We were willing to have them share with us the right to fish but not satisfied with equal rights they have yearly made additional obstructions to prevent our catching fish, by setting traps, and placing piling around the grounds. They have driven us from our old camping ground on the beach and have so treated us that we feel we must now appeal to you for assistance. In our treaty with the government we were given the first right to hunt and fish on our old grounds and we know too well that the good government that has so far protected our rights will not permit us to be trodden upon simply because we are Indians."[375] The native complaints cited Point Roberts fishing rights more than anywhere else. The tension between reef netting and fish trapping symbolized the development of the salmon fishery in the Salish Sea.[376]

When a government patrol found three fish traps stitched together creating a trap over a mile long, protests erupted from the Coast Salish as well as white purse seiners and gillnetters. The result was the first regulations on fish traps. Washington's first state legislature met in spring of 1890, creating a State Fish Commission, with a State Fish Commissioner appointed by the Governor for four years. The Commission began licensing fish traps in 1893, with the funds raised going to salmon hatcheries, such was the early concern about the depletion of the huge salmon runs. Regulations were introduced for all aspects of fish traps, where they could be placed, the type of mesh allowed, and the seasons in which they could operate. The commission even authorized peace officers who could arrest without writ, rule, order or full due process. Trap mouths had to be six hundred feet apart and leads were limited to 2500 feet. Fish trap owners responded by creating "experimental" traps, partially built traps which looked complete from above the water but without the actual netting. This was done to claim space in the waters to dissuade others from coming in or to create so many fixed structures the seiners had no room to lay out nets.[377]

The Canadians were far more restrictive in order to protect the Fraser River salmon runs and despite the creation of the Washington State Fish Commission, the Canadians watched the overfishing happening at Point Roberts with dismay and concern. In 1903, the

B.C. Fisheries Commissioner blamed the fish traps at Point Roberts for the collapsing salmon runs, citing the reason for it resting "principally, if not wholly, at the door of the state of Washington, as the unbridled fishing conducted in her waters is indefensible and unjustifiable, and, if continued, will wipe out the salmon fishery of the Fraser."[378]

Sustainable salmon fishing is an issue at the forefront of the present day, but concerns about overfishing date all the way back to the 1870s. The Coast Salish people were vocal in stating their concern about how whites were harvesting more salmon than the fishery could support. One Point Roberts trap caught 680,000 salmon between July 10 and August 29.[379] Far more fish were trapped than there was processing capacity. The excess was wasted; the majority of salmon trapped at Point Roberts that year were simply thrown away. Ripe rotten salmon carcasses were used to start beach fires.[380] Barges overloaded with thousands of dead salmon were towed into the middle of the Salish Sea and tossed overboard, to the dismay of the Coast Salish.[381]

Figure 61: A fish trap extends off South Beach, with the Tule in the foreground. Photo by Whatcom Museum, 1996.10.6652; Bellingham, WA.

Where the Coast Salish had managed the fishery in a sustainable manner for thousands of years and had been promised the right to fish at Point Roberts in their treaties, the commercial white fishery simply hijacked Lily Point for their own gain. Thousands of years of reef netting at Point Roberts came to an end, utterly stolen by the white commercial fishery. The Lummis used reef nets at Lummi Island until 1917 but by 1921 reef netting by the Coast Salish was essentially over.[382] A few reef net licenses were sold after 1920 at Point Roberts but they were sold to whites who hired a few Coast Salish men to use them. In their natural tendency to share, the native people taught their usurpers how to fish where they once had, using the method their ancestors had invented at Point Roberts.

CANNERIES

As you walk the beach at Lily Point you will encounter rows of decaying pilings, some ten feet tall, lining the beach hinting that wharves of something major had been here. Walk carefully, as some rusty metal pieces poke out between beach pebbles, often hidden by garnishes of seaweed. Other pieces are enormous hulking machinery, dotting Lily Point like a rust-colored outdoor sculpture garden. This is no curated garden; these are remnants of a major cannery which operated for a quarter century at Lily Point from 1892 to 1917.

By 1892, long before the days of refrigeration, the fish traps had been catching vast quantities of salmon for fourteen years. Massive amounts of fish needed to be processed before they would spoil. It was inevitable commercial interests would establish canneries along the Salish Sea to complete the supply chain.

The American salmon canning industry began, not coincidentally, in the same place the where the first fish traps on the west coast were trialed, on the Sacramento River in California. Hapgood, Hume and Company built a cannery floating on a barge in 1864. Early attempts wasted half the output, but by 1866 the salmon runs on the Sacramento River were already depleted to the point the cannery was unprofitable, so George Hume moved to the second salmon fishery in the United States, and the first in Washington, and opened a cannery along the shores of the Columbia River at Cathlamet. By 1868, they had tripled their production from the Sacramento River, from two thousand cases in a season to a robust 6800 cases. When the term case is used in descriptions of cannery output it should be noted a case referred to forty-eight *one-pound* cans. That equates to 150 of today's typical five-ounce cans, meaning the Cathlamet cannery produced the equivalent of over one million of today's cans in its very first season. Most of the output was shipped to Australia, England, Germany and France.[383] Five years later a cannery opened at Astoria in 1873, and by 1874, just a year later, there were thirty-five canneries on the Columbia below Portland. Across Young's Bay from Astoria in Hammond, Oregon, two business partners, G. H. George and W. H. Barker, bought the Point Adams Packing Company in 1885, and operated it under the name of George & Barker Cannery.

It didn't take long for these entrepreneurs to move further north. Soon the commercial salmon fishery moved into the Salish Sea. A cannery at Lily Point was built in 1892, the fourth salmon cannery to open in the U.S. portion of the Salish Sea, after the first one at Mukilteo in 1877 and big canneries at Semiahmoo which opened in 1882 and 1891. The Drysdale Cannery of Blaine packed over 8800 cases of salmon in its first year of operation in 1891. New canneries popped up each year. One opened at Friday Harbor on San Juan Island in 1894, one at Bellingham in 1895 and Lummi Island in 1896. With no regulation, there were no caps on how many canneries could open, no licenses were required, and other than purchasing the tidelands, there were no restrictions on where a cannery could be located. By 1900, Whatcom County was the capital of salmon canneries on the west coast, producing two-thirds of Washington's total salmon production.[384] By 1902, ninety per cent of the state total of salmon was caught within twenty miles of Point Roberts.[385] The top eleven canneries in the state were all in Whatcom County. Blaine had no less than a half-dozen canneries and there were five in the Fairhaven area of Bellingham. Point Roberts had its second salmon cannery by then as well. Things were also developing north of the border. A cannery had opened on the Fraser River as early as 1864, but it would take nearly a decade for a second cannery to open. These canneries bought fish caught in Point Roberts-area fish traps before the U.S. canneries opened. By the mid-1890s, canneries lined the Fraser River, especially near the river's mouth at Steveston.

The canning process sounds simple, but in reality is quite involved. Various fishing vessels, scows, tugs and steamboats would tie up at the cannery's wharf at Lily Point. Once ropes were tied to cleats, the cannery crew snapped into action, grabbing long-handled picaroons whose hook was used to snag salmon one at a time, tossing the fish into a rotating wheel which counted the fish and moved them inside the first building. Once in the slaughterhouse, the salmon were routed to cutters. Chinese laborers were cutters in the cannery here at Lily Point. Wielding sharp knives in long ten hour shifts they deftly cut the fish in a specific way to facilitate the canning process. The cut fish were washed in salt water and taken by cart to the main cannery building where automated machinery lined up the fish and cut the fish into can-sized chunks. Manual labor scooped up small pieces of fish to pack into the can by hand, filling in all the little gaps, requiring rapid agility. A small amount of salt was placed in the can. This required a ready supply of salt, and salteries were located at Lily Point for this purpose. Cans were weighed, and a lid was manually placed on top, where a topping machine soldered it to seal the can. The cans were stacked and carried to the steam room where the cans were pressure-cooked for a half hour under 220 pounds of steam. Next, the cans were pierced with a fine point, where experienced workers watched for steam to hiss out, and those which did spray were soldered back shut again and pressure-cooked for another hour under 245 pounds of pressure. If the can didn't emit steam or water, the can was pulled from the line and redone. The cans were washed in lye water to get rid of grease from the machinery and then brought to a cooling room. After chilling for several hours they were dipped in a varnish wash to prevent rust before workers manually glued on the label.[386]

Individual fishermen sold fish to the canneries often under a contract with a cannery. The cannery would provide a boat and fishing gear, docking the rental cost from the sale of fish. Some contracts required supplies and even food to be purchased from the cannery. Of course, the rates were inflated, meaning many fishermen under those contracts made little at the end of the season.[387]

In the 1880s Edmund A. Wadhams owned a cannery on the Fraser River at Ladner, and also frequently traveled to Point Roberts to buy fish. One day his steamer *Winifred* was seized by U.S. customs officials for moving salmon over the border. Wadhams protested, insisting he had bought fish at Point Roberts and brought them back to his cannery at Ladner for many years and knew of no law to the contrary. It was a nice story until officials noticed quite a few of Wadhams' cannery boats had had previous run-ins with the law and had even been seized over the last three years for this very reason. Officials pointed out another boat owned by Wadhams, the *Emma*, had been involved in fish piracy.[388] Sick and tired of the hassle of the border which separated his Ladner cannery from all the salmon action at Point Roberts, Wadhams sold the cannery at Ladner in 1890 and moved to Point Roberts to live closer to the salmon. He set up some fish traps, and in December 1892, signed a contract with Kate Waller to lease her property so he could build a cannery at Point Roberts. By the next spring the cannery was well under way. It would remain open for twenty-four years, initially managed by his son Arthur.

The competition for salmon was intense at Point Roberts and it soon became litigious. Wadhams was sued by Joseph Goodfellow for improperly trap fishing in the summer of 1893. Washington's fish trap regulations required licenses for fish traps on the Columbia River and in Puget Sound. Wadhams won by arguing Point Roberts is not on Puget Sound, but rather was on the Strait of Georgia. In another case, Wadhams was acquitted of having his traps too close to other traps. The lawsuits didn't slow down Wadhams. His Lily Point cannery together with the Semiahmoo canneries collectively canned a record 100,000 cases of salmon by the end of 1893. The salmon industry in the U.S. side of the Salish Sea was catching enormous quantities of salmon: eleven thousand cases were packed in 1891, jumping to 66,000 in 1893, 248,000 cases in 1894, doubling again in 1895 to 423,000 cases and 871,000 cases in 1899. *The New York Times* wrote in April 1896, "Fisheries of the Pacific will soon be one of the greatest industries of the world."[389]

CANNERY POINT, POINT ROBERTS, WASHINGTON, 1895, SHOWING THE CANNERY ESTABLISHMENT AND THE STRING OF THREE TRAP NETS EXTENDING OFF FROM THE POINT.

Figure 62: The APA cannery in 1895, the year after the APA acquired it from Wadhams. Photo by Richard Rathbun, Review of the fisheries in the contiguous waters of the state of Washington and British Columbia, Report of the United States Commissioner of Fisheries, 1899, Washington, DC: Government Printing Office, Freshwater and Marine Image Bank [Public domain], via Wikimedia Commons.

Figure 63: The Alaska Packers Association cannery at Lily Point in its final year of operation. Photo by John Nathan Cobb [Public domain], via Wikimedia Commons.

As more and more canneries opened and competition grew, canneries started to merge together to have more muscle in the consolidating market. In February 1893 twenty-five canneries in Alaska merged to form a major corporation called the Alaska Packers Association (APA). It was nothing short of a cartel, controlling three-quarters of the Alaska canneries, and was also a dominant force in the Salish Sea fishery into the 1960s. With its newly-formed corporate power, it bought out Drysdale in Semiahmoo and in early 1894 Wadhams at Point Roberts. By 1900 they owned thirty-six canneries. Locals kept calling it Wadhams Cannery after the APA buyout, possibly due to the fact Arthur Wadhams continued to serve as cannery manager. The APA also owned thirteen fish traps off Lily Point.[390]

With increasing power as a mega-corporation, the canneries acted as though they were above the law. Many U.S. customs agents were unarmed and could not force wealthy cannery owners to obey their orders. The manager of the APA cannery at Point Roberts swore revenge on the local U.S. customs agent for fining one of his company scows, stalking the agent and lobbying for his removal.[391] Many small canneries closed in 1902 due to the purchasing power of the APA cannery at Lily Point.[392]

The Coast Salish also protested the commercial salmon operations to the Bureau of Indian Affairs, but the BIA did nothing about their complaints. Convinced the Coast Salish should quit fishing and take up agriculture, the BIA applied steady pressure for the Coast Salish to farm their reservation lands. With their protests ignored by the BIA, the Coast Salish next turned to the white courts to enforce the new fish trap regulations to restore their treaty-guaranteed fishing rights at Point Roberts. Lily Point was the subject of the most famous case of all. The Lummi Nation sued the APA in 1895 for interfering with their right to fish "in their usual and accustomed places." The Lummis hired their own legal counsel out of Bellingham and pressured the BIA to request the U.S. Attorney General to take the case to court, which eventually happened. *The United States et. al. v. The Alaska Packers Association* was heard by Judge Cornelius Hanford.

In the proceedings the Lummis declared themselves lowly fishermen dependent for generations on the special reef at Point Roberts for subsistence. A ninety-year-old Lummi testified during his whole life he fished at Point Roberts, dried salmon on racks, and brought salmon home to the Lummi winter village at the mouth of the Nooksack River for rest of tribe. He also described gathering cranberries and blueberries in the marshes of Point Roberts. He said it was at Point Roberts where "all the Indians, both those of B.C. and of the Sound (sic), fished every year."[393] The APA's defense focused on three points. First, the APA used the border against the

Coast Salish. Their witnesses testified the Coast Salish people who used Point Roberts were not Lummis, but were Saanich and Cowichan from Canada. Canadian Coast Salish had no rights in U.S. waters and thus the APA couldn't be encroaching on rights they didn't have in the United States. Secondly, APA's witnesses testified the Coast Salish sold large quantities of salmon to the APA

Figure 64: A scow unloads sockeye at the APA cannery at Point Roberts in 1895. Photo by Stefan Claesson, Gulf of Maine Cod Project, NOAA National Marine Sanctuaries; Courtesy of National Archives.

cannery at Point Roberts, countering the Lummi claim they were poor and fishing for subsistence. The farcical attempts by the BIA and article thirteen of the Point Elliott Treaty to train fishing-centric Coast Salish to become farmers arose in the trial, with witnesses claiming that legally under the treaty the Coast Salish were farmers with no need to fish for salmon. They argued the Lummis were successful farmers who only rarely fished and had no claim to the Point Roberts reef as a traditional fishing spot. Lastly, the border was again used as an issue, with the APA arguing the Lummi didn't sell fish exclusively to the APA, and instead sold a lot of their catch to Canadian canneries competitive to the APA cannery at Point Roberts. As an APA stockholder, Wadhams testified, arguing Lily Point was the last chance to catch salmon before they rounded peninsula and entered Canadian waters at the Fraser River. If the Americans didn't catch and process the sockeye, Canadians would get the bounty instead. APA stoked fear by arguing they produced jobs and if they had to remove their fish traps the Lummis would get more of the catch, sell more in British Columbia, and impede the growth of the new state.

Judge Hanford was appointed by President Harrison as the first federal United States Judge for the District of Washington February 25, 1890. He had previously been the Chief Justice of the Territory of Washington. Hanford had been the chairman of the Republican Party of the Territorial Government during the 1888 elections. During his judgeships in Washington he became known for incorrectly interpreting native treaties pertaining to fishing rights, always in favor of non-Indians. In 1905, the U.S. Supreme Court even overturned a ruling Hanford made in 1896 – at the same time as the Lummi case – against the Yakama tribe. He got caught up in more controversy in 1912 when he stripped U.S. citizenship from an immigrant because he was a Socialist. The United States House of Representatives began impeachment proceedings, hearing testimony of Hanford's chronic alcoholism, and more importantly, of accepting bribes from the Northern Pacific Railroad in exchange for rulings which would lower their taxes. Hanford resigned in disgrace before the House could impeach him. Besides his judgeship, Hanford was also the president of a power utility and irrigation company. A small town was settled in 1907 on land in Benton County along the Columbia River in eastern Washington purchased from Hanford's irrigation company and utility. The settlers named the town Hanford, but were forcibly evicted from their homes thirty-six years later with thirty days' notice by the federal government, who in 1943 established the Hanford Nuclear Reservation during World War II.

Hanford did not bother to recuse himself from the Lummi case despite owning salmon fishing operations in Whatcom County and having invented the can crimper and can capper machines used by the defendants in the canning process. He decided the case against the Lummis. Hanford ruled under the Point Elliott Treaty the Coast Salish retained equal rights but not special privileges such as permanent protected locations. Despite the testimony of the unique nature of the specific Point Roberts fishing locale to the Coast Salish, Hanford found APA's traps didn't stop the Lummis from reef netting on other reefs in the Salish Sea. Lastly, he ruled it would actually hurt the Lummis to rule against the APA because the Lummis sold much of their fish to the APA cannery and if they were put out of business as a result of the lawsuit, the Lummis may not be able to sell their full catch at another cannery.

The Coast Salish pursued the matter again in 1897 by having the BIA appeal Hanford's ruling. In this trial, the Lummi Nation's counsel testified, "In the first place, we wish to mention that about two years ago the APA, a fish canning company, operating in Point Roberts, Washington, have been interfering in many different ways to prevent the Indians to fish on the Point Roberts reef, which from time immemorial, had been occupied by our ancestors and ourselves for fishing purposes."[394] Through various trials and rulings, the Lummi Nation's case was appealed all the way to the U.S. Supreme

Court. However, for unknown reasons, on May 22, 1899, the U.S. Attorney General advised the BIA to drop the case, and submitted a motion to the Supreme Court to dismiss the appeal, which the Court subsequently did. The outcome was the Lummis, and all Coast Salish groups, lost their treaty-protected fishing grounds on the Point Roberts reef to the wealthy fish trap and cannery owners. The Lummi had to abandon Cheltenem and eke out a living off their reservation in Bellingham Bay. Even fishing there brought discrimination. The state government started requiring the native people to have a license to fish but only citizens could get licenses. The Coast Salish people were not considered U.S. citizens, thus putting the Lummis in a catch-22.

In the boom-bust cycle of pre-Depression capitalism, APA profits spiked and dipped. In one downturn, the APA cannery closed in 1917 and the empty buildings at Lily Point lay abandoned for decades. The company employed a guard in the 1940s who lived in a house on the Lily Point lowlands with a guard dog. In the late 1950s and early 1960s people started taking lumber from the decaying buildings. A barge was floated across Boundary Bay to salvage anything remaining of value. Around 1962, a fire got out of control of some partying kids, which leveled the remains of the APA buildings at Lily Point.

No longer a presence in Point Roberts, the APA continued on. The salmon processed at Lily Point after 1905 were marketed under the Argo brand. After a 1916 merger, the brands Del Monte and Pioneer were used. Indeed, Del Monte bought out the APA in the 1960s. APA's regional offices for the Salish Sea were in Seattle and later at Semiahmoo. The cannery at Semiahmoo closed in 1964; though salmon can labels were printed at Semiahmoo until 1974. The APA kept a boat repair yard at Semiahmoo until 1981, when they transitioned all of their Semiahmoo property, including buildings, artifacts and records, to Whatcom County Parks and Recreation. APA was renamed in March 1982 as DMC Properties and is still in operation in Alaska as a subsidiary of Del Monte Corporation.[395]

A second cannery opened on Point Roberts in 1899 at the foot of Gulf Road on the west side of Point Roberts, built by Leonard Pike. George and Barker left Astoria and settled in Point Roberts, buying out Pike in March 1900, calling this cannery, like the one near Astoria, the George and Barker Cannery. They brought along as foreman Henry Teller, who had been foreman in Astoria.

Figure 65: Net tarring machine at the APA Cannery in 1918, the year after it closed. Photo by John Nathan Cobb [Public domain], via Wikimedia Commons.

The cannery employed eighty people in 1914 who were hired seasonally in the summer months, renewing the seasonal salmon congregation at Point Roberts started by the Coast Salish. George and Barker's workers would often camp on the hill above the cannery. The *Blaine Journal* described the scene in 1909: "The girls and boys who have been at work since early in the morning come out and go to their homes, or to the many camps that have been made on the bluff, for Point Roberts's population is largely a floating one and it camps there during the summer."[396] When fish arrived for processing at Pike's dock, the cannery foreman would blow two long blasts of a steam whistle, heard all over Point Roberts, to signal the labor workforce to come down the hill to work. Much of the time, the George and Barker cannery would have bought their fish from a different kind of fisherman than the Alaska Packers Association cannery did. George & Barker were not as successful as the APA because they came late and missed the best fish trap locations. They sent fish-buying scows around the Salish Sea, as far as Gig Harbor.[397] Located on the west side of Point Roberts just south of the mouth of the Fraser River, George and Barker specialized in serving a niche market. They advertised their salmon buying operation specifically to Canadian gillnetters. In Canada, these gillnetters were in contracts which required them to sell the salmon they caught in specific quantities to a specific Canadian cannery. The fishermen would sneak over the border to Point Roberts and sell their surplus salmon to George and Barker for cash under the table. A steady force for three decades, George and Barker's operation was long a thorn in the side of customs officials, who eventually cracked down and threatened a full investigation. George and Barker shut down in 1930.

When the fish traps were outlawed in 1934, Archie McMillan, a long time trap operator, and Walt Waters built a cannery on the west side of Point Roberts south of the former George and Barker cannery. Their new cannery, the Point Roberts Lighthouse Packing Company, began canning salmon bought from purse seiners and gillnetters, as we learned in Chapter 2.

These salmon canneries in Point Roberts were owned by whites with access to capital to purchase modern fishing technology. They quickly supplanted the native fishery, dominating access to the vast salmon runs. The bigger ones came to own the processing of the salmon from net to tin; indeed many canneries, including the APA, also owned fish traps. Like many corporate monopolies before them, control of the entire cycle meant, as cartels do, they could control prices and profits.[398] Indeed, it wasn't merely coincidence the canneries were located at prime native fishing locations. The cannery owners had realized most whites were interested in logging; to place canneries in profitable locations they emulated native fishing behaviors, especially near the border at Point Roberts, usurping those sites for themselves.[399]

Conversely, it didn't take long for the Coast Salish to figure out how the canneries and the corporate control of their former fishery worked. They quickly realized the white man's border cut precariously close to Point Roberts and the APA cannery. No fools themselves, they quickly learned to exploit the binary nature of the border at Point Roberts. The canneries were where the money was, and Coast Salish people throughout the Salish Sea began to fish closer to canneries. Prior to the arrival of the white fishing operations, all sites in the Salish Sea belonged to an elder and somebody wanting to fish at a site would ask permission; the owner would grant approval partly based on sustainability. In this new era, traditional resource boundaries were gone. Another change to which the Coast Salish had to become accustomed was the dependence on cannery contracts. Canneries often stipulated natives set aside their traditional canoes and use cannery-provided skiffs, of course with the condition their catch was sold exclusively to that cannery. It took time to realize the cannery advances on food and supplies weren't handouts and had to be paid back from their wages. The Coast Salish were well aware this came at the expense of losing their traditional and accustomed fishing grounds. By the 1910s the commercial salmon industry had restructured the Fraser River fishery in Washington to shut out the Coast Salish people. In 1912 a lawyer for the Pacific American Fisheries, owner of the largest salmon cannery in the world[400] at Bellingham, went so far as to boast openly that he and other large canners' legal counsel had essentially written the fishery statutes of Washington.[401]   It employed so many people in Bellingham from 1898 to 1965 it was commonly referred to as "Pay After Fishing."[402]

The legendary Fraser River sockeye salmon runs collapsed by the end of World War I. By 1920 only eleven canneries were still operating in northwest Washington. In just twenty-five years, white capitalized commercial fishery operators moved in, appropriated a millennium-old fishery from the native people, formed a cartel to monopolize the industry, over-fished the runs and created pollution and tremendous waste.[403] Sheer greed wiped out one of the world's largest salmon fisheries. Too little too late, Washington and British Columbia finally got serious about working together to manage the fishery, a novel idea the Coast Salish people had been shouting for all along.

LABOR HISTORY

Chinese laborers arrived in the 1880s to work in salmon canneries on the Salish Sea. They were a dominant force in British Columbia canneries.   Canneries   in   Washington   had   more automation, so the Chinese workforce wasn't as large as in B.C., but nonetheless thousands toiled in Washington canneries, about half the total Chinese and Japanese population of the state in 1902.[404] Most Chinese had been expelled from the state after race riots, but the canneries continued to quietly use Chinese labor by outsourcing staffing to a hiring agency.

The Blaine Journal in 1895 wrote about the Lily Point cannery, where "sixty whites are at work and 130 Chinese."[405]   Charles Snyder was the U.S. Immigration Inspector for Point Roberts. In 1901, working on tips from local fishermen, he raided the APA cannery, busting Chinese supervisors who moonlighted in human trafficking. Their going rate was one hundred dollars a head (over $2,600 today) to smuggle a Chinese laborer into the United States through Point Roberts.[406] The case shed light on how large numbers of Chinese still worked in the canneries even after they had been expelled from Whatcom County. A Chinese laborer in Canada would be put in touch with the coyote from the APA cannery at Lily Point. They made their $100 payment, and the coyote would meet them on the Canadian side near Ladner, lead them at night through the marshy delta lowlands by foot into Point Roberts. Waiting just north of the cannery below the Lily Point bluffs until it was safe to proceed, they would either stay at Point Roberts to live in the Chinese dormitories and work at the APA cannery or they were taken onto boats to take them further afield into the United States. A common route for the next handoff point was Sucia Island, easily seen from the south shore of Point Roberts, where they would hide in the natural sandstone caves at Shallow Bay. Generations of my family have played in these caves during summer holidays. The coyotes in the APA cannery also handled Chinese laborers heading northbound too, because the Chinese were never banned in Canada as they were in Washington after the Chinese Exclusion Act of 1882, which made the smuggling of Chinese more intense. It was high-risk, high-reward, and from all accounts many met unfortunate ends. If the pirates encountered the authorities on the water, devious skippers would rid themselves of incriminating evidence by tying weights to the Chinese and throwing them into the cold, deep waters off Point Roberts. A news brief in the *Seattle Post-Intelligencer* on April 8, 1884 was typical of the era: "Another five Chinese men were captured off Point Roberts."

The organization of Chinese labor at Lily Point went through a Chinese-owned agency. The agency signed a contract with the Alaska Packers Association, agreeing to pack a given number of cases of sockeye salmon in a season for a flat fee. The agency hired, paid, fed and housed the number of Chinese workers they wanted to take on to meet the quota yet still make a profit. Inspection of the old contracts shows the contracts were typically for between 20,000 and 50,000 cases of salmon, at a rate of forty-five cents per case ($12.50 today). Some fifty to 132 workers would be hired to fulfill such a contract.[407] The workers weren't paid until the end of the season when they were on the scow leaving Point Roberts.[408] A Chinese worker made an average of $274 for the season in 1915 ($6600 today), compared to $363 ($8800 today) for a white worker but a lot more than the average $83 ($2000 today) pay for a Coast Salish worker.[409]

There was a separate dormitory for Chinese workers here at Lily Point for the APA cannery. Rhubarb and apple trees still grow from the garden they planted.[410] At the George and Barker cannery, a building called the China House was built on the hill above the cannery. The Icelandic settlers wrote about seeing the Chinese leave the cannery at the end of their shift, carrying their lunch pails and butcher knives, ascending the hill, the sounds of Chinese language filling the air, mixing with the Germanic sounds of Icelandic and English. At night their camp fires lit the hilltop, and singing could be heard accompanied by guitars, banjos and mandolins. Many slept outside on beds made of fir boughs.[411]

One Chinese worker in particular deserves note. Ah Fat was born in 1841 in China. There are records of him at Semiahmoo working for John Elwood. When the Chinese population was expelled from Whatcom County, Ah Fat eluded deportation and came to squat on the military reservation at Point Roberts and work for the George & Barker cannery. Most Chinese workers focused on washing and cutting fish, but Ah Fat had a unique skill. He could use the machine which punched the hole in the cans to see if steam hissed out, and he would then solder it sealed again. He built his own house near Lighthouse Marine Park, complete with picket fence and gardens brimming of vegetables and flowers.[412] In 1905 he bought a restaurant. Though the Chinese had been driven out of Whatcom County, Ah Fat had openly registered with officials, as he was required to do. However, there was a mix-up in his paperwork and he was arrested for not registering. He was respected by the community and had been a fixture in Point Roberts for years; no fewer than ten members of the community testified in his defense. They very hour he was to be deported, a telegram came in confirming his registration paperwork had been found, allowing him to stay in Point Roberts, one of only a couple of Chinese officially allowed to stay in Whatcom County after the expulsion. Residents of Point Roberts to this day speak affectionately about Ah Fat, helped by the fact he went out of his way to assimilate into the community. He spoke English and dressed in western clothes, calling himself Charlie Chinaman to make it easier for the locals. He was often seen scavenging the flotsam and jetsam on the beach, cork being a favorite find. One day some chopsticks washed up on shore, which Ah Fat used to make an elaborate Chinese musical kite. His kite whistled in the wind, amazing the Icelandic settlers who had never seen such a contraption. He died in 1915 and is buried in Bellingham.[413]

Eventually technology eased the need for Chinese labor. Perhaps the most important innovation in the canneries was the Smith butchering machine. It could behead, eviscerate and de-fin enough fish in a single ten-hour day to fill two thousand cases of salmon, one fish per second. It worked like this: a worker would feed a fish into the machine. First, the salmon's tail was pinned down and cut off. The fish moved up a wheel where the belly fin was removed next. The following blade removed the back and dorsal fin. After that, the fish was opened by a splitting saw at the top of the machine. Moving down the other side of the wheel, the abdominal cavity was cleaned and then a scraper removed the kidney. At the bottom of the wheel, brushes cleaned the salmon. The salmon exited the machine onto a conveyor belt on its way to the sliming table. This 1903 invention replaced much of the manual Chinese labor in the canneries, giving it the decidedly politically-incorrect name The Iron Chink. This device was invented by Edmund A. Smith and first used in the sprawling Pacific American Fisheries cannery at Fairhaven in 1903. It immediately eliminated the need for fifteen up to as many as fifty cutters in the average cannery. The machine was highly profitable, though its name was offensive to those who worked with it. Further innovations included can-filling machines, washing machines, can-soldering machines, can crimpers, all of which reduced the need for workers in the Point Roberts canneries.[414] Profits for corporate owners soared and stress on the sockeye salmon fishery intensified.

The year 1902 was the peak year of Chinese participation in the cannery workforce at Point Roberts. Immigration crackdowns, tax increases and automation in the canneries caused many Chinese to return home. By the end of the decade the Chinese were on the decline and Japanese fishermen were attracted to come to work in the Fraser River canneries. The trick was getting in to Canada. Samuel Walker, U.S. Customs Inspector in 1903, reported to his superiors hundreds of Japanese coming north to the Fraser River that year, the favorite route for getting into Canada was through Point Roberts.[415]

At its peak the APA cannery employed nearly 300.[416] Women had their own dormitory at the APA cannery, named "Seldom Inn." Children were also used in the cannery labor force. Children as young as nine years old worked in both the APA and George & Barker canneries,[417] where they put empty cans in trays, earning ten cents per hour (about $2.38 per hour in today's money) in ten-hour shifts. In a "Point Pioneers in Review" series of articles in the early 1970s, Bill Olson wrote of his parents, "Father (Magnus) worked at the George and Barker Cannery until he died in 1907 when we children were still very young. Mother Olson worked in the cannery too, during the summer months, like most of the ladies – and young people too – in the old days at Point Roberts."[418]

The harsh conditions in the canneries and in their treatment of labor attracted socialists to the Salish Sea who saw an oppressed workforce ripe for recruitment into labor unions. Washington was renowned for having quite a few of these socialist societies, and was home to some of the strongest labor movements and some of the most violent repression of socialists in U.S. history. It had become illegal to be a socialist or spread socialist information during World War I. Laugi Thorstenson recalled in his memoirs being chosen as a deckhand on a coal steamer which fished off Point Roberts. He found himself working alongside a coal fire man and cook who were Wobblies, members of the Industrial Workers of the World, who advocated for niche leftist groups to unite into One Big Union.[419] Thorstenson mentions the Wobblies attempted to recruit him into the anarchist-leaning union. The IWW was the leading actor in the famous free speech fights of the American West, which sought to be allowed to openly avow socialism and anarchism. Spokane was the scene of a large free speech fight in Washington. Over a dozen people, mostly socialists and anarchists, were murdered in vigilante mob massacres in Everett in 1916 and Centralia in 1919, and Seattle was home to one of the largest general strikes in American history in 1919.[420] The Salish Sea was home to so much radical labor history U.S. Postmaster General James A. Farley was prompted to offer this toast during a visit to Seattle in 1930: "To the forty-seven states and the soviet of Washington."[421]

Another group of socialists who fished at Point Roberts were members of a socialist colony in Samish Bay at present-day Edison, Washington named Equality Colony. Equality was the largest socialist colony in Washington, and was such a big deal the Socialist Party moved its national membership office to Edison. Equality Colony was vocal in its opposition to the corporate salmon canning cartels, including the Alaska Packers Association. In order to catch salmon to feed their members, earn some money and take a share of the catch from the APA, Equality colonists fished at Point Roberts in 1898. For $150 Equality bought the eight-ton sloop *Progress* and had a few smaller boats. In late July they went north to Point Roberts for sockeye salmon each year from 1898 to 1900, in the shadow of the fish traps and the massive corporate cannery at Lily Point.[422]

The APA was so notorious for its corporate power and domination over the workers a radical labor song was written by J.W. Sparrow & Joe Debenedictus called "The A.P.A. Jig."[423] Sung by the workers as they worked the fish traps and toiled in the cannery, the lyrics tell of working for the corporation:

> We'll fish all night, and smoke all day, seining up the salmon for the APA. Come all ye lads from the 48, sign on now, don't be late, fish all night and smoke all day, seining up the salmon for the APA. Let me out of the noise and stink, don't hand me a can from the old Iron Chink. Give me a skiff and a line of pay, seining up the salmon for the APA.

Salmon fishing had been something ordinary people had done at Point Roberts; the barrier to entry was lower than most professions. After the introduction of fish traps and modern canneries, regular Joes were shut out and only big corporations with capital had access to the salmon. White workers did not aggressively pursue unionization in the Salish Sea fishing industry. British Columbia had a fishermen's union in 1899, but it didn't last long. In Washington, whilst mining and forestry workers were more commonly organized in unions,[424] fishermen were more solitary. Those who used a specific fishing gear type tended to stick together. The Slavonian purse seiners didn't get along with the Scandinavian and British gill netters, who found each other destructive and pressed for fishing regulations which would benefit their own gear type. This in-fighting within the fishing industry prevented unionization.[425]

The tide turned when fish traps were banned by the state of Washington in 1934. This dealt a hard blow to capitalized interests like fish trap and cannery owners, but was a boon to individual fishermen, leading to a rise in purse seining and gill netting. They previously hadn't been able to compete with large corporate owners and one-sided contracts. After the passage of the fish trap ban, demand spiked for harbor space in Blaine's Drayton Harbor, the closest marina to Point Roberts. Soon more individual white fishermen were fishing at Point Roberts than ever before.

PIRATES OF POINT ROBERTS

In chapter two we discussed how Roberts Town was a hotbed of smuggling. When we think of smuggling, we think of booze. Smuggling was repeatedly reported at Point Roberts from the 1850s all the way into the middle of the twentieth century. The *Victoria Colonist* reported in 1926 Point Roberts was the "scene of much lawlessness especially smuggling."[426]   Beyond booze, a major object of smuggling was salmon. Nowhere in the Salish Sea was salmon smuggling more rampant than at Point Roberts.

Three groups were involved in salmon smuggling: the Coast Salish, Canadian fishermen and fish pirates. The Coast Salish ignored the white man's artificial boundary and caught fish where they were abundant and sold fish where the price was good, regardless of which side of the invisible line they were on. In the early years of white presence in the fishery, the high prices were in British lands; Canadian prices were fifty per cent higher than they were in the United States. The Northern Straits Coast Salish, whose homelands spanned the border, often caught fish at Point Roberts and sold it to canneries along the Fraser River or to middlemen in the upper Canadian portion of Boundary Bay. "It will be very difficult to prevent English boats from anchoring in Boundary Bay, close to the line, and receiving fish from Indian canoes," observed U.S. Customs officer A. L. Blake in 1883.[427]   The articles in the Point Elliott Treaty prevented the Coast Salish from crossing the border, but they continued to trade across their traditional homeland spanning west and east shores of the Strait of Georgia, being savvy enough to know how to exploit the border for their benefit.

The Coast Salish were not the only people to exploit the border. The international boundary, scant patrols and fluctuating economic conditions all resulted in movement of white fishermen across the border, with Point Roberts the common denominator in the middle. Canadians were active in smuggling salmon at Point Roberts. It was easy for them to dip below the 49th, fill up their boats with salmon in U.S. waters at Point Roberts, and then quickly escape back to the safety of Canadian waters. In August 1895, George Webber, U.S. Customs Inspector at Point Roberts, said of Canadian salmon fishing boats, "If you try to get to them, they will steam away for a hundred yards across the line and then lay and laugh at you."[428] Frequently observing Canadian smugglers, Webber tried to apprehend and get on board as soon as they entered U.S. waters at Point Roberts.

From the mid-1890s prices evened out, and the situation reversed: Canadian fishermen caught fish north of the border and in defiance of their cannery contracts, came south of the border to sell their catch to the Point Roberts canneries. One Fraser River cannery investigated and found twenty of their contracted fishermen selling at Lily Point. After the George and Barker Cannery opened, the situation escalated. Another Canadian canner spied no fewer than forty-three boats he had provided to Canadian fishermen selling thousands of sockeye salmon to George and Barker in Point Roberts. George and Barker were liable for duty on these salmon but since sockeyes all look the same charges were hard to prove. Nonetheless in 1912 they were forced to pay $15,000 in unpaid duty, the equivalent of $366,000 today.

The third group of salmon smugglers at Point Roberts was fish pirates. We tend to think of pirates in the Caribbean dealing with gold and treasure chests, but in the Salish Sea salmon were the gold, and there were at least as many pirates around Point Roberts as in the hotspots in the Caribbean. It was the fixed fish traps off Lily Point which tempted folks to get into salmon piracy. The salmon were already caught and stuck in the spiller. It was all too easy for fish pirates to ignore, and since Point Roberts had more fish traps than anywhere else, Point Roberts had more pirates than anyplace else.

The pirates of Point Roberts came out at night, sneaking among the fish trap pilings emanating from the reef. Lights and motor switched off, the moonlight guided them to the spiller full of salmon. Working swiftly, the pirates filled their boat with thousands of fish before making their getaway into the night.[429] One of the most notorious fish pirates at Point Roberts was Bert Jones. Jones knew how to pirate the salmon because he himself had worked as a fisherman for the canneries, and had insider knowledge of how the canneries and fish trap operators worked. On a typical piracy run Jones would nab 2500 salmon, with one night's work netting as much as $1800.[430] That would be $43,000 today, all in one night. Jones' knowledge of the Point Roberts reef was essential to his success as a pirate, "I run without lights altogether. I wouldn't run onto no rocks because I knew where to go."[431]

In an early form of economic populism, salmon piracy was largely driven by monopolistic practices of the big salmon corporations. The more they exerted control by lobbying for laws which protected them at the expense of all others, and offered take-it-or-leave-it one-sided contracts, the more pirates they spawned. Though the salmon fishery was theoretically owned in common by all people in Washington, with fish traps costing over $5000 to create and as much as $90,000 to purchase and owners leveraging their power to shape fisheries law, regular fishermen were shut out. The traps were ruthlessly effective at trapping salmon, lessening the need for canneries to buy from individual fishermen. These factors led many to turn to piracy.

To level the playing field, pirates took the share to which they felt they were entitled but couldn't realize due to the corporations' monopolistic control of the commons. Indeed, most fish pirates passed by fish traps owned by individuals and smaller outfits, instead preferring to exact revenge against the fat cats.[432] The corporate-owned traps became a target of the pirates at Point Roberts just as the corporations had stolen Lily Point from the Coast Salish and put independent fishermen out of work. Grabbing a few to get back at them couldn't hurt, they reasoned.[433] We're not talking about one or two bad apples. The Whatcom County sheriff estimated there were no fewer than five hundred pirates working between Point Roberts and Bellingham Bay in 1902. Not a day went by during salmon season where a piracy-related theft of a fish trap was not reported.[434]

Whilst at Point Roberts, pirates mostly stole salmon, but with the border so temptingly close, some expanded their piracy to steal nets, equipment and boats from the APA cannery dock.[435] The pirates became more brazen over time. Pirates shot out the windows of one watchman's shack on an APA-owned trap at Point Roberts in 1903 and in 1908 at an APA trap the pirates got off their boat, climbed onto the trap ledge and stormed the guard's shack. They wrestled the watchman's gun from him, leaving him bound and gagged.[436] The Pacific American Fisheries cannery of Fairhaven found their fish traps at Point Roberts had been robbed one evening by three boats, each with four to six pirates on board.[437] In one incident in 1909, no fewer than forty armed pirates attacked fish traps at Point Roberts, filling multiple scows with sockeye and escaped to Canadian waters beyond the reach of U.S. authorities where they sold the loot to B.C. canneries. Although some trap owners had employed watchmen earlier, it was after this raid that owners of most Point Roberts fish traps began hiring night watchmen, who were now universally armed with guns and searchlights and instructions to kill any pirates caught in the act.[438]

After the introduction of night watchmen, pirates changed their methods. Whereas before they had simply stolen live fish from the fish trap spiller, this was no longer possible with an armed guard literally sitting atop the trap. However, the trap owners paid the watchmen poorly, and the pirates began bribing the guards who were all too often eager to cooperate with the pirates, even guiding them to the spiller with signal lights. One Bellingham trap watchman accepted a $500 bribe ($12,500 today) to look the other way as pirates raided over 10,000 salmon from the spiller, and even helped the pirates get the last fish loaded into their boat. With that kind of cash, he actually rode back to shore with the pirates, effectively walking off the job, since the pirates had just paid him more than he would've made for the rest of the season.[439]

Another tactic used by the pirates at Point Roberts was to ram their boats into the fish trap pilings and webbing as an act of vandalism. Their goal was to damage the traps, causing the owners to have to spend their profits repairing the structures. With their night watchmen bribed and repair costs escalating, the trap owners made the next move in the Point Roberts piracy chessboard. The trap owners came to realize older trap watchmen tended to be former fishermen who fostered resentment against their employer for having forced them out of their former profession. The owners countered this problem by scheduling two night watchmen, the second typically a younger fellow who would be more loyal to the trap owner, and who would prevent or at least report piracy.[440]

Resentment of fish trap and cannery owners was a major driving force and justification for the Point Roberts pirates. Bert Jones admitted piracy was theft, but rationalized this by viewing the trap owners as thieves as well. Jones reminisced later in life, "Oh gosh, I used to be a crook, but I wasn't any more crooked than they were. They fished their traps during the closed season and were just as bad as me... It is all right for a fish trap to catch 60,000 fish on one tide, but if I got 2000 I was a pirate."[441] Jones touches on a key rationalization of the piracy at Point Roberts. The corporate owners of fish traps off Lily Point were obligated to close the entrance to their traps at specified times each week for conservation purposes, but many slipped their night watchman a little extra pay to open the trap entrance as long as the government patrols weren't nearby. This exploitation of the commons riled the pirates.

Fish piracy wasn't actually illegal in Washington until 1915[442] and as late as 1912 only four government boats patrolled the entire state.[443] The Canadians were also concerned about piracy at Point Roberts, but had much stronger patrols. As early as the 1890s one boat was dedicated just to the small stretch of coast between the mouth of the Fraser River and the Point Roberts boundary; a constable was stationed near Point Roberts in 1903 for quick response to piracy, and by 1915 no fewer than twelve patrol boats were used along the border at Point Roberts.[444]

With the pirates now in possession of so many salmon, their next problem was how to offload their ill-gotten loot. Pirates stole so many salmon from traps at Point Roberts the canneries went looking for more salmon to catch. Inevitably, the two met. Canneries dispatched boats to weave through the network of fish traps off Point Roberts to buy more sockeye. Soon individual fishermen pulled up to the cannery tenders to sell them fish, only these "fishermen" were the pirates, who were selling back to the canneries the fish they had stolen from the cannery's own fish traps!

The general public often took the pirates' side. On the rare occasion pirates were detained they were typically released based on public sentiment. The citizenry was irate that the canneries got to ignore the law whilst police cracked down on individual pirates. Pirates put on trial argued the fish caught in the traps were still in the commons until they were lifted from the water and one lawyer set three salmon on the courtroom table and asked the trap owner to identify his property; when he couldn't the case was dismissed.[445] One Point Roberts resident working as a fish buyer for APA in 1931 reported a typical comment from one seiner was, "I tell you Mike, I throw my fish overboard before I sell to Alaska Pack."[446]

Most people would be surprised to know how much seafood piracy still happens at Point Roberts. In just two days in September 2015, 675 illegal crab pots were seized by fifteen officers from the Washington Department of Fish and Wildlife and Coast Salish native police, who used several boats to comb the waters between Point Roberts and Blaine. The crab pots were hoisted up out of Boundary Bay and brought to Blaine, where it took ten truckloads to haul them away to be auctioned off by the state of Washington.[447] Most were owned by Canadians, illegally crabbing in U.S. waters without licenses.

Piracy at Point Roberts took many forms. Salmon piracy is not as well-known as other smuggled goods, yet was arguably the most-common form of local piracy for several decades. If nothing else, it's a fascinating if under-told part of the history of Point Roberts.

AFTER THE FISH TRAPS

People from Croatia's coastal area along the Adriatic Sea who called themselves Slavonians were experiencing unrest as World War I loomed in the 1910s. Many were fishermen, with quite a few coming from the island of Vis. These men left their homeland before the draft started. One young man named Dom Moskovita, my great-grandfather, traveled with other Slavonians to New Zealand. There they got jobs as gum diggers, digging in the ground below giant kauri trees for resin. The first Slavonians arrived in the Salish Sea in 1895. News of a Slavonian community making a living by purse seining at Point Roberts eventually reached the Slavonians in New Zealand. This fishing technique had been used in the Adriatic Sea for generations and adapted well to the Salish Sea. Slavonians were so dominant in the purse seining fishery that it provoked state fish commissioner Darwin to remark in 1917 they should be prohibited from the fishery because they would fish the salmon to extinction and return to Europe with the profits.[448] That year, $8 million of the $12 million in salmon was caught by non-Americans and non-Canadians, chiefly these newly-arrived Slavonians.[449] Moskovita gave up gum digging, left New Zealand and arrived at Whatcom County in 1910, settling in Bellingham. He crafted a crude crab pot and tried his luck one day in Bellingham Bay, pulling up a huge quantity of Dungeness crabs, enough for the family to eat and plenty left over to sell. He soon quit his day job and began fishing for Dungeness crab full time. My grandfather, George Moskovita, was born in 1913 and from an early age worked in the crab fishery with his father. He was often late to school because he was busy working in the early morning hours.

Figure 66: Dom Moskovita at his Bellingham home. Photo: Author's collection.

The purse seiners were making a good living, so the Moskovitas augmented the crabbing with salmon fishing at Point Roberts. My grandfather described the scene off Lily Point in his memoirs: "We fished around Point Roberts. They had lots of fish traps in those days between Point Roberts and Blaine. Boundary Bay was just full of them. Each company owned their own sites and placed their traps there. These fishing traps were made of pilings driven into the bottom, a whole line of them, maybe as much as a block long. In between the pilings was a wire mesh. They used the wire to lead the salmon into the fish trap. Each trap had a shack on it with a watchman. People would come and try to rob the traps. When the fish were in the water, they didn't belong to anybody, so there was a lot of trouble with trap robbers. There were times a watchman would sell a load of salmon to the fish pirates. So, the fish trap owners put on patrol boats to stop this kind of business. There was one guy who was so mistrusted they offered him $250 a month ($4500 today) to just sit in front of the cannery office so they'd know he wasn't out pirating their traps. Then they finally outlawed the traps and then everything was purse seining and gillnetting from then on."[450]

It seems grandpa knew a lot about the salmon pirates. That might be because he was a pirate too. My grandfather wasn't a salmon pirate; he was a clam pirate. As a teenager, he stole over 300 pounds of clams a week at Semiahmoo Spit to use as bait for the family's Dungeness crab pots. In his memoirs he writes, "We'd go sometimes to dig clams for crab bait up at Blaine. We had a little boat and we'd go across to a little spit where there was a clam reserve owned by the Alaska Packers. They didn't allow anyone to dig clams there. But, almost every week we'd

Figure 67: George Moskovita. Photo: Author's collection.

go out at night and use a gas light and dig three- to four-hundred pounds of clams. We'd sneak over there because it was fast digging and the clams were better than other places. Sometimes they'd come down and kick us out but then we'd go back. I guess they got used to us... I think one of the reasons we did so well in the crab business was we used good bait."[451]

My great-grandfather was more of a cautious fisherman than my grandpa. He wasn't as aggressive, didn't take opportunities to cork another fisherman, and stayed off to the side of the run rather than try to crowd in the middle of the run where everybody was jostling for position. He had been a crab fisherman since arriving in the Salish Sea in 1910, and purse seining was more of an action sport than the decidedly sedentary activity of throwing a crab pot in the water and waiting for the crabs to come to you. By 1935, my grandpa had been fishing at Point Roberts (and elsewhere in the Salish Sea and in Alaska) since he was a sixteen. In this anecdote about fishing with his dad at age twenty-two, I can hear him yearning to get out on his own and be his own captain: "My dad used to run the boat to Point Roberts for salmon. He was the sort of guy who didn't like competition. A lot of the boats were taking turns at the light at Point Roberts. On the ebb tide you'd wait about twenty minutes for one boat to lay out their net, and then he'd drift out of the way and the next boat could lay out. I told my dad, 'Why don't you go over there and get in position and get a chance to get some of those fish? Those guys are doing real good.' But he didn't like the competition. He'd go on the outside of the guys. His net wasn't deep enough so he never caught much. So, I used to argue with him a lot and he'd kick me off the pilothouse. I always insisted, 'You'd better go over there with the rest of the guys or you're not going to make anything.' But he wouldn't listen to me. So, finally he let me run the boat. When I was running the boat, I'd go fish where I thought we needed to be. In order to catch fish, there's a lot of dog eat dog. Everybody's out to cork you. Two boats see the same fish jump. One skipper starts to lay out his net and the other guy lays out about the same time, except he's in front of you. Since the guy in the second spot wouldn't catch a thing, he has to stop and pull his net in. There's no use laying your net outside of him."[452]

Eventually my grandfather got his own boat and made his living purse seining off Point Roberts. He recalls, "Most of the time we fished off Point Roberts. It was a good place to fish because when the fish leave the San Juan Islands, they have to come up through

Point Roberts to get to the Fraser River in Canada, so we had a pretty good crack at the fish there… On a big ebbing low tide and a westerly wind, the fish would back down into U.S. water. We called them blowbacks. We'd have a man up in the mast, and he would be able to see these big brown spots in a mass as the fish were in big schools. We'd go up there (to Point Roberts)

Figure 68: George Moskovita posing in 1936 with the Durant he bought from money earned fishing at Point Roberts. Photo: Author's collection.

and lay the net out and go right around the fish. Sometimes you could almost load up a boat this way, there were so many fish."[453]

Purse seiners placed their nets in front of the fish traps at the Point Roberts reef, intercepting the sockeye salmon and catching a larger and larger share of the catch. Several armed incidents between capitalized interests versus the purse seiners escalated the tension in the waters off Point Roberts. The legislature in Olympia sat by, doing nothing. By the 1920s, purse seiners caught more fish than traps, and the tide began turning. In the face of inaction from Olympia, the purse seiners saw an opportunity to use initiative process to get fish traps banned, so they could get more of the salmon catch. To build a coalition of popular support, the seiners reached out to sport fishermen. The force which finally got fish traps banned was not the legislators, but the people. Initiative 77 was on the 1934 ballot and called for the banning of fish traps and other fishing methods and created fishing seasons. The text appeared to the voter as: "An Act relating to fishing; prohibiting the use of fish traps or other fixed appliances for catching salmon and certain other fish within the waters of the State of Washington; prohibiting the taking or fishing for salmon and certain other fish within a certain area therein defined and created by any means except by trolling, regulating trolling in such area, and permitting the operation of gill nets therein under certain conditions; providing for open and closed seasons, prohibiting drag seines and limiting the length of gill nets in the Columbia River; prescribing penalties; and repealing all laws in conflict therewith." It passed with sixty-four per cent of the vote. The use of salmon fish traps continued in Alaska, but with a diluted impact on the fishery because they were spread over a much greater area than in the Salish Sea, until 1959 when they were banned with statehood.

My grandfather left the Salish Sea and went on to a life at sea. He crabbed in Alaska, seined for tuna and sardines in Mexico, and pioneered Oregon's ocean perch fishery out of Astoria. He saw the Columbia fishery he helped to build be devastated by foreign factory processing ships.[454] Nearing retirement, in 1976 at age sixty-four grandpa returned to Bellingham and bought a gillnetting boat. The first place he went to fish for salmon was at Point Roberts. My Aunt Kathy fished with grandpa in 1977 and 1978. One day they found themselves in a major storm off South Beach. The boat was rocking back and forth so much she was sure it was going to capsize. The boat's galley had huge wooden drawers, so heavy in regular conditions my aunt could barely open them, but these drawers were effortlessly sliding open and shut with each rocking wave. They were just able to make it to safety in the newly-built marina to wait out the storm.[455] She wasn't sure what would have happened had the marina not been there.

For the next eight years, my grandpa and grandma both fished for sockeye salmon off Point Roberts. He writes of my grandma June, "From 1978 to 1986 June fished with me for sockeye salmon. Most of the time we fished around the Point Roberts area... where most of the seine boats and gillnetters worked. Being Norwegian, she had fishing in her blood and made a good boat puller. It was awfully nice to have your cook aboard as well."[456] In August 1985, I fished with him a few times during sockeye season, always off Point Roberts. After a lifetime of fishing, my grandfather began and ended his long career at Point Roberts. He retired the next year at age seventy-three and lived until 2004. He is buried near Astoria, less than five miles from the original George & Barker Cannery.

The Coast Salish people had had enough by the early 1970s, and in 1973 thirteen tribes, eventually joined by the federal government, sued the state of Washington, the Washington Department of Fisheries, the Washington Game Commission and the Washington Reef Net Owners Association. Judge George Boldt ruled in February 1974, finding the 1855 Point Elliott Treaty's famous phrase "in common with" meant the Coast Salish people were entitled to a guaranteed allocation of salmon, and he ruled that share to be fifty per cent. Boldt emphasized the Coast Salish owned the fishery aboriginally and through the treaty had relinquished only a portion; in other words, native fishing rights were reserved to the Coast Salish whereas fishing was a privilege non-natives were granted. Earthshattering for the white commercial fishery, it put many out of work at a time the fishery was already in decline. The Boldt Decision was intended to clear up once and for all the matter of Coast Salish fishing rights; its impact was to make things more complicated than ever. The state of Washington fought the decision through the courts, all the way up to the U.S. Supreme Court, which upheld the decision in July 1979 in a six-three ruling.

My mother, Georgene Swenson, supported the Boldt Decision which restored aboriginal fishing rights. After the court decision, she arranged for the Coast Salish people to get a fishing boat to leverage their restored fishing rights. She worked with famed Coast Salish leader Esther Ross, who I remember visiting our home on many occasions. My mother helped to link Ross with the National

Indian Lutheran Board in Washington, D.C. to campaign for a fishing boat in order to fish for their share. This boat campaign was meant to be the spark for other tribes to get their own fishing boats as a result of the Boldt Decision.[457] Ross was a frequent visitor to Congress where she walked the halls making her views known; indeed, one Washington Congressman famously exclaimed as he walked through the Capitol in Washington D.C., "Oh God, here comes Esther Ross."[458] Mom helped Ross raise money to pay for the trip to the nation's capital to fight for the boat. The campaign was successful and a gillnetting boat was purchased in Bellingham.[459] Needless to say, it was a contentious issue in my family; my grandpa being a Whatcom County commercial fisherman and his daughter campaigning for natives to get half the salmon for which he had previously fished. I have vivid childhood memories of these family debates.

The Coast Salish people continue to fish at Point Roberts with purse seining and gillnetting gear. Commercial fishermen are also seen fishing today right off the beach. During the peak days, it's like a city on the water with so many fishing boats in the waters surrounding the Point, each jockeying for a good spot. The sound of their diesel engines and the pop of the plunging poles echoing off the shore is an iconic Point Roberts experience.[460]

On September 13, 1994, Washington closed the sockeye salmon season early. The Lummis claimed they were owed 225,000 fish worth two million dollars, and chose a site to stage a protest: Point Roberts. Gathered on a flotilla of over forty boats at Point Roberts, they were quickly joined by the Coast Guard, special agents from the National Fisheries Service, the Lummi tribal police, and of course TV crews. Seattle's NBC affiliate even sent its news helicopter. The Coast Guard cited two Lummi boats, but found no illegally caught fish. In a celebrity appearance, the Lummis attracted the support of Russell Means, who came to Point Roberts to protest for the Lummis. As the national director of the American

Indian Movement (AIM), Means was one of the best-known Native Americans. He participated in the Alcatraz Occupation, the fourteen-month AIM occupation of Alcatraz Island in San Francisco Bay. The U.S. government forcibly ended that occupation in June 1971. Means led AIM protests which occupied the *Mayflower II* in Boston Harbor in 1971 and Mount Rushmore and the Bureau of Indian Affairs offices in Washington in 1972. Means is perhaps best-known for his involvement in the seventy-one-day Wounded Knee occupation in 1973. He has been active at the United Nations, ran for U.S. President in 1988 and starred in the 1992's *The Last of the Mohicans* and was Chief Powhatan in Disney's *Pocahontas* in 1995, a year after his visit to the Point. The protest ended with the burning of a skiff at Lighthouse Park.[461] Point Roberts continues to be a central lightning rod for competing interests in the management and utilization of the salmon resource in the Salish Sea.

Point Roberts is at the junction of the border and salmon. The Point was home to innovations like the Coast Salish reef nets and the sockeye fish traps. Had greed not overfished it, there should have been enough for everybody. As salmon were canned by the million, the APA used its capitalized power to manipulate the government to protect their stranglehold on the supply chain; the Coast Salish people and the pirates exploited their home field advantage by using their familiarity with the natural ecosystem to acquire salmon. Point Roberts was the epicenter of all this and bore the brunt of economic, class, ethnic and international pressures between corporate cartels, native people, purse seiners and pirates.

SAVING LILY POINT

Walk along the beach to the north to explore the northern public tidelands. The orange-hued sandstone cliffs tower over public tidelands. Scattered along the beach are pieces of rusting slag, some six feet tall, stubborn relics of the Point's industrial history. This is the area of Goodfellow's saltery. In the spring waterfalls trickle down the cliff sides along the tidelands almost up to Maple Beach, the noisiest of which is year-round Cheltenem Falls as it meets the beach after a two-hundred foot cascade down the ravine.

Return to the grassy lowlands of the park. Find a trail from the beach on the north side of the lowlands which traverses the flat area

Figure 69: Cheltenem Falls cascades down the ravine and off a cliff onto the beach at Lily Point Park. Photo by Mark Swenson.

once home to the APA cannery. The Point Roberts Historical Society has placed an informational marker about the cannery along this trail. Explore the lowlands to find relics from the cannery, including concrete foundations, rusting equipment and a wooden water tower. Return to the parking lot by climbing the switchback trail and twenty-four stairs, and then turn left at the main intersection and head downhill on the loop trail. It will loop around and then head back uphill along the backyards of cute tiny homes and cabins on Claire Lane.

Now that you know all Lily Point Marine Park has to offer and understand its cultural and historical significance, it's time to reflect on the fact Lily Point was very nearly lost to private development. To consider private greed could have taken this site from the public is gut-wrenching. It cannot be overstated how close the community came to losing Lily Point. Before it became a park by being purchased by the Whatcom Land Trust and the Nature Conservancy in two deals in 2008 and 2009, the 230 acres of land and ninety-six acres of tidelands were owned by private owners who worked hard to keep the public out of such a big area.

After unfettered access to Lily Point into the 1970s, eventually fences were put up in the 1980s. Guard dogs were used. Security systems were installed. The sheriff patrolled the forest, ticketing trespassers. None of these attempts to ban the local community from the lands were successful; generations of locals have cherished Lily Point, risking fines and injury to commune with nature in the footsteps of history.

The owners were responsible for the property and cited the inherent risks of the public using the land. Besides people falling off the cliffs, the risk of fire was always present. In 1981 five acres of the grassy lowland area was burned by careless partiers.[462] In August 2006 three acres of the lowlands were burned in a fire set by a person setting financial documents on fire. With no roads to the lowlands, it took the fire department over an hour to get on the scene with equipment. During this time residents filled water bottles one at a time from the beach to contain the fire; others were stomping out the huge flames by foot.[463]

There were development proposals for Lily Point off and on for years, and Point Roberts came very close to losing the town's crown jewel forever. In the mid-1970s a major development was planned for Lily Point to be called Seacliffe Estates. Touted as "one of the best pieces of real estate on the entire Pacific coast,"[464] it would have built ninety-nine homes, 124 condos, three wells, a security gate, and fencing around the entire property, including the beaches to keep the public out of all of Lily Point. The project was approved in February 1978, and logging began in summer 1979 and continued into spring 1980 to clear trees for the roads and underground utilities.[465] The main trail would have been the private road through the single-family homes which were to have been built cliffside.[466] As you walk down the main gravel path imagine dozens of residential lots with homes between the trail and the cliff. In February 1984 the front page of the local newspaper announced construction would start in April with the headline, "Lily Point Development Soon a Reality."[467]

Although some welcomed the development for the jobs and increased population it would produce, many were horrified Lily Point could really be off-limits. In true Point Roberts fashion, the community bounded together and initiated a furious letter writing campaign to save Lily Point. Just as construction was imminent, in a surprise move what appeared to have been a done deal was called into question when in April 1984 the final hearing examiner voiced concerns with the project, saying he had to "carefully consider all information we got." He cited letters received describing maple trees which were growing at the time George Vancouver walked the park. There was shock when the developer seemed indifferent and said they couldn't guarantee the historic maples would be saved,

Figure 70: Logging in Lily Point in February 1980 to build an exclusive gated subdivision. Photo: *Ocean Star*.

with a limp "We'll try." It was also pointed out the cliffs lose several inches – up to a foot – each year. Not only would this require buyers to sign special cautionary paperwork, it could also have left the public with a big tax bailout liability in the future.

Another concern was the condominiums, which were to be built on the lower lands all along the beach. The engineers had worked out the best grade they could find was between twelve and thirteen per cent, but the maximum allowed was twelve per cent, so it wasn't certain the road from the uplands to the lowlands could even be built. The importance of the road was driven home when it was pointed out for the 124 condos, there was no alternative exit.[468] After the developers spent over $800,000 at the county's request on studies, by August the first indication surfaced the road slope would be rejected.[469] It's probably a good thing they didn't go with the road. Today, the fencing near the southern viewpoint in Lily Point Park blocks off where the road would have descended to the beach.

It was the main trail to the beach before the stairs were built. Today it's impassible as there has been major erosion and minor landslides in the road's path. Indeed, the condos actually would have been cut off.

Seacliffe Estates had been approved in 1978 but those permits expired in 1982.[470] The community geared up for more hearings in late 1984 when developers sought approval again. Although still endangered, sixty bald eagles had been counted by then. Concerns were raised about the impact development would have on the protected birds. This time the developers offered a concession that the public could walk on the beach and in some of the trails, but security would prevent the general public from walking on most trails and driving cars or parking on the property. Some asking why, if the public would be allowed to walk on some trails in the development, why there was currently fencing, guard dogs and security systems in place to keep folks out. The optimism of the ability to walk the beach at Lily Point was doused when adjacent land owners voiced their opposition to the public crossing their land to get to Lily Point.[471] Not liking what they were hearing, the development foes crossed their fingers and hoped for the best. Hopes were dashed when word came in December the development was approved, but it got mired in red tape and Seacliffe Estates was never built.

In February 1991, a new proposal was made to develop Lily Point. The Resort at Lily Point would feature over two hundred condos, a two hundred room hotel and a 126-acre golf course. Almost all of the trees in the entire property would be cut down, with the developer's plan calling for 166 of the 196 acres to be developed, leaving only seventeen acres of forest for preservation.[472] Step by step, the project advanced through the approval process. By the summer of 1994 the county had approved the unit development plan, contingent on the developer setting aside ten per cent of the lands for cultural, historical and scenic purposes, including a small museum of the Coast Salish village Cheltenem.[473] The threat of losing Lily Point again galvanized many in the community. Committees were organized to write letters, attend hearings and contact government representatives. In addition to the people of Point Roberts, the Lummi Nation also protested the development. From their perspective they faced a no-win choice of losing Cheltenem to developers or having their culture displayed behind plate glass. Neither acceptable, the Lummis gave a passionate defense of their former home in a Whatcom County Council Planning Commission meeting in March 1993, "We're talking about our way of life, our *chilangin*. Our people, reef net sites, petroglyphs, archaeological sites, burial sites, tree burial sites... The place where we stored our sacred regalia. You look on what's that, where that line's at, the border, even standing at Point Roberts you can see the rows of shell middens, our burial sites."[474] Again the Lily Point protectors were dismayed to learn in June 1997 their anti-resort appeal had been rejected.[475] Permits were soon issued and it seemed Lily Point was doomed. However, this project too got stuck in bureaucracy, due in part to the challenges of the Point's exclave status. The original permits issued in 1997 were not extended when they expired; several financial partners died and investors lost interest.[476] The Resort was dead by November 2003, after keeping Lily Point – and the community – in limbo for twelve long years.

With the resort proposal dead, Lily Point went back on the market. This time, it was no longer marketed as a golf course or a housing subdivision; it was now positioned as a private estate for a tech billionaire, or as a large university facility. Subdividing wasn't ruled out, but Lily Point's recreational potential was now the focus. A December 2004 ad in Canada's *National Post* featured the property for $2,950,000.[477] As late as 2007, new development proposals were raised. In July that year another developer announced plans for a private development of Lily Point would build 106 elite luxury mansions. Today's north trail and the beaches would have been available for public use, but most of it would be developed, fenced and gated.[478]

Organized efforts to raise money to buy Lily Point for a park began to galvanize. In June 2008, many groups came together to make a public purchase of Lily Point to create a park. The Whatcom Land Trust raised $3.5 million to buy a hundred acres of forest, ninety acres of shoreline and forty acres of tidelands. Washington Governor Christine Gregoire established a salmon restoration program as part of the Puget Sound Partnership, which donated many funds, as did the Department of Ecology, Whatcom County and the Land Conservancy of British Columbia.[479]

To mark the momentous occasion, a community walk was organized. Members of the Lummi Nation attended and spoke of the park's significance to native people. Lummi Nation Council member Sherilynn Williams noted, "Lily Point has been a refuge of abundance for the Coast Salish people." Another tribal member added, "A lot of our ancestors are buried there."[480]

The era of greed at Lily Point was finally over. Exploited from 1878 to 2008, an incredible 130 years of use by settlers, corporations, smugglers, pirates and later, private owners and greedy developers, this priceless property is now safely in the commons.

 Leave Lily Point Park on A.P.A. Road.

A.P.A. Road's name confuses visitors and outsiders. Locals know it's an acronym for the Alaska Packers Association, but visitors try to pronounce it as a word, like *AY-puh* or *AH-puh*. This amuses the local Icelandic population, as "apa" means ape in Icelandic.[481] Google Maps also shows the road as a word "Apa" with a lower case p and a, which exasperates the problem. There was even a petition raised in December 1980 to change the name of A.P.A. Road to Fernwood Road, the original name of this street, which was named after the street on which the Icelandic settlers had lived in Victoria.[482]

CHAPTER 5 • SERVICE, PLEASE!

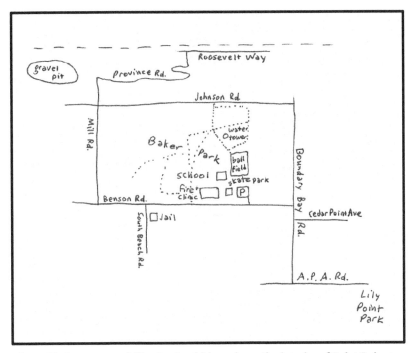

Figure 71: Route map of Chapter 5, which explores the interior of Point Roberts. Start at Lily Point Park, travel west on Benson Road, and take Mill Road to Province Road down to Roosevelt Way. Distance: 2.9 miles (4.1km)

Community services are essential for public order, well-being and safety. Unincorporated Point Roberts has had its challenges getting services provisioned, often exasperated by its exclave status. Its isolation means it doesn't get as many services from the county and state government as its population would warrant. Without solutions from the government, Point Roberts has been left to its own devices and special districts and community groups have filled the void.

COMMUNITY REPRESENTATION

Of the nineteen communities in Whatcom County recognized by the U.S. Census Bureau, both incorporated and unincorporated, Point Roberts ranks thirteenth in population.

Rank	Census-Designated Place	Population
1	Bellingham	80,900
2	Lynden	13,500
3	Ferndale	12,700
4	Birch Bay	8,400
5	Sudden Valley	6,441
6	Blaine	5,056
7	Marietta	3,906
8	Peaceful Valley	3,324
9	Everson	2,600
10	Geneva	2,321
11	Nooksack	1,480
12	Sumas	1,373
13	**Point Roberts**	**1,314**
14	Custer	366
15	Deming	353
16	Maple Falls	324
17	Acme	246
18	Glacier	211
19	Kendall	191

Point Roberts represents just 1300 people out of over 200,000 in Whatcom County. Its position off the mainland keeps it out of sight, out of mind. The isolation means the Point's residents are acutely aware they pay more in taxes than they feel they receive back in services from the county. Blanket regulations passed on the mainland cause difficulties for life in the exclave, and when Point Roberts does ask for assistance, help from the county is a long time in coming. Serious proposals to incorporate as a city have come up before. The local chamber of commerce funded the cost of putting the question on the ballot in 1981, but when locals saw the cost of having a municipal government, the proposal failed.[483]

Incorporation not feasible, Point Roberts joined many communities and created special-purpose districts. These entities are independent government units which exist separately from county and city government, carrying substantial administrative and budget independence. They often proliferate where county governments fail to address community-level needs, giving more autonomy to citizens at a local level, featuring governing boards and using public funds to execute work assigned by the legislature. The first special district was a sewer district in England in 1532. Today there are over 40,000 special districts found across the United States, managing entire communities and providing public operations such as airports, roads, transit, firefighting, libraries, stadiums, parks, cemeteries, hospitals, water and sewer, utilities, tribal reserves, etc. Services once supplied by municipalities and counties are increasingly fulfilled by special districts. Due to their public foundation, and thus public control, special districts have the power to tax, and states allow them to act autonomously with little supervision. Because they possess a civil office board holding a delegation of sovereign power from the state, they're perfect for communities like Point Roberts, which has its share.

The late 1960s saw the growth of community organizations and special districts on the Point, although a few committees pre-date that. The variety of these organizations meant more and more residents were represented by at least one of the groups. The Point Roberts Community Association was created in 1968 to present a central function for facilitating decisions about the community's needs, including zoning, road-widening and permits. Acting as a liaison between the community and governmental entities, it coordinated discussions about growth and development. Its representation of both Canadians and Americans helped it take an international perspective to local challenges.[484] The role of special districts and the Community Association became all the more important when Whatcom County dissolved the Point Roberts Township in 1969, which ended a decades-long institution which had been the local government. At the association's annual general meeting of 1971, 400 people attended, basically the entire population of the town.[485]

After the first Point Roberts Plan was adopted 1979, the next two decades saw the community grapple with balancing development and the rights of private property owners with the retention of tree cover and other environmental concerns. This was a time when the town's look and feel was hotly debated. After a 1988 plan to log trees near the heron rookery, the Heron Preservation Society pushed Whatcom County to adopt tighter controls on tree cover on the Point to protect the herons. In January 1990, a new Point Roberts Subarea Comprehensive Plan contained goals to preserve environmentally-sensitive areas, vegetative stands, cultural and archaeological sites, and "maintain existing natural vegetative cover to the maximum extent feasible." It provided for an advisory committee of two from the local chamber of commerce, one from the voters association, one from the taxpayers association and one at-large member. In May 1990 a law was passed which mandated the retention of trees over eight inches in diameter to the maximum extent possible. In January 1993 the Point Roberts Character Plan Committee, armed with a mandate by the Whatcom County Council,[486] proposed a tough sign ordinance in hopes Point Roberts could form a themed look. The committee was inspired by the look and feel of New England fishing villages and Hilton Head, South Carolina. Backers envisaged wooden pilings wrapped in rope, galvanized metal lamps and carved wooden signs.[487] Point Roberts was growing rapidly in 1994, with development sites popping up all over the Point. One hundred acres, almost fifteen per cent of the Point's forests, were logged, cleared or had been given permits to be logged. Residents were alarmed when it was learned only 750 acres of forest were left,[488] further galvanizing many to protect the Point's trees, leading to the county council to approve the Character Plan. Land for the herons was purchased in December 1995. At the Seabright Farms location, logging began at the corner of APA Road and Pauls Road in December 1996 but a stop-order was issued in January, perhaps triggered by vandalism of construction equipment causing damage over $100,000 in February. In June 1997 over one hundred people turned out to a town meeting calling for tighter regulations on tree removal. The rules were confusing, but throughout 1998 one sepcific case tested the rights of property owners against the desire by some to keep its tree cover. The permits to log four lots had been denied and were appealed on grounds the land use rules on the books stated they only applied to Lily Point. The issue divided the community as debate raged into 1999. Some wanted to get rid of all tree retention regulations and let property owners log as much of their own private property as they saw fit. Others wanted significantly tighter environmental regulations passed to keep the maximum number of trees possible. Backers pointed to a poll taken at the time which found the Point's "natural beauty" one of its top five assets. Others wanted zoning to keep the Point's cottage look and feel. Some residents derided the pro-tree and pro-cabin camps for stubbornly reminiscing about the 1950s summer cottage vibe when they felt the Point needed investment, growth and jobs.[489]

Current attitudes continue to try to balance growth and character. An October 2000 survey found the top three desires of the local population were sewers, sustainable growth and a pier. The findings showed most wanted to preserve the local character and for more overnight accommodations to be available. A 2002 poll of economic priorities for the Port of Bellingham found most wished to preserve and improve the quality of life by balancing provisioning of services with environmental and recreational opportunities.[490] A public trail system on Point Roberts was called for by the Whatcom Trails Association in 2002.[491] Local committees have controversially enforced rules which prohibit residents from living year round in RVs on empty residential lots; such lots are commonly seen on the Point.

In 2010 the Point Roberts Community Advisory Committee was formed and took over the Character Plan Committee. At its first meeting, like the city advisors in a SimCity simulation computer game all advocating for special interests, ideas began pouring in for what was needed to be done to make life easier in Point Roberts. To cite one example, the issue of local taxes is handled by the committee. The Point's residents endure inconveniences from border traffic and a border-influenced economy, but most of the sales taxes generated in Point Roberts from that commerce go to the mainland. The only portion of that tax revenue which is directly earmarked to benefit the exclave is the town's local gas tax from the Point Roberts Transportation Benefit District (TBD). TBD funds must be used for road construction, maintenance and repair, but voices in the community wanted to spend some of the roughly $7,000 a month the TBD receives to fund a special school bus which would serve the kids who stay after school on the mainland to attend sports and school events. That idea was deemed too far out of scope and the 2014 funds were spent creating a sign-posted scenic loop around the exclave. In 2017, after thirty-eight years in one form or another, the Character Plan was dissolved with its provisions put into standard zoning codes.

Point Roberts has a vast array of community organizations. There is something for everybody. Prominent organizations in the community include a chamber of commerce, a taxpayers association (which includes Americans and Canadians), a voters' interests group (just for Americans), an emergency preparedness group, a seniors program and food bank. A transportation committee organized community van service in 2003. There is a garden club, a historical society, a society to lobby for a lighthouse to be built at Lighthouse Park and a walking group. Several groups advocate for animals, including groups for orcas, herons and eagles.

Residents are opinionated and there are some partisan camps with regard to taxation, county governance, private property, community landmarks and environmental concerns. Some guard against zoning changes which would lead to rapid development and growth; others are trying to stimulate the economy and bring jobs to the community. These viewpoints often clash when development proposals and zoning law changes arise. It gets all the more interesting in a small exclave like Point Roberts, where everybody knows everyone and their business. A quick run to the supermarket often leads to running into somebody and getting caught up on all the gossip. Lest one think it's just small town squabbles, not only are there frequent verbal arguments and shouting matches at meetings, but an actual fistfight broke out at a water board meeting in April 1995.[492]

Politically, Point Roberts is more of a swing-city than other towns. Whereas Bellingham tends to vote for the Democratic Party, and agriculturally-based towns in Whatcom County like Lynden and Ferndale are strongly Republican, Point Roberts has a mixed voting record. In the 2016 general election, Hillary Clinton received 512 votes (66%) compared to 211 votes for Donald Trump (27%).

President Obama carried Point Roberts in both 2008 and 2012, with 58% and 55% of the vote respectively. However, in the 2000 election, the Point narrowly swung Republican. George W. Bush carried Point Roberts narrowly over Al Gore, 47% to 46%. The 1996 election was a Democratic year on the Point, but the non-establishment vote was very present. Bill Clinton won 45% of the vote in Point Roberts (compared to 49% nationally), Bob Dole captured 42% in Point Roberts (compared to 41% nationally), and Ross Perot received votes from 13% of the Point Roberts electorate, far above the 8% he won nationally that year. In 1992, Perot came in second: Clinton got 128 votes (43%), Perot 83 (29%), Bush 80 votes (27%).[493]

Third party candidates capture a larger-than-average share of votes on the Point. Point Roberts has a large progressive voters block; in 2016, Jill Stein of the Green Party came in third with 30 votes (3.8%). In one of his campaigns, Green Party candidate Ralph Nader captured nearly seven per cent of the vote in Point Roberts, compared to only 2.7% nationally. A large libertarian bloc on the Point voted for Gary Johnson in 2016 with 21 votes (2.7%); the Libertarian Party vote often hovers at three per cent in Point Roberts, significantly higher than its national average.

 Turn right on Boundary Bay Road. In a half-mile or so, pause at Cedar Point Avenue.

Boundary Bay Road was originally named Goodman Road, and still is called that north of Johnson Road.

ROADS

Some early roads were built within the exclave by the Icelandic settlers in the 1890s, but the first graded roads within Point Roberts were built by the township in 1914.

Well into the 1920s, most people got to Point Roberts by water. Transportation to and from the exclave by land was a long journey from anywhere. People walking or riding horses used trails to go to Ladner Landing for any supplies not available in Point Roberts. By foot it was a three-hour trek each way, basically a full day trip. Going to the U.S. mainland by land involved a trip along the beach, which, with a laden domestic animal in tow, could take a day and a half each way. It wasn't until 1919 the first road reached Point Roberts from the outside world.

Enterprising locals bought graders and found employment creating and maintaining dirt roads for the township. This continued until the mid-1930s when the county took over responsibility for road construction and repair, dealing the locals an economic blow, compounding the recession caused by the closure of the fish traps.[494] Residents grumbled that the county put them out of work and insisted on maintaining the roads, but then complained about the costs and logistical issues with maintaining a crew to repair the roads in the remote exclave. Hard surface roads first appeared in 1945 when a rock crusher was brought from Bellingham.[495] Today the five square miles of Point Roberts contain thirty miles of paved roads.[496] At fifteen miles, our tour covers half the roads on the Point.

The mundane topic of road works sometimes gets exciting. Case in point: the June 22, 1970 Battle of Point Roberts. A Point Roberts property owner, Philip Sopow, hired Ernest Astells, a Canadian grader operator from Burnaby, to create 1000-foot Cedar Point Avenue for his residential development. Judging the work shoddy, Sopow refused to pay the $680 bill (about $4,300 today), and told Astells, who had come over the border with his grader to collect payment, he had resorted to hiring another firm from Vancouver to fix the work. Astells told Sopow he would tear up the road if payment wasn't made. Thinking it a bluff, Sopow nonetheless phoned the police. Deputy Sheriff Chad Caswell pulled up just as Astells, at the controls of his grader, tore up the asphalt of the new road. Caswell maneuvered his patrol car in the grader's path, but Astells plowed on forward, careening into Caswell's vehicle, which led to many more police arriving on the scene. Several local citizens were quickly deputized. Astells fled for the border in the grader followed by the police in a low-speed chase at thirty miles per hour down Benson Road and up Tyee Drive. The officers blasted a hail of bullets at the grader's large tires to apprehend Astells before he reached the boundary line. In a scene reminiscent of the Dukes of Hazzard racing to safety across the county line, Astells slipped across the line back into Delta unscathed, with the American police following him through the border and the Canadian officials just watching them all go by. The grader finally died at the bottom of 56th Street. Apparently, there is no extradition treaty for malicious cul de sac damage or reckless grader driving.

The Battle of Point Roberts is a modern-day Salish Sea folk story and it appropriately has a folk ballad to go along with it. Folk musician Paddy Graber thought Astells would go down in Salish Sea legend as a folk hero, prompting him to write a folk song about Astells called "The Re-Grading Tale of 1970." Graber wrote in 1978, "This is a song that crosses back and forth from Canadian Territory to American Territory... a true account... We have very, very few local folk heroes, and I'm sure this particular character is bound to become one."[497] The song, played to the tune of the traditional Irish song "The Holy Ground," begins, "Oh, the yarn I'm goin' to spin you occurred in the month of June, The twenty-second was the date, and it ended 'round about noon. It's about a grader operator, by now you know him well. He lives in beautiful B.C. and his name is Ernest Astells."[498] The song goes on for forty more lines of rhyming verse, telling the tale of the Battle of Point Roberts.

Point Roberts' address system is easy to figure out. Most streets which run north-south have two or three-digit house or building numbers. Numbers start at the border at 0 and increase going south toward South Beach. On east-west roads, four-digit building numbers increase from 1000 on the western side and reach the 2000s on the Point's eastern side. Building numbers are generally odd numbers on the south and west sides of the street, as in the rest of Whatcom County.[499]

Many homes, most of which were mere cabins, had no house numbers originally. Many homeowners were more likely to post a cutesy cabin name than a house number near the front door. As late as 1983 public officials were pleading with residents to post house numbers and even took out ads in the paper which offered the phone numbers for officials who could help you figure out what your house number was, as evidently large numbers of homeowners did not know. A fire official at the time said in over fifteen per cent of all emergency calls the first responders had trouble finding the house because of lack of house numbers.[500]

The top speed limit anywhere on the Point was lowered to thirty miles per hour (fifty kilometres per hour) in May 1983, and other than a handful of main roads, most streets are twenty-five miles per hour (forty kilometres per hour).[501] Regardless, the lanes are narrow, the cabins dense. People stroll and bike in the street and kids chase balls and pets. Many drivers are senior citizens. With all these obstacles, you'll find yourself naturally slowing to a crawl in the narrow lanes in most residential neighborhoods; it's just that kind of place. Indeed, the Point has the lowest accident rate in Whatcom County.[502]

A common complaint about the roads in Point Roberts is the lack of sidewalks and street lights. When the sun sets before 4 P.M. in the winter, Point Roberts is a very dark place indeed. With only a handful of streetlights, the isolated feeling in Point Roberts is amplified by this darkness. Visitors and seasonal residents have gone home, so the cottage neighborhoods are dark, their narrow lanes deserted. Many year-round residents say it's their favorite season. One really feels the isolation of exclave life in the long, dark, windy, wet, winter evenings.

 Turn left on Benson Road.

Benson Road is named for Kristjan Benson, the first Icelandic settler in Point Roberts. Confusingly, Benson Road was originally called Boundary Bay Road.

Travel west on Benson Road for three-tenths of a mile. Turn right into Baker Community Field; its sign will be facing away from you. Park in the lot and take the trail through the forest to the community field.

PARKS

When the old township system was dissolved in 1969, much of the township's property was transferred to the Parks district.[503]

Preserved for the community's use, this eighty-acre park includes a large tract of forest which extends all the way north to Johnson Road. The native forest is crisscrossed with trails.

The park also features a large sports field, named Baker Community Field. The Baker for whom the field is named was John Baker.[504] Baker was born in March 1900 and moved to Point Roberts in the 1920s. Boys would commonly play ball on Baker's field (elsewhere on the Point; this was not his field). Baker would come out and play with them and he eventually formed and coached the first baseball teams on the Point. He saw it as giving back: he thought kids busy with sports would stay out of trouble. The Point Roberts Pirates baseball team was formed and Baker raised $211 ($3000 in current money) in the community for uniforms and equipment. Dubbed "the man behind the Pirates," Baker was still handing out trophies into the 1970s. In 1972, the Pirates won twelve straight in the South Delta Amateur Peewee division to take the John Baker Cup, the league championship trophy; Baker himself presented the trophy named after him.

The land for the park was acquired by the township for eighty dollars in 1936 in a delinquent tax sale; that would be $1400 today.[505] For years it was undeveloped forest, but also home to a gravel pit and the town's dump. The park has never had a formal name, even to this day. For many decades this land was simply called "Garbage Dump Park"[506] because in its midst was the town landfill. There was no gate; folks would simply drive into the forest and dump their trash into the huge pile of garbage in a clearing. The open landfill attracted huge numbers of rats; complaints about the rats are frequently seen in township meeting minutes going back to the 1940s. In winter shallow swampy areas surrounding the dump froze over, offering a chance to ice skate, but long-time residents tell of skates hitting rats frozen in the ice.[507] The unfortunate Garbage Dump Park moniker actually hampered efforts to formalize the park and create the ball field. In the early 1970s, town voters approved a $35,000 levy to develop the park and clear land for the ball field, but the matching funds needed from the county hit a snag due to the presence of a garbage dump. In what the Point Roberts Community Association described as "difficulties,"[508] the parks district learned health regulations dictated the dump be removed if county funds were to be used to create a park. Folks remarked that only in Point Roberts could it apparently be easier to get the county to move an entire landfill than to cough up a few grand to widen a forest clearing into a ball field. The community could not afford the cost of moving the dump – there aren't many alternative locations in the five square miles of the peninsula – and in the end the county government on the mainland withdrew the matching funds. Volunteer labor from the community had to be used to create the ball field.[509]

Today Baker Community Field offers a baseball diamond with bleachers, a large grass field and a playground surrounded by forty acres of forested trails. The original plan called for a 100-foot long concrete slab to accommodate outdoor dancing and shuffleboard, which could be flooded in winter for ice skating, hockey and curling, but the loss of the matching funds meant it was never built.[510] During certain hours of the day, the ball field is the only off-leash area on the Point where dogs can run free. A skate park opened in 2005. In late summer, acres of blackberry bushes hang laden with fruit. (A local adage questions whether the blackberry should be the official fruit or official weed of Point Roberts.) At the northwest corner of the field a trail leads into the interior of the park, past the old dump site, now one massive blackberry patch. A large trail junction forks with one path going west to the Point's mobile phone tower, with more trails in forest beyond. Another trail goes north through the forest to Johnson Road, and one extends east toward a large cylindrical water tower. This is the highest elevation on Point Roberts, at 235 feet above sea level. The one million gallon water tower was filled with water from local wells and today sports some amazing graffiti.

The park features public washrooms, built in June 1988.[511] During the Canadian Era, with up to 10,000 visitors on a summer weekend – many drinking copious quantities of beer in the big taverns and on the beaches – public urination was a big problem. In 1969, a survey of the population found no fewer than 93% of residents said they were extremely concerned there were no public washrooms on the Point. It wasn't uncommon for strangers to go to private homes to ask to use the toilet. Today there are five public washrooms on the Point, one per square mile.

SCHOOL

The lucky youngsters of Point Roberts get to go to school in this park. The Point has had a school since 1886. Enrolment in 1890 was twenty-seven, but when the first Icelanders began arriving in large numbers, the school grew big enough to become School District 68 in 1893. Attendance shot up to eighty-three kids by 1908, requiring four teachers who earned $30 to $45 per month ($750 to $1120 today). A bigger four-room school was built in 1909, but only after a community meeting generated some passionate opinions about funding it; a favorite town legend still told today recalls one guy told another he was so narrow between the eyes that he could look through a keyhole with both of them.[512] Macroeconomic impacts on Point Roberts' population were seen again in the 1930s. In 1931 the school enrolment was still in the

Figure 72: Baker Field and Point Roberts Primary School. Photo by Mark Swenson.

eighties. But after fish traps were banned in 1934, enrolment plummeted by half. In 1938 there were only forty-four students, just in time for the new school built by the New Deal's Works Progress Administration to open in 1937. That school was today's Community Center on Gulf Road. The Point Roberts School District was merged with the Blaine School district in 1940.[513]

After seventy years of having a local school, this community institution closed in 1963 when attendance fell to just a handful of kids. There would be no school in Point Roberts for the next thirty years, meaning all the schoolchildren, even in the little kindergartners, had to endure an hour on a school bus each way to the school on the mainland in Blaine, going through the formalities and waits at four international border crossings every single day. By 1978, population growth on the Point meant there were fifty-eight school-aged kids.[514] As attendance grew, a new school was built behind the fire hall in September 1993 on land donated by the parks district.[515] It has two classrooms, educating students from kindergarten and first through third grades. The school is staffed by one full time teacher and a full-time assistant who also serves as school secretary. The Point Roberts Primary school is designated by the state of Washington as a "Remote and Necessary School" which entitles it to special funding. It can accommodate thirty-five students, but enrollment averages fifteen and service levels are revisited annually, meaning a grade can be added or dropped each year. Currently, at fourth grade the kids go to school in Blaine, a fifty mile round trip every single day. Sports, drama, music, dances and similar extracurricular activities require parents to make evening runs to the mainland in dinnertime rush hour. Some local kids go to private school in Tsawwassen or are home-schooled rather than face the ordeal of four daily border crossings. In 2005, a smuggling operation involving a sixteen-year-old was busted; the teen had been smuggling eight pounds of pot a day in her book bag, and her friends who were in on it collectively moved as much as thirty pounds of pot a day.[516]

FIRE DEPARTMENT

The local fire hall is next door. In Chicago, it's Mrs. O'Leary and the cow in 1871. In San Francisco, it's 1906, Seattle, 1889, Vancouver's was in 1886. In Point Roberts, the year 1908 is known as the year of the big fire. In August 1908 much of the south and east of Point Roberts, including this area, burned in a crown fire, the treetop flames jumping from tree to tree. Every available man on the Point dropped everything to put it out, including the cannery workers,[517] and quite a few of the women and children pitched in as well. After an all-night effort to put it out, the devastation became clear. The cedar fence posts which had taken the settlers so long to drive in to the ground were gone. Burned spikes of fir tree trunks, their top greenery charred off, covered the blackened landscape. The hard work paid off; most structures were saved. There are trees on the Point today which show evidence of the 1908 fire.

Figure 73: Fire Hall and Medical Clinic.

In the early summer of 1945 with World War II still underway, another large wildfire threatened much of the Point. A large grass and brush fire was threatening many homes and quickly grew to the point outside help was called in. That help would come from the Boundary Bay Royal Canadian Air Force Base just northeast of Tsawwassen. There was a sense of urgency from the base staff since quite a few RCAF personnel had rented homes in Point Roberts. The local fire department was busy using bulldozers to create fire guards around the homes. The RCAF guys were asked to get a fire hose set up to douse the flames. Fortunately, it was a minus tide that day at Maple Beach allowing the RCAF 1940 International pumper to drive a third of a mile (500m) out onto the sandy tide flats so their pumper could suck in water from Boundary Bay and propel it through a hose onto the homes lining the shore. Soon water was flowing and other fire departments arrived, connecting to the RCAF pumper. But the air force crew from the base were landlubbers and not aware of the concept of tides. Soon Boundary Bay was lapping at the floorboards of the pumper and the crew, mostly from Winnipeg, was surprised to find the water had nearly reached the engine's battery. Trying to drive the pumper back to shore quickly resulted in it being stuck in the mud.[518] It was finally towed off the beach to help extinguish the fire.

The current fire department was organized in January 1955 after Ladner announced they would stop handling fire calls for Point Roberts.[519] In August 1956 the fire crew bought a used pump, five hundred feet of fire service hose and a used fire truck from the state surplus property division. Almost immediately, there was a serious beach fire threatening the long line of driftwood along the shore. Seawater was sucked up through the newly-acquired equipment, making quick work of the fire, but the pump was ruined by seaweed and gravel. Local ingenuity was used to repair the pump. Thereafter, water was pumped from wells or ditches. By November the fire department had procured a siren, buckets, axes and a two-wheel trailer to tow all the gear.[520]

In 2013, Fire Chief Christopher Carleton announced the fire hydrants in the exclave were in bad need of repair. Most had faded after years of neglect. With paint peeled off the drab color was camouflaged in the tan dry grass, making them hard to find in emergencies. He announced the public was allowed, even encouraged, to paint the fire hydrants of Point Roberts. A Cow Parade-like community art project was born. Carleton made it a contest. Using fire department-provided paint and supplies, residents competed for prizes. The result is over 150 hand-painted fire hydrants across the community, each a unique work of art. The Point is slowly becoming known in the Salish Sea for its quirky, colorful hydrants. Visitors make it a game to try to find as many of the

Figure 74: Point Roberts fire hydrants are a community art project. Photo by Mark Swenson.

hydrants as they can; several websites enable visitors to map out a hydrant tour, and upload photo collections. As you drive along this tour, be on the lookout for the Point's creative fire hydrants, whose fun designs include the Vancouver Canucks, Tigger and R2-D2.

A fire hall opened in January 1958 on Gulf Road, and this one opened in 1979. A bingo operation had started at the Breakers tavern in 1973 and later the fire hall used to hold bingo games and sell pull tabs to fund its operations. Over the years proceeds were cashed in to buy new fire equipment in 1970 and in 1976 bingo profits funded the addition of the western wing of the fire hall. The Point's ambulance and quick response vehicle were bought with bingo funds. Hurt by the 2005 ban on smoking in bingo halls, the state reviewed its license after two quarters in the red and the bingo operation closed in November 2007.[521]

HEALTH CARE

Health care is a critical service for a community, but as late as 2003, there was no doctor or health care facility in Point Roberts. Its isolation meant there were major impediments to providing health care. Mainland doctors essentially couldn't come to Point Roberts due to complexities with customs regulations when crossing the border.[522] State law prevented Canadian doctors from establishing practices in Washington, so physicians in British Columbia were essentially only permitted to respond to emergency calls.[523] Prior to the opening of the clinic, locals had to go to the mainland to see a doctor, usually all the way to Bellingham. This sixty-mile round trip with four border crossings to see a health care professional meant many residents struggled with transportation or would weigh the severity of the health condition against the time and expense of such a long trip. Many health issues went without treatment. The lack of local health care services was a major factor in stunting the growth potential of Point Roberts. An April 1995 survey of voters found the second-most requested improvement wanted in the exclave was a medical facility; only a pier and ferry to Blaine scored higher.[524] Some residents purchase a special Point Roberts insurance policy for emergency helicopter service from Point Roberts to the mainland, which can cost $10,000.[525]

The Ayden Wellness Clinic was created in 2003. The only one of its kind in the state of Washington, it was sponsored by the local fire district but funded by federal grant. This saddled the clinic with many rules to meander, but at least health care had finally arrived to the Point Roberts. The initial grant ran until April 2005, so a new special district was proposed to provide the services permanently. In February 2005, the Point Roberts Public Hospital District special district was passed by 80% of voters.[526] A nurse practitioner is employed along with a part-time nurse and assistants. Housed in the western end of the fire hall, there's a helipad next to the clinic for helicopters from Bellingham for use in emergencies. The availability of primary and urgent care available contributed to recent growth of year-round residents. Residents can alleviate trips to the mainland for ancillary services and lab work. In the course of a year, the clinic has over 1200 visits, on average one visit per person on the Point.[527] Time your illnesses and injuries if you can; the clinic is only open Mondays, Tuesdays and Thursdays. There are no pharmacies in Point Roberts, and U.S. prescriptions usually can't be filled in Canada, so locals must travel to the mainland to fill most prescriptions.

 Continue west on Benson Road until you come to South Beach Road. Turn left.

PUBLIC SAFETY

The compound encircled by a chain-link fence on the left is the only actual administrative local government presence on Point Roberts, not counting of course the federal government's presence at the border crossing. This is where the local sheriff deputies work and live. Border towns inevitably spend more of their budget on law enforcement than other towns; it's just the cost of having an international border in your town. Persons not granted entry across the border are handed over to local law enforcement, driving up public protection costs. A study in the early 1980s found Blaine spends roughly double the Washington state average on law enforcement. With its much smaller population – Point Roberts is one-quarter the population of Blaine – law enforcement costs in Point Roberts are triple the Whatcom county average.[528] For years there was just one deputy assigned to Point Roberts, but public pleas for greater police presence amid all the sometimes-rowdy visitors and population growth led to a second deputy. However, the population of Point Roberts is not the same as how many people are physically present, and these same two deputies patrol the one million Canadians who cross the land border into Point Roberts each year. Over 35,000 Canadians can come to Point Roberts during a single Canadian long weekend and unlike Blaine, where many of the millions of Canadians who cross the border into that town continue their journey onward to Bellingham, at Point Roberts they are in Point Roberts because they want to be. Aside from some outbound marina traffic, those throngs stay in Point Roberts as there is nowhere else to go with one road in and one road out.

You should feel safe in Point Roberts. The overall crime rate in Point Roberts is sixty-three per cent lower than the national average and seventy-two per cent lower than the Washington state average. Point Roberts is often referred to as America's largest gated community, and with everybody's identification checked and face and car license plate photographed, local business promoters have claimed it has the lowest crime rate in all of Washington, with some claiming it's even the lowest in America. The statistics show Point Roberts is safer than eighty-one per cent of cities in the United States based on the violent crime rate. Property crime is seventy-one per cent lower than the Washington state average.[529]

Figure 75: The Point Roberts Jail. Photo by Mark Swenson.

Situated within the compound near the road is a small cinderblock building. This is the Point Roberts jail, built around 1964.[530] Despite the low crime rate, the occasional arrest is made where the accused is taken into custody. However, detainees generally cannot travel through Canada, and this jail is used to hold people either until air or boat transportation directly to the U.S. mainland can be arranged or extradition proceedings can be approved. Up to eight people can be detained in the jail, so hopefully no criminal baseball teams visit the Point.

JOHN MEIER

The most famous person to be detained in the Point Roberts jail was held there August 9, 1973. The story starts when John Meier took a job for Howard Hughes in Las Vegas in the mid-1960s. Hughes moved to Nevada for its low taxes but became concerned about nuclear radiation being so close to where the Atomic Energy Commission (AEC) was conducting atomic weapons tests in the desert. He decided to use his power and influence to try to kick the AEC out of Nevada; Meier was his right-hand man. As a result of the anti-AEC campaign, the Meier story spawns four tentacles. First, Meier witnessed a million-dollar bribe; second, Meier reached out to the presidential candidates on behalf of Hughes to buy influence; third, Meier's work on the anti-AEC campaign was associated with left-wing politics and thus as a political enemy to Richard Nixon; lastly, Meier would search for Hughes' whereabouts after he left Nevada to escape radiation. In the midst of all of that, Hughes had Meier invest in gold mines in Nevada for Hughes Corporation in anticipation of the U.S. leaving the gold standard. These five paths unfurl and then weave together in a story of international intrigue and high-stakes political drama, eventually leading through Point Roberts.

As part of the AEC campaign, Meier met with Thomas Murray Jr., son of a former AEC chairman, for his connections. Murray mentioned Air West was for sale and wondered if Hughes would like to buy it. Hughes' love for the aviation industry is well-known, and Meier was sure Hughes would be interested.

Hughes sent Meier to Miami on March 9, 1969. Meier emerged from his hotel room's bathroom as Ken Wright, the head of Hughes' charity, the Hughes Medical Institute, and Nixon friend Bebe Rebozo were exchanging an open briefcase containing a one million dollar bribe – equivalent to $6.6 million today – to fast-track the approval of Hughes' acquisition of Air West. Meier had just been implicated in an exchange which would hang over Nixon's presidency.[531]

Another prong of the anti-AEC campaign was to influence 1968 presidential candidates to shut down the AEC. President Johnson had been offered money to shutter the AEC. Hubert Humphrey turned down an offer to bankroll his entire presidential campaign if he would close the AEC. Meier had an appointment to meet with candidate Robert Kennedy in Los Angeles June 6, 1968, canceled by his assassination the evening prior. To connect with the Nixon campaign, Meier met with Rebozo and Richard's brother Don whilst he was in Los Angeles. Don wanted access to Hughes for a potential job offer and to get dirt on the Democrats from Meier; Meier tolerated the obnoxious Don to influence Richard Nixon.

After Don kept pestering Meier for intel on the Democrats, Meier and Humphreys concocted a plan to misguide Don and the Republicans. Meier told Don he could share advance copies of Humphrey's campaign speeches. Don thought he'd hit the jackpot when his leaked speech was later delivered verbatim by Humphrey. Don went back for more. The next step in the ruse was to leak to Don a Democratic Party election playbook. Of course, this time it would be fake, full of misleading data on the Democrats' polls, budgets and strategies.[532]

After Nixon's 1968 election, Meier's work on the anti-AEC campaign put him in the crosshairs of Nixon's Chief of Staff, John

Ehrlichman, for political payback. Meier was under federal government surveillance and the administration ensured the IRS took an extra-long look at his tax returns. Meanwhile, in the late 1960s, Hughes sensed the U.S. would go off the gold standard, leading to a spike in gold prices, so he instructed Meier to buy gold mines on his behalf. Shuttered gold mines are everywhere in the west and Hughes planned to lobby for federal subsidies to reopen them.

Fast forward to the end of Nixon's first term, in November 1971 Meier baited Don Nixon over dinner by mentioning the Democrats thought they had a good shot at winning the 1972 election because evidence of the Nixon-Hughes bribe had been turned over to the Democratic National Committee (DNC). Meier went on to say he was mulling a run for Senate and planned to disclose the bribe in his candidacy. Debriefing with Humphrey a few days later, the two of them surmised Richard Nixon would, assuming the worst, panic and do something crazy on the scale of his paranoia if he thought the IRS was going to discover his bribe.[533] Why smear Nixon if he'd smear himself?[534]

Meier turned down repeated offers in 1972 from the IRS to have them back off if Meier would disclose what info he had given the DNC. Meier's refusal coincided with the timing of the orders given by Nixon for the Watergate burglaries. Getting the Democrats' playbook was the cover for the break-ins, but only Nixon knew the real goal: making sure the Democrats didn't have info on the Hughes bribe. Of course, the irony was DNC Chairman Larry O'Brien had no info in his office about the bribe; Meier and Humphrey's ruse was just to make everybody think he did.[535]

Meanwhile, Meier's work on the gold mines came back to haunt him. A Hughes company sued Meier in March 1972 claiming Meier had laundered millions of dollars in the transactions. Meier had only negotiated the terms of the deals and never touched any cash, but Meier knew he needed Hughes' help to clear his name. Hughes had left Nevada in 1970 over concerns about radiation and his whereabouts were unknown. Meier finally tracked him down. Hughes was hiding out just twenty-five miles north of Point Roberts, in the Westin Bayshore Hotel in downtown Vancouver. Hughes was one week in to what would become a six month stay in the hotel's penthouse. Meier tried to get to him but was blocked by security. He left Vancouver for Albuquerque the next day, returning to a ransacked office and bugged phones and a final offer from the Nixon administration to share what info he gave the Democrats in exchange for an end to the IRS action.[536]

After three previous break-ins or attempted break-ins in May, the Watergate burglars were apprehended in the DNC offices June 16, 1972. The plan hatched by Meier and Humphrey to bait Nixon into doing something extreme to cover up the Hughes bribe was a success as Nixon's operatives were found in the act, pursuing the false trail, political theatre at its best. Meier told *Playboy* in 1976, "I'm fully convinced that one big reason for the break-in wasn't to get something on McGovern but to find out what I was telling the friends of O'Brien about Richard and Don Nixon and Hughes, to see if anything was going to break before the election."[537] Despite the urging of his advisors, George McGovern didn't have the balls to use the Air West bribe in the 1972 presidential campaign, and Nixon went on to reelection.

Things were serious. Nixon used IRS intimidation to silence Meier from giving harmful testimony about the Air West bribe in Watergate hearings, and the alleged tax evasion from the mining properties served to wreck Meier's credibility. The CIA used their connections to Hughes to intimidate Meier. The million-dollar bribe Meier had witnessed was so powerful three of the most powerful institutions in the world were colluding amongst themselves to keep him quiet. Facing four more years of Nixon harassment, Meier moved to Canada, settling just north of Point Roberts in a suburban home in Tsawwassen. The move was meant to avoid extradition for civil proceedings against him on the phony tax evasion charges and to try to regroup with his family in a new country. As we've seen from the unguarded border already on this tour, the imaginary line on the 49th parallel was not going to stop the feds, and Meier soon felt the heat.

It was still morning on August 9, 1973 and it was already swelteringly hot. Meier gathered his children, Johnny, aged 16, and Jimmy, who was celebrating his second birthday, his wife Joanne & Floyd Hargan, a family friend visiting from California and drove in his white Mercedes to go crabbing at a secret tide pool in Point Roberts. The family had been going down to Point Roberts frequently that summer to set the crab pot and play on the beach. They'd opened Jimmy's presents that morning and had a few hours to go crabbing before returning home for lunch, hopefully with some Dungeness crabs. As Meier pulled out of the driveway, he noticed two men who seemed to be watching them, and then followed them as they drove to the Point Roberts border crossing. Another car did a U-turn and followed until they pulled into U.S. border station. Normally there was just one official but today there were four, two in suits. Meier had an uneasy feeling and wanted to turn around and go back home, but the kids were thirsty so they drove into Point Roberts to get sodas. Two men in suits and sunglasses followed them in to Ben's Store. Meier knew something serious was going to happen, so he urged the family to leave and they piled into the car without the pop. Meier slipped his wallet and address book to Johnny, and quickly drove back up Tyee Drive to the border. As they approached the Canadian border booths, three police cars were parked broadside blocking the road, with several officers aiming drawn weapons at them from behind the barricade. Meier had to slam on the brakes to avoid colliding with the cars, and after the car lurched to a stop it was surrounded by officials. He lowered the window to ask what was up, and a revolver was pushed in against Meier's head. A voice said, "Get out of the car." Meier opened the door and stepped out onto Tyee Drive. He noticed two IRS agents in plainclothes pointing guns at him as he was handcuffed. Officials showed their power by addressing Hargan by name. Jimmy became hysterical as the family watched in horror at Meier's arrest. The others were released to go home and Meier was taken to the Point Roberts jail. Inside the two men in sunglasses from Ben's Store were sitting at a desk. He was locked in a small cell. He asked repeatedly why he was being held, but was ignored. The IRS agents and the sheriff left the room and two new men came in. Meier's heart sank when he saw from their badges they were Secret Service. Nixon had him.[538]

Meier was told if he cooperated, he could go home, otherwise it would get rough. Under arrest for income tax evasion, the price of freedom was to surrender all his documents in his and his lawyer's possession relating to Hughes, Nixon, the CIA and other federal agencies. In his book based on Meier's diaries, Gerald Bellett writes, "This was the shopping list the Watergate burglars had been given some fourteen months before. Incredible as it was, the search which had started in the nation's capital had now come to an insignificant corner of the United States... The White House was now hoping to prevent Meier from giving his information to the Watergate committee."[539]

Officials refused to allow Meier to call his lawyer or even his wife. Meier could not view his arrest warrant, but was given five minutes to agree to the terms. Meier declined. The Secret Service left and the IRS and sheriff's officers returned. The phone rang, and the officer told the caller, "No, he's not here. He's been taken to Seattle." Hanging up, he callously told Meier it had been his wife on the phone. One hour later Meier was taken from the Point Roberts jail, feet shackled and his hands in cuffs, driven to a dock and lowered into a small powerboat. The weather had turned rough, and Meier tried to steady himself in the choppy ride, but he fell to the floor. As he tried to stand up, a guard put his foot on Meier's back, keeping him face down as the oily bilge water splashed in his face on the bumpy ride across Boundary Bay. The guards had their guns drawn on him the entire trip to Blaine.[540]

Meier was arrested on income tax evasion, but his IRS case was still in front of a grand jury in Las Vegas. On the likelihood Meier would be indicted, the IRS and Secret Service had placed their operatives in Point Roberts. Their arrest of Meier was before the indictment was in and they had no legal warrant, but Meier's chance crossing into Point Roberts was an opportunity they simply could not pass up. Had Meier been in Canada when the indictment was handed down, all he had to do was not set foot in the United States and he would have been able to avoid arrest.[541] The allure of Point Roberts' beaches was Meier's downfall.

From Blaine, Meier was driven to Everett and arraigned in Snohomish County District Court. The CIA arranged news reporters and photographers to record his perp walk. He was then taken to Seattle where he appeared before a U.S. magistrate. The charge was failure to report income of $2.3 million earned from 1968 to 1970, most of it Meier's alleged share of money paid out by Hughes for mining properties. Roger Foley, the judge who ordered his arrest was the brother of an important witness against Meier, Joseph Foley, who had done the conveyancing of the mining properties for Hughes. Meier was allowed to post bail and returned home to Canada.

The CIA report from one of the agents involved in the operation that day in Point Roberts reads,

"August 6 1973 CIA follower flew to Vancouver when it was decided with the IRS and Intertel to do something about Meier. We were told by Intertel that he had been visiting Point Roberts with his children. On August 9 1973 Meier made the journey with three children and a man called Floyd Hargan. He was followed and the local law officers told to prepare to block the road if Meier attempted to leave before we were ready. As Meier left two armed officers arrested Meier. Arrangements had been made for a secret grand jury to hand down a tax charge indictment that day. Meier was held at Point Roberts jail for some hours while I debated with the IRS but they wanted to keep him themselves. I had not realized the IRS was working closely with Intertel and was unable to lay hands on Meier without a smell. Meier was taken to other jails and August 10 I arranged for some photographers to be at the jail to wire out picture of Meier in shackles."[542]

Essentially, what culminated at Point Roberts that August day in 1973 was the daunting resources of the Secret Service, IRS, police, courts and state agencies turned loose against a political enemy. Meier was apprehended in August 1973; it was that month the Watergate inquiry was careening toward the Nixon-Hughes bribe connection. These were the last panicky months of the administration; Nixon would resign within seven months.

George Boldt had written his Coast Salish fishing decision and was ready for his next case. Meier received a phone call in early 1974 telling him the dismaying news Foley had been replaced with Boldt, who now was given charge of his income tax evasion case. Meier was charged with conspiracy and income tax evasion from his 1969 tax return. Boldt is famous in the Salish Sea for his fishing decision, but he was already well known nationally in the early 1970s as the chair of Nixon's wage review board. It was an unpopular partisan committee designed to keep prices in check, but labor groups complained it did nothing to stop inflation but rather kept wages down. After government goons from the U.S. embassy barged into his hotel room in the London, a spooked Meier flew home to Tsawwassen, missing a hearing before Boldt; in so doing he became a fugitive in January 1975.[543]

The phone rang in the Meier home in Tsawwassen on May 23, 1975. The man calling was sure Meier would remember him, or one of the many mutual friends he claimed they had, but Meier couldn't place him. The caller proclaimed he was one of the best sound technicians and wiremen in North America and was offering to install a system in Meier's home whereby he could tape all his phone calls. The caller, Reice Hamel, rattled off many celebrities for whom he had worked including Barbra Streisand, the Who, Joan Baez and Frank Sinatra. He offered to drive his van to Meier's home in just a few minutes because he was nearby, calling from Point Roberts. Meier was wary, but agreed to a free consultation. Upon arriving, Hamel barged into Meier's living room, warning Meier his home was bugged. Concerned, Meier called B.C. Tel to report the bugs. When the phone company heard Hamel's name, they dispatched a technician to the Tsawwassen home immediately. Hamel was a pioneer in sophisticated remote recordings. He was known to B.C. Tel for having phone equipment in his possession which allowed users to make free long distance calls. B.C. authorities were looking for Hamel, who had slipped into Point Roberts. Local police on the Point were monitoring Hamel themselves, as he had a .38 automatic and a hungry Doberman in his van. The B.C. technician found and uninstalled Hamel's illegal equipment at Meier's home. This prompted Hamel, who was monitoring the lines he installed from back in Point Roberts, to phone Meier to complain about him squealing to B.C. Tel. Meier was sensitive to the fact a strange man had installed equipment in his home which allowed his phone to be monitored without interception, and kept B.C. Tel informed of Hamel's comments. B.C. Tel responded by tapping Hamel's line in Point Roberts, since B.C. Tel provided the phone service to Point Roberts in those days.[544]

Less than two months later, three Whatcom County sheriff deputies and a B.C. Tel security official arrested Hamel on July 18, 1975 in Point Roberts. Officers searched Hamel's property and found state-of-the-dart bugging equipment; his van was nothing less than a high-tech mobile surveillance unit. The equipment was so cutting edge the cops had never seen it before; they were covetous of its capabilities like tapping a phone just by dialing its number, and equipment which self-destructed like in the movies. Hamel was charged with having toll fraud devices in his possession and freed after posting bail. Hamel phoned Meier in the middle of his famous interview for *Playboy* magazine. "I'm gonna come round there and kill you," he raged. Meier called the RCMP to report the threat, who arranged for the Delta police to grab Hamel as he crossed the border from Point Roberts. They seized a handgun and escorted him back into Point Roberts warning him to stay away. This troubled the RCMP to the extent they changed all the phone lines at their Vancouver headquarters.[545]

There are no more Point Roberts references – our scope – but Meier's fascinating story goes on much further. It is well-worth reading his full account, a man with such an amazing story to tell.

He ended up being found guilty – against overwhelming evidence in his favor – in the tax evasion case in 1976 and was extradited to the United States in May 1979 [546] after being held under a one million dollar bond; at the time only Patty Hearst had faced such a high bail amount.[547] After thirty months in jail, Meier was paroled in January 1981. In the middle of all that, Meier ran for the Democratic nomination for Senator of New Mexico in 1972. Meier finally found Hughes in a Bahamanian cryonics chamber Meier himself had purchased five years earlier, leading to Hughes officially being declared dead. He sold bonds to build a harbor and airport in Tonga for King Taufa'ahau Tupou IV against the U.S. government's wishes and faced retaliation from the U.S. In a series of events worthy of a spy movie, connections in Australia arranged for him to visit a Chinese restaurant where he was then directed to the Cuban embassy, who directed him to a nearby public plaza where a contact handed him a New Zealand passport with a fake identity. With this he was able to get back home to the Roberts peninsula via Europe.

Among his other accomplishments and adventures, Meier found time to write the official book for the first Earth Day in 1970, *Speaking for the Earth*. Years later, his friend U.S. Senator Mike Gravel, who ran for U.S. president in 2008, credited Meier with preventing the spread of nuclear weapons[548] and stated Meier had been persecuted by the U.S. government for being "the man who knew too much about too many bad people." Those bad people caught up with John Meier on a chance crabbing trip to Point Roberts in 1973.

 Turn around and go back to Benson Road, turn left, and then turn right on Mill Road.

RESOURCE EXTRACTION

From their peak between 1914 and 1917, logging camps and a busy sawmill harvested the Point's old growth forests. Mill Road was originally a skid road, where logs were slid to Joseph Largaud's sawmill. Mill Road was originally part of Johnson Road.

 Continuing north on Mill Road. At the stop sign at Johnson Road, go straight.

This extension of Mill Road between Johnson and Province Roads was added in 1970. On the left hand side of the road, just beyond the intersection with Province Road is the Point's largest gravel pit. It was an active sand excavation pit operating under a strip mine permit in the early 1970s with a steady stream of trucks coming and going. Each of the huge dump trucks carried ten cubic yards of fill as part of an operation which was removing a total of 300,000 cubic yards. The sand would not benefit any infrastructure projects on the Point; it was all trucked out through the border crossing.[549] The entire area has a one million cubic yard potential, but repeated attempts in recent years to get permits to extract more from the site have been unsuccessful.

Figure 76: The Point Roberts gravel pit was a large active work site in 1972. Source: Point Roberts Guide.

At one time there were several gravel pits on the Point. The current refuse transfer station on Johnson Road was formerly a gravel pit. There was a gravel pit at the entrance to Lily Point Park on the north side of APA Road. Diefenbaker Park in Tsawwassen just north of the boundary line was the largest gravel pit in South Delta. Local kids loved playing in the unfenced pit, considered a blight on Tsawwassen and the entrance to Point Roberts. Tragedy struck in January 1973 when a seven-year-old Tsawwassen boy went missing. A Point Roberts sheriff was among the search teams. Five hours later the boy's body was found; he had fallen through the ice into four feet of water and drowned. This accident galvanized earlier proposals to close the pit and turn it into a park and garden. Approved in 1975, Diefenbaker Park opened in September 1980, beautifying the Roberts peninsula and the approach to the Point.

 Turn right onto Province Road.

After meandering through a residential neighborhood, Province Road turns into Point Roberts' own version of San Francisco's famous Lombard Street, billed as the crookedest street in the world. Difficult to maintain, it was dubbed the "roughest section of road in Whatcom County" in 1978. The road snakes back and forth as you descend the ridge down to the next stop, Maple Beach. (If this steep switchback is difficult for your vehicle, turn left onto Province Road from Mill Road.)

At the bottom of Province Road, you come to a T-junction at Roosevelt Way. Turn right. You were on Roosevelt Way at the beginning of this tour on the west side of Point Roberts; you are now on Roosevelt Way on the east side. Roosevelt runs along the U.S. side of the boundary; the homes on the right side of the street are in the United States and the homes on the left side are in Canada.

CHAPTER 6 • HANGIN' OUT AT THE POINT

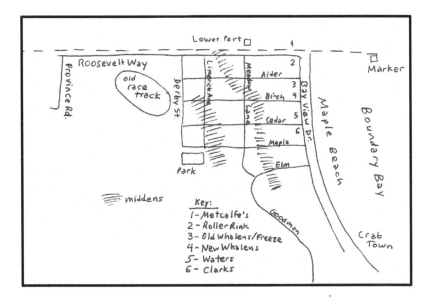

Figure 77: Route map of Chapter 6. Explore Maple Beach. Distance: 1 mile (1.6km).

Maple Beach is a community within a community. Occupying the northeast corner of Point Roberts, it holds much historical and cultural significance. For thousands of years it was the home of the Coast Salish people and in the 1890s it was settled by the Whalen family. For decades this neighborhood was known as Boundary Bay, thought of by some as a separate community than the rest of Point Roberts. The cottage community continues on the opposite side of the border. Today the U.S. side is called Maple Beach, but the neighborhood on the Canadian side is still called Boundary Bay. We'll use the term Maple Beach for consistency with its current name. Maple Beach grew as a place for recreation; in its heyday, it offered camping and cottages, a half-dozen businesses and seaside recreation on a warm water sandy beach. It was a popular destination for generations of Canadians.

 Go three blocks and turn right on Derby Street.

RACETRACK

The large grassy field to your right ringed by a split-rail fence once was a racetrack. The original horse stables, a long low-slung blue building, still stand along Roosevelt Way. The half-mile track was owned by Mike Whalen and Frank Farrell and operated from July 1951 to 1954. Thoroughbred horse harness racing was on offer every Sunday, with betting. The races attracted over two thousand spectators to the grandstands each Sunday, seven times the local population.[550] Complaints mounted about the dust from the track coating the cabins in Maple Beach. They hosed down the track, but this took most of the water pressure for the whole community. Business declined, and to reinvent itself, car racing was introduced but this generated more dust than ever. The track quickly closed after that.[551] For the next half-century this space was an RV park, which closed in 2008. Its closure meant dozens of families had a month to dismantle summer hideaways they had spent years building since the 1950s.[552] Both the track and the RV park are examples of how Maple Beach flourished on fun.

At the end of the street is Maple Beach Community Park. Owned by the local homeowners association, it has a picnic shelter, basketball court, playground, grassy field, benches and even a Little Free Library paperback book exchange. It's a charming and cozy park nestled up against a steep forested hill. For thousands of years, the Coast Salish people also found this very spot cozy and protected.

 Turn left onto Maple Street.

MIDDENS

The most common archaeological remains around the Salish Sea coastline are middens. Middens are physical remnants of ancient communities or seasonal camps. Middens are made up of large piles of discarded shells; fire-altered rocks, ash and charcoal; housing ruins, such as hearths, storage pits, household artifacts and post moulds; and skeletal remains of humans and animals. Human remains are commonly found in Salish Sea middens.

One major Salish Sea midden to which all other middens are compared is the Great Marpole Midden, named for the Vancouver neighborhood in which it was located. This midden was the site of an ancient Musqueam village inhabited continuously from 4000 years ago to 200 years ago, and is one of the largest pre-contact middens in western Canada. The Marpole village embodied a distinct and unique culture type called Marpole Culture, which dates from 2400 BP. The midden was first disturbed by white settlers in 1884 for road construction. Charles Hill-Tout did extensive excavations there in 1892 for the Art, Historical, and Scientific Association of Vancouver.[553] Interest in middens exploded after 1892. Harlan Ingersoll Smith, an archaeologist from the American Museum of Natural History working with the Jessup North Pacific Expedition from 1897 to 1899, dug through the midden looking for human remains. It would be Charles Edward Borden, a professor of the University of British Columbia, who would connect the remains and artifacts found at Marpole with the contemporary Musqueam First Nations people in archaeological digs in the 1950s and 1960s.[554] Most of the remaining sections of the midden were destroyed when the site became the Fraser Arms Hotel at the foot of Granville Street despite the midden having been recognized as a National Historic Site of Canada in 1933.[555] As recently as January 2012, condo construction in the area uncovered intact remains. (The condo development was halted.) When other middens are excavated in the region, comparisons are made to the Marpole midden. Most midden artifacts show parallels to the Marpole culture. But before Borden excavated at the Great Marpole midden, he got experience with midden excavations in Point Roberts, right here at Maple Beach Community Park.

Maple Beach is largely tidal sands and silts which built up when Point Roberts was an island 10,000 to 5,000 years ago. Land filled in about 4,500 years ago, rendering Point Roberts a peninsula.[556] That's about the time the earliest settlement at Maple Beach is known.

Maple Beach is the home of one of the most-famous middens in the Salish Sea, and it remains "an important enigma in the literature of Northwest Coast archaeology."[557] The site, known as the Whalen Farm Middens, is immense. There were two separate midden areas. The western midden was 1000 feet long, two residential lots wide and nine feet high. The top of the midden piles were made up of larger shells including horse clams, butter clams and some mussels. The lower levels had many more mussel shells along with basket cockles.[558] Closer to the beach was a much longer midden. This midden was a long, skinny 2500 foot long line of shells, one residential lot wide and at least six feet tall, higher in some areas. Many other smaller middens dotted the area, and much of the Maple Beach neighborhood was scattered with midden shells, and the complete shell ridge extended over the border as well.

The name of this site comes from Mike Whalen, who had a farm on the site, as did his father, P.J. Whalen, who originally squatted on this land in 1891. There were minor agricultural disturbances to the site until 1955 when most of the middens were destroyed as Maple Beach expanded from just a few seaside buildings to a full cottage community four blocks inland. Local resident Edgar Dunning recalled that in his youth in the late 1920s, "One summer us kids camped on what we later found out was an Indian midden. They came and excavated it" several years later.[559] Bulldozers ripped through most of the middens in the 1950s; an archaeology student who happened to be there found the bulldozer blade had exposed human remains. Today, the bulldozing and housing development would be immediately halted; back then it wasn't understood these were sacred archaeological and cultural treasures. Nonetheless, there are still remnants of the midden today. The western midden is totally leveled now, but a ridge between Meadow and Bay View Roads is the remnants of the eastern midden.

Several excavations of the middens have brought archaeologists to Maple Beach to study the ancient societies which first inhabited Point Roberts. Harlan Smith was the first archaeologist to study the Whalen Farm site, issuing papers as part of the Jessup North Pacific Expedition in 1901, 1903 and 1907, and then a larger study in 1925 for the Canadian Museum of Civilization. In this study Smith found several deep and large pits amongst the middens thought to be sites of longhouses. Smith found net-sinking stones used in reef netting, club-like weapons, and clam-digging tools made from antlers. Burial cairns were also discovered on Smith's excavations. At the point where the middens meet the tall ridge towering over Maple Beach, pits around four feet deep and ten feet long were found covered by boulders. At the bottom of the pits, caked in two feet of mold and pieces of wood, perhaps a decomposed casket of some form, were human skeletal remains.

The most-famous dig occurred in the summers of 1949 and 1950 by Charles Borden and his crew. Mike Whalen had dug up skeletal artifacts whilst plowing in July 1949. He contacted the Archaeology Department at the University of British Columbia.[560] Borden was on the scene quickly, conducting a formal dig. And just in time; in 1951, much of the inland portion of the midden was bulldozed for the race track. Borden's objectives at Whalen Farm were to "recover as complete a picture as possible of the life and culture of ancient people at various periods of their history" and "follow their migrations and attempt to determine the nature of their relationships with other groups."[561]

They focused on the inland midden, cutting a large trench through the midden ridge. The dig essentially cut a slice through the midden three residential lots wide, beginning at the present-day intersection of Limerick and Maple Streets, continuing east along Maple Street for a third of a block. Using pointed mason trowels, grapefruit knives, spoons, dentistry tools, and one-quarter inch screens, Borden reported finding a large hearth and eleven post molds ranging from three to eight inches wide. About 450 artifacts were found, including cutting blades made of stone and beaver teeth. The archaeologists discovered various artifacts including spear fishing, barbed antlers, harpoons, carvings and ornaments. Micro-blades were found; the first ever in the Salish Sea. One discovery provides a clue to how the people adorned themselves. The team catalogued necklaces, earrings, and even a lip ring upper-class women would wear.[562] There was evidence of weaving from 3000 years ago.[563] Borden also found human skeletal remains; the dig revealed thirteen of them over the two year effort. In the older burials the remains faced west, but the newer burials contained remains facing east. A study of the bones in 1958 found a couple cases of arthritis and tooth abscesses.[564] At the time, it was thought the middens were only a couple hundred years old, but solid carbon dating of charcoal samples performed in 1952 at the University of Saskatchewan put the age much, much older. The lower parts of the midden were reported at 2450 ± 160 BP, and a sample from the middle of the middens came in at 1580 ± 140 BP.[565] In 1997, the more accurate radiocarbon process was used at Washington State University on another charcoal sample from the site, placing the date at 2110 ± 65 years BP. Essentially, all these readings indicate use of Maple Beach by the Coast Salish people dating back to four thousand years ago.[566]

As late as the 1970s, there were still intact middens in Maple Beach.   One respectful homeowner contacted Simon Fraser University's Department of Archaeology in 1972 informing them of his intention to bulldoze one of the last large intact portions of middens.   Brian Seymour and a crew rushed to the site to perform salvage excavations on Maple Street just east of Meadow Lane. Seymour dug several pits into the top of the midden, three to six feet wide and up to twelve feet deep.   Based on the kinds of artifacts Seymour's team found and the age of the middens, this was thought to be from a native Marpole culture.   Three additional burial remains were found, including one of a teenage boy.   The burial cairns were covered by rocks, and boulders on top of the rocks. Unlike Borden, Seymour catalogued animal remains.   Besides the shells, Seymour noted dog bones (over eighty per cent of the faunal remains other than salmon were dog), deer, wapiti, marten, harbor seal, porpoise, ducks and geese.   Other excavations on the middens on the Canadian side in the 1980s found food processing centers, steaming or storage pits, cooking stone piles, and the like.   Ten more burial sites were found.   Nobody knows how many were lost in the construction of the cottages in Maple Beach in the 1950s, but it is likely dozens or even hundreds of human remains were bulldozed and lost forever.   Some Maple Beach residents may even still have artifacts and remains thousands of years old under their lawns; they're found in modern times.

Borden separated the midden findings into two eras.   The lower, older part of the midden he called the Whalen I phase, and the newer part of the midden – the shells in the top half or so of the piles – he named Whalen II.   Borden traced the harpoon styles in the lower strata of the middens to Alaska, as they resembled Inuit harpoons.   However, artifacts found among the newer shells at the tops of the middens seemed to prove to Borden the Coast Salish people of Point Roberts came from interior lands down into the Salish Sea basin.   He had found wood-working tools, specific beads, and a preponderance of chipped stone tools as opposed to ground slate tools, stone bowls and stone carvings. In the 1970s, archaeological scholars started to criticize Borden's work, questioning his contention a new understanding of prehistory had been made. Borden wrote an article – his last – in 1978 where he addressed his critics. Gone was his theory of interior peoples settling on the Salish Sea. He now felt the newer portions of the middens showed a merging of Marpole and another culture named Locarno Beach into the Coast Salish culture, which Borden called the Whalen II phase. This was soundly denounced by other researchers, who feel nothing merged with Marpole culture and that the Whalen Farm site is merely an example of Marpole culture alone.

Borden seemed enamored with the idea he had found a unique phase at Maple Beach in the Whalen II remains. Another of his theories questioned whether Whalen II is Marpole (which ended 1400 BP) or a culture named Stselax I (a later phase around 660 BP). Borden wrote the fact he didn't find a lot of ground slate knives or stone carvings caused him to conclude Whalen II was unique. This is strange because Borden did actually catalogue stone carvings, including a small pestle with carvings all over it and a frog-shaped carved stone bowl. Seymour later found a carved stone bowl with a face carving on it. Nonetheless, Borden felt he had discovered a Whalen II culture phase between Marpole and Stselax, populated by people coming down the Fraser Valley from the interior. The chipped stone he found is present in Marpole culture but not Stselax. Bone tools and ground stone are common in Stselax but not Marpole. It's unusual that Whalen Farm middens had very few flake-edged tools. Archaeologists today surmise this is due to bias in Borden's research interests and methods. Borden didn't tabulate his artifacts as thoroughly as modern conventions now dictate. Critics cite Borden's use of one-quarter inch screens, through which small objects such as beads and flake-edged tools would have fallen, compared to one-eighth inch screens which would have found flake edge tools. Neither would have caught beads and thus none were found in Point Roberts, which is an unfortunate omission because beads were exceedingly common in Crescent Beach and Tsawwassen excavations. The result is Borden could make conclusions about burials, housing and structure but not diet and sustenance.

In his writings in the 1970s and 1980s, Borden favored a theory of a "fusion" of cultures; this has now been soundly rejected. Borden based this theory on finding wood carvings (common in Marpole) and harpoons (common in Locarno Beach). Later researchers have found a fusion over hundreds of years is not sufficient to explain cultural change; they theorize the Whalen Farm site in Maple Beach area of Point Roberts was merely occupied continuously for well over one thousand years from Locarno Beach times through to the end of Marpole. Borden's harpoons were probably introduced in Locarno times and used continuously into early Marpole eras. As they faded out, wood elements slowly phased in. In essence, the change was gradual, not denoted by a sudden change as though a new population had arrived. Experts now believe there were variants of Marpole, not a rigid change of culture. These shortcomings in Borden's work have resulted in an enigma of Salish Sea archaeology. The reasons for Borden's scant detail is common throughout his career; in the 1950s as the Salish Sea rapidly urbanized, Borden felt pressure to do a quick dig, do initial reports on his findings, and quickly move on to another site before archaeological evidence was destroyed. The fact Maple Beach was developed just a few years after Borden's Whalen Farm dig supports the urgency Borden felt; indeed, the race track was built just a year later in the same area. Every summer he moved on to new sites, in a frenzy to find Salish Sea's rapidly vanishing history. The summer after Whalen Farm, Borden moved on to excavate at Tweedsmuir Park in Surrey. Archaeology fails when research isn't thorough; projects which lack a complete cataloging of artifacts result in faulty analysis. If collections aren't properly documented in field notes, maps, photographs and field bag numbering, the research can lead to improper conclusions. In Borden's research, artifact numbering was duplicated; artifacts went missing or were separated from the main collection. In his rush, Borden had no time to assess his new finding with older evidence and draw holistic conclusions. This has tainted his conclusions of what he found in Point Roberts.

Present day archaeologists now conclude Whalen Farm was definitely Marpole, with dates between 2110 and 1580 BP. Certain artifacts are now believed to be early Marpole, not a separate Whalen II phase. For years, archaeologists consistently cited Borden's Whalen II phase, but this is now disused in archaeology. Indeed, no other Whalen II sites have ever been found. Although Lily Point was occupied in summers, archaeologists feel Maple Beach was inhabited from early autumn to late spring because it is similar to artifacts found at Deep Bay, Shoal Bay and Crescent Beach where greater evidence suggests winter occupation. The scale of archaeological sites and artifacts in Point Roberts is significant. There are five times as many archaeological sites in Point Roberts alone than in the rest of Whatcom County combined.[567]

The entire Maple Beach area still contains many archaeological artifacts. Mike Whalen's son Pat told Richard Clark in a 1980 TV interview, "A good portion of the homes you see back here are sitting on middens," gesturing to the lanes of cottages in Maple Beach. Artifacts are occasionally encountered when people dig on their property to install a septic tank, swimming pool or fence posts. In October 2002, there were a half-dozen active projects in Point Roberts on hold due to the discovery of Coast Salish remains. One owner digging a septic tank encountered human remains. Lummis visited to inspect the artifacts, but contractors ordered them to leave. The Lummis escalated to Whatcom Health Department who told the contractors they would be legally liable if work continued without tribal agreement. That same month a swimming pool project found human remains in Maple Beach. Lummis excavated and removed the remains. The homeowner could also have hired their own archaeologist, but at a cost of thousands of dollars. State law dictates artifacts found on private property and anybody who disturbs Indian graves *inadvertently* through construction and mining must reinter them with supervision of the appropriate tribe. *Knowingly* disturbing remains is a felony leading to five years imprisonment and fines up to ten thousand dollars.[568] These protections came after decades of indifference and ignorance as to archaeological remains. Longtime residents recall thinking native artifacts they found were dropped there, not buried there with their owners. In those years it wasn't known so many archaeological treasures were at the Point and how important they were in Salish Sea history. The idea of a midden wasn't well known – they were often viewed as where Indians had dumped clam shells – though there was a general feeling they were special. Some people kept artifacts they found.[569] Some may have been ignorant, but others were outright disrespectful. Construction of Marine and Edwards Drives simply plowed through innumerable bones.[570] One man found a skull with an arrow through it, which he affixed to his car as a hood ornament. If you ever come across Coast Salish artifacts, consider this: nearly a century ago, a local boy brought home a skull with an eerie chipped tooth which he had found at the middens. His Icelandic parents were respectful of the native culture, and insisted he take the skull back to where he had found it and rebury it. A few days later, this boy fell off his bicycle and chipped is own tooth exactly the same way as the skull.[571]

Continue to the intersection of Maple Street and Meadow Lane. The rise just beyond Meadow Lane on Maple Street is the site of the 1972 Seymour excavations of the longer eastern midden.

   Turn left on Meadow Lane.

The midden ridge parallels Meadow Lane, seen as a slight rise in the land to the right. After Birch Street, Meadow Lane goes over a slight hump, part of that same midden as it veers to the west. Back at Roosevelt Way, Meadow Lane used to continue into Canada. There was an official crossing here for four decades from 1936 until the spring of 1976.[572] This crossing was called the Lower Port, and the main crossing on 56th Street and Tyee Drive was called the Upper Port. The building with a porch on the Canadian side is the old customs building, now a private home. It is identical to the Canadian border station which opened at the Upper Port in 1935.[573] The Lower Port was closed at night and operated from April to Labor Day, and two days a week in the winter.

AMERICAN BOYFRIENDS

A scene from a movie was filmed in Point Roberts here at the Lower Port. This old border crossing was a scene in the film *American Boyfriends*. Shot on December 1, 1988, it was the sequel to the 1985 smash Canadian film *My American Cousin*.[574] After *My American Cousin* won six awards at the Seventh Genie Awards, including Best Picture, Best Director, Best Original Screenplay, Best Actor, Best Actress and Best Film Editing, its sequel was eagerly anticipated.

As seems to happen with these things, the filmmakers took some liberties, resulting in Canada and the United States being reversed in the film. In the movie, the teens are heading from Penticton, B.C. to Portland, Oregon, and setting aside the fact you can't get to Oregon by car from Point Roberts, the scene shows the car driving north down Meadow Lane into Canada when the story has them entering the United States. A U.S. border officer comes out of a colonial-style building a couple of structures north of the border supposedly being U.S. customs. Later in the film when they're returning home, it's reversed again. To reenter Canada, the film shows them driving from Canada into Point Roberts, again stopping at the "wrong" customs house, the aforementioned Lower Port building. *American*

Boyfriends was directed, produced and written by Sandy Wilson, who had directed, produced and written *My American Cousin*. Margaret Langrick and John Wildman reprised their starring roles as Sandy Wilcox and Butch Walker. It was released September 11, 1989 in Canada. As a sequel, *American Boyfriends* didn't have quite the success its predecessor had, but the film's soundtrack was nominated for Best Original Song for "Restless Dreamer" by Barney Bentall and the Legendary Hearts and Best Sound Editing at the Eleventh Genie Awards.

Turn right on Roosevelt and continue to its end at Boundary Bay, under the tall "C" border marker. Park in one of the public parking spots at the foot of Roosevelt; more public parking spots are available just off Bay View Road on each of the "tree streets" (e.g. Alder, Birch, Cedar, etc.) perpendicular to the beach.

MAPLE BEACH

You've arrived at Maple Beach. Since 1899 people have been flocking to Maple Beach for rest and relaxation. Patrick Whalen was the first American to settle in Maple Beach, arriving in 1891 with six kids in tow. At the end of the military reserve he was granted 160 acres including most of Maple Beach along Boundary Bay. Whalen set up a farm near a spring.[575]

Cut off from the rest of Point Roberts by a steep ridge, the Shangri-La-like seaside plain seemed an ideal spot for camping, and Whalen offered just that. During the military reservation years, Canadians had camped in the area, pitching canvas tents near today's Maple Beach Community Park. Whalen offered tent camping to visitors from the beginning of the twentieth century. When the first bridge over the Fraser River was built at New Westminster in 1904, Canadians could get to the Point much faster. Some would come for a day to attend a church social or picnic, but many would camp for weeks in the summer. With few stores in the area, they brought everything they would need for the summer.

Like the Gilligan's Island castaways, odd possessions were deemed necessary: cars were laden with china dishes, enormous Hudson's Bay Company picnic baskets, heavy canvas tents. That's tents plural, as men had separate tents than women, and there were dedicated tents for cooking and eating.[576]

Although the bridge at New Westminster was drawing more people, it was still relatively difficult to get to Boundary Bay from Vancouver. The *Delta Optimist* complained about the how hard it was to get to Point Roberts on September 17, 1910, "Popular as the district is at present as a summer resort, its popularity would be greatly increased were the disadvantage of inaccessibility removed... and Vancouver brought within two hours distance. In time it could become the premier summer resort of British Columbia." Notice was taken and passenger ferry service over the Fraser River began before the close of 1910 between Steveston and Ladner. The ferry ran twice a day year round, with a third daily sailing in summers. Electric tram service extended from Vancouver to Steveston, greatly shortening the time for Vancouverites to travel to get to Boundary Bay, and alleviating the need to travel all the way east to New Westminster to cross the Fraser. Vancouver and Delta lobbied for a crossing to be built from Steveston to Ladner (so the electric tram could reach Boundary Bay), but that would take another half-century.

Volume quickly grew to the point that by 1913 a car ferry was needed. A ferry terminal with a car ramp was built at the bottom of Number 5 Road in Richmond at Woodward's Landing, with sailings to Ladner. This cut the time for a car to travel from Vancouver to Point Roberts to under two hours. Access to Point Roberts improved again when White Star Motor Company began jitney service in 1922 with ten-seat vehicles meeting all ferries in Ladner and shuttling vacationers to Boundary Bay.[577] A forty-car ferry ran the route into the 1930s. Larger ferries were added and ran this crossing until 1959 when they were replaced by the Massey Tunnel.

The Ladner ferry was not the route one would take to get to the U.S. border at Blaine in those years – that was done from New Westminster, so the origins of the ferry were primarily to bring traffic just to Ladner, Boundary Bay and Point Roberts. Word was spreading in Vancouver about the sandy beaches, warm water and camping available at Boundary Bay. The *Vancouver World* heralded the "coming summer resort." Whalen took note and realized his land could be the basis of a significant resort for the Lower Mainland.

For Canadian veterans from the Great War convalescing at the Canadian side of Boundary Bay, Whalen organized picnics on his farm, and the veterans helped to build cabins for Whalen's emerging resort. Soon the beachfront road sported two large camp buildings. Each had a kitchen, living room, bedroom, and a sleeping veranda. Just after the end of World War I, another camp, Glenfield Lodge, opened on Birch Street.[578] Its owners had been in Europe with the war and were familiar with the European plan in hospitality, where one rate included lodging and meals. They brought this novel concept to Point Roberts, with the central lodge offering afternoon tea. Many camps shut down at the end of summer but Glenfield Lodge remained open into autumn for hunting excursions.[579] After the World War II, the Silver Sands Motel opened across the street from the Glenfield Lodge site.

Whalen divided his land into tiny lots, each reasonably priced with enough space for a small cabin and beach rights included. Whalen dammed the spring to create water pressure to provide piped water to the cabins. In the 1930s, refrigerators were prohibitively expensive for a small beach cabin used only a few weeks a year, so a truck would visit to sell ice and rent iceboxes. The narrow lanes and cute cabins Whalen created are still reflected in the look and feel of Maple Beach today. Shingled cottages sport Adirondack chairs on porches and decks, none more than four blocks to the beach. It's the kind of place where people give their cozy cabins cute names like "It'll Do" and "Dunwurkin'."

Figure 78: Swimming platform on Maple Beach. Photo by Corbett, Whatcom Museum 833; Bellingham, WA.

As families arrived each summer, the first job was to gather wooden planks washed up on shore from the dismantled fish traps. These boards were perfect for making all manner of things. Planks were used to repair winter damage to cabins. They were joined together to create a swim platform, allowing swimming within a square of floats.[580] Others created the infamous "cozy corners," three-sided beach shelters like small cabanas, which shielded one from the wind.[581] At night families would sit in the cozy corner singing songs around a beach fire. After the grownups went to sleep back in the cabin, cozy corners were alternatively-known as "love nests" for young lovers.[582]

There was always something to do. After checking the tide chart, families would go crabbing and gather many varieties of clams, raking the sandy beach for cockles with which to make chowder, much as the Coast Salish had been doing at Maple Beach for centuries. It's said boys wading in the tide flats merely picked up crabs by the hundreds. A short stroll led to the spring on Whalen's farm where drinking water was collected and laundry washed. Each August from the 1920s a sports day was organized. A team of horses would drag a log along the beach to clear it of debris, creating a more-or-less smooth sports field. A band was hired and prizes awarded for competitions including greased pig wrestling, swimming between floating docks, diving off driftwood platforms and canoe races. The sports included practical skills such as live saving and rescue techniques. In 1926 a biplane even landed on the sand bars to give rides to the holidaymakers.[583]

Lining the beach were several businesses to serve the summertime community. Locals have fond memories of these businesses which completed the resort feel. Let's take an historical tour of the bayside strip.

At the north end of the beachside strip, the first building was actually on the Canadian side. Before World War II, the beach lot on the Canadian side of border was empty, separated by a picket fence. In 1948 Metcalfe's was built, literally right up to the last millimeter on the boundary line.[584] Perched on a seawall directly over the beach, Metcalfe's offered dancing and slot machines. The snack bar offered twenty-five cent fish and chips. The door to this Canadian building opened into Point Roberts in the United States. One stepped into Metcalfe's through a door right on Roosevelt Way. Later the door was closed but a takeout window still allowed customers standing in the United States to order fish and chips from the Canadian clerk.[585] The owners lived over the business in the boxy two-story building. In more recent years it was a squash club where top B.C. players trained. One of the last commercial buildings of Maple Beach's resort past, it was torn down in the autumn of 2016, after sixty-eight years as an icon of Maple Beach.

Next, the beachfront townhouse condominiums at the corner of Roosevelt Way and Bay View Road used to be another resort business. In 1928 the Whalens constructed a mini-golf course but after a decade in 1938 this corner became the home of an outdoor roller skating rink. The rink had wooden decking around it, ringed by a wooden fence. Covered picnic shelters were rented and local boys hoped to get a plum job as a skate boy. This meant they skated for free and helped customers put on their rented roller skates.[586] Loudspeakers blared music non-stop from ten in the morning until dusk, and skating continued into the evening with the rink lit up at night.[587] Longtime residents recall "White Silver Sands" was one of the songs played over and over at the rink, all day long from 10 A.M. to 10 P.M. on the outdoor P.A. system. The song was a *Billboard* #7 hit for Don Rondo in 1957, but a cover by Pat Boone is the version remembered by folks who owned cabins next to the rink, who can still hear Boone croon in their heads. When World War II was declared, Whalen paused the music to make an announcement over the PA system. The rink occupied this corner until 1958.[588]

Figure 79: Looking south from Roosevelt Way on Bay View Drive in 2017. The condos at right were the outdoor roller skating rink. The "New Whalen's" store is seen a block south. Photo by Mark Swenson.

Figure 80: Looking south on Bay View Drive in summer 1947. Boundary Bay was crowded with people visiting six beachside businesses. The "New Whalen's" building at right still stands, today a private residence. Photo by Whatcom Museum, 2005.97.1391; Bellingham, WA.

During World War II, Maple Beach had a perfect view of military aircraft coming and going from Boundary Bay Airfield just north of Point Roberts. The Airfield would later become the Operational Training School of the Royal Canadian Air Force. The constant roar of flights filled the air from April 1941 to August 1945. Bomber pilot practice missions were conducted right offshore, with Mitchell B-25 and Liberator B-24 planes flying very low over the sandbars on practice missions, firing machine guns into the water. Americans were brought in to provide training, and Maple Beach played an important role in providing housing for these men who preferred living on Yankee soil. Canadian personnel also rented homes at Maple Beach during the war, staying all winter and providing a source of badly-needed income during the off-season. Maple Beach was also a popular day trip from the base. Its beach resort amenities provided the perfect place for the troops to enjoy some R&R. Troops horsed around on the beach, roller skating at Whalen's rink and dancing with local girls. Besides,

Canada had wartime rations, and so many came over to Maple Beach's stores to shop for goods they couldn't get just a few meters north, including beer.[589]

Across Alder Street, 43 Bay View Drive was the site of the original Whalen store. Mike Whalen opened The Bungalow here in 1920, renaming it to The Palace in 1923. The store offered ice cream, candy, cold beverages, tobacco and the like. This was also the real estate office where folks could rent a Maple Beach cabin or buy a lot. It even had a formal tea room. Whalen used beach stones as paper weights to hold down piles of cash as he counted the day's take. Students were hired to run the store each summer, a rite of passage for many of the old-timers still living on Point Roberts. A Texaco gas pump was installed in 1931.

Early success prompted the Whalens to open a pier directly across from the store. The pilings stretched out into the bay over the sand bars; the pier surface was made from fish trap planks. The pier became a focal point on the beach, and Whalen hoped to attract fishing boats to tie up and come into the store for supplies. The end of the pier was also to have been crowned with a dance pagoda, but it was never built. The pier itself was relatively short lived. The constant need of upkeep was challenging during the war years and soon after the end of World War II the wharf had deteriorated beyond use, but its pilings are still visible at low tide.[590] After World War II this site was a snack bar named The Freeze which opened in 1949 and continued for over two decades until 1972, offering hot dogs, fried seafood and soft-serve ice cream.[591]

The large home at 51 Bay View Drive is the "new" Whalen's Store. In the 1940s Whalen moved the store into these larger digs and over the years it has been a Maple Beach landmark housing soda fountains, a lunch counter, resort supplies and a real estate office. It was a Mexican restaurant in the early 1980s and a pizza parlour in the late 1980s. In 2003, a business named Whalen Beach

Figure 81: The Freeze was a beachside institution for 23 years. This ad ran in its last year of operation in 1972.

Café Wine Bar and Country Store was the last business in this structure. This site of Point Roberts history is also now a private residence, as are all of the former beachside businesses.

Across Birch Street at 63 Bay View Drive was the site of the first business on Maple Beach. G. H. Waters opened a store here in 1916, named Waters Mercantile and Dance Hall.[592] Whalen's vision for a dance pavilion never materialized but Waters had one. Point Roberts had class from the very early days; couples paid a buck to dance to the house orchestra and feast on Dungeness crab. It's not a new phenomenon that Canadians come to Point Roberts for cheap gas; Waters also had a gas pump here from the very early years. Tragedy struck in 1936 when a fire destroyed it all, killing an employee, along with torching the original two camp lodges next door. An establishment named No Dice was in this spot from 1946 to 1947.[593]

Anchoring the southern end of the strip at Cedar Street was another retail store at 81 Bay View Drive, originally opened in 1932 as Maples Store, owned by Eggert Burns. The store was named after the tall maple trees which towered over an earlier holiday camp on this lot.[594] Tom Clark bought it in 1957 and changed the name to Clark's.[595]   Even as Whalen's stores came and went, Clark's was open seasonally throughout the years. Tom died in 1980 but Clark's continued; as late as 1992 they installed a new deli and were offering fried chicken and burritos, jojos, corn dogs, pizza pockets and egg rolls.[596] The building was ultimately condemned and with too many structural issues for conservation, and it was torn down in May 2006.[597]

The beach at Maple Beach was privately-owned by the Whalen family. When they sold lots from as early as 1912 the buyers were given "free and unlimited" beach rights as part of a community association. But with over two thousand feet of shoreline it was hard to patrol entry to the beach. Fencing was installed in the 1970s to control access to the beach, and admission fees were charged for visitors from outside Maple Beach. By the end of the 1970s the fence had fallen down, and the public had unfettered access to the beach. Rowdy visitors left garbage, made noise and got aggressive after excessive drinking on the beach. Some camped out all evening. The cabin owners, mostly families, were intimidated if not outright hassled by what the local newspaper described as bums, drunks and bikers. The paper lamented "things are too rough down at the beach."[598] To return order to the private beach, in May 1981 Pat Whalen installed a five-foot-tall, 1250 foot long chain-link fence along Bay View Drive, blocking access to the beach (and marring the bayside views). The public now had to pay a fee at a gate in the fence in order to access the beach. Admission was $1.50 for a full day's access per adult (that would be $4.20 today), and kids over six were fifty cents. Kids under six and seniors, and of course Maple Beach homeowners, were free. A family could buy a year's pass for twenty dollars. Clark complained the only gate to the beach was right in front of Whalen's store, creating a big inconvenience for Clark's customers who had to walk several blocks north to the gate to get to the beach. Clark suggested hiring extra police instead of the blight and constrained access of the chain-link fence.[599]

Clark needn't have worried, the fence wouldn't last long. On December 16, 1982, a major winter storm hit the Point. The flooding caused by the eighty mile-per-hour winds was the worst in fifty years. Eighty per cent of Lighthouse Park was under water, closing it for a month. There was extensive damage along Edwards Drive with the back yards of homes choked with driftwood and three homes knocked off their foundations. The beach-level cabins on Crystal Water Beach suffered extensive damage. Here at Maple Beach, Elm and Fir Streets had standing water. The fifty-year-old wooden seawall, the chain-link fence and large sections of Bay View Drive were simply washed away, the exposed cabins behind strewn with logs.[600] Because it was a private beach, federal aid funds were not available, causing the community to form a special district to raise funds for repairs.[601] A federal grant finally made up the rest, but it took a long time, isolated Point Roberts yet again out of sight, out of mind. The neighborhood simply went without Bay View Drive for an incredible year and a half. Waves just rolled up to the homes from December 1982 until June 1984 when finally the current 2300 foot-long, one foot-thick concrete wall was installed.[602] Winter storms easily top even this current seawall. Driftwood and seaweed often carpet Bay View Drive during the winter.

The beach and tidelands are public now, donated in January 2000 by the Whalen family to the Whatcom Land Trust.[603] Maple Beach County Park has two thousand feet of beach and tidelands, extending out for a kilometer into Boundary Bay, though the park has no facilities.

HAVING FUN

Point Roberts is a place where people come to play. For most visitors, besides spending time at one's cabin, most outdoor recreation is oriented to the beach. The Point's beaches are where people have played for generations. One kilometer off shore is a large concrete boundary line marker. In summer on very low minus tides, the water recedes so far you can walk to the towering concrete structure 3500 feet offshore. A quintessential Point Roberts activity involves strolling out to this marker. Beachcombers take care when wading through thigh-deep eelgrass-choked tide pools between the rippled sand bars (if you're planning a visit, bring some saltwater-friendly beach footwear). The low tide traps crabs, sometimes seen scurrying into the eelgrass beds for safety. In summer these are some of the warmest waters in the Salish Sea, helping present-day visitors to understand the allure of the warm water beach resort which thrived here throughout the twentieth century. Some claim it's one of the top beaches in the United States, and most locals wouldn't disagree.

If there's a minus tide the day you visit, you really must walk on the beach – it's the most iconic thing to do on Point Roberts. With long stretches of sandy beach exposed, building sand castles is a popular pastime. Low tides also make tide pooling possible on all of the Point's beaches. In the summer, the warm water makes swimming possible – a rare feat in the chilly Salish Sea. Point Roberts has a long history of beach recreation; in the 1960s, a rectangular set of rafts were built at Crystal Water Beach and floated to Maple Beach, creating an enclosed swimming pool. A swim club formed, offering lifeguard-supervised swimming and swim lessons.

Today many come to Point Roberts for easy access to the beach for boating-oriented activities. It is now commonplace to see stand-up paddle boarders, kite surfers, skim boarders, surfers and kayakers. Out on the water, Point Roberts is well-known in the Salish Sea as a top fishing spot, with anglers vying to hook salmon, rockfish, lingcod, mackerel, smelt, perch, halibut and sturgeon. Annual fishing derbies have been organized for many years. Clamming and crabbing are very popular, but check for any red tide warnings when you get your license. The marina makes water-based excursions possible including sailing, cruising, jet-skiing and whale watching.

From the shoreline, birding is another popular hobby. Point Roberts is one of the best birding locations on the Salish Sea. Boundary Bay lies on the Pacific Flyway, a bird migration corridor between the arctic and Latin America. It is visited by millions of birds each spring and autumn. Boundary Bay is on the list of Important Bird and Biodiversity Areas (IBA), which are internationally-recognized bird areas; indeed, it is Canada's top IBA. The mud flats and eelgrass are home to marine life which provides food for the 150 species of birds which come through the Boundary Bay Pacific Flyway. In a single day at Lily Point, ninety-four species of birds were once catalogued.[604] There can be over 100,000 birds in the bay on any given day during the migration which sees five million birds visit the Point's shoreline. Boundary Bay is especially known for its fifty species of shorebirds. A large share of the global population of the western sandpiper, the smallest shorebird, stops at Point Roberts on its migration. Massive numbers of dunlin (with a black belly), black-bellied plover (with a black belly and neck) and red-necked grebes overwinter on Boundary Bay. Hundreds of thousands of ducks and geese winter here. Many types of waterfowl, trumpeter swans, jaegers, turkey vultures, owls, and harlequin ducks also call Point Roberts home, not to mention dozens of great blue herons and bald eagles as we've discussed earlier.

Eventually the tide comes in and beachgoers become landlubbers. Point Roberts still offers a lot within its five square miles. Hikers enjoy crisscrossing the Point on forested trails. Wildlife abounds, from orcas to eagles to deer to herons. It's hard not to see a bald eagle on a trip to Point Roberts. The southwestern quadrant of the Point is made up of flat bike-friendly lanes, and there is an active walking group. Horseback riding is possible along the quiet lanes, forest trails and beaches of the Point.

Geocaching is a popular outdoor activity in Point Roberts. This form of recreation is a high-tech game of treasure hunting involving participants using Global Positioning System apps on mobile devices to find containers called geocaches using geographic coordinates. There are geocaches hidden all over the world, including some three dozen of them on Point Roberts. Geocaches can be found in all four county parks and in the forest behind Baker Field. Geocachers find a waterproof container and sign a logbook with their code name. The fun comes from the thrill of the hunt, the moment of finding the geocache, and the customary small token trinkets inside the geocache for trading.

One outdoor activity not permissible in Point Roberts is hunting with guns. The Point is one of twenty-two "no shooting zones" in Whatcom County. Guns may only be discharged in self-defense, to kill a livestock predator, to put down an injured animal or by law enforcement in their line of duty. To hunt animals whilst in the exclave, licensed hunters may use a bow and arrow, but not in county parks where all forms of hunting are banned.

Despite a small and transient population, the community manages to put on several annual events worth attending if you can

Figure 82: Beaches at Point Roberts are lined with driftwood, perfect for building forts. Photo by Mark Swenson.

time your visit. Given its exclave status, the most iconic event on the annual calendar in Point Roberts is its annual Fourth of July parade. The American exclave proudly dons its red, white and blue along the Gulf Road parade route which has been an annual tradition since the early years of the last century. There's an annual belt sander race at the local hardware store, salmon derbies, an annual garden tour has been hosted since 1999,[605] sandcastle-building contests, a summer kid's program, New Year's Day polar bear swims, summer markets and winter holiday fairs. Former events included a late-summer annual arts and music festival held for over four decades beginning in 1973. There was an annual Blackberry Festival for a few years in the early 1990s. The late 1980s saw a children's festival at Seabright Farm. The marina hosted a boating festival in 1996. There have been seafood festivals, and in earlier generations, salmon, crab, clam and oyster bakes were a popular way to attract a crowd.[606] In 1986, 1200 people, far above the population of Point Roberts, held hands in a chain stretching across the peninsula during the Hands Across America campaign. They almost even got the border officials to join in.[607]

Because a lot of people are on vacation when they come to Point Roberts, it helps Point Roberts feel like a festive holiday location. Lucky Point Roberts gets to celebrate double holidays, both official U.S. holidays and the Canadian holidays to boot. In many years there are double fireworks displays in July, once on July first for Canada Day, and then an encore show on the Fourth of July for U.S. Independence Day. Point Roberts also celebrates two Thanksgivings, Canada's on the second Monday in October and U.S. Thanksgiving on the fourth Thursday in November. An international flair is added with fun long weekends commemorating holidays like British Columbia Day (cleverly in the middle of summer on the first Monday in August), Victoria Day (which falls on the Monday preceding May 25 to celebrate Queen Victoria's birthday, adding a second long weekend in May, usually the week before U.S. Memorial Day) and Family Day (for many, a skiing weekend falling on the second Monday in February). Easter is only a Sunday event in the U.S. but is part of an official four-day weekend for Canadians. Four holidays are the same on both sides of the line: Christmas, New Year's Day, Labor Day and the second Monday in November, the holiday known in the United States as Veterans Day and in Canada as Remembrance Day. The good time vibe is felt in the air and the cabins are fully occupied, though Americans in the exclave quickly become familiar with British Columbia statutory holidays to not get caught in huge traffic lineups on holidays and three-day weekends.

The Point's exclave status and isolation has made some holiday traditions hard to execute logistically, requiring creative workarounds. Take Christmas. For many years, Santa Claus delighted kids at the grange hall, but exclave bureaucracy being what it is, sometimes he had a hard time getting out to Point Roberts. In the early 1950s the Point's kids weren't forgotten by the Bellingham Junior Chamber of Commerce. They organized a Santa Ship to bring treats to the kids of remote islands in the Salish Sea. Starting in 1951, the Jaycees trimmed a ship from bow to stern adorned with plastic reindeer and all.[608] They hired two men to skipper the boat loaded up with 1300 toys and 1500 bags of candy[609] and headed out to remote Salish Sea communities. In the first year, they stopped at Orcas and Shaw Islands and at Friday Harbor. In their second year, they added a new port of call: Point Roberts. As they approached the Point, the Jaycees plugged in a huge Christmas tree on the boat. In the December darkness, the tree lit up the night sky. The ship arrived at the Gulf Road dock with carols blaring through a loudspeaker. Of course Santa Claus was on board too, delighting children as he handed out candy, nuts and oranges. It then sailed off, making stops at Patos Island for the lighthouse keeper's family, then Waldron Island, Friday Harbor, Orcas, Shaw Island, Doe Bay and Gooseberry Point on the Lummi Reservation, where 300 kids gathered in a warehouse, before returning to

Bellingham.[610] The pier at Lopez Island was too small to support all the activity, but the ship sailed into the harbor and the community lit a huge bonfire on the shore. With hot cocoa all around, kids gathered to see the Santa Ship, all lit up and glowing. Santa came ashore in a dinghy to greet the kids.[611]

The following year for the 1953 Christmas season, the Santa Ship got stuck in a fierce southwester and couldn't get around the Point at Lighthouse Park. It had to sail on to the rest of the San Juan Islands without stopping at Point Roberts.[612] The Jaycees made up for it the next year, and eventually expanded the route to include, with customs permission, the Canadian Gulf Islands, adding Saturna, Mayne, Galiano and Ganges Islands to the route. Later in 1963, Canada joined the fun, and organized a Santa Ship to leave Victoria and travel throughout the Salish Sea, visiting both the U.S. San Juans and Canadian Gulf Islands. The two ships would then meet up at a chosen port for a big party. A spokesman for the

Figure 83: The Santa Ship leaving Bellingham for Point Roberts in 1952. Photo by Whatcom Museum 1995.1.31418; Bellingham, WA.

Victoria Jaycees said, "We can't have you Yanks being nicer than we are."[613] We think of the San Juans today as the playground of the wealthy, but in the early years the San Juans weren't so developed, and many residents were actually poor families eking out a living on the remote islands. The Santa Ship was the highlight of the year; these kids actually thought Santa arrived by boat, not sleigh. The locals would often decorate their dock with festive lights. Santa would go onshore, sit in a large chair, mobbed by the island's youngsters who wanted to sit on Santa's lap. The ship faced many storms and rough seas; the Christmas tree was even lost overboard one year. It sometimes had to pull into a small harbor and stay at a local's home overnight. One Slavonian fisherman from Bellingham, Tripo Costello, volunteered to be Santa for thirty-eight years. At its peak, it would become a multi-day, one hundred mile trek with thirteen stops.[614] The Lions Club took over in 1997 with a ninety-six foot ship. Santa today is joined on board by pirates, clowns and Mrs. Claus. It arrives in the afternoon to use the daylight for selfies and photos for posting to social media. The tradition continues, though the boat hasn't called on Point Roberts for many years because of the thirteen mile detour it requires north of the San Juans.

 Go to the intersection of Bay View Drive and Cedar Street.

BAREFOOT BANDIT

The Barefoot Bandit is a pop culture icon. The subject of a Hollywood movie, a viral YouTube video (*The Ballad of Barefoot Harris*), well over 60,000 Facebook fans, themed merchandise for sale online and awestruck articles in *Outdoor* magazine and a four-page spread in *Maxim*, the Barefoot Bandit is Colton Harris-Moore. Known as Colt to his friends, at age seventeen he evaded a three-country, continent-wide law enforcement dragnet for exactly twenty-one months, from November 11, 2008 to July 11, 2010. His legendary spree took him through Point Roberts, proving people continue to use the Point to hide out even in modern times, much as they have been doing for 170 years.

Colt's foray through Point Roberts occurred almost exactly halfway through his time on the lam and less than one month after reality TV personality Ryan Jenkins came through town. The specific leg which brought him to the Point began in the San Juan Islands. One night in early September, 2009, Colt stole a small airplane from the Friday Harbor airport and crash-landed it a few miles away at the Eastsound airport on the north coast of Orcas Island. Eastsound is the closest U.S. town to the south, fourteen miles from Point Roberts. On September 7, Colt burglarized a bank and five stores in Eastsound, including the Island Market store, which sustained over $25,000 in damage when Colt used a forklift to ram the store's ATM machine. He even stole a rifle from a cop car. He was spotted by police on September 12, who gave chase, but Colt outran the cops and slipped into the woods. The next day, he stole a twenty-eight-foot boat from Brandt's Landing marina in Eastsound, and cruised out into the Salish Sea north toward Point Roberts. Colt caused $2,000 in damage when he hit the reef at Lily Point, where he abandoned the boat. Escaping through Lily Point Park, he burglarized a home right outside the entrance to the park. He was trying to meet up with a friend he knew from juvie who lived in Point Roberts, but once in Point Roberts he learned his buddy had moved to Vancouver. Colt tried to get into a house in the South Beach area but failed, so he made his way to Maple Beach.

He hit two homes in Maple Beach, one on Cedar Street and one on Bay View Drive, so standing at this intersection retraces Colt's path. A home right here on Bay View attracted Colt's attention. He forced the lock on the front door and walked right in. In true Goldilocks style, he spent the night after taking a shower and eating canned food he found in the kitchen. At a home on Cedar Street, he broke the lock on an outdoor refrigerator, taking $82 worth of food.[615] After a few days in Point Roberts, he slipped across the border, smuggling himself into Canada. On the Canadian side, Colt stole a BMW, met up with his buddy in Vancouver who was impressed by the wad of cash and firearms Colt showed him. Colt would resurface next in Creston, British Columbia, in the far southeast of the province as his cross-continent adventure continued.

Harris-Moore grew up in the Salish Sea, about fifty miles south of Point Roberts on Camano Island. Camano Island, first explored by Whidbey and Puget in May 1792, is a lot like Point Roberts. To reach Camano Island one must drive around a large bay, arriving on the island via the only road in and out. The island is chock-full of vacation homes and small cottages very similar to the cabin culture on Point Roberts. Colt grew up dirt poor with an unemployed, abusive and substance-abusing single mom who seemed incapable of showing him the unconditional love mothers are expected to extend. Colt began burglarizing Camano's vacation homes in 2004 at age thirteen. By age sixteen Colt was supporting himself financially on burglaries.[616]

He was a careful and even courteous burglar. He learned from an older kid how to pick locks, case houses, escape through the woods and avoid getting caught. He didn't pull off jobs too frequently; just a couple times a month would he break in, grab jewelry, mobile phones, MP3 players, laptops, credit cards, TVs and especially food. Often using the mark's own car to haul away the goods, he would fill it up with gas and return it with prints wiped away. Being inside these clean and well-appointed homes showed Colt a life he did not have, so rather than dash off, he began to stay a while, removing his shoes, noshing on food and juice, and watching the tube or using the wifi to go online. Surfing the net, he learned how to get PINs for credit cards, and even ordered merchandise, having it shipped to the vacant homes, including lock-picking tools and credit card readers. He also spent time online researching aviation. His friends and family remember him being fascinated by planes. He could identify planes flying overhead, and he used his time surfing the web to read Cessna manuals and play with online flight simulators. Despite the fact he was stealing property and whiling away afternoons in other people's houses, Colt showed a softer side of criminality with an almost respectful behavior in these homes, cleaning up his messes and even leaving notes. Despite his criminality, he was a good kid in the sense he didn't drink or use drugs, and he loved animals, especially dogs.

Colt wasn't getting rich off his loot; he hoarded the goods on his mother's five-acre Camano Island property on which the dilapidated mobile home in which he grew up sat. The cops found his stash in September 2006, after tracing one of his online purchases made with a stolen credit card. Before he could get arrested for what Camano police estimate was over $1.5 million in cumulative property loss, he became a fugitive for the first time, and for most of the next four years he would be on the lam.[617]

That four-year stint was interrupted only once. After a couple close calls when he had to outrun police into the woods of Camano Island, Colt was finally caught in the act. An observant neighbor called the cops after seeing a light on in a vacation home in February 2007. Whilst holed up in the home with the police outside, Colt called his mom on a mobile phone. She spent an hour on the phone convincing him to surrender. He was convicted of burglary in June and sent to a couple of halfway houses. Colt escaped from a low-security facility in Renton, Washington on April 29, 2008 and never looked back. He went back to what he knew, burglarizing cabins on Camano Island. He was spotted by the cops driving a Mercedes. Pulling over, Colt ran from the car into the woods. Inside the car, police found Colt's backpack. A digital camera showed a selfie Colt had taken of himself lying on his back amidst ferns, listening to tunes on a stolen iPod, wearing a Mercedes polo shirt and his signature smirk. This photo would go viral on social media, becoming the photo of a confident, successful teen doing quite well thank you on the lam.[618] Cops thought he was living in the woods, but dog teams found no trace. He more likely lived in empty vacation homes or crashed with friends.

In November 12, 2008, Bob Rivers, the longest-serving radio disc jockey in Seattle history who had a loyal following of listeners in Point Roberts to his morning show on various Seattle classic rock stations over the years, received news that a Cessna plane he kept at the Eastsound Airport had been stolen. After dreaming of flying all his life, and having practiced simulators and read manuals for hours, but never having actually flown before, Colt successfully stole and took off in Rivers' Cessna 182 from Eastsound in the early dawn. Getting up was easy; finding a place to land was another matter. After three-and-a-half hours in the air and 250 miles southeast of Eastsound, Colt found a field on the Yakama Indian Reservation on which to land, so as to avoid attention at airstrips. The crash-landing was hard, but Colt walked away alive, disappearing into the Cascade Mountains. He had done it; he had flown an airplane. More than a mere bucket list stunt, Colt had achieved his life-long number one passion.

Colt would lay low for the next eleven months before he stole his second plane in September 2009 in the San Juan Islands, which led to him stealing the boat at Eastsound and continuing his escape through Point Roberts. By this time he was being called the Barefoot Bandit, after retail store security cameras recorded him in bare feet as he went through the Eastsound store.

After Point Roberts, Colt's run on the lam from law enforcement continued for another nine months. Colt surfaced in Creston, B.C. on September 24, 2009. After several burglaries there, he slipped back into the United States, stealing a plane at Bonners Ferry, Idaho on September 28. Colt crashed this plane near Granite Falls, Washington, after running low on fuel from having taken a scenic tour of eastern Washington. That Colt walked away from the crash alive is a miracle. This plane theft was sufficient to get picked up by the national news wires, whose articles referred to a fan page a Seattle writer had started on Facebook after himself having seen the news of Colt's crash landing in local media. After only one day the fan page had over one thousand followers, and would later surpass twenty thousand. Fans wrote on his wall comments like, "Fly, Colton, Fly!", "Colton is a true hero," and "You're a modern day Jesse James."[619] Girls were offering to go on dates or even hide him. Colt t-shirts appeared online by entrepreneurs trying to cash in. His mom, still on Camano Island, was deluged with calls from media around the world.

A gun stolen from one of Colt's burglaries in Creston was found at a campsite in the woods on October 2, 2009. A week later the police issued an official warrant for Colt's arrest, causing Colt to lay low for several months through the autumn. It would be February before Colt would again attract attention. On February 10, 2010, Colt stole another plane, taking off from the Anacortes Airport thirty-six miles southeast of Point Roberts. The world's attention was on Vancouver that week as it hosted the Winter Olympics. As a result, there were temporary airspace restrictions in place. Not knowing this, Colt flew directly toward Point Roberts and the no-fly zone, but skirted the restricted airspace at the last minute, and had a decent landing at Eastsound. Colt was well-aware of his media reputation. He is attributed to a burglary the next day at Orcas Homegrown Market, where he took $1200, a cheesecake, and some chalk with which he drew 39 footprints on the floor, an apt signature for the Barefoot Bandit. He burglarized the Orcas Island Hardware store at the end of February, which led police to receive three Colt sightings that day, but he still eluded them.

In May, still on the lam, Colt appeared on San Juan Island where he stole a boat and navigated through Cattle Pass, one of the most dangerous waterways in the Salish Sea with incredibly strong currents. Colt was able to get through the pass, landing across the channel at Shark Reef County Park on Lopez Island. Only the day before he had been the subject of a long article in *Rolling Stone*, further building his fame and outlaw status. Colt had evaded capture so far, but hiding on islands left limited options for escape. Although he knew these islands really well, Colt left the San Juans for the last time. He was now headed on a transcontinental trip, with cops and the FBI on his tail.

On May 28, 2010, staff at a veterinary medical clinic in Raymond, Washington, arrived at work to find their facility had been burglarized. As an animal lover having had dogs growing up on Camano Island, instead of stealing cash, the Barefoot Bandit left one hundred dollars and a note reading, "Drove by, had some extra cash. Please use this cash for the care of animals." Colt continued down Highway 101 toward the Columbia River. He could have simply driven over the Astoria Bridge, a 4.5 mile long bridge spanning the Columbia River, to Astoria, Oregon. The Columbia River empties into the Pacific Ocean near here. The Columbia River bar, a series of dangerous shifting sand bars, have claimed many ships and lives in what is known as the Graveyard of the Pacific. My grandfather lost boats at the mouth of the Columbia, and had to swim to shore in gales. For some unknown reason, Colt didn't drive over the Astoria Bridge. He made his way to Ilwaco, Washington, a town just inside the mouth of the Columbia, and on June 1 stole a boat from the Ilwaco marina and in a risky solo crossing, somehow navigated the boat across the bar to the Oregon side. Colt reached Astoria's western suburb of Hammond, near the site of the original George & Barker cannery, and made his way to the Astoria Airport. Colt looked around at the planes there, but ended up stealing a car.

Colt's movements now started happening more rapidly. Ten days after his car theft in Astoria, he stole another car at McMinnville, Oregon, which he drove across Oregon and abandoned in Ontario, Oregon, near the Idaho border. On June 11, a car was stolen in Boise and recovered in Cody, Wyoming. He stole a car at Buffalo, Wyoming on June 12 which was recovered at Spearfish, South Dakota on June 14. On June 16, another car was stolen in Spearfish, later recovered at the Yankton, South Dakota airport. Following his old Salish Sea M. O., Colt broke into a home to rest, but on June 18, the family returned from vacation, finding the six-foot five-inch Colt nude in their home. He pointed a laser pointer at them, frightening them thinking it was a rifle scope. He escaped, stole a car on June 20 from Yankton, and drove it to Norfolk, Nebraska where he abandoned it. June 21st would be a busy day for Colt. Another car was stolen in Norfolk, which was found later in the day at Pella, Iowa, and yet another car was stolen that day in Pella, later recovered in Ottumwa, Iowa. On June 24th, a car was stolen in Ottumwa and later found at Dallas City, Illinois. Colt surfaced July 3 in Bloomington, Indiana, apparently tiring of stealing cars – he had stolen at least ten in a little over a month. In Bloomington, Colt returned to his passion, stealing a Cessna and flying southeast. He would stay in the air for twelve hundred miles, about the same distance as Point Roberts is from the Mexican border. He had a hard crash-landing in a swampy area of Abaco Island in the Bahamas. This landing activated the plane's emergency locator beacon, which alerted the local authorities and the FBI. Colt burglarized some restaurants but didn't stay on Abaco very long. He stole a forty-foot boat and made his way south to Eleuthera Island, where he burglarized more properties. Eventually, on July 11, 2010, he stole yet another boat, cruising to Harbor Island, but the police were catching up and his cruise became a high-speed chase. In the midst of the action, Colt hit a sandbar, and his eighteen months on the lam came to an end. As Colt desperately tried to get his boat off the sandbar, police caught up to him and shot out his engines. After some negotiation where Colt threatened to shoot himself, he was captured.

Colt was charged with: interstate transportation of a stolen aircraft, interstate and foreign transport of a stole gun and interstate transport of a stolen boat, bank burglary, flying a plane without a pilot's license, attempting to elude, being a fugitive in possession of a gun, burglary, identity theft, illegal entry, illegally landing a plane, malicious mischief, motor vehicle theft, possession of stolen property and theft by unlawful taking or disposition. Although the cops tried to paint a predictable narrative of "he's not a folk hero, he's a criminal," Colt had a knack as a crowd-pleaser. His determination and ingenuity were infectious; every time his escapades made the news, a legion of fans were hoping he'd get away. After a six-and-a-half-year sentence in a Federal Detention Center, he was released on probation in 2016. He signed a movie deal whereby all the proceeds will go to restitution to his victims. Colt may have spawned a copycat; in 2004, a sixteen-year-old was arrested for burglarizing over twenty cottages in Maple Beach and stealing boats from the marina.[620] The police report didn't mention if this thief was wearing shoes.

CRAB TOWN

The southern end of Bay View Drive becomes a private lane, which in old times was called Crab Town. Point pioneer Jeppe Thompson owned this lane and the land at the top of the bluff above it. Thompson turned to crab fishing after previously working in the APA cannery. Each Sunday he set up a huge tank on the beach and cooked crabs. Canadians came over the line to Crab Town to get an order of hot crabs wrapped in newspaper. His daughter Dora recalls, "All the children would gather, waiting for what would surely come their way – a crab hot from the pot."[621] Thompson shipped his crabs to Seattle and took the rest in the back of his Ford truck to sell in Vancouver.[622]

Like Lily Point, Maple Beach too was almost lost to development. In the early 1960s a considerable portion of Maple Beach was to be filled in and developed as a major residential and industrial complex. Bay View Drive would have become a street far inland from the bay. The $68 million proposal (that's an incredible half-billion dollars today) would have dredged Amsterdam-style canals perpendicular to the beach to create boat-to lots.[623] A group called Save the Beaches was organized to block the development.

Leave Bay View Drive on Elm Street, the original walking path from the beach to the Whalen farmhouse, which sits in front of you at the stop sign at the three-way intersection of Elm Street, Meadow Lane and Goodman Road. A wooden windmill sits in front of the farmhouse, originally created in 1918 but installed here in the spring of 1999. It was purchased from a farm in Little Fort, British Columbia, where it had been lying in a field for fifty years.[624]

In May 1979 the West German TV series *Huck Finn and Friends* was filmed at the old farmhouse. The white clapboard exterior of the Whalen Home stood in for the estates of Hannibal, Missouri. Ladner was used for the river scenes, and more filming occurred in Burnaby. Many of the steam-powered sternwheelers featured in the series were at the time working ships on the Fraser River and tourist boats operating in the harbors of Vancouver and Nanaimo. In the twenty-six episodes Tom Sawyer was played by Sammy Snyders, Huck Finn was Ian Tracy, and in a casting coup, Brigette Horney played Aunt Polly. Horney was a famous German theatre and film actress known for her role as Empress Katherine the Great in 1943's *Baron Münchhausen*. Bob Stabler was the producer, who also did *Hopalong Cassidy* and *Gunsmoke*. Many of the guest directors were from the *Beachcombers*.[625] Although it merged into one story what Mark Twain had written as separate stories, today it has a cult following after airing in countries around the world, helped by reruns which aired well into the 1990s. Today, fans can buy the four-DVD box set, introduced in the UK (region 2 format) in 2007.

Go up the hill on Goodman Road.

As you head up Goodman Road there is a good view of Boundary Bay to the north and the productive Delta polders. A huge source of light brightens the entire northern night sky during the long winter nights. Situated on the northwestern shore of Boundary Bay just three miles north of Point Roberts is a massive greenhouse which is the epicenter of British Columbia's tomato industry. Founded by a Dutch immigrant in the 1950s, Houweling's Tomatoes is still a family business run by the founder's son. The company is the largest tomato plant propagator in all of North America. Their ten-acre greenhouse complex grows millions of seedlings annually. In December and January each year enough tiny seedlings are produced at Houweling's to fill over 400 semi-trucks. The operation plants tomato seeds on a continual basis until they are seedlings, when they are shipped to greenhouses across North America. They also grow some seedlings to maturity, including beefsteak, Roma and heirloom tomatoes, among other tomato varieties. Inside the greenhouse, the tomatoes are grown hydroponically, not in soil but in crushed coconut which keeps the roots moist. Water and nutrients are cycled through via an ebb-and-flow system which floods the plants' roots on a periodic basis around the clock. In summer months, natural light streams through the greenhouse roofs and walls, but in winter artificial lights keep the growing cycle a year-round operation, guaranteeing British Columbians tomatoes any time of year. Houweling's tomatoes are occasionally seen in the Point Roberts supermarket, though most of the time the Point's tomatoes come from Mexico. The output from the 765 acres of greenhouses in British Columbia would require a traditional farmer to plant over 7500 acres of land, well over twice the size of Point Roberts.

Turn right on Johnson Road.

Johnson Road is named for Thorleifur Johnson, an Icelandic settler who came to Point Roberts in 1900.

CHAPTER 7 • EXCLAVE LIFE

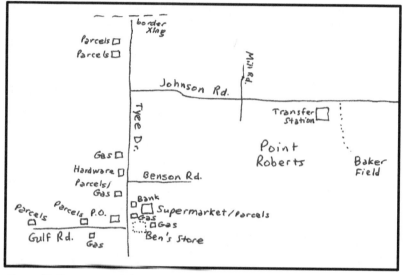

Figure 84: Route map of Chapter 7. Start at Johnson & Goodman Roads and end at Tyee Drive & Gulf Road. Distance 2.5 miles (4km)

It's hard to imagine what it would be like to live in an isolated exclave unless you've experienced it. Life is often a hassle: stifling bureaucracy and insurmountable logistical snafus pop up all the time threatening basic services, economic growth and freedom of movement. In this chapter we'll explore life in an exclave from three perspectives. First, we'll explore the challenges of providing essential services to an exclave. Then we'll examine how external economic forces make for a limited range of businesses and a volatile economic climate to which Point Roberts has had to adapt. Lastly, we'll look at the opportunity for Point Roberts to leverage its position as the closest access point for Metro Vancouver to the United States economy.

Point Roberts is not just a border town, it's an exclave. The reality of life in an exclave means you're cut off from the mainland's infrastructure. Most exclaves are small, out of sight and out of mind, and expensive to serve for a very small population. For instance, perhaps no town in America has struggled with utility services more than Point Roberts. County and state authorities on the mainland have struggled to provide utility services to Point Roberts for decades. When bidding opens to contractors to provide services on the Point, sometimes nobody steps forward because of the logistical barriers of serving Point Roberts. Border regulations impact how services can be tendered. Its small population and challenging logistics keep it perennially at the bottom of county works priority lists. Some on the mainland deprioritize investments in Point Roberts because they are perceived as primarily helping Canadians. Residents have fought hard to get the services which exist today. Garbage, phone and water services have been controversial, each with periods of restricted service levels and availability, making life difficult for locals. The availability of utilities, or lack thereof, has limited the amount and scope of growth and economic possibilities more than any other factor since the end of the big salmon runs. Garbage, phone service and especially access to water were all severely disrupted at one time or another and subject to frantic, confusing and agonizing bureaucratic hurdles to get resolved. For much of the 1970s and 1980s, utilities were the subject of contentious debate which dominated all aspects of daily life. Point Roberts reached its watershed moment in 1988 when sources for two major utility services were each resolved after years of uncertainty.

UTILITIES

Point Roberts is considerably cleaner and greener than it used to be. For many years, garbage lined the streets and ditches. The dump was a landfill only open a couple times a week, and cabin owners needed to dispose of their garbage when they were leaving their cabins. If the dump wasn't open on the day they were leaving, and they might not be back for several weeks or even months, the garbage couldn't just sit there. If the dump isn't open on the day you are leaving or you don't feel like paying the fee, which is only payable in U.S. currency, many visitors would just dump the garbage in a ravine or along the side of the road. Day trippers need to jettison trash before they reach the border crossing. Tyee Drive used to be lined with beer bottles people had thrown out the window as they drove toward the border. In the late 1970s and early 1980s, the community organized clean-up crews who would spend many hours on designated weekends bagging trash and beer bottles in an effort to clean up after Canadian visitors.[626]

It's been hard to keep a solid waste provider in Point Roberts. The town landfill was formerly on Benson Road behind Baker Field. It was open one day a week, on Sundays so Canadians leaving their cabins for the weekend could dump their garbage for fifty cents on the way out. A residential garbage pickup service started in 1968, charging $18 per year for weekly pickup. The county briefly closed the dump in May 1969 because a bureaucrat in Bellingham felt it was too close to the water towers, but he hadn't considered that left no garbage option. You can't just drive to the next town's dump; garbage isn't allowed over the border. Garbage soon piled up in the woods and ditches all over the Point and the county reversed course and reopened the dump.[627] Containerized trash collection began in February 1986.[628] After a decade-long campaign, in May 1991 it was announced the Benson Road landfill had to close because it was not up to code and needed to be cleaned up.[629] During August the landfill was covered in a plastic dome for environmental cleanup. Today it's the mother of all blackberry bushes, the size of a football field. A new facility opened in a former gravel pit on Johnson Road.[630] On September 16, 1991 Whatcom County introduced mandatory garbage collection. Canadian homeowners who only use their cabin for a few weeks in the summer didn't want to pay for garbage collection service year round and tried to file exemptions, but exemptions were only available for those who could prove they were disposing of garbage in an environmentally sound manner.[631]

By 1995, the Point Roberts solid waste facility was the only one still run by Whatcom County, who wanted to privatize it like all the rest. Some residents proposed, since Canadians generate most of the Point's garbage, approaching Delta to take the garbage at the Vancouver landfill in Burns Bog, but this was rejected by Delta.[632] In May 1995, a private company took over the local garbage contract. Garbage pickup rates soared as much as eighty per cent in March 1996, because too few people subscribed to the service, well below estimates. Offering residential curbside recycling pickup on all of the small narrow lanes in Point Roberts was expensive. The vendor was required to provide the service under county rules, but only seventeen per cent of residences in Point Roberts participated in it. Recycling pickup service was cancelled but it was free to bring recyclables to the transfer station. Locals protested throughout 2008 they were being discriminated against because of their location in the county.[633] The county ruled the vendor's changes to be an insufficient service level and for six *months* in 2009 there was no garbage service at all on Point Roberts until a new contractor could be found. Today debate continues about mandatory garbage service, closing exemption loopholes and upgrading service.

Residential phone service came to the exclave as late as 1955. The Elskan House, a purple home on Benson Road, was the first in Point Roberts to have a phone. Constructed partly from salvaged pieces of fish traps washed up on the Point's shores, this home also holds the distinction of housing Point Roberts' first and only dentist, something the Point doesn't have today.[634]

Point Roberts used to have free calling throughout Metro Vancouver but everything in Washington was long distance. This was great for Canadians but for the Americans in Point Roberts it meant they were not listed in the Whatcom County phone book and any call to the U.S. mainland was long distance. To pay the phone bill, American residents had to get their proof of identity, drive across the border into Tsawwassen, go to the bank to exchange money into Canadian dollars and pay the phone bill at a certain drugstore only in Canadian funds. They even had to pay a five per cent provincial social services tax required on all phone lines provided by B.C. Tel,[635] who had been providing phone service in Point Roberts for eighty years. They had connected the first canneries' phones and by default kept installing residential phones over the years. Incredibly in 1985, a small telecommunications company from Whidbey Island, Whidbey Telecom, discovered B.C. Tel was not legally a phone provider in the state of Washington. B.C. Tel had a franchise certificate at the county level with Whatcom County, but all the proper regulatory papers had not been filed with the state of Washington and as a result they weren't recognized by the state government.[636] Apparently, for years nobody questioned why a foreign company was a phone provider in U.S. territory. Once again, forgotten Point Roberts, thankful for any service it could get, had basic services challenged by outsiders and got caught in a bureaucratic nightmare by people who cannot imagine the impacts on an isolated exclave their decisions have. This challenge to its phone service provider caused the local newspaper to proclaim, "Dramatic Bid to Take Over Point Roberts Phone System."[637] On June 30, 1986 the Washington Utilities and Transportation Commission declared Point Roberts an unassigned telephone territory. B.C. Tel's assumed monopoly to provide service in Point Roberts was rejected and overnight they lost Point Roberts as part of their coverage area.[638] Bids were solicited for a new service provider. A locally-based community phone cooperative formed and submitted bids for the contract, along with Whidbey Telecom and the provider serving the San Juan Islands.

Whidbey won in the end. Their office is here on Johnson Road, just down the road from the transfer station.[639]

After the June 4, 1988 switch to Whidbey Telecom,[640] having a basic phone line became a lot cheaper, but Point Roberts lost its free calling areas. Today, the only place you can call for free from Point Roberts is Point Roberts. All calls to anyplace else – whether just a few meters to Tsawwassen or to mainland Whatcom County, are long distance. This change in provider meant Point Roberts had to switch from British Columbia's 604 area code to what was western Washington's area code at the time, 206. Today Point Roberts' area code is 360 and its phone prefix is 945. This 945 prefix still stems from B.C. Tel days. In 1960, Tsawwassen was assigned prefixes 941 and 943 and Point Roberts was essentially the third Tsawwassen prefix with 945.[641]

Should you need to look up somebody's number, it won't take long. The Point's white page listings in the phone book are all of eleven pages long but they're hard to find, tucked like an appendix behind the yellow pages way in the back of the South Whidbey Island phone book. Even tiny Hat Island, a small island near Everett with a population of forty-one, is listed up front before the yellow pages. Yellow pages are different; Point Roberts businesses are mixed in with Whidbey Island businesses. When urgently looking up, say, plumbers, you have to sift through most of the listings which are for businesses on the southern end of Whidbey Island, where Whidbey Telecom is based. Ads in the yellow pages catch your eye, but upon closer examination most are located in Langley, Greenbank, Freeland or Clinton, a 120-mile, two-and-a-half-hour drive necessitating four international border crossings round-trip. Local residents take it in stride; as late as 1988 Point Roberts phone listings were printed in a Canadian phone book. Whilst local phone service was wrest from Canadian hands, that hasn't happened with the local cable TV provider. The Point has had cable TV service since 1971[642]; its provider is Canadian to this day, meaning many popular U.S. channels aren't available.

In case your mobile phone isn't getting good reception whilst on the Point, and it won't on most United States carriers, there is a phone booth at the Community Center on Gulf Road and at the Whidbey Telecom office on Johnson Road, built in March 1988. Canadian mobile phone subscribers have better service; Canadian signals blanket most of the Point. Not all B.C. subscribers have a calling package which includes roaming in the United States, and American devices often roam onto Canadian carriers, so visitors should check their plan before visiting or turn off cellular data to avoid bill shock. For years there was no U.S. mobile phone tower. A Verizon mobile phone tower was finally built at Baker Field in April 2013, but American users of other carriers will likely roam or have no service. If that's you, try getting a signal at the lookout in Lily Point Park.[643]

Point Roberts did not join the electrical grid until 1932 when power lines finally reached the exclave.[644] Arni Myrdal was the first to have electricity in his house on the Point. At the time residents could buy electric stoves. Although this seems like a wonderful convenience to modern ears, many of the cooks on Point Roberts preferred cooking on a wood stove, and several residents purchased hybrid models which had both electricity and a wood-burning option. For many years, electricity was actually furnished by B.C. Hydro, but Canadian law didn't allow export of electricity, so the service was branded as a franchise of Puget Sound Power and Light for many years. The result was neither company had maintenance staff on the Point, so outages had to wait for Puget Sound Power and Light personnel to come from the mainland;[645] every home on the Point had a good supply of candles. Today, electricity is supplied directly by Puget Sound Energy.

The census reports four in ten people in Point Roberts heat their homes with electricity, twelve percentage points lower than the state average of 53%, but higher than the national average of 37%, owing to the dominance of hydroelectricity as the source of the electric grid in the Salish Sea area. Besides electricity, residents keep warm in strange ways. The second most common home heating fuel is bottled propane gas, used by an incredible three in ten on the Point, far exceeding the national average of 4.8%. Eleven per cent even use kerosene. Wood-burning fireplaces account for a full sixteen per cent of home heat in Point Roberts, four times the state average of four per cent and eight times the national average of two per cent. Point Roberts often sees burn bans in summer, but with so many houses having wood as their only heat source and thus exempt from the bans, the risk of fire is always present.

Probably no issue occupied so much attention, so much angst and was as pivotal to the development and future of Point Roberts as the availability of water. The fight for water was a long-term community-wide effort which required fighting bureaucracy, conducting international diplomacy and evaluating scarce feasible options. With no lakes or rivers, its only natural water source was seven wells. The stakes rose in the early 1970s as two wells ran dry and the water table declined in the other five.[646] When the population spiked in summer with all the Canadian visitors, demand regularly exceeded supply.

The first century of European settlement on Point Roberts was marked by severe water limitations. The wells dug by the original settlers were still being used decades later, but they pumped water which smelled and looked bad, leaving rusty mineral deposits in sinks and tubs. These wells would frequently run dry in the summer. The water issue affected all residents of the community in their daily lives. As cabins were built on Point Roberts after the war, Canadians would frequently bring dekaliters of their own water to their cabin from home because summertime saw wells run completely dry.[647] The Point Roberts Water District Number Four was formed in December 1956. Pipe installation started in 1964, continuing for fifteen years, but sufficient water to supply the pipes was tenuous. Severe drought struck in 1973, and by mid-summer that year, there was no more water. A half-million gallons of water had to be imported from Blaine in milk trucks. The water district appealed to the city of Vancouver for a connection to its water system, but was refused by the Canadians, who said it was against Canadian law to export water to a foreign country, clearly not wanting to start a precedent. Desperate, the Point Roberts water district retaliated by threatening to cut off water to hundreds of Canadian residents on Point Roberts unless water access was supplied. "Canadians Go Home" and "Disaster Area" signs popped up.[648]

Point Roberts has much potential for development, but proposal after proposal fell through because there wasn't enough reliable water and no sewers. After trying to push through a sewer proposal without sufficient study, and tired of smelly water and the iron-colored stains, voters kicked out the water board. The entire board was recalled in a vote December 28, 1976, the first successful recall election in Whatcom County history.[649] In April 1980 the water level in the main well fell from eighteen to ten gallons per minute, and another well fell to only five gallons per minute. The early 1980s was a time where the water situation was getting serious and significantly hampering everyday life let alone supporting any new growth. A moratorium on new building construction was implemented due to lack of water. What little water there was in the wells was found to be tainted with sea water in 1981.[650] A 1981 land boom following talk of a big resort on the Point crashed due to water limitations. With small but steady population growth in the 1980s, the urgency of finding a water supply intensified.

The water issue was covered on the front page of the local newspaper nearly every issue for years on end. Point Roberts had three realistic options: it could buy water from Canada, build an underwater pipeline from Blaine or build a desalinization plant. Viability studies were conducted and slowly options were eliminated. In March 1981, local water district officials travelled to Hong Kong to study the water desalinization plants in use there.[651] Once the price tag was known, this was quickly ruled out. More overtures to the north offering to pay cash for water from Delta were made in 1981 and 1982. To assuage Canadians who wouldn't export water, an even trade was proposed. If the Greater Vancouver Regional District sold water to Point Roberts via Delta, Blaine would sell an equivalent amount of water to Canada via Surrey. Locals were dismayed when this kind of fair and even trade was not even acknowledged by the Canadian authorities.[652] [653] With water running seriously low, hookup charges for new water accounts were hiked seventy-five per cent in February 1983. A new well many were counting on to provide relief disappointingly failed in March 1983. Looking at the rest of their potential well sites, the water board came to the uneasy conclusion only three of eighteen sites were at all promising and the chance of locating water locally was "remote."[654] The idea for building an undersea water pipeline to Blaine was first seriously studied in July 1984, but whilst it seemed simple, the logistics weren't viable. There were continuous cutbacks in water service through late 1986. Residential water usage restrictions were introduced in the 1980s. Water restrictions are the ultimate irony because not only is Point Roberts surrounded by water, it is the fact it is surrounded by water which causes it to exist as an exclave, yet as an exclave, there isn't enough fresh water, and no easy way to get water to the exclave from the rest of its homeland. The invisible manmade line on the map never felt as real.

Finally, the community's efforts reached a tipping point of momentum in getting the attention of senior levels of government about the water situation. The local water board escalated its case to every level of government, eventually leading to an agreement. It took no less than the following bodies to come to the table to provide water to Point Roberts: the International Boundary Commission, Governor General of Canada, the Canadian Transport Commission, British Columbia provincial ministries and its legislature, the local Delta government, U.S. Department of Agriculture, Washington State Department of Social and Health Services, Washington State Department of Ecology and its environmental impact statements, Whatcom County, U.S. Congressmen & Senators, State Senators and Representatives and British Columbia Premier Vander Zalm.[655]

On August 28, 1987, the water district completed final negotiations and secured $4.7 million (over $10 million in today's money) in funding, needed for an endless list of legal costs, engineering, construction of water reservoirs, water lines and a pump station. On April 19, 1988 it signed a half-century agreement with the Greater Vancouver Water District to draw 840,000 gallons of water per day from a reservoir a few hundred meters north in Tsawwassen[656] for a $2.2 million connection fee; and you thought your last water bill was high.[657] And just in the nick of time. Days later the Solomon well, which had been providing a full thirty-five per cent of Point Roberts' water, went dry.[658] The main reservoir you passed in chapter 1 on Roosevelt Way was built on 3.5 acres in August 1988 and holds 2.5 million gallons. With a water supply secured, development was immediate. By the end of the year, border crossings were up 18 per cent, soaring to a record 1.4 million crossings. "Probably never before in history has such a small community and water district been required to comply with such a multiplicity of international, domestic and foreign national, state and provincial, county and municipal laws and regulations," wrote Glennys Christie in the local paper.

With a water source secured, community debate raged as to whether Point Roberts should be opened up for rapid development, Tsawwassen-style as a long-awaited way to kick start the economy, or whether it should retain its identity, with its idyllic, slow-paced rural feel. As soon as water was available, development proposals popped up everywhere. Construction, condos, hotels, a gravel pit and especially logging were all in the works. After a twelve year county moratorium on building permits, the arrival of reliable water caused building permits to jump 25 per cent.[659] Locals who need to make a living at Point Roberts welcomed new jobs. But newcomers who had fled development and urban sprawl wanted to keep the Point as a bucolic retreat. The lack of a community zoning charter exasperated the situation. The community realized they had fought for water for so long, but had not prepared for the changes it would bring. It was grappling with the impacts of having water in an ad hoc way. Many landholders who had long wanted to develop their land but were waiting for water now had water but couldn't log their land, because the water deal coincided with the peak of the heron rookery, and development anywhere near the nesting area was still prohibited. Were it not for the border, Point Roberts would be as developed as Tsawwassen, fully built out. The balance between development and character is a debate which has never been solved, continuing to this day trying to perfect a delicate balance.

But the lesson of Point Roberts is to not get too cozy with the current situation. Decisions outside its control can and do happen at any time. Point Roberts uses less than a third of the water it buys on any given day.[660] When demand for water was highlighted as a political issue in recent years, the British Columbia legislature passed an updated law stating no water could be sold to anybody outside Canada. Point Roberts was suddenly back to having its water supply being threatened, but dodged the bullet as a clause to honor current contracts was included. When water restrictions hit the Lower Mainland of British Columbia during a drought in 2015, Vancouver media incorrectly reported residents of Point Roberts had unlimited use of Metro Vancouver water. The resulting uproar neglected to mention unlike Vancouver, Point Roberts customers have water meters and are charged based on the volume of water they use.

There is water supply today but no sewers except around the marina. Septic systems are the norm and must be factored in to how lots are improved. Hundreds of zoned lots cannot be built on due to swampy land where septic tanks won't be approved. Most residential lots date from the late 1950s and early 1960s, and the original half-century-old septic tanks are failing. A public vote to fund a sewer system failed at the polls in 1976, fifty-six to forty-four per cent. There were serious talks of installing a sewer system from 1990 to 1992, but the motion died.[661] A water district vote to approve a sewer system was voted down in September 2003.[662]

The availability of water has probably done more for the recent growth in Point Roberts than any other factor. Beachfront condos, a golf course, a resort and larger homes for year-round families are examples of what having access to water has meant for Point Roberts. Having water transformed the possibilities for development in Point Roberts, and the Point has quickly and steadily grown since then. The water district currently provides service to over 2000 customers.

Continue along Johnson Road, going straight at the stop sign at Mill Road. This section of Johnson Road between Mill Road and Tyee Drive is the newest major road in Point Roberts. It was proposed in July 1991, offering residents in the Point's northeast quadrant convenient access to the border, but came at the expense of the closure of Roosevelt Way at the border.[663]

Turn left at Tyee Drive, the north-south main drag through the Point. After its narrow lanes and deep ditches claimed many cars, it was widened with shoulders in May 1977.[664]

POINT ROBERTS ECONOMY

The Point Roberts economy is driven by its exclave status. All land-based trade must cross an international border subject to inspection, importation rules and taxation. As early as 1939 residents protested the need for those hauling freight to unload at Blaine and again at Point Roberts. A system was introduced using tamper-proof seals placed on freight. For a while in the 1960s the flavor-of-the-week idea was to designate it as a free port, a la Monaco. A flurry of proposals in 1964 urged that the Point be designated a duty-free international port. As a tax haven, Point Roberts would attract industry and the infrastructure to spur growth.[665] As Canada developed the Roberts Bank Superport, it increasingly made sense to leverage Point Roberts' close proximity to Vancouver as an international port, complete with a trade fair and exposition center. A 1965 planning study for the Whatcom County Council envisaged Point Roberts as an integral component of Canada's Roberts Bank Superport.[666] By 1969 a proposal gained steam to move the Washington State International Trade Fair, built in 1962 at the Seattle Center for the Seattle World's Fair, to Point Roberts as the anchor the free port concept. The proponents described a grand exposition center in Point Roberts to "meet the region's needs for a great business and industrial showplace for foreign buyers or sellers."[667] Never built, it is a good example of the potential Point Roberts could play in its strategic position between Vancouver, Victoria and Seattle.

In December 1969, Canadian customs officials 2700 miles away in Ottawa started cracking down on Point Roberts residents buying stuff on the U.S. mainland and taking their goods home by driving through Canada. For years, Point Roberts-bound travelers would simply mention they were in-transit to the exclave and it was all good. Suddenly, they threw a book of strict and perplexing import regulations at goods in-transit to Point Roberts. When a Point Roberts resident shopped on the mainland they had to purchase a twenty-five cent seal (imagine paying $1.70 per bag in today's money) for specific sizes and types of plastic bags. These sealed goods were placed in the trunk when entering Canada and the seal would be checked when arriving at the U.S. border to enter Point Roberts. Itemized receipts or inventories in triplicate of goods going through Canada are still technically required to this day. Residents are worried there is nothing stopping a rule crackdown at any time from a federal government in Washington D.C. or Ottawa which could severely complicate life in the exclave more than it is already. Mainlanders cannot imagine facing these federal regulations to merely come home from the store, yet this is daily life in Point Roberts.

Tradesmen on the U.S. mainland often decline work requests from Point Roberts. Even simple jobs require the crew have passports and have no arrests or DUIs on their record in order to pass through Canada. There is a gauntlet of customs procedures to get their goods, supplies, tools and equipment documented and sealed to cross the border. The crew, on the clock, is inspected at both border crossings coming and going. Bonded trucks and freight forwarders often need to be arranged, whose services between the Point and the mainland date back to 1934.

Similarly, business owners on Point Roberts endure similar challenges getting supplies, none more so than the grocery store and restaurant owners due to the involvement of fresh food. It's far easier to ship food from the U.S. mainland, even with shipping costs from as far away as Seattle, than it is to get something from just across the boundary line in Tsawwassen. Sourcing in Canada involves duties and inspection checks associated with the importation of goods. The pre-9/11 era was relaxed and local practices were tolerated. Today, edicts come from a centralized, federal level which have huge impacts on everyday life in an exclave. The terrorist attacks of September 11, 2001 and the creation of the Department of Homeland Security resulted in far-more stringent rules governing the border. Many new national security laws were passed, some with daunting paperwork for things which used to be a common nod at the Point Roberts border. For the first time, travelers had to have a passport to enter Point Roberts; for years driver's licenses or birth certificates sufficed. Thousands of people were turned away from the border, denied entry because they hadn't heard the news and hadn't brought their passport, or didn't have a passport to begin with. Forty per cent of Canadians and sixty-four per cent of Americans don't have a passport, and couldn't drive to Point Roberts until the introduction of the enhanced driver's license. Local restaurants depending on Canadians for their customer base were decimated as their patrons couldn't get in to Point Roberts; most tables during the dinner rush were empty a year after the new passport rules were introduced.[668] The restaurants had to phone Canadian customers holding reservations to remind them to bring the new documentation.[669] In 2002, the Bioterrorism Act was introduced to protect the nation's food supply. It required the Food and Drug Administration to be notified by anybody importing food for more than personal use two to eight hours before the food's arrival at the border, and the manufacturer of the imported food must have previously registered with the Food and Drug Administration. This stroke of the pen in Washington, D.C. essentially criminalized the ability of a Point Roberts restaurant owner to run over the border and buy a few loaves from a specialty bakery in Tsawwassen.[670] These new regulations also introduced the prohibition of firewood and plants from importation into the United States from Canada, ending trips by locals to nurseries in Delta, and prompting a nursery to open in Point Roberts. The local newspaper painted a dark mood in February 2002 in the wake of 9/11. It lamented the Breakers nightclub had closed, another popular bar was now closed mid-week and had shortened hours overall. It described the drive down Gulf Road, supposedly one of two commercial strips, as a "dark drive." The Canadian dollar was weak, the economy was in a recession, breathalyzers were frequently used on people leaving the Point, visitor traffic was down over fifty per cent and it was a dreary winter to boot.[671] The response to the discovery in 2003 of mad cow disease in North America changed daily life in Point Roberts for years. The United States had banned beef imports from Canada in May 2003, and in December Canada forbid beef imports from the United States, meaning no beef could travel through Canada to get to Point Roberts. A wholesale grocery supply truck on its way from Bellingham to the Point Roberts Marketplace on December 29, 2003 was turned away at Blaine. The truck's contents, frozen dinners, soups, pet food and nutritional supplements, some with just traces of beef fat far down the ingredients list, were all prevented from entering Canada. The supermarket in Point Roberts had to scramble to arrange shipments of groceries by ship and air.[672] Locals were skimming ingredients lists on everything they bought on trips to the mainland. After a duck in the Fraser River valley caught avian flu, all uncooked poultry was banned from being brought over the border in January 2006, further complicating shopping by Point Roberts residents.

External economic forces can in an instant create sweeping impacts on daily life and the economy in Point Roberts. The community has had to adapt several times to totally remaking its economy based on frivolous decisions made far away in WOVO: Washington, D.C., Ottawa, Victoria and Olympia. Canadian economic policy, currency exchange rates, border policy in an era of terrorism, labor strikes and U.S. laws written for mainland life or the southern border have had unintended ripple effects in the exclave. This unpredictability has resulted in a limited range of businesses on the Point, and a volatile economic climate to which Point Roberts has had to adapt.

Much of the rest of our tour of Point Roberts will focus on the Point Roberts economy, largely comprised of retail trade and services. The local economy ebbs and flows based on the strength of the Canadian dollar and national taxes and regulations in both the United States and Canada. Being a border community, Point Roberts capitalizes on being the closest American town to Vancouver, but is also at the mercy of decisions made by politicians with no accountability to Point Bob's residents. This book has discussed a number of these already: border blasters who wanted to mar the beauty and safety of Point Roberts to get around Canadian broadcasting regulations; Canadian infrastructure projects such as the Massey tunnel bringing more car traffic; racial policy spurring human trafficking; the Roberts Bank Superport increasing the risk of spills and environmental damage; the struggle in keeping garbage service and recycling; the challenges in providing water. In this chapter, many more stories of how decisions made afar impact daily life and economic prospects in Point Roberts will paint a picture of a community which has had to reinvent itself repeatedly, with both defensive adjustments to its economy as well as seizing proactive opportunities to leverage the difference in laws and economic policies on either side of the border.

Retail trade is the oldest business on Point Roberts. From the retail stores outfitting miners in Roberts Town, to the company stores of the canneries and the early mercantiles, to the beachside resort stores, retail trade served residents in an isolated locale the goods and services needed to keep a community supplied.

Agriculture, canneries and summer camps came and went, but retail trade has been a constant presence in Point Roberts throughout its eras. For much of the pre-war era of Point Roberts, locals tended to be self-sufficient, able to build or grow things for themselves. They would collect odd bits of flotsam and jetsam which washed up on shore. The Point's retail stores were there to fill the gap as best they could. Still, even to this day, for many common needs, locals must go to Vancouver-area stores, or to the U.S. mainland.

Although over one hundred businesses are registered with the local chamber of commerce, one of the major consequences of being both an exclave and a border town is Point Roberts has a limited number of business categories. Depending how you count there are three dozen customer-facing retail businesses in Point Roberts, but there are only fifteen distinct categories of businesses. There is a supermarket, hardware store, liquor store, country boutique, a couple salons, auto repair, mini-storage, bike rental, art gallery, marina, two banks, five real estate offices, five gas stations (three with mini-marts), four restaurants (some open seasonally) and the largest plurality of any store type in Point Roberts, parcel receiving, with six locations offering this service.

The Point's small population can't support much of an economy, especially since in the winter only a few hundred people remain. Between seventy-five and ninety per cent of customers are Canadians, who can have different shopping missions than locals. This leads to businesses geared to visitors, not the needs of the local population. There's lots of gas, beer and wine, cheese and parcel pickup, but many essential goods for local year-round residents are simply not available. At the average U.S.-Canadian border crossing, forty per cent of Canadians say they are visiting the U.S. for shopping, but at Point Roberts, only seven per cent say they're coming to the Point to shop 'til they drop.[673] There is a long list of what there isn't. There are no dedicated stores for clothing, shoes, consignments, picture framing, crafts, office supplies, music, books or toys. There is no dedicated bakery, Mexican or Asian of any kind, health food, pizza delivery, drive-through or food truck. No barber, hotel, gym, cinema, travel agent, florist or Uber drivers. There isn't even a duty-free store. Despite being legal in Washington, there is no cannabis retail store in Point Roberts. Cannabis cannot travel over the international boundary through Canada, so Point Roberts has yet to experience legal pot as on the mainland. The lack of business type diversity means having to make frequent trans-border errands, with their lineups and declarations. Besides gasoline brands, the utter absence of chain stores (it seems like the only town in America without a Starbucks or Subway restaurant) gives the Point a quaint mom and pop feel.

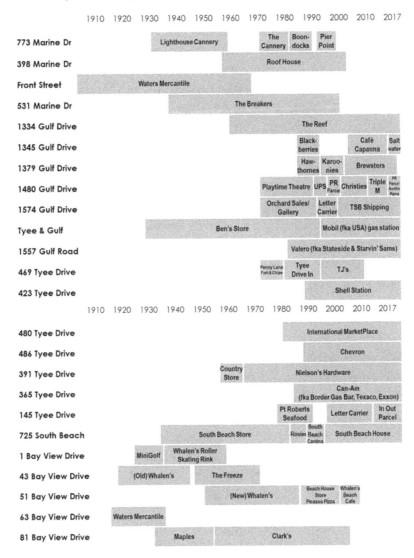

Figure 85: Gantt chart timeline of key Point Roberts businesses shows the shift from waterfront businesses to a commercial strip on Tyee Drive and Gulf Road. Graphic by Mark Swenson.

Until the 1930s, the easiest way to get to and from Point Roberts was by water. As a result, until the 1980s most businesses on Point Roberts were along the shoreline. Canneries, dockside mercantiles, resort and beachside stores, neighborhood markets, beer halls and nightclubs lined the beaches of the Point. From the 1980s commercial trade began to shift inland to the Tyee Drive and Gulf Road corridors, away from a water-based connection to the outside world and toward a road-linked connection to Canada. The Point Roberts Character Plan covered these two commercial streets, dictating the appearance of commercial businesses on these two streets in an effort to prevent tacky commercial blight and to create a conforming range of maritime, historical and Northwest contemporary veneers. There are few businesses on the beach today; with only a couple notable exceptions, waterfront lots are almost all residential. That leaves the two inland main drags as home to the Point Roberts economy. The Gantt chart in Figure 85 shows the shift from waterside businesses to the central commercial strip along Gulf Road and Tyee Drive.

GAS STATIONS

The single largest category of cross-border visits to Point Roberts is drivers coming to purchase gasoline. A full forty per cent of border-crossers are coming to Point Roberts to fill up on gas.[674] Gas stations are popular on Point Roberts because gas is significantly cheaper than in Canada, due to lower taxes. The border serves to put the two countries' tax systems side by side, where societal & governmental priorities are different. Point Roberts benefits from its lower tax rate next to Canada's higher taxation for well-funded social services, which the U.S. lacks.

Driving south down Tyee Drive the first gas station is the busy Can-Am station, which sees steady business because it is the closest gas station to the border. Originally called Border Gas Bar and then operated under several brands, it opened in June 1985. Automated pumps allow 24-hour fueling and its close position to the border means Can-Am's sixteen pumps are usually occupied with Canadians filling up on cheap U.S. gas.

The retail gasoline business accelerated in the mid-1980s in Point Roberts. As recently as 1983, Point Roberts had only two gas pumps. In March of that year, gas prices spiked thirty per cent in British Columbia from 37 to 49 cents per liter. Overnight, the two gas pumps at the Point's lone gas station were offering gas for sale forty cents per gallon cheaper than just over the border in Tsawwassen. This station, Ben's Department Store, sold eight thousand gallons of gas in a normal month, but now the store was selling 19,000 gallons a week.[675] Seeing the chance for huge profits, in June 1983 a second gas station in Point Roberts opened on Gulf Road. Local media gushed at the thought of twelve cars filling their tanks at the same time.[676] By the late 1980s, the retail gasoline industry on Point Roberts had grown to the sixty pumps which exist today, one for every nine residents in 1983 and one for every twenty-two residents today. After more gas stations opened, in February 1989 a large contingent of Point Roberts residents traveled to Bellingham to complain about the number of gas stations at a Whatcom County Council meeting. Locals wanted to preserve the natural beauty in Point Roberts, and felt the Tyee Drive strip was becoming tacky and commercialized, especially with large signs advertising the cheap gas prices. Residents complained about long lineups of visitors crossing the border to buy gas, and the heavy tanker trucks supplying the gas stations which clogged the border in the days before there was a dedicated truck lane. Pleading for help to stop the commercialism of Point Roberts, they succeeded in getting a moratorium placed on new gas stations, which is still in effect today.

The impact of retail gasoline sales in Point Roberts is felt far and wide. In December 1991, a gas tax was approved by voters. The proceeds were intended for the establishment of ferry service to Blaine. That never happened, but in February 1994 the funds were used to add a center turn lane down the middle of Tyee Drive between Benson and Gulf Roads.[677] In February 1989 strict weight restrictions were imposed on Tyee Drive. Exemptions were made for school buses, emergency vehicles and perishable food, but the big gas tanker trucks which regularly supply local gas stations were too heavy for the weight limit. As supplies dwindled, Ben's and an Exxon station made a killing because only their gas supplier's trucks were light enough to comply with the weight restrictions.[678] Today, over 3.75 million liters of gasoline are sold every month in Point Roberts. That's over 769 gallons per month for every person in Point Roberts, giving you an idea of how much the local economy is dependent on visitors from Canada. Complaining of lost taxes, the city of Port Moody, British Columbia actually sent the Canadian government a letter estimating ten per cent of all gas consumed in Lower Mainland was bought in Whatcom County, much of that in Point Roberts.[679]

That so many Canadians will wait in long lineups just to cross the border to save on gas means the savings must be worth it. Prices fluctuate independently in each country, so a rise in gas prices on one side of the border doesn't always mean the other side has also risen, but on average the savings are between sixty cents and U.S.$1.25 per U.S. gallon from the stations next door in Tsawwassen. As I wrote this chapter, gas was U.S.$2.89 per U.S. gallon in Point Roberts versus U.S.$3.71 per U.S. gallon in Tsawwassen. Canadians can save twenty to forty dollars on a fill-up. I quote gallon statistics here for American readers, but it should be noted gas is sold by the liter in Point Roberts, perhaps the only American town to do so. Since Americans are used to seeing gas prices in the two or three dollar range, seeing the gas prices in mere cents is quite a novelty to Americans visiting from the mainland, adding to the exotic feel of the exclave. Since we're discussing gallons and liters, a bit of a backstory on the metric system is warranted.

We don't think of the U.S. as using the metric system. It's used in specialized industries and technologies, but other than a two-liter bottle of pop very few instances of the metric system reach the average American. Indeed, many Americans make fun of the metric system. After dabbling with it in the 1970s during the Carter administration, the U.S. cut funding for metric conversion in the 1980s.

Figure 86: Looking north on Tyee Drive in 2016, a gas station and convenience store sit at the former site of Ben's Store. Note the price of gasoline is in U.S. cents by the liter. Photo by Mark Swenson.

The liter-based gas prices make Point Roberts feel like a metricated town, thanks to the fact Canada switched to the metric system over forty years ago, starting in 1975. Prior to that, when Canada used the imperial system of measurement, things were confusing, because most units were the same in the United States and Canada except for the gallon. Canada used the imperial gallon, which is 4.55 liters, whilst the United States uses the U.S. gallon, which is 3.79 liters. (In agriculture, bushels are also different, the Canadian bushel having one more liter than a U.S. bushel.) Switching to liters in the metric system alleviated that confusion, but introduced new confusion in that Canada and the United States today use different weights and measurement systems, and Point Roberts is, as ever, caught in the middle.

France was the first nation to adopt the metric system, in the 1790s. The most recent country to convert was Saint Lucia, which switched to the metric system in 2005. That left only the United States, Myanmar and Liberia not using the metric system today. Canada's metrication program was eased in over several years in the late 1970s. Metric product labeling arrived in 1976 (except milk, which switched in 1980). Temperature in Celsius was instated in April 1975 and precipitation switched in September of that year. Road signs converted all in one month across Canada, in September 1977. Fuel switched from gallons to liters in Canada in 1979.

Aviation is blended across systems. At YVR, the airport code and common nickname for the Vancouver International Airport located just eighteen miles (29km) north of Point Roberts, your luggage is weighed in kilograms, but runways and altitude are measured in imperial feet. When aviation fuel switched to metric, this caused a famous aviation accident on July 23, 1983. A pound-to-kilogram mistake led Air Canada Flight 143, a Boeing 767 twin-aisle jumbo jet flying from Montreal to Edmonton, to run out of fuel mid-flight over Gimli, Manitoba. Out of gas, the jet had to glide to the ground, giving the incident the moniker Gimli Glider. Like Point Roberts, Gimli was settled by Icelandic immigrants and today is the largest concentration of Icelanders outside Iceland and home to a major annual Icelandic festival. The Canadian government reserved a large tract of land called New Iceland in October 1875 for Icelandic settlers, whom they apparently had to pay to settle there. It was governed locally by the Icelanders until it was annexed by Manitoba in 1880. Icelanders still make up a solid 2.5% of Manitoba's population.

Although Canada feels to Americans like a very metric country, it is not fully metric by world standards. Canadian driver's licenses show height in centimeters, but many Canadian adults still verbalize their height and weight in imperial measurements. TVs are measured in inches. Lumber is still sold in imperial measurements.

Nails are sold by the gram but sized by the inch. Paper and photo sizes are in inches in Canada, following the U.S. "letter" and "legal" paper sizes, not the A4 size used in the rest of the world. However, the Canadian government uses a proprietary paper sizing system which is close to the American 8.5 inch by 11-inch letter paper size, but rounded to the nearest five millimeters. The Canadian Football League and golfers measure their sports in yards, not meters. And in the kitchen, Canadians usually cook with imperial measurements and Fahrenheit oven temperatures, despite appliances and metric measuring cups and spoons being commonly available.

Just a kilometer north of Point Roberts, Canadian supermarkets in Tsawwassen are blended. Some specials are advertised by the pound in the weekly flyer, but sold in the store by the gram. In the center aisles, packaged goods are packaged in round imperial units but labeled in metric; this is why there are so many Canadian packages sized at 454 grams, which is one pound, a practice known as "soft metric" (as opposed to "hard metric" which sees the metric system adopted throughout the supply chain resulting in packages in round numbers of metric measurements, like 500 grams instead of 454). Cans of pop are soft metric at 355 mL, the equivalent of 12 U.S. fluid ounces since the 1990s.

As a result of shopping in Canada, listening to Vancouver radio and interacting with Canadians on the Point, residents of Point Roberts are quite adept at switching back and forth between meters and feet, grams and ounces, acres and hectares, m.p.h. and km/h, and Fahrenheit and Celsius. Whilst the gas-by-the-liter signs feel metricated to American visitors, what's actually surprising is that Point Roberts isn't more metricated. One would think with four-fifths of drivers being Canadian the county would add speed limit signs in kilometers per hour, but the only such dual-speed sign is a tiny one right after the border station. Directional signage on the Point does not list distances in metric, as in "Marina, 1 km." There is no digital signage displaying the temperature in Celsius. The tide table in the newspaper lists water levels in feet. The binary nature of the border keeps Point Roberts deep in an imperial measurement mindset, liters at the gas pump notwithstanding, sometimes causing missed opportunities to cater to the perspective of an international customer.

SHOPPING

With 22,000 people living just meters away in Tsawwassen, it is a bit surprising there aren't more retail stores in more retail categories in Point Roberts to tempt Canadian shoppers. Whilst the Americans in Point Roberts grumble about how expensive everything is in Point Roberts compared to the U.S. mainland, prices in Point Roberts are a bargain for Canadians. When the corporate folks decide where to place new retail chain stores, they use U.S. census data which shows Point Roberts as an isolated town of 1,300, not a strategic town of 23,000 if you put Point Roberts and Tsawwassen together, a reasonable thing to do given they are both perched on the Roberts peninsula sticking out in the Salish Sea.

You're entering the current commercial core of Point Roberts, a couple of blocks long with a hardware store, grocery store, bank and several gas stations and parcel receiving depots. On the northwest corner of the intersection of Tyee and Benson is one of the oldest continuously-operating brick & mortar businesses in Point Roberts. Nielson's Building Center, the Point's hardware store, opened in 1963. With tools, hardware, lumber, gardening supplies and other home improvement supplies, Nielson's is busy with customers fixing up their cabins and homes. Before 1963, Laugi and Ella Thorstenson operated The Country Store at this location, selling gas and groceries.

Continue straight through the intersection of Tyee Drive and Benson Road, protected by one of the Point's two flashing red stop lights; there are no full red-yellow-green traffic lights on the Point.

Next on the right is the Shell Center, which opened in June 1985.[680] A four-in-one business with gas, dairy, coffee roasting and parcel receiving, it adds eight more gas pumps to the Point's total. Across the street, the empty field on the left side of the street was the old Benson homestead. From 1977 into the early 1980s it was a golf driving range.

Next on the left is the International Marketplace, the Point's supermarket. Originally proposed in December 1979, it opened September 1, 1982 and was originally called Mark & Pak,[681] switching to the Marketplace name in November 1985.[682] The arrival for the first time of a proper supermarket, a step above a neighborhood market, was heralded in the community and local newspaper. Businesses throughout Point Roberts and Tsawwassen – some of which competed for food sales – ran ads in the paper welcoming Mark & Pak. Residents gushed about the novel concept of being able to buy ice cream for the first time; previously, ice cream bought on the mainland would melt all over the car in fold-up cartons before you could get it home to Point Roberts. By the late 1980s the store was part of a regional Northwest chain of grocery stores called Brown & Cole, based in Bellingham. The Point Roberts outlet was the largest Brown & Cole store outside the city of Bellingham.[683] An expansion in October 1991 saw the square footage grow from 14,000 to 35,000 square feet and new point of sale scanners installed. The expansion brought a delicatessen with seating, larger butcher shop, video rentals, general merchandise and even shoes offered for sale. The renovation "incorporated genuine rope-wrapped pilings as its front entrance" to conform to the Character Plan.[684] The north entrance's mural of a map of Point Roberts, meant to give the store the look of a "vintage country store," was painted June 1995.[685] Marketplace became one of the six parcel receiving businesses in Point Roberts when it began providing postal service in 1991.[686] The bank inside the supermarket opened in March 1996 in a space formerly occupied by a travel agency. Today, the Marketplace serves as a community hub, with the local food bank drop-off and a community bulletin board. Canadians mob the place, where groceries are about thirty per cent cheaper than in Tsawwassen. Canuck kids gush at the exotic American candy bars, whilst parents stand agape at the greater assortment of goods stocked in each product category than found in Canada. The cash registers have dual cash drawers for both U.S. and Canadian currency. The staff takes care to keep up to date on border regulations, posting signs in the produce and meat sections indicating which products are prohibited from crossing the border.

ENGLISH
CUCUMBERS
$1.69 EACH GROWN IN
MEXICO
231
PROHIBITED from crossing border

Figure 87: Signage in the supermarket informs shoppers whether goods may cross the border. Photo by Mark Swenson.

When a household's needs require a greater supply of goods than can be purchased in Point Roberts, locals shop outside the exclave. Prices are high and selection is limited in Canada, so many residents make the trek to Bellingham for large stock-up trips. The challenges of living in an exclave often are told in stories about utilities, contractors and dealing with the border, but everyday shopping is often overlooked as one of biggest ways living in an exclave is tough. Let's follow two average shoppers, one a typical mainland American family, and one in Point Roberts, to appreciate the challenges of living on the Point.

Betty Blaine and Point Polly are busy soccer moms. Each with two kids, one thirteen and one aged nine years, they both live in three-bedroom split-level homes and drive minivans. They each leave their house one Saturday morning to go to a big box store in Bellingham. Each mom starts prepping for the shopping trip. Betty and Polly both jot down a quick shopping list, find coupons they've clipped and pile the kids in the car. Just as they're getting ready to leave, each mom coincidentally gets a similar text from a frantic neighbor pleading to watch her son for a few hours due to a sudden situation. Betty says sure, and the neighbor kid joins Betty's clan. It's not so easy for Polly. The neighbor delivers her kid along with a notarized letter signed by both parents, kept handy which informs the border officials her child is knowingly with Polly. Parents routinely keep this kind of letter handy for neighbors and babysitters who watch their kids.

Because the neighbor kid doesn't have a NEXUS card, Polly must use the regular border lanes at the border crossings. Because she wants to arrive at the Bellingham store right when it opens at 9:00, she must leave an hour early to account for border lineups plus the forty-five minute drive, meaning the minivan pulls out at 7:15 A.M. Betty can sleep in and get by with leaving her home in Blaine at 8:45. Betty opens the sliding door to the minivan and as kids pile in, a moldy apple slice and a half-eaten hamburger from a forgotten

Happy Meal fall out onto the driveway, disgusting, sure, but no big deal for Betty. Over at Polly's house, this could never happen. Polly plans enough time to inspect the car from end to end. She opens the glove compartment, the center console and sun visors. Though she did a similar inspection a day or two ago, she still takes time to reach under every seat in the car, ensuring no apple, onion or Happy Meal remnants are lurking beneath. She feels inside the seat pockets and does a full inspection of the rear cargo area. To cross the border, it is critical she knows everything in her vehicle and no restricted good is inadvertently on board in case she is sent into secondary inspection at any of the four international border crossings for this shopping trip.

Once at the big box store Betty loads up her shopping cart with the retailer's weekly promotions. Attractive end-caps display items on sale, saving Betty money on her weekly shopping trip. Over in the wine department, the store is having a sale on New Zealand Sauvignon Blanc, so Betty puts four bottles in her cart. Polly happens to be in the same aisle and notices the wine sale. She'd like to take advantage of the sale too, but that promotion would exceed her duty limit, so she can't avail herself of the offer. Point Roberts customers routinely have to forego savings opportunities on the mainland due to restrictions in bringing home the goods. Kids grow fast, so in the shoe department Betty buys one of her kids a new pair of sneakers. Polly's kid also needs new shoes, but the duty can be very high on footwear and she skips the shoe department making a note to buy the shoes online, hoping the sneakers will fit. If the shoes don't fit, she'll then have to go to the hassle of shipping them back, but at least Point Roberts has a plethora of shipping outlets.

In the food section, Betty adds items to her shopping cart with little care, buying impulse items, seasonal produce, items on sale, ingredients for recipes and healthy school lunch items. Polly must be much more careful. Before the trip to Bellingham, she queried government web sites to get the most-recent list of restricted goods.

If she gets caught crossing the border with prohibited food, the old excuse she didn't know which specific apples which were OK in the past but are now banned won't hold up. It is Polly's responsibility to know what can be brought across the border. They don't make it easy to know what's on the current list as the rules keep changing. Some foods are only banned seasonally and others are OK only if packaged in a certain way. For instance, Polly knows never to peel off the country-of-origin stickers on produce before she gets to the border. It's common to learn about new restrictions from neighbors who had had their goods confiscated or taxed. Polly is especially careful on trips where she uses the NEXUS lane. A small mistake can result in having one's card taken forever, with no realistic appeals process available. Like many people in Point Roberts, Polly is concerned about inadvertent misunderstandings. To ensure she's in compliance with the current rules, Polly has printed them out and brought them along. This week's list indicates prohibited goods include live plants, firewood, soil, meat, eggs, whole spices, fruit and vegetables from outside North America, but fruits from certain British Columbia valleys which are also a no-no. Loose oranges are banned even with stickers on them, but OK if they're bagged and organic. Canadian potatoes are OK to come into the United States unless they're from Prince Edward Island or Newfoundland. The rules are especially sensitive regarding apples, plums and maize. Polly must be very particular when dealing with nuts and seeds, which are permitted if shelled and roasted. If they're raw they can only come from Canada or the United States. Sandwiches and salads are allowed, but not if they contain fruit. Fully cooked prepared food and canned meats are okay unless they have beans or rice in them. Baked goods are allowed; pet food and pet treats are not. In the floral department Betty buys a beautiful bouquet of tulips, but Polly doesn't dare bring freshly cut flowers over the border as they could be confiscated. With complex rules like that (and that's just the U.S. rules, Polly also has the Canadian rules handy), changing frequently, Polly gets used to not carrying any fresh meat or produce over the border, no matter how tempting the store displays and low prices are.

The big box store has a gas station in the forecourt. Betty has a half a tank and so she skips the lineup since she can always fill up in Blaine. Polly also has a half-tank but she takes the opportunity to wait in the queue to buy gas as it is twenty-five cents per gallon cheaper than on the Point. A fill-up on the mainland is a must regardless of how full her minivan's tank is. On the way home Betty sees a farmer's stand selling fresh berries. Whatcom County is one of America's largest blueberry, raspberry and strawberry producers, and a flat of berries is inexpensive, fresh and makes a healthy dessert for her family. Polly sees the same stand and would love to buy fresh local berries, but she's worried about getting them across two borders so she passes the opportunity. Betty has been home for over an hour as Polly finally is ready to head out of Bellingham back toward Point Roberts. However, she needs to stop at a coffeeshop to create her inventory list and organize her receipts. She has brought along carbon paper to hand-write a detailed list of everything she purchased in triplicate; just listing "groceries" is not sufficient. If the item has a serial number of any kind, that too must be written down on the inventory list. Goods travelling from the mainland to Point Roberts are technically being imported into Canada, even though they're really in-transit through Canada for a half-hour or so. Often the border guards will wave through in-transit items, but sometimes one encounters a border official who evaluates purchases as imports. The Canadian Border Services Agency's District Director told a community meeting in April 2010, "There is no in-transit provision in our books."[687] One reason for forming the sister-city relationship with Campobello Island is to widen the campaign to authorities in both countries to create a policy provision for exclaves. Polly also checks the latest currency exchange rates, as she must also calculate the total value of the goods she's bringing over the border in both Canadian and U.S. currency, as she may be asked that amount at each border crossing, each official wanting to know the value of the goods in their own currency. Though Polly's daily life is more of a hassle, but she wouldn't live anywhere else.

Pop into the Marketplace and pick up a copy of the local newspaper, the *All Point Bulletin*. Free copies of this monthly newspaper are available inside the store. Published since May 1985, of interest to visitors are the tide tables and events calendar. The *All Point Bulletin* succeeded the previous monthly newspaper, *The Ocean Star*, which published from 1976 to 1985. Earlier newspapers included the *Point Robert Guide*, published between 1970 and 1972, the *Point Roberts Beacon* and *The Pointer*. Between monthly editions of the newspaper, folks in Point Roberts keep themselves informed by a group email service called Point Interface. Everything from lost dogs to garage sales to requests for contractors to community organization meeting reminders gets posted to the Point Interface, run by the Point's animal welfare society. Seemingly everybody in the exclave has signed up to receive the dozen-or-so postings every day. The Point Roberts Business and Tourism Council hosts the website pointrobertsnow.com for visitors and newcomers. Other websites pose problems for Point Roberts. When locals post ads to Craigslist.org in the Bellingham page, nobody responds because Point Roberts is so far away. When locals post ads to the Vancouver page, Canadians often flag the listings as listed inappropriately in a Canadian page, even though the poster was specifically targeting buyers just across the line in Delta.

The grocery store's forecourt has a Chevron gas station which opened in the spring of 1989,[688] and an Umpqua Bank branch. In the spring of 1981 residents became more vocal bemoaning the lack of a bank. In an era before debit cards, automatic teller machines and Internet banking, all banking required driving all the way to the mainland. This bank opened September 1, 1982, the very same day as the Mark & Pak, and has been owned and operated under many different brands over the years. In June 1998 it was a Sterling Bank branch, and the bank's corporate owners filmed a TV commercial here.[689]

Next door, a gas station sits facing the head of Gulf Road, taking advantage of being at the busiest intersection within Point Roberts. This prime spot was the sixty-three year home of legendary Ben's Store from 1928 to 1991. Named after original owner Ben Thordarson, for years it was the main general merchandise and food store on Point Roberts. This was the quintessential mom and pop store, where the proprietors knew all customers by name and their preferences; the original customer relationship management. Old timers recall Ben's Store with fond memories of getting gas, groceries, fishing tackle, ice cream and candy. Thordarson, formerly the accountant of the George & Barker Cannery until it closed in 1929,[690] opened Ben's Store. Ben's offered a cup of coffee and a chat 363 days per year. It was the go-to place for essentials like tide tables.[691] In the early years, Ben realized the local population, mostly fishermen and small farmers with scarce income much of the year and then windfalls during harvests, needed extended credit. When customers brought their bill current at the end of the month, Ben would slip in treats for the kids and a cigar for dad. Kids couldn't wait for the surprise when somebody came home from a trip to Ben's.[692] As other stores closed, Ben's Store expanded in 1934 with the annexation of a half-acre of land. During World War II gas was strictly rationed in Canada, so there were big lineups at Ben's for its single gas pump during times gas wasn't being rationed in the States. A manual pump, one's hand was sore after filling the tank because of how tightly the pump had to be gripped. But the Canadian visitors couldn't shop for much in the store as they did not have U.S. ration books, so business was tight during the war.[693]

Ben's served as one of the hubs of the community. During wartime, scrap metal drives were organized at Ben's. Before

Ben's
Dept. Store, Inc.
• • •

GROCERIES
FRESH MEAT
— VEGETABLES —
FRUIT

SEE US FOR TOOL RENTALS

•Ladders Up to 40'   • Elec. Drills

"THE COUNTRY STORE
WITH THE FRIENDLY SMILE"   •Belt Sanders   • Circ. Saws.   •Router

POINT ROBERTS, WASH.

OPEN 7 DAYS A WEEK
Phone 945-2833

Figure 88: Ben's Store in a 1971 ad and the same view in 2017. Top photo from ad in the Point Roberts Guide. Bottom photo by Mark Swenson.

residential phone service began in 1955, in order to call somebody in Point Roberts, you called Ben's Store, who had the only generally-available phone on the Point. The canneries had phones but they were not for public use. Ben and his wife Runa would take a message, no matter how mundane or personal, trivial or urgent, and get in their car and drive to the person's home to personally relay the news. Runa learned to drive to be able to deliver these messages.[694] Calling itself the "biggest little store in Washington," in 1947 it was leased to Ken Waters. In 1954 it was sold to Carl Julius who owned it until 1966. Julius expanded the twenty by fifty foot store, so it could carry not only staple foods but also TV sets, appliances and clothing, renaming it Ben's Department Store with a new neon sign perched atop the roof.[695] The store had a series of owners after that. Mr. Chips, a fish and chips stand, was tucked behind the store from 1984 to 1986.

Crowning the top of the T-junction at the head of Gulf Road was a great location for a general purpose retail store. The store's gas pumps were right out front very close to the road on Tyee Drive, and immediately across the intersection from the end of Gulf Road. Locals had always feared a car coming up Gulf would T-bone into the gas pumps, fearing the worst. It inevitably happened on September 28, 1987. A car approaching the end of Gulf Road failed to maneuver the turn onto Tyee Drive, instead, slamming into the gas pumps and canopy support. The guy had been coming from the Point's big taverns and was drunk. He somehow got the car into reverse, pulled out of the wreckage, and raced off toward the border. The police pulled him over but didn't arrest him, and he was allowed to continue to the border and return to Canada. The local deputy sheriff took a little heat after admitting the driver should have been arrested, but the hassle of organizing an air lift to Bellingham that night played a factor in his decision not to detain the guy.[696] Ben's Store survived that crash, but four years later it happened again. On October 10, 1991, a car again hit the gas pumps directly, taking out both pumps, careening through the wall of the store and again collapsing the overhang canopy which covered the gas forecourt.[697] In March 1992, it announced it was temporarily closing to repair, remodel and expand the store and gas pumps.[698] However, on August 17, 1992, it was announced it would not reopen after all. When news spread the landmark would be torn down, locals came to get a piece of the wood to save a piece of iconic community history. They had to be quick; the current gas station was open within a month of the announcement Ben's would close.[699]

WHEN VANCOUVER SNEEZES, POINT ROBERTS GETS HEALTHY

Sometimes external macroeconomic changes favor Point Roberts. The North American Free Trade Agreement of 1989 liberalized rules under which Canadians could own and operate businesses in the United States. This brought new business owners to what had been a relatively closed market. Two years later, Canada introduced the Goods and Services Tax which generated a big spike in Canadians coming over the border to avoid paying the GST. It's no wonder 1991 was the record year in border crossings, at 2.6 million, a million more than current volumes.

Besides macroeconomic policy, currency fluctuations have an enormous impact on the Point Roberts economy. At most places on the Point except the post office and the dump, you can pay with Canadian money. Perhaps no other town in the United States so happily accepts the Canadian dollar. Several of the gas stations display gas prices in both U.S. and Canadian cents. Folks in Point Roberts have to keep up with changes in currency, especially Canadian money. The paper Canadian dollar note was withdrawn at the end of 1989 and replaced with the eleven-sided gold Loonie coin. The two dollar Twoonie was introduced in 1996. The Canadian penny was withdrawn in 2012, so prices are rounded to the nearest five cents. Canada is the largest country in the world to use polymer banknotes. These colorful notes depicting innovators were introduced in 2011.

The economy in Point Roberts lives and dies by the Canadian dollar. Business booms when the Canadian dollar is strong, making the gas and alcohol and cheese all the more cheaper for Canadians. Perhaps no other community in Washington is so heavily reliant on the morning's exchange rates. When the Loonie is weak, even the

Point's low prices are costly. The local economy can dive by a fourth or more based on swings in the currency. After doubling each year from 2010 to 2014, the Loonie's nosedive in 2015 decimated Point Roberts business by a quarter. But no panic is evident; Point Roberts business owners have seen this before. Many business owners actually plan for a cyclical Loonie and plan upgrades to their facilities during these downturns.[700] Historic lows in the value of the Canadian dollar are milestone events in Point Roberts history. The Loonie was worth only 69 cents in 1986 during Expo 86, 63 cents in 1998, 61 cents in 2002, and it fell below 70 cents in 2016, each time hitting Point Roberts hard. In just the last five years the Loonie has swung from a high of US$1.06 in July 2011 to a low of 68 cents in January 2016. Such is life in an exclave economy.

Labor actions in Canada often have ripple effects in Point Roberts, which cleans up by exploiting its position near Metro Vancouver. During Canadian postal strikes, hoards of Canadians come to Point Roberts as the closest U.S. post office to Vancouver, in order to send mail to keep their business going. That may not sound like it's that big of deal until one realizes from 1967 to 1979 there were no less than seven postal strikes in Canada. During the 1975 strike there were enormous lineups at the border and during the 1976 strike, three clerks and the postmaster worked six days a week into each evening to process all the mail sent by Canadians.[701]

Brewery strikes are another lucrative event for Point Roberts. There are big brewery strikes in B.C. every few years. In one case, the three big brewers locked out 1500 union workers July 26, 1980.[702] The last time there had been a brewery strike in 1978, liquor stores still had beer because imports from the U.S. continued. This time, the liquor store clerks' union was threatening to refuse to handle imported beer. It was going to be dry. Thousands of Canadians made beer runs to the United States, and Point Roberts being the closest U.S. town to Vancouver, the border was clogged. The strike coincided with a provincial holiday long weekend in the middle of the hot summer, as Terry Fox was running across Canada. There were huge lineups, and special border lanes were opened up to cope with the crush of thirsty visitors. Canadian customs confiscated fifteen hundred cases and twenty-four kegs of undeclared beer.[703]

There was another liquor worker strike in November 1983. The Point Roberts liquor store went from a normal day of $600 in sales to selling on November 10 over $13,200. In all of November 1982 the local liquor store had $27,000 in sales, but from November 1 – 21, 1983, sales had already tallied $79,700. This strike broke the record by eighty per cent for number of people paying duty at the border.[704]

The process happened all over again in 1985. This time, the strike would go on for a dehydrating seven months. Between a ban in British Columbia on Sunday beer sales, and major brewery strikes every few years, Point Roberts remained the go-to place for Canadians who couldn't buy beer when they wanted it, which fortunately for Point Bob, was quite often. To locals, it seemed Point Roberts' ability to fulfill British Columbia's beer cravings would never end, just as the salmon were thought to be inexhaustible. Once again events outside Point Roberts' control would fundamentally change the Point Roberts economic model. Its number one retail product would dry up overnight in 1986, like the sudden end of the Fraser River gold rush in 1859 and the banning of fish traps in 1934, but a new service people could hardly fathom in the late eighties would by the early 1990s replace beer sales as the number one business in Point Roberts. Again, the Point's ability to exploit its closest-to-Vancouver location would transform the retail landscape.

Of the top three Canadian metropolitan areas, Vancouver is closest to the U.S. border. Point Roberts is the closest U.S. town to Canada's third-largest economy. Laws, prohibitions, strikes, corporate control, price rises, taxes, general availability and intellectual property controls can all generate cross-border traffic. Nowhere in the United States do these situations have a higher impact to the local economy than in Point Roberts. With the swoop of a pen from officials in distant capitals, entire business categories can be wiped off the map in the exclave, but they can also be created overnight.

Being the closest piece of the U.S. economy to Vancouver means lots of cross-border trips are made to Point Roberts by Canadians to get things they can't get in Canada, either permanently or temporarily. As mentioned, strikes are one example of when Canadians cross the border to Point Roberts to get goods like beer or mail service impacted by strikes. Similarly, big Powerball lottery jackpots draw huge lineups of Canadians to Point Roberts.

On average, most quick trips by Canadians over the border involve buying gas, cheese, milk, wine or beer. Point Roberts represents convenient savings for those who live close enough to swing by; the fact there are millions of them is what drives the Point Roberts economy.

There are no traffic stoplights in Point Roberts, but the Tyee Drive commercial strip ends at one of two flashing red lights on Point Roberts, governing traffic at the intersection with Gulf Road since 1989.

 Now, turn right on Gulf Road, traveling west.

POSTAL HISTORY

The first building on Gulf Road to your right is the local post office for ZIP code 98281. The first post office on Point Roberts was set up in 1894. Strangely, the name of the first post office was Brewster, Washington, likely because it was located on Horace

Brewster's land. Prior to this, residents had to walk nearly three hours each way to Ladner to get the mail, basically a full-day round trip.[705] The first postmaster was Peter Bruhn in 1894, followed by Arthur Wadhams in 1895 and George H. Waters in 1896-97 who renamed the post office Point Roberts. A regular mail boat came from Whatcom, at present-day Bellingham. Until 1967, all postmasters who had served Point Roberts in the last seven decades had essentially come from three families.[706] This current post office

Figure 89: Commemorative cachet covers created in 1961 to celebrate the centenary of boundary marker number 1, postmarked on the first day of issue on July 30. Author's collection.

– Point Roberts' sixth – was built in 1984. There were originally 184 post office boxes. It was expanded to 424 boxes in the 1970s,[707] and in 1982 grew to 610 boxes,[708] almost one for every two residents at the time, but most rented by Canadians eager to have a U.S. address. The post office is clogged with Canadians bringing mail and parcels to mail to U.S. addresses with domestic postage. Woe to the customer who stands in the lineup behind a Canadian eBay-er here to ship dozens of parcels to her customers. Having a post office box allows Canadians to have a presence in the United States with a bona fide U.S. address. Their U.S. customers can mail them with a standard first class U.S. stamp, rather than the global rate. In a quirk of living along our international border, it costs as much to mail a letter from Point Roberts to Tsawwassen as it does to Mauritius, the country closest to the opposite side of the globe from Point Bob.

Introduced in July 1963, the ZIP code is used not only by the United States Postal Service, but in many areas of the American economy, including credit card security to banking loan approvals to teen chic along the lines of Beverly Hills 90210. The ZIP in ZIP code is an acronym, standing for Zone Improvement Plan. The "improvement" replaced the previous postal zones, introduced in 1943, which 178 large cities used, such as "Seattle 4." The five digits of the 43,000 U.S. ZIP codes represent a hierarchy for automatic sorting machines to sort mail. Point Roberts' ZIP code, 98281, can be dissected as follows. The 9 represents the west coast. All ZIP codes in Alaska, Washington, Oregon, California, Hawaii, as well as Pacific Ocean dependencies start with a 9. The next digit represents a state or portion of a state. All western Washington ZIP codes start with 98. The third digit is for a "sectional center facility," basically a regional distribution center. In this case, 982 represents the SCF at Everett, where the Point's mail gets handled. Ironically, brick and mortar stores and post offices handling physical mail were supposed to die out with ecommerce. But in an only-in-Point Roberts twist, ecommerce has spurred the growth of postal services and brick and mortar businesses. U.S. mail is down thirty per cent nationwide since 2007, but it's only down fourteen per cent in Point Roberts. With so much mail, local letter carriers struggle with crammed mailboxes. Many people don't come down to their cabins for months on end, but advertising circulars and other junk mail clogs up mailboxes. The post office pointed out an arcane rule which states mail must be collected within three days or it would be held at the post office for a few more days before being returned. It's hard to think of another town where this rule would need to be applied.

Figure 90: Special postmarks were created in 1997 to commemorate the salmon fishery and on June 15, 1996 to commemorate the sesquicentennial of the Treaty of Washington which created Point Roberts in 1846. Author's collection.

Point Roberts is also home to the world's only relational database of the world's postage stamps. Philatelists, also known as stamp collectors, can identify, track and analyze their stamp collections in the cloud. The database is compiled and maintained in Point Roberts.

Across the street is the final gas station on our tour. It is the oldest continuously-operated gas station in Point Roberts. It opened in June 1983 with the first self-service pumps. Originally called Stateside gas, it had "computerized pumps" which could fill a car's tank in a fourth the time of the old manual pumps at Ben's. When it opened Point Roberts overnight went from two to fourteen gas pumps.

PARCEL RECEIVING

After Sunday beer sales dried up in the late 1980s, a new invention debuted on August 6, 1991 which would change Point Roberts and the world. The World Wide Web ushered in the modern era of the Internet, and with it, ecommerce. The Internet would grow quickly; in 1995 there were 120,000 registered domain names. By 1998 it would mushroom to over two million. Amazon.com, eBay and Yahoo! started in 1995 followed by PayPal and Google in 1998 and Facebook in 2004.

Canadians use the Internet to research purchases and compare prices at the same rate as Americans. However, the share of digital purchases is much lower in Canada. Canadians want to shop online, but Canadian retailers have not rolled out digital innovations and last mile delivery to the extent U.S. retailers have done, meaning Canadians' ability to shop online in the Canadian market is comparatively hampered. As a result, there is a digital divide between the U.S. and Canada.[709] Point Roberts fills that gap. For many Metro Vancouver residents, Point Roberts is their connection to the vast array of goods available in the U.S. ecommerce market. Compared to the multitude of big box and superstore hypermarket formats and an endless array of online websites in the United States, Canadian retailers offer a narrower assortment of goods. Throw in higher prices, limited shipping and slow delivery compared to American service levels, and it's no surprise Canadian consumers look for better solutions in the United States. Prices are so low Canadians usually come out ahead even when the cost of paying duty and driving to Point Roberts is factored in. The Internet's proverbial "last mile" to a consumer's home runs through Point Roberts for over a thousand Canadians a day.

Canada Post says seventy-six per cent of Canadian households shop online. The average Canadian spends $954 per year online, about six per cent of all retail sales in Canada. With three quarters of Canadians living within 100 miles of the U. S. border, Canadians are fully aware of the selection of goods in the United States. Back home, the range of offerings in Canadian shops by comparison doesn't compete. Canucks love to grumble about the shortcomings of Amazon.ca, the inferior Canadian version of the popular Amazon.com web site. A full twenty-four per cent of Canadians shop online at Amazon.com instead of Amazon.ca for its vast product selection and much lower prices than the much-reviled Canadian version.

Naturally, Canada's sparsely-populated and vast size contributes to the expense for retailers of rolling out advanced marketing and distribution networks. Canadian retail stores pull inventory from fewer distribution centers covering a wider geographic area than any other country globally save Russia. The result is frequent out-of-stocks and shopping trips where Canadian shoppers can't take home their merchandise on the same trip; the goods must be ordered from another store or from the warehouse. A March 2016 Deloitte survey found Canadians can take home their merchandise in one visit to the store only fifty-five per cent of the time. Eighteen per cent of Canadian consumers want to be able to order online and pick up their purchases from a local retail store, but consumers reported to

Deloitte this was only possible ten per cent of the time in Canada, resulting in an eighty per cent gap in expectations.[710]

It's not just a wider selection which drives Canadians to American online websites. U.S. retailers lead their Canadian counterparts in using ecommerce, social media and mobile applications to offer a cross-channel shopping experience for their customers. American retailers also offer more digital and mobile payment and account login options. As a result, U.S. marketers know their customers better and use these data to deliver a better digital shopping experience in an era when consumers have more information and choice than ever before. During an online shopping mission, customers leave data breadcrumbs about themselves and their intentions. With more digital shoppers, American retailers outpace their Canadian counterparts in using those data and analytics to offer a fully-personalized and optimized shopping experience, driving up profits which can be reinvested in more digital innovation, thereby widening the digital divide with Canada even further. Indeed, the Deloitte survey of over two thousand Canadians explores how consumers north of the border are using, and wish to use, digital touchpoints during shopping trips in physical retail stores. Half of Americans are swayed by digital marketing, but only four in ten Canadians are. Nearly a third of Americans use mobile phones during their shopping journeys whilst less than a fifth of Canadians do.[711]

Of course, for many shoppers price reigns supreme. Even before the Loonie-Greenback exchange rate is taken into consideration, prices are steep in Canada. An item on Amazon.ca can be double the price of the same thing on Amazon.com. So, there is strong demand to use the U.S. version of popular websites, but to avoid international shipping and automatic duty, a shipping address in the United States is needed. For this to work, a Canadian would need to be close to a place in the U.S. where they could receive the shipment. Due to the Point's proximity to Vancouver, it was a natural somebody would open a business to receive parcels for Canadians.

Parcel receiving is the most common retail business in Point Roberts today. They all work pretty much the same: register on one of their web sites, and then use their address as your shipping address. They'll contact you when your package arrives so you can pick it up. The basic fee for a standard-sized package ranges from $2.50 to $4.00, and fees go up from there for larger parcels. In doing so, Canadians evade the steep shipping charges American ecommerce sites often charge for international shipping to Canada. It's a game of averages. The Canadian Border Patrol isn't staffed to process duty paperwork from everybody coming across the border, so most are waved through, even for some who declare what they've picked up. And even if duty is charged, Canadian customers often still come out ahead. With a convenient option like Point Roberts located within Metro Vancouver, B.C. retailers are vulnerable to losing customers to American options which are keeping pace with advances in digital retailing and marketing.

Rivaling retail gasoline sales for dominance in the local economy, parcel receiving is big business in Point Roberts. These facilities have databases of upwards of forty thousand customers, ninety-eight per cent of whom are Canadians. This block is the epicenter of a Point Roberts industry which generates over a fifth of all cars coming over the border from Tsawwassen. Nearly a thousand people cross the border every day for parcel pickup, making up twenty-six per cent of all regular lane crossings. "Overall, the largest increase to traffic at Boundary Bay (Point Roberts border crossing) that we have seen over the last six months is due to Internet shopping and people shipping parcels to Point Roberts for pick-up," said a spokesperson for Canada Border Service in September 2009.[712] Indeed, though Blaine, Lynden and Sumas all have parcel receiving outlets, no other border crossing in

Washington has a higher per cent of crossings for parcel pickup than Point Roberts.[713]

The idea of musty mail rooms in Point Roberts initially seems so very analog in these digitally-disrupted days, but at the end of the day after consumers have shopped til they dropped on the web, all of those online orders have to be shipped, and for tens of thousands of Canadians, those packages all come through Point Roberts, on purpose. The parcel receiving industry had a nascent start with the opening of a mailbox rental shop, appropriately named The Mail Box, at the marina in February 1989.[714] They found a following from their newspaper ad which asked a simple question, "Do you need a U.S. address?"[715] Many did. Some estimates indicate twenty per cent of Lower Mainland B.C. residents have a post office box in the United States.[716] The business grew, was sold and eventually became The Letter Carrier in 1992. In the early years, the focus was on mailbox rentals, and parcel receiving services were free! Today, fees to pick up a parcel have become the chief revenue source at the Point's six locations, which makes parcel depots the largest plurality of retail business in Point Roberts, with more retail locations than restaurants or its famous gas stations.

For some Canadian customers, parcel shipping and receiving via Point Roberts has become a way of life. Many are eBayers and Etsyers and other home-based and small businesses. After the most recent downturn in the value of the Loonie, by and large the same customers were still coming down to Point Roberts, they were just receiving fewer packages. For many Canadians the assortment available in the U.S. market is too broad to stop coming down to Point Roberts to get goods unavailable in Canada, at least at a reasonable price, but the splurge happens less often. "For Canadians to forego online shopping, they are also foregoing product variety and retail options," says Laurie Trautman, associate director of Western Washington University's Border Policy Research Institute.[717] The tipping point seems to be the when the value of the Loonie falls below seventy-five U.S. cents. Point Roberts is a no-brainer when the Loonie is worth eighty or more cents but if it falls below 75 cents the difference generally seems to change shopping and shipping decisions. Point Roberts retailers have seen this kind of boom and bust cycles for years and know how a one cent change in exchange rates will impact their cross-border business.

Although the methods and goods have changed over the years, one thing which hasn't changed is people using Point Roberts as a smuggling route. Borders cause people to reevaluate each country's rules and the cost of doing business, which can cause them to change their behavior. From smuggling liquor, fish and Chinese laborers in years past, today smugglers use the parcel receiving services to send prohibited goods to a convenient pickup place and then move the goods over the border where the movement of the goods can blend in with general traffic. With the Internet, the type of goods being smuggled over the border at Point Roberts now runs the gamut. In 2014, a major rhinoceros horn smuggling operation was busted. A 39-year-old from Richmond, B.C., Tony Guan was sentenced to thirty months in prison for smuggling endangered species parts through a parcel depot in Point Roberts. Guan was swept up in a sting operation named Operation Crash in March 2014. Approached by undercover American agents from the U.S. Fish and Wildlife Service, Guan agreed to come down to the U.S. and pay $45,000 for two rhino horns. With an accomplice doing double-duty as an interpreter, they went to an express mail store where the agents observed Guan send the horns to a parcel receiving business in Point Roberts labeled as "handicrafts." He told the agents one of his employees would drive down to Point Roberts from Richmond to retrieve the parcel and smuggle it into Canada, a practice he admitted he had done many times before. When Canadian authorities raided the Richmond business, they found more wildlife objects, many of which had evidence of having been smuggled through Point Roberts.[718]

Despite all the ways Point Roberts is so utterly unique, the lesson of the people who survive daily life in an isolated exclave is they don't think they are so different and they actually just want to be so utterly normal. They just want to be treated equally, like all other residents of the county and country. Tired of being discriminated against based on how they drive to their home, the residents of one of the continent's strangest towns struggle to not be defined by that strangeness, but instead overcome it in a quest for respect, empathy and accommodation for the government's inconvenient and invisible line on the map.

CHAPTER 8 • FORBIDDEN FRUIT

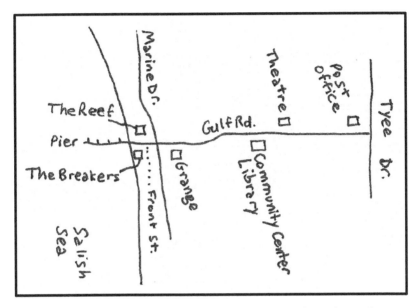

Figure 91: Route map of Chapter 8. Start at Tyee Drive and travel west down Gulf Road to the beach. Distance 0.6 miles (1km)

The border causes Canadians to come down to the Point to have experiences they can't do back home. At one time, Point Roberts was known for babes, beef, beer, bands and betting in ways Canadians could not get back home, or in some cases still can't. In the 1970s and 1980s it was variously called Sin City, the Las Vegas of British Columbia and even Vancouver's Tijuana. Community supporters were outraged at such disparaging comparisons, though with both Point Roberts and Tijuana being border towns without sewers perhaps they're not so different after all![719]

POINT ROBERTS PORTRAYED IN THE MEDIA

You would be hard-pressed to find another town of its size which features so frequently in national media as Point Roberts. Hardly a year goes by where Point Roberts isn't profiled by a big city newspaper or media outlet in an inevitable "look at the crazy little town we found" feature. It's been happening for decades. *Billboard* magazine wrote a profile piece as early as 1943, describing the changes in Point Roberts in a piece called "Canadians Go South for Fun."[720]

The big issues of the 1970s and 1980s began to attract regular media attention. When Canadian officials were cracking down on Point Roberts residents bringing home goods from the mainland through Canada, the *Spokane Spokesman-Review* on March 1, 1970 marveled at the detailed inventory forms in triplicate the people of Point Roberts were required to fill out to come home from the store, strictly enforced in those years. *The New York Times* profiled Point Roberts as a result of John Meier's capture on August 9, 1973 in a piece entitled, "Canada's Nationalism Hits an Isolated U.S. Town."[721] One week later, the water issue brought the Canadian media on August 16, 1973, alarmed at the thought of a Canadian resource being exported to Americans, in a *Globe and Mail* editorial titled "Water is Not for Sale."[722] Letters to the editor of the local newspapers in Point Roberts have long complained about these media stories. A 1971 letter complained, "At regular intervals, feature writers visit The Point, take a series of unflattering pictures, and return to whence they came to compose a story telling of an area where there is virtually no police protection and the school children must rise at six each morning to travel to a school several light years from their home. We who reside at Point Roberts continue to be amazed by the amount of misinformation which a single writer can amass during one afternoon's visit to our area. We have come to expect being subjected to regular appearances of these articles depicting us as an Appalachian area of the northwest, whose barefoot and ignorant natives are watched over and ministered to by Big Daddy in the form of British Columbia. Most quote Canadian rather than U.S. officials and residents concerning our 'unique' situation. Nary is a mention made of the attractions of The Point other than beer. Conspicuous by their absence are comments on our climate, beaches, sport fishing, and the aura of tranquility which can be found here if one looks in places other than the taverns."[723]

The reporters kept coming. Canada's national broadcaster *CBC News* came to town in February 1981 to report how Point Roberts struggled to attract growth.[724] The *Los Angeles Times* followed suit on October 5, 1986 with a similar theme in a piece titled, "A Bit of U.S. Clinging to Canada, Point Roberts Waits for Boom."[725] They returned three years later to follow up with, "A Woodsy Northwest Retreat Gets the Water it Wanted, with a Flood of Development."[726] Many of the more recent national news articles about Point Roberts write about the paradox of exclave life. The *Philadelphia Inquirer* sent their own staff reporter to Point Roberts in December 1988 to write about the "dual way of life" in an exclave;[727] and *The Seattle Times* profiled the Point in September 1991 in an article entitled "Point Roberts: Foot in State, Heart in Canada."[728] The *Christian Science Monitor* wrote about Point Roberts in December 1994, headlining the article, "As U.S. Cracks Down on Its Borders, Canada Records a Rise in Illegal Migrants."[729] Point Roberts even popped up in the pages of the *National Enquirer* in April 1988 in a story about a local Afghan hound holding the world's record for longest dog ears.[730] National Public Radio featured Point Roberts in its 1998 "Life on the Border" series, which saw *All Things Considered* producer Art Silverman come to the Point to interview several local residents for the feature which aired in December 1998.[731]

Then came the big one: that icon of geographic enlightenment finally discovered one of the most geographically-interesting places in the country. *National Geographic* featured Point Roberts in

August 2004 in a monthly feature which profiles one specific American ZIP code. All two hundred copies of the magazine at the supermarket sold out immediately. Four years in the making, the article caused an uproar among Canadian readers for dissing Tsawwassen as "strip mall hell."[732]

These news articles about Point Roberts appear in a steady cadence. In more recent times, *The Washington Post* wrote "The Border's Right Here, but the Debate is Many Miles Away," on July 20, 2006.[733] The headline in Toronto's *National Post* read, "Point Roberts, Washington: A Little Slice of the U.S., Only Accessible through Canada" when they wrote about Point Roberts on February 27, 2012.[734] When the Canadian dollar fell in value most recently, the *Vancouver Sun* wrote on January 15, 2016, "Point Roberts Feels the Squeeze of the Low Loonie."[735] Ken Jennings of *Jeopardy!* fame even wrote some short quirky facts about Point Roberts in a guest article in *Conde Nast Traveler* in October 2012.[736]

We've discussed how, in the 1950s, Point Roberts switched from an orientation toward the United States to a Canadian-facing economic link. This hinged on supplying goods to Canadians more cheaply than they cost in Canada. The Point's economy also offered experiences not available north of the border, like the parcel receiving services as a conduit for Canadians to shop in the U.S. online market. For some, Point Roberts provides a chance to experience things forbidden north of the border. For five decades, the local economy centered on British Columbians doing things they couldn't or wouldn't back home. This led to what some felt were unseemly businesses. Had it come to this? Stuck on a stunningly beautiful peninsula, the price for jobs and growth was to tolerate smut and drunkenness. Residents muttered that nobody said living in paradise was going to be easy or glamorous. For decades, if you played name association with somebody from Metro Vancouver and said "Point Roberts," the first thing many people would say would be cheap gas, Sunday beer or the X-rated movie theatre. On

September 7, 1979, NBC aired a seven-minute segment about Point Roberts on *The Today Show*. The Point's local paper decried the angle, "There were predictable shots of beer, taverns and Canadian money."[737] More coverage of porn and beer halls came from the *Louisville Courier-Journal* in a typical piece entitled "Getting to the Point: Canadians Like to Hang Out Where the U.S. Hangs On," published May 31, 1981.[738] On October 3, 1982, the *Seattle Post-Intelligencer* ran their infamous article about Point Roberts being Vancouver's Tijuana. It painted a negative and seamy description of the exclave, calling it Tijuana of the North to the dismay of local civic supporters and realtors. It described the big taverns, the trash, the smuggling, and porn. Six years after the *P-I* piece ran, the community lived through it all over again when the story was picked up by the Associated Press December 28, 1988 and the "Tijuana of the North" article ran in papers across the continent.

PORNOGRAPHY

During the 1970s and 1980s, three different porn stores operated or nearly opened in Point Roberts, all of them here on this stretch of Gulf Road. If Point Roberts had had one, which it never did, this would have been its red light district.

In 1984, the building at 1574 Gulf Road nearly became a porn supercenter unlike anything else in the Salish Sea. It was to be an enormous project. It would have featured an adult bookstore, a movie theatre showing feature-length X-rated films, thirty-six individual booths with coin-operated screens showing several channels of porn flicks, and most disturbing to the community, live nude dancing, all under one roof. Like the KRPI towers which snuck through the permitting process and public hearings with the community only learning of it at the last minute, this had happened earlier with this porn palace. The new owners of this building in late 1983 got all the papers filed to open the porn center. It was already zoned commercial so no new permits were needed which would have required a public hearing. It was only because of an anonymous tip June 27, 1984 to *The Bellingham Herald* seven months into the process and at the eleventh hour the community discovered it was happening. Locals galvanized an effort to try to stop it from opening.

With a capacity of 110 customers and open nudity, a county health inspection was ordered to ensure sanitary conditions. The Point's good old utility challenges saved the day. Without a sewer system, a sprawling facility that huge was not approved.[739] For once, the lack of standard public utilities was a good thing. By October, the porn supercenter had addressed the sewer issue and was getting closer to opening, and locals were getting desperate. They wanted to ban pornographic businesses from being able to open at all in the exclave. *The Ocean Star* reported, "The Registered Voters Association of Point Roberts has asked the county prosecutor to introduce some type of law which would make it impossible for such businesses to operate at Point Roberts."[740] But legally, this was not a good approach as it surely would contravene First Amendment laws. The prosecutor wrote back and said he wouldn't go after them because of the type of business they are, but suggested they should consider lobbying for laws which would discourage prostitution and drug sales, which could indirectly target the type of business. This didn't make sense in Point Roberts; with the federal government guarding the entrance to town, those types of problems associated with other X-rated theatres weren't a problem in Point Roberts.

Nonetheless, protests kept coming from Point Roberts, so Whatcom County began enacting countywide restrictions on nude businesses. They were prevented from serving alcohol, required employee background checks ensuring no violent crime or felony convictions, no touching of live nude dancers by customers or vice versa, including a ten foot separation which prevented lap dances.[741] The prosecutor's advice proved fruitful: to survive constitutional challenges, the technique was not to ban the business on the basis of what it did, but instead control it and clean it up.[742] Faced with this amount of bureaucracy per employee, the porn palace gave up and the Orchard Gallery, which had previously occupied this space, re-opened, selling homewares and art until October 1992. After a brief stint as a shoe store, in July 1994 it became a parcel depot.

Continue along the broad Gulf Road, which was widened with paved shoulders for parking in May 1987, past Teller Road. Teller Road is named for August Teller, a German settler who had arrived in the United States in 1888, originally settling in Astoria, Oregon where he was a fisherman. August moved to Point Roberts in 1901 with his brother Henry Teller, who was the supervisor at the George & Barker Cannery and first chairman of the Point Roberts township. Henry Teller was also an early school board chairman in 1908.[743] Stop at 1480 Gulf Road, currently a large two-story blue building.

Figure 92: The building at 1480 Gulf Road in 2017. This was the most-profitable X-rated theatre in America in the 1970s & 1980s. Photo by Mark Swenson.

From 1971 to 1989, this blue building was one of the businesses which led Point Roberts to be called Sin City and the Tijuana of the North. This was the Playtime Theatre. In the days before porn was available to take home on videotape, X-rated cinemas were one of the only ways people could view adult video entertainment. In the 1970s pornographic films could not be shown publicly in Canada.

To satisfy Canadian (and American) demand, many porno theatres opened in U.S. border towns, Point Roberts included. The Point's X-rated theatre was the closest to Vancouver, it attracted a loyal following of customers who came to watch feature-length porno films. These flicks showed the full-Monty, "XXX-rated" in the parlance of the day.

The Point Roberts Playtime Theatre was the only indoor X-rated cinema in unincorporated Whatcom County.[744] In 1981, the theatre manager reported the Point Roberts theatre was the most-profitable X-rated cinema in the United States.[745] The theatre was jammed with Canadians sixteen hours a day, seven days a week. Canadian authorities refused to permit the films to be brought over the border, so the heavy movie reels in metal canisters had to be brought in by boat or plane.[746]

There were efforts in the summer of 1977 to close it. Local residents brought their case to force closure of the cinema to the county commissioner. It led to some scrutiny by the county for a while, and a manager was prosecuted for some misdemeanor indecency charges, but courts allowed the theatre to reopen because laws required a distinct case to be prosecuted separately for each distinct film shown, making it essentially impossible to use those laws to close the theatre.[747] For many in the community it wasn't a problem. It had no large or garish sign, no flashing red lights. Patrons were embarrassed about others knowing they had come to Point Roberts for porn (and gave all manner of reasons other than a sex-positive desire to see adult entertainment to the border officials for their visit), but the local paper described a "seemingly always-full porn theatre parking lot" in June 1982.[748] Point Roberts got attention from across Canada when the theatre was featured in a 1981 CBC radio broadcast, but there were actually very few complaints about it; the overwhelming attitude was to completely ignore it.[749] Nonetheless, because of the Point Roberts theatre and threat of the new live nude dancing venue, Whatcom County passed a new countywide ordinance not to ban porno theatres, but to control them to the point nobody could meet the criteria to open one, a goal lawmakers openly admitted.[750]

Its owner, Playtime Theatres, was a chain of porno theatres based 100 miles south of Point Roberts in Renton, Washington. In 1985, Playtime Theatres was party to a lawsuit which went all the way to the United States Supreme Court and is frequently used as case law across America to this day. The case concerned the company's theatre in Renton, but the actions in Renton were driven by previous actions in Whatcom County regarding the Point Roberts theatre. Eyeing the situation with the Point Roberts theatre in Whatcom County, in 1980 Renton's mayor asked the city council to pass a law to regulate zoning of adult entertainment businesses, even though none existed in Renton at the time and none were proposed. The council passed a 1980 ordinance prohibiting businesses which sell, rent or exhibit adult entertainment. This was followed in 1981 with another ordinance which restricted zoning for adult entertainment. It established adult theatres could not be opened within one thousand feet of any residential area, park, school or church. Theatres were specified; the ordinance did not impact adult book stores, topless bars or massage parlors. Ninety-five per cent of the land in Renton was now off-limits to where adult theatres could be situated. Playtime bought two theatres in downtown Renton in early 1982. After initially being shut down, they cited First Amendment protections and were allowed to resume showing films.

The case was eventually argued at the U.S. Supreme Court on November 11, 1985, and focused on where X-rated theatres could be located. The city of Renton had enacted a zoning ordinance prohibiting theatres which screened adult movies from situating within 1000 feet of "any residential zone, single- or multiple-family dwelling, church, park or school." Playtime Theatres Inc. challenged the law and sought a permanent injunction against its enforcement on the grounds it violated the First and Fourteenth Amendments. Taking the case from the United States Court of Appeals for the Ninth Circuit, the Supreme Court handed down its verdict on February 24, 1986. It found in a seven to two decision that Renton's zoning ordinance did not violate the First and Fourteenth Amendments, holding that the law was a form of time, place and manner regulation, not a ban on porno theatres altogether. Writing for the majority, William Rehnquist's opinion argued Renton wasn't banning the film content, "but rather the secondary effects of such theaters on the surrounding community." The Court found the law served a substantial government interest in preserving the quality of life and allowed for "reasonable alternative avenues of communication." Thurgood Marshall and William Brennan Jr. dissented for Playtime. After the decisions, many municipalities and counties in the United States introduced zoning laws for X-rated theatres, moving them off to seedier parts of town away from the innocent eyes of children.

In 1981, a U.S. immigration officer indicated in an interview with a visiting newspaper reporter that when he asks visitors the purpose of their visit to Point Roberts, the top three answers were "to drink beer," "to gamble," and "to see a dirty movie."[751] This traffic-driver led some locals to happily tolerate the local economic boost it generated, and not everybody in Point Roberts opposed the theatre. Letters to the local newspaper in the 1980s commented that nobody had been raped in Point Roberts by a customer who had just seen porn content in the local theatre, whereas the thousands of Canadians who came to drink were a major nuisance, with clogged roads and border lanes, rampant public urination, discarded beer bottles and drunk driving, many of which are much more serious and widespread problems than the embarrassed theatregoer who just wanted to slink home after the movie without seeing anybody.[752]

It was not moral decay which eventually closed the theatre. With porn widely available on videotape, the profitability of such cinemas was gone, and the Playtime Theatre closed in 1989. The local newspaper was gleeful in announcing the new tenant would erase the building's "sordid past."[753] The building's blue façade seen today is from a March 1991 remodel. It was a retail boutique in the 1990s, a real estate office in the 2000s, and at various times has also held, and currently holds, the sixth Point Roberts parcel service, as well as a country store-style retail shop.

Figure 93: In 1979, when a second porn business opened selling and renting porn on the then-new video cassette tape, the community put its foot down. Photo by *The Ocean Star.*

In the late 1970s and 1980s there was yet another adult business on Point Roberts, across the street. The adult book store owners had first approached the county with a proposal to open an adult book store at the western end of Gulf Road.[754] That attempt was not approved but the owners were able to open at 1461 Gulf Road. As chronicled in the movie *Boogie Nights*, the decline of X-rated theatres sharpened in the early 1980s, replaced by the availability of adult content on inexpensive videotape. Now, porn videos could be brought home. Videotape changed the porn industry and laid the groundwork for the democratization of porn which would come a decade later with the Internet. It was natural that videotaped porn would be a big seller in Point Roberts, and relatively early in 1979 a porn store quietly opened. Now Canadians could visit nearby Point Roberts to discreetly buy porn in a small package, slip it into a pocket and take the porn home with them. This was revolutionary at the time but fit perfectly with Point Roberts' role as the purveyor of forbidden fruit. The local newspaper lamented another smutty store on Point Roberts' main drag was selling "video tapes payable by Visa and Mastercharge… across the street from the Point Roberts hard core porno theatre."[755] This time, the community put its foot down. Not wanting to ride videotape to a new era of porn profits, the community pressured the county to withdraw permits, and the store eventually closed in July 1980.[756] Had the videotape bookstore stayed open and the porn palace opened, Point Roberts would have had three X-rated businesses in one block – few if any cities other than Seattle could make that claim statewide – and Gulf Road would have been the Point's little red light district. That never happened, but porn as forbidden fruit for Canadians was an undeniable part of the Point's history and economy for eighteen years.

COMMUNITY CENTER

On the left you'll come to the brick Point Roberts Community Center. This building originally housed Point Roberts' school, but

Figure 94: The Community Center holds many community meetings and events, and the local branch of the Whatcom County Library System.

today it is the Community Center, which hosts the parks district, seniors society, a seasonal information kiosk and meeting rooms where local community organizations hold meetings, including the local historical society, active since November 1977.[757] The grounds include a playground and community garden. It's also the local branch of the Whatcom County library system. One of the busiest and oldest branches in the county,[758] the library opened in and has operated from this very room since 1946. The library is open three days per week (and a fourth day during summer season).

The first school was conducted in a person's home in Freeman Beach off Marine Drive. The second school, and first actual schoolhouse was on Benson Road where a mobile home park sits today. A one room white wooden schoolhouse was constructed in 1900 on the parking lot and playground area of today's Community Center. In the 1930s the Works Progress Administration provided funds to build a new brick schoolhouse, built next to the old wooden school in 1937. In 1954 there were 24 students in grades one to six all in one room. A local school bus service was organized to fetch kids from various parts of the Point. After grade six all students were bused to Blaine. By 1962 only eleven students remained. The school was closed and all students were bused to Blaine, or went to private school in Tsawwassen. After closing as a school, this building became the Community Center owned and administrated by the parks district.

Although the Works Progress Administration is credited with building the Community Center, the WPA is more famous locally for building something else at Point Roberts during the Depression: outhouses. Locals would often rate outhouses, and WPA outhouses were well built and always topped the list of best biffies. The most-famous WPA outhouse in Point Roberts was the twelve-hole structure at the APA cannery.[759]

Figure 95: An automated salmon processing machine on display at the Point Roberts Community Center. Photo by Mark Swenson.

Behind the Community Center is a lawn planted in the summer of 1980, introducing a bocce ball court,[760] and today hosts the rusting hulk of the Smith automated salmon processing machine. As we saw in chapter 4 at Lily Point, canneries initially hired Chinese laborers to can the fish by hand, but a machine was invented to automate much of this process. A model of the type used in Point Roberts canneries is on display on the grounds, just behind the Point's community garden. It could process over three thousand salmon per day.

Continuing down Gulf Road, just as it veers slightly to the left, is Julius Place. Margaret Laurence's home was just off Julius Place, and further down is the Point Roberts Fellowship Camp. The land for the camp was donated in memory of Emma Wilbee in 1948 and has been operated by various Baptist groups over the years.

DOWNTOWN POINT ROBERTS

Around the bend you enter the last couple blocks of our tour. For decades the west end of Gulf Road was considered downtown Point Roberts. In its heyday, there was a concentration of businesses lining the streets in a way which does not really exist today on the Point. In the early 1930s this downtown area had a mercantile, barber shop, Goodyear service station, Shell station, restaurant, hotel and even a Kodak shop.

Figure 96: The downtown of Point Roberts in the mid-1930s was at the foot of Gulf Road below Marine Drive. The Maple Leaf Tavern in the photo sits where the neon sign in front of The Reef tavern is today. Photo by Corbett, Whatcom Museum 820; Bellingham, WA.

These businesses opened here because in the 1890s, Horace Brewster parceled out his land for a commercial district, creating lots along Gulf Road. Starting near the jog on Gulf Road, there were several buildings originally built by the George & Barker cannery as homes for their managers. In the early 20th century, Point Roberts was often called a company town. The first building you come to at 1385 Gulf Road, today a real estate office, was built in 1913 and originally housed the cannery bookkeeper. At one time was the home of the sheriff. From time to time prisoners would spend the night in a stockade building behind the home before transportation to Bellingham the following day.[761] The historic building at 1379 Gulf Road, one of the oldest in Point Roberts, was built in 1911 to house cannery families. An early resident was Henry Teller. It was a private home until a restaurant, Hawthorns Restaurant and Tea House, opened in 1982. After that it became Karoonies Seafood House and Bar from 1991 to 1994. From 1996 to 2016, it was a restaurant and country food store named Brewster's. A bit farther down on the right-hand side was Blue Heron Gallery, an art gallery and gift shop, which operated from 1993 to 2017, and was an outlet for the work of local artists. Next door is a bike store. Since 2009, they have rented a variety of bikes for visitors to the Point. The southwest quadrant of Point Roberts, basically chapters two, three and eight of this book, is generally flat and the slow lazy roads are ideal for biking. Don a helmet for safety if you prefer, but they're not required by law for adults in Point Roberts.

Across the street is the grange hall, built in 1902.[762] It played a big role in Point Roberts history. During most of the twentieth century, Washington had townships for communities which weren't incorporated as cities. Point Roberts became a township in 1911 and the de facto township hall was this building, which also housed the Point Roberts Social Club, founded in 1902. Church services were held here beginning in 1913 before the church was built. The grange society took over in 1929.[763] The grange was the place where community meetings were held. In 1943 it was the site of a debate among residents on a proposal for Canada to annex Point Roberts. During World War II, it was the site where locals organized care packs & gift baskets for the troops,

Figure 97: Point Roberts Grange Hall. Photo by Mark Swenson.

including first aid kits, knits, rolled bandages and the like. Eighteen local kids were in the service during the war.[764] As it was the only sizable building on Point Roberts where large gatherings of people from the community could gather, it was the scene of many social events in the lives of the local population. Everything from the annual Christmas party and bazaar, fashion shows, school programs, Halloween parties, dances and wedding receptions were all held here, in addition to grange meetings of course.[765] Plays were held in the grange, in the early years, performed in Icelandic.[766] A basement kitchen supported these events until the lean-to addition was added in the early 1960s with a modern kitchen. The grange society would eventually pass the building to the parks district in the late 1960s, at the same time the parks board was reorienting community meetings to the Community Center. A carnival, concerts and a game night attended by over one hundred were held in the grange hall into the 1980s.[767] In that decade Gulf Road was widened with a parking lane added to each side of the street, effectively transforming it from a narrow two-lane road lined with ditches to a wide curbed two-lane road with parking lanes on each side, essentially four lanes wide. Today the grange hall still stands, though it sits awkwardly close to the widened road. It was sold by the parks district in February 1989.[768]

Beyond Marine Drive was the heart of the downtown for decades. At the bottom of the hill just past the realty office was another cross street named Front Street. The corner of Gulf Road and Front Street was the site of Waters Mercantile. It was opened by Captain Curtis in 1896, who hired George H. Waters, who went on to buy out Curtis, who went on to buy a sloop and made supply runs between Point Roberts and Semiahmoo, Bellingham and Lummi Island for Waters.[769]

In the early years Waters Mercantile was the main general store on Point Roberts. In the early part of its seventy-year presence, it bought butter and eggs from local farmers. The Point's first post

Figure 98: Looking east from the pier to the businesses at the foot of Gulf Road. Photo by Corbett, Whatcom Museum 832; Bellingham, WA.

Figure 99: Looking east from the foot of Gulf Road in 2017. Photo by Mark Swenson.

office opened July 22, 1897 inside Waters store, ending the need to walk seven miles to Ladner to pick up mail. The post office would move out of the store into a new building built next door in the 1930s. The Waters family lived upstairs above the store. It was a major retail presence on Point Roberts for decades, eventually closing in 1967.

Point Roberts has had trouble keeping hotels operating over the years; they kept burning down. We noted in chapter two how there was a close call when the owner of Roberts Town's hotel saw his other business, a retail store, burn down in 1858. In May 1900 the *Blaine Journal* reported the Point Roberts Hotel burned completely to the ground, charring everything inside. The fear of everybody present was that the fire would jump to the George & Barker Cannery, whose structure was a mere fifteen feet from the hotel. All hands available pitched in to save the cannery, which suffered only minor damage. The hotel was leased to Robert Lord. Lord owned the hotel's saloon, but Lord's saloon license had expired a few days before the fire. He had traveled to the mainland to renew the license at the time of the fire. Lord lost his entire inventory valued at $900, which amounts to over $21,000 in today's money, and he held no insurance. Suspiciously, the fire originated in Lord's room in the hotel, but he swore he could not have been responsible as he was not in Point Roberts that day and had no flammable materials in his room. Fifteen boarders were rendered homeless. In the 1930s another hotel on Front Street, the two-story Bayview Hotel, was destroyed by fire. One young man died in this fire after going back in to the hotel to fetch belongings.[770]

Also perched above the beach on Front Street was the Bureau Saloon. Attached to the saloon was the Point's first dedicated restaurant, the Saddlerock Chop House, owned by Ah Fat which opened May 27, 1905. Ah Fat died in 1915, but the restaurant's sign was still visible as late as 1937, years after it closed.[771]

All these businesses were located here because this was the front door of Point Roberts, home to its pier. The pier's pilings at the foot of Gulf Road are still there, standing at attention, hinting at a once-important purpose. For much of the first half of the twentieth century, the pier was the portal into the community, receiving passengers, mail and freight. Most days fishermen would tie up along the pier and come in to the nearby taverns. It was first constructed by Leonard Pike, and then upgraded by the George & Barker Cannery.

Steamships served the Point Roberts route for many years. After selling his store to Waters, Captain Curtis ran supplies to the pier from Blaine on the *Effort*. Later, larger steamships made direct service from Seattle possible beginning in 1904, bringing in huge quantities of supplies for the canneries, endless stacks of lumber for the fish traps and picking up the Point's exports: agricultural products and salmon. All manner of goods were seen at the pier, even crates of live hogs for the Chinese workers.[772] Many U.S. ships stopped at the Point Roberts pier as the last American stop before heading to Alaska, and first stop in the U.S. coming from Alaska laden with resources.

The steamers *Erna* and *Ella* came three times a week. They had been designed for distance, originally built for the Dutch royal mail service between the Netherlands and its colonies in Indonesia, and ferried goods from Point Roberts to points across the Salish Sea and as far away as Mexico. Sometimes the notoriously slow side-wheeler *George E Starr* called at the dock as part of a Seattle-Fairhaven-Whatcom-Blaine-Point Roberts route.[773]

Later, Waters himself bought the sixty-five foot *Tulip*, a boat which would bring mail and supplies from the mainland up to six days a week for many years. The *Tulip* ran between Point Roberts and Bellingham, sometimes with a stop at Lummi Island and on Thursdays stopping at Patos Island to serve the lighthouse staff. If the seas were rough and it couldn't pull up to the dock without being smashed into it, the crew would toss the mail bag onto the dock on an incoming swell, and a team on the dock would likewise toss the outgoing mail bag onto the ship as it bobbed and swayed in the rough surf. It's said nobody ever missed.

By the early 1930s the *Tulip* was aging and frequently in dry dock for repairs. When it was out of service, my grandfather, George Moskovita, was the backup guy who brought the mail and supplies to Point Roberts from Bellingham on his boat, *New*

Zealand. Since salmon fishing was a seasonal job, my grandfather was thankful for earning an income during the off-season. He describes in his memoirs how he secured "a job carrying the mail and freight for the Waters Brothers. I took the mail from Bellingham to Point Roberts... Usually the 65-foot *Tulip* made the mail run each day. When it went on dry dock for repairs, we took over. There wasn't much work for the salmon boats during the winter months except for dragging for bottom fish. Most of the skippers had to pull their boats out of the water for the winter, so we were pleased to have some work."[774]

Figure 100: George Moskovita's *New Zealand*, on which he brought the mail and supplies to Point Roberts from Bellingham when the *Tulip* was in dry dock in the early 1930s. Photo: Author's collection.

With heavy use, it was inevitable the pier would see its share of accidents. At the end of the pier, a long spur stuck out diagonally to the southwest. On a foggy night in 1930 the S. S. *Riverton* ran into the dock and destroyed this spur. Wedged into the dock, it had to wait until next high tide to float free. In 1932 the Iwersen brothers began canning seafood in a building built on a spur halfway down the pier, sticking out to the north. A fire in 1937 destroyed the Iwersens' building on the dock; at the time it was leased by an

Anacortes company. The brothers rebuilt both the dock and building. An airplane taking off from Victoria Airport crashed into the dock during World War II. The pier was operational into the 1950s until a fire in 1959 destroyed a large part of the end of the pier. The old "front door" to Point Roberts shut for good, yielding that title to the Tyee Drive border crossing.[775]

BURGERS

Gulf Road is home to most of Point Roberts' restaurants. Next door to the grange is Saltwater Café. In the 1980s this building was a clothing boutique called Blackberries and in 2004 became the Caffe Capanna restaurant.

One guilty pleasure available at the restaurants of Point Roberts which cannot be enjoyed north of the border is a medium-rare hamburger. Most Americans are shocked when they venture north of the 49th and try to order a medium-rare burger to learn this sandwich, so common in America, is essentially illegal in Canada. Attempts by Americans to order one in Canadian restaurants often result in shrugs and blank stares. This seems odd to Americans since Vancouver is home to literally hundreds of cheek-to-jowl sushi restaurants and raw oysters on the half shell are celebrated as some of the world's best. Even raw beef in the form of steak tartare and Ethiopian gored gored are fine to order in Canada, but not medium-rare or rare hamburgers. In Canada, many diners shun them, restaurant owners fear making patrons sick, and health inspectors are on the lookout for any restaurant violating the ban. Everywhere in Canada, provincial and municipal law requires hamburger to be cooked to seventy-one degrees Celsius. A medium-rare burger typically raises the mercury to only sixty-three degrees. The concern is E. coli. Canadian health inspectors often point to the four customers who died of E. coli after eating burgers at Jack in the Box in the United States in 1993. Seven hundred more customers got seriously sick. When any bit of pink is found in a burger during Canadian health inspections, not only does the burger get sent back, so too does the bun which must be thrown out, and a clean plate is required to boot.

It wasn't always so. Older Vancouverites can recall a time when it was legal to order a pink-inside burger in Canada. This ended in 1974, when Canadian TV featured an investigative report which tested hamburger in Ontario and found lots of staphylococcus and fecal coliforms. In the resulting public outcry, the federal health minister admitted the country's ground beef supply chain could not be fully inspected, and his advisory to cook burgers to seventy-one degrees has remained ever since.

Burger aficionados hate the shoe leather texture of dry Canadian burgers. The forbidden fruit of the burgers leads to foodie social media sites which post tips of Canadian restaurants who perhaps with a nudge, nudge, wink, wink will serve hamburgers medium-rare. Occasionally restaurants will actually promote pink burgers on bar menus, but this usually results in a swift visit from the health inspection agency. In the Lower Mainland of British Columbia, Vancouver Coastal Health conducts inspections at restaurants, sticking thermometers into burgers to ensure the meat is over seventy-one degrees.

Ground up steak comes from one piece of beef, and if the meat is from a quality source and ground on premise with very clean utensils and prep space, the risk of illness from medium rare meat is very low. A sear for a few minutes on a steak kills most E. coil. Ground beef in hamburgers on the other hand is another story altogether. Meat in burgers is made up of the remains of hundreds of cows raised in factory farming feedlots hundreds of miles apart.[776] The contents of the meat include the leftovers from the abattoir including intestines, sinew and gristle, prime breeding grounds for E. coli., which get pressed into the interior of the burger where only high temperature can kill the contamination. As corporate factory farming has taken over the North American food supply, the risk of contamination has exploded over the years, often stemming from frozen hamburger patties. Add to that the low wages paid at corporate fast food restaurants attract staff who serve food not as culinary experts but as assembly line cogs and it's easy to see why the United States is one of the few industrialized western nations still to offer medium rare burgers, and why for many Americans, burgers just don't taste the same when traveling overseas. For Canadians, it's a no-no today, a novel risk to be attempted by the daring on trips to the States, much like one plays casino games only on trips to Las Vegas. But that could all change. Medium rare burgers bans have started taking hold in the United States. Medium-rare burgers are now illegal in North Carolina and even in beef-loving Wyoming, and in South Carolina, you have to be eighteen to order one. Daring Canadians need not fear, all restaurants in Point Roberts with hamburgers on the menu will serve a medium rare burger.

ALCOHOL

Since the dawn of the nineteenth century, alcohol has played a constant role in the Point Roberts economy. Alcohol powered the early smuggling days, fueled the booze-soaked miners in the Roberts Town saloons, profited from the Prohibition years, attracted generations of Canadians to cavernous drinking halls, and continues to drive today's trans-border lineups to buy cheap beer and wine. This ongoing linkage with alcohol earned Point Roberts a reputation among many British Columbians as a place for drinking. When you traveled south from Monument Park on Marine Drive past the golf course to Gulf Road earlier in chapter 1, you were on an historic smuggling trail. All the beaches on the Point were used in rum running. One early resident recalled a 1920 Point Roberts during Prohibition, "I remember one day when I was about twelve years old and was helping my father with the crab pots. We went down the cliff from the old house very yearly in the morning, to get into the skiff to go out to lift the pots and there, on the seat of the skiff was a twenty dollar bill and a note saying, 'Thanks for the use of the skiff' with no signature. Since this was during Prohibition, though we didn't know who had used it, we knew why, and how, the skiff was used."[777] That twenty dollar bill is the same as $250 today, such were the profits made by smugglers at Point Roberts. In short, nowhere in Washington has alcohol dominated a town's economy more and for so long than Point Roberts.

In the United States, Prohibition was born out of a time when American society was searching for order. In the 1910s many people were demanding from government the same moral stewardship they received from religion. When legislators did not act, or act quickly enough on several moral issues of the day, citizens demanded political techniques to advance their aims. Out of this movement the citizens' initiative process was born. The very first initiative put on the ballot in Washington was about alcohol, having to do with saloon licensing.[778] The initiative process enabled anti-saloon politicians to get elected to the legislature. Rather than immediately ban alcohol, their first order of business was to approve a constitutional amendment allowing women to vote. Beyond the goal of women's suffrage, extending the franchise to women had the side benefit of enlarging the pro-Prohibition voting bloc. By 1916, three years before the 18th Amendment, Washington was one of twenty-three states to go dry. Some had been dry for decades. For many in Washington, Prohibition was "a belated confirmation of their early wisdom."[779] During the years the U.S. was under Prohibition but Canada was not, young men from Point Roberts would visit the doctor in Ladner for fake coughs to get prescribed cough medicine.[780]

Point Roberts was the first town in Washington to open taverns after Prohibition was repealed, ushering in a fifty-year era of large taverns on the Point. Ye Olde Tavern was opened in 1933 by Walt Waters and Hy Martin in a house just east of the grange hall. Waters & Martin held the first liquor license in Washington after the repeal of Prohibition. It served beer in ketchup bottles – Prohibition had gone on so long barware was in short supply – and then moved down to the George & Barker site when the cannery building was torn down, changing its name to the Maple Leaf Tavern. It burned down in 1944.[781] Ye Olde Tavern was quickly followed by Kate Beadleston's Green Lantern Café in the empty lot across from the Grange Hall, and the Iwersen brothers' Breakers in 1934,[782] the latter two also among the first post-Prohibition taverns in Washington.

Point Roberts has British Columbia to thank for decades of profits from the alcohol trade. The province has long had a thing with alcohol. A bizarre history of anti-alcohol attitudes treated alcohol like a toxic substance, with bizarre laws unheard of elsewhere in North America. Since Prohibition ended in Canada in 1921, British Columbia has only liberalized alcohol laws ten times, and where those ten laws are concerned, describing the changes as "liberalizing" is a bit of a stretch. Minor tweaks have left British Columbia with North America's most-restrictive, even draconian, alcohol laws.[783] After four years of total Prohibition, in 1921 the B.C. government set the drinking age at twenty-one years, and banned drinking in public. Even those over twenty-one years of age had to buy an annual license for five dollars, the equivalent of sixty-two dollars in today's money. Vodka was completely banned because it was odor-free, which caused officials to worry they wouldn't be able to tell when juvenile delinquents had been drinking. The goal was to not replicate any aspect of the pre-Prohibition "wild west" saloon, and to not do anything which encouraged or made it easy to have a drink.[784]

It wasn't until 1925 when beer parlors were allowed, but only in hotels, and women weren't allowed inside. After some protest, in 1927 women were allowed in beer parlors, but only in a separate area from men. Music and dancing were forbidden; wine and whisky could not be served. For over a half-century, B.C. patrons had to remain seated at all times. As the U.S. ended Prohibition in 1933 and alcohol became easily available to Canadians near the border, British Columbia stayed frozen in time with archaic laws. It would be over two decades after U.S. Prohibition before the province further liberalized alcohol laws. In 1954, beer parlors were given the unprecedented freedom to serve sandwiches. Vodka was legalized in British Columbia as late as 1960. It wasn't until 1962 that liquor stores were reformatted with the product on open shelves, where customers could browse and pick up their own bottle and bring it to the cash register, unheard of before. Furthermore, women would work in liquor stores for the very first time. British Columbia would stay in the alcohol dark ages well into the 1980s. In 1970, a government commission made an eye-raising recommendation that social mores were changing and succeeded in lowering the drinking age to nineteen. Liquor sales had always been banned on Sundays, but the 1970 law allowed for one tiny exception: British Columbians could buy a drink on a Sunday only if it was served with a paid meal in a restaurant. The year 1974 would bring a further concession: neighborhood pubs were allowed, opening a new category of service establishment besides liquor stores, hotels, restaurants and beer parlors. And, quite revolutionary at the time, patrons were for the very first time allowed to stand whilst they drank their beer. That's right, 1974.

Forty years later, British Columbia still has illogically restrictive alcohol laws resulting in Canada's most-expensive booze.[785] Let's say you want to go out and enjoy a drink with friends in British Columbia. The bar you go to was really hard for the owner to open, especially if it doesn't serve food. The application process is long, complicated and very expensive, and if the application is rejected, as apparently many are, all the application costs are forfeited. An enormous list of regulations is daunting for an individual proprietor; as a result, most of British Columbia's major bars and nightclubs are owned by a few very large corporations who can afford dedicated staff to deal with micromanagement by the province, hire alcohol consultants who help navigate the bylaws, and respond to the ever-changing regulations and scrutiny. The result is B.C.'s bar scene is a dull set of cookie-cutter establishments all feeling oddly similar. Driven by a province-dictated narrow template of what a bar can be, this predictable nightlife scene spawned a 2010 documentary movie about Vancouver titled *No Fun City*. By European standards, indeed, embarrassingly even by *American* standards, Vancouver is widely known for its ho-hum, home-by-the-eleven-o'clock-news entertainment scene.

It's time for you and your friends to order your drinks, but don't look for alcohol from other Canadian provinces. For eighty-eight years, alcohol has been banned from being transported across provincial borders in Canada, much to the chagrin of the British Columbia wine and craft beer industry, Canada's oldest.[786] Furthermore, foreign alcohol cannot be served at private events; foreign wine tastings are impossible. Booths at trade fairs can serve food from their home country, but no alcohol to complete the cultural experience. No ouzo with spanakopita, no Coronas with tacos, no Prosecco with your penne, no wine-and-cheese pairings. To serve local alcohol, staff for events like conferences, fairs, weddings and fundraisers must purchase their beer, wine and spirits at provincially-run B.C. liquor stores. Stories abound of visiting event organizers – and attendees – being shocked to arrive at dry events. Global visitors to international events held in Vancouver are dumbfounded by the draconian laws – the likes of which they have never seen across the many years of attending events around the world, even in dry countries. Their hands tied, B.C. event planners routinely lose business.

The last six years have seen some cracks appear in the anti-alcohol province. In 2014, British Columbia made it legal to carry a glass of wine from a restaurant's lounge into its dining room, for customers to order a drink without food in restaurants and for a farmer's market stall of offer samples of craft beer. Everybody likes to save a buck or two, but happy hour is a relatively new phenomenon in B.C., finally legalized in British Columbia in 2014. Discounts during specific times of day had been illegal on the pretense the government wanted to "free" businesses to help patrons make responsible choices, saying they wanted to promote the "freedom and independence" to imbibe any time of day.[787] After happy hour, you decide to go see a musical act. If the band seems uptight, it may be because musicians weren't allowed to drink on stage in British Columbia until 2011, and though no longer a law this is still enforced as a policy at many Vancouver venues.

It's still illegal in British Columbia for bars to offer loyalty programs because you can't use loyalty points to pay for alcohol in British Columbia. You still can't drink beer and play bingo at the same time in Canada, which Point Roberts capitalized on for many years. Only ten per cent of liquor stores are open on Sundays to this day,[788] which still generates traffic to Point Roberts for Sunday drinking, just nowhere near the levels they used to. B.C. wine is still cheaper on the Point than in B.C. Not being fools in the backyard of Canada's third-largest metro area, Point Roberts cashes in big time on B.C.'s backward view on alcohol.

THE BREAKERS

One law in particular, in force from the 1920s to the 1980s, dominated the Point Roberts economy after World War II: the B.C. ban on Sunday drinking. During this time, a major Point Roberts landmark, The Breakers, opened in 1934 by Gus and Ing Iwersen. Previously the site had been the location of the George & Barker Store, which served residents but also the workers who toiled in the cannery across the street. These workers would draw purchases against their wages. A shoe store was upstairs, something Point Roberts doesn't have today. Sitting empty today, the Breakers played a major role in Point Roberts history. The Breakers is famous to many Vancouverites because for over six decades, from

1934 to 2000, it was a major drinking hall packed with Canadians, especially on Sundays.

Business got off to a strong start from the very beginning. During World War II beer was rationed in Canada and the Breakers had a ballroom. Canadians loved to dance to the music of Andy Cleghorn on the Wurlitzer organ. Cover was fifty cents, and locals got in free because the doorman knew everybody in Point Roberts. Thousands of jugs of beer were purchased for fifty cents and lavish smorgasbords were popular.[789] As early as May 8, 1943, *Billboard* ran an article on Vancouverites coming to Point Roberts to drink. "According to an illustrated feature story published in *The Vancouver Sun* on April 5, over 500 Canadians in 150 automobiles cross the border on Saturday nights to drink beer and dance to juke box music in the single and over-crowded tavern in Point Roberts, Wash. It's all because beer is rationed in British Columbia, and The Breakers, the tavern operated by Gus Iwersen, has unlimited quantities of unrationed beer. The Canadians are not allowed to take more than five dollars per person across the line, but Gus says they don't need that much. The average spent in his tavern on beer, food, cigarettes and music is only two dollars. The news item reported that the Canadian customers seem to like best the fact that they can drink, eat and dance in one establishment. Under the heading, 'Vancouver Jitterbugs Relax to Juke Box and U.S. Beer,' there's a picture of two couples dancing to the music of an automatic phonograph. The caption repeats the claim that beer and dancing on the same premises is one of Point Roberts's greatest attractions."[790]

For decades Canadians poured into the Breakers on Sundays to watch sports on giant screens with a cold one. The huge facility could seat 1000 customers, and did: during peak hours it was so packed you could barely move around inside. The venue had two bar stations. The large wooden bar at the south end was one hundred years old and was brought to the Point from Sumas.[791]

Troublemakers weren't tolerated; Iwersen would get rid of them Point Roberts-style, escorting them out to the huge parking lot wrapped up in fishing net.[792] He retired and sold the Breakers in the late 1960s, but couldn't stay retired and went on to reopen his old Lighthouse cannery as a nightclub called, naturally, The Cannery. With the Breakers, the Reef and the Cannery, from 1972 to 2000 tiny Point Roberts supported three enormous drinking halls and nightclubs.

The decades of the 1970s and the first half of the 1980s saw Sunday drinking entrench itself as a weekly ritualistic pattern for life on the Point. One Canadian customs inspector in 1981 reported, "The Point goes bonkers every Sunday. Traffic is stacked up every Sunday for hours, with Canadian cars waiting to clear the American border station. Bars are not open Sundays in B.C. At the Point bars are going full blast Sundays with live rock bands."[793] On Labor Day 1985, over 16,000 people in 7,000 cars came across the border to Point Roberts, population 500 at the time. So many intoxicated people ran off the Point's then-narrow roads that an enterprising resident sold "See You in the Ditch at Point Roberts" t-shirts.[794] According to one of the sheriff deputies in the 1980s, "Drunks are our biggest problem. The drunks are a pain in the neck. Our jail can hold only eight people. We collect the most obnoxious drunks and push them across the border and let the Canadian cops worry about them."[795]

The king of the bars on the Point was the Breakers. A major landmark in a tiny isolated town, the Breakers was the largest tavern on the Salish Sea. Harry Johnson owned it in the 1970s and said he used to get by just with Sunday sales.[796] To keep the crowds coming, the Breakers kept up with the times, adding more reasons for Canadians to make the trip down to Point Bob. In a January 1977 newspaper advertisement, the Breakers' ad proclaimed the "grand opening of the latest in disco."[797] A bingo hall was refurbished in summer of 1977,[798] offering Canadians something else they couldn't do back home: drink whilst playing bingo.

With a cavernous room and a bar, it only made sense for to use these huge taverns for rock concerts. For a third of a century these taverns brought in big-name Canadian rock bands. Some bands saw the potential of Point Roberts and made it a base. In the 1970s two globally-known rock bands lived in Point Roberts, arguably its most-famous residents ever. Canadian rock superstar Randy Bachman had been in The Guess Who, who had a big number one song in the U.S. & Canada with "American Woman," the first U.S. number one hit by a Canadian band. Randy financed a new group in Winnipeg in 1971 called Brave Belt, investing $97,000, his life savings from The Guess Who, to record their first album in 1972. By the end of 1972, Bachman had moved to the West Coast and set up shop in Point Roberts and Vancouver. Brave Belt began regularly playing concerts at the Breakers. Bachman was shopping around for a label, and Mercury Records had just lost artists Uriah Heep and Rod Stewart. A Mercury executive heard Bachman and saw potential, sending Bachman and his band back to the studio to remix the album with more prominent guitars. They recorded two new tracks with the heavier sound popular in the day. Signing to Mercury in 1973 during the time they were actively playing the Breakers, Brave Belt became Bachman Turner Overdrive. Determined to make it bigger than The Guess Who, Bachman wanted to break into the American market, so BTO spent 330 days of their first year together on the road. Between road trips Point Roberts was home, so they were frequent headliners at the Breakers, hoping to attract the attention of anybody in the audience who could help them expand further in the United States.

American success came with their second album, *Bachman– Turner Overdrive II*. It was released in December 1973 and became a huge hit in the U.S., peaking at number four on the American charts. The album produced two of their best known singles, "Let It

Ride" and "Takin' Care of Business." Randy had already written most of "Takin' Care of Business" under the name "White Collar Worker" whilst he was in The Guess Who, but that band didn't feel it was their style of tune. When a Vancouver DJ introduced the song as "We're takin' care of business on C-Fox radio" (still a popular rock station heard in Point Roberts to this day), Bachman used "takin' care of business" in place of "white collar worker" in the song's chorus, and the song "Takin' Care of Business" was born. Point Roberts was one of the first places where the new megahit was played in front of a live audience.

During this time, Bachman and the band used the Breakers as their mailing address. Long before the Point became flush with mailbox rental facilities in the 1990s, Bachman had the idea of having a U.S. address for the convenience of Americans. Their base in Point Roberts gave them the idea of playing other border towns to balance playing to their Canadian fan base at the same time they were getting exposure to the U.S. market. BTO took that idea born in Point Roberts and soon started booking gigs in Detroit and Buffalo to facilitate their transborder goals. After several temporary departures, Randy Bachman was eventually replaced formally by Randy Murray in late 1991. The reconstituted version of BTO proved to be its most enduring as they toured together from 1991 through 2004. Ever drawn to their old home at Point Roberts, the new lineup kicked things off with a three-day gig on the Point September 9-11, 1991 before going on to play Seattle September 12.

A couple of years after BTO, another major rock group lived in Point Roberts. The band Heart, one of the most commercially-enduring hard rock bands ever with top 10 albums in the 1970s, 1980s, 1990s and the 2010s, lived in Point Roberts early in their career in the mid-1970s. Despite lineup changes, the band has long centered on headlining sisters Ann and Nancy Wilson. They've sold over 35 million records globally, had twenty Top 40 singles, seven Top 10 albums and four Grammy nominations.

The band which became Heart was founded in Bothell, Washington in 1967. After several changes to the lineup and a few different names, Ann Wilson joined one of the original members, Roger Fisher, in 1970. Roger's brother Mike was about to be drafted into the Viet Nam war and ended up in Canada. In 1972 Mike entered the United States to see family and met Ann at a concert, and they became an item. Ann decided to follow Mike when he returned to Canada. Other band members moved to Canada as they finished school, including Roger. Ann's sister, Nancy, joined them in Canada and soon became romantically involved with Roger. For a time Ann, Nancy and Roger settled in Point Roberts as their Vancouver-area base to be close to Mike. By then they were playing under the name Heart, including many shows around Metro Vancouver. During their time living in Point Roberts a demo tape was cut which turned into Heart's 1976 debut album named *Dreamboat Annie*, which would go on to reach number seven on *Billboard*.

The debut single from that debut album was "Crazy on You," which epitomizes the signature sound of Heart's early years. The song is known for two things: its blend of Heart's original hard rock with the folk rock Nancy brought to the band, and its famous acoustic guitar intro. The result of this mashup of rock and folk, electric and acoustic, a duality largely perfected during their time in Point Roberts, has been described as the essence of the band and evident in the song's intro, known as Silver Wheels. The song begins with Nancy strumming an almost-classical acoustic guitar solo on a Guild Jumbo. Its intricate moves required Nancy to use a thumbpick in conjunction with her fingers. "Because that first part was a solo piece, I had to get the whole thing down in one take," says Nancy. "I didn't want to do a punch-in because it would have been obvious. So by the time I got it right all the way through I had blisters all over my fingers. It felt like they were going to fall off!"[799] Nancy's acoustic intro fades into Roger Fisher's big hard rock riffs. Roger Fisher recalls, "I remember when they were writing "Crazy On You" we were living in an A-framed house in Point Roberts, Washington and Ann and Nancy were working on this song and they said, 'You know Rog, we've got this acoustic guitar part that goes like this... We want something on top of that, what would you do?' So I listened to them play it. And I said here, this is what I hear, and I played; ("Crazy on You" was born) just like that."[800]

Meanwhile, Ann got busy with lyrics for the new melody. The four of them were under a lot of stress in Point Roberts because Ann was partnered with Mike Fisher, stuck over the border in Canada. Ann's lyrics describe wanting to be near a loved one in order to forget problems, at the time sparked by the Viet Nam war and social unrest. Ann writes, "The words were straight out of the scenes of the wild sexuality that went on in our cottage."[801] Nancy shared that Ann "was singing about the world being really out of whack, when all you want to do is just be with the person you love instead of dealing with all the insanity going on around you... We had to deal with a lot at that time — it was a tough period for the band."[802]

"Crazy on You" was released as a single in October 1975 and would go on to be Heart's first commercial hit, and an enduring signature song for the band, heard daily on classic rock radio stations across North America to this day. It peaked at number thirty five on *Billboard*, and rose to number twenty-five in Canada and number thirteen in Belgium, number two in the Netherlands and number one in France. In 2013, the original lineup of the band performed the song for their induction into the Rock and Roll Hall of Fame, their first performance together in over thirty years. It has been used in many media. It has been featured in seven Hollywood films and on video game *Guitar Hero II*. Network TV often uses its riffs when going to commercials, and it's been used to sell Dodge Chargers.

On November 21, 1983, the Breakers burned down in a major fire causing half-million dollars damage. The fire raged for fourteen hours, completely destroying over three quarters of the structure.[803] Fire investigators confirmed the blaze was caused by arson. The owners immediately announced plans to rebuild. Whatcom County leveraged the situation to make changes to the foot of Gulf Road. Before the fire, each weekend the foot of Gulf Road and several blocks of Marine Drive were completely clogged with parked cars. First responder vehicles in some occasions couldn't get through to respond to emergency calls. For the new Breakers, Whatcom County officials required parking for 206 cars and a venue capacity limit of 999 customers. The old Front Street, a Point Roberts fixture for decades cutting across Gulf Road below Marine Drive, was to be eliminated. In return for vacation of Front Street so Breakers could build the enlarged parking lot, a "visitor area" giving public access to the beach at the base of Gulf Road was required; the access is the small stretch of land between the Gulf Road curb and the Breakers' fence.[804] The Breakers reopened on Labor Day weekend in 1985.[805] Unfortunately, its reopening was only a few months before the retail alcohol industry which had dominated Point Roberts for over half a century came to a sudden and unexpectedly abrupt halt.

EXPO 86

Back in 1978, a casual mention during a lunch meeting in London between a British Columbia provincial cabinet minister and a Canadian diplomat who happened to sit on the board of the International Bureau of Expositions (IBE), an organizing body which gets the fun duty of picking which cities get to host world's fairs, would bring an end to an era in Point Roberts. No city had claimed rights to be an official world's fair for 1986 (the IBE organizes all of this, ensuring there can only be one world's fair in any given year), eight years in the future. The year 1986 is significant for Vancouver because the year 1886 had two big events, the incorporation of Vancouver as a city, and the Canadian Pacific railroad reached Vancouver, completing for the first time in Canada a rail link from the east coast to the west coast. It was felt a reasonably-sized fair could celebrate both of those centenaries and put Vancouver on the map, heralding it from sleepy timber port to a city on the world stage, a jewel on the Pacific Rim, with astounding beauty and plentiful resources and infrastructure. Due to the connection with the railroad reaching Vancouver, transportation would be the theme and the fair would be called Transpo 86. The Social Credit government of Bill Bennett was trying to get out of a recession and a fair was a tangible way to show progress and a new mind set for the Vancouver region. Seattle's 1962 world's fair was the only fair to turn a profit, and just four years before the initial planning got underway, Spokane had hosted the 1974 world's fair relatively successfully. What could go wrong?

When the fair was first announced, the local Whatcom County media was giddy in anticipation of the riches which were to be made from the fair coming to Vancouver. The *Ocean Star* newspaper wrote in November 1980: "It could be the chance of a lifetime for communities in Whatcom County... All agreed that intensive planning is needed now to capture the opportunities for tourism in 1986."[806] Little did folks know, but the Transpo fair which would become Expo 86 would end a decades-long economic industry and change life in Point Roberts forever.

With no experience in major expositions, the Transpo organizing committee hired an American theme park expert, Michael Bartlett, to manage the show. Not only did he know how much beer – and urinals – would be needed, but as President, Bartlett brought a big vision that this event shouldn't just be a transportation trade show, but could radically change the future of Vancouver as a full world's fair with top notch entertainment, roller coasters and cutting edge technology.[807] He was known for saying, "You get 'em on the site, you feed 'em, you make 'em dizzy, and you scare the shit out of 'em." Bartlett probably saved the fair, but also drove the budget to explode, resulting in his sacking halfway through the prep phase.

Initial estimates put the show's cost at $78 million (it would end up costing a whopping $1.2 billion dollars). The provincial government wanted the city of Vancouver to pick up 25% of the fair's cost overruns should the cost exceed the budget. But with recent over-budget events in recent memory such as the 1976 Montreal Olympics, Mayor Mike Harcourt declined the offer, preventing the city from being on the hook for the eventual huge cost overruns.

Expo 86 was almost cancelled twice. The BC government proposed cancelling the fair in 1981, and in April 1984 the fair's own director recommended the fair be cancelled due to conflicts with labor unions on whether the fair's construction site would be a closed shop. Even with $80 million already sunk into the effort, the director recommended the province cut its losses and prevent further ones. But Bennett feared this would embarrass the Social Credit government and cause the party to lose the next election, so he overruled his hand-picked director and heralded that the show must go on. Any overruns would be made up from a new provincial lottery.

The original plan was to copy the 1962 Seattle world's fair. The site of Transpo would be the Pacific National Exhibition fairgrounds in east Vancouver, and like Seattle a monorail would be built along Hastings Street to connect the fairgrounds to downtown. At the same time, the Canadian Pacific Railroad's vast lands along the north shore of False Creek had turned into an urban blight in the center of Vancouver, an industrial junkyard of forgotten railroad tracks, factories and lumber mills. By comparison, people pointed to the south shore of False Creek as a success story. In the 1970s, a similar industrial area on Granville Island had been revitalized – we say gentrified now – into a public market, with art galleries, artist studios and entertainment venues. And there were coincidental calls for a covered stadium like Seattle's Kingdome.[808]

Soon it was realized the PNE fairgrounds were too small for a world's fair. Incredibly, the city of Vancouver proposed filling in Coal Harbour between today's Convention Centre and Stanley Park where the float planes take off, allowing the fair to be held downtown. The TV show *The Love Boat* had shot an episode in Coal Harbour showing Vancouver's run down docks, which did not portray the city in a good light, and tearing those down and using a land-filled Coal Harbour for the fair site would solve the problem. Thankfully, the False Creek area was ultimately selected by IBE, who officially changed the name from Transpo to Expo. Due to the transportation theme, a proposed mass transit system had been proposed to help move millions of visitors around the city, and relieve Vancouver's famously congested streets and lack of freeways. To boot, a mass transit system would attract extra federal funding. When Transpo became Expo, the transportation theme was widened to become a transportation and communications theme, with a slogan of "World in Motion; World in Touch." Expo 86 would be the largest urban renewal project in North America, ever.[809] Queen Elizabeth II conducted a kickoff ceremony in October 1983, turning the key to a cement mixer and conveying Vancouver's "invitation to the world." Work then promptly stalled for five months in labor disputes.

Officially opened by Prince Charles and Princess Diana, fifty-four countries had pavilions. Canada's pavilion was not on the False Creek site, but rather across downtown on Burrard Inlet, in what today is Vancouver's convention center. It was the next-to-the-last time two dead countries, Czechoslovakia and the Soviet Union, would appear at a world's fair. The Soviet Union, Cuba and Viet Nam even issued postage stamps commemorating Expo 86. Fourteen mega-corporations including General Motors, Coca-Cola, Minolta, Kodak, Canadian National, Canadian Pacific, McDonald's and Royal Bank of Canada had showcase pavilions, filling a huge part of the budget with their sponsorship funds. Besides Charles and Diana, notable attendees included the crown prince and princess of Norway, the prince sultan of Saudi Arabia, the prime minister of Canada, Margaret Thatcher and then-vice-president George Herbert Walker Bush.

The theme World in Motion, World in Touch carried on after the fair. Vancouver's Skytrain subway system and the cruise ship terminal are legacy transportation projects, emblematic of the original Transpo focus. The convention center, B.C. Place stadium and Science World are all legacies Expo 86 bestowed upon Vancouver which are integral to the city today. By tying all these infrastructure initiatives together into a combined world's fair project, Vancouver was able to tap into federal monies and realize more than if it had tried to secure funding without the fair. Because the fair was tied in to a larger infrastructural project, it propelled growth at a time when Vancouver was searching for its potential on the Pacific Ring of Fire amidst big growth in globalization. Expo 86 was the last world's fair to be held in North America. After the financial disasters of the 1982 world's fair in Knoxville and the 1984 world's fair in New Orleans, Vancouver's world's fair proved world's fairs could be successful, but nobody in North America has risked it since. Brisbane hosted the next world's fair after Vancouver, in 1988. Europe and Asia host most IBE-sanctioned world's fairs; of the eighteen world's fairs since Vancouver, Europe has hosted eleven of them and Asia six.

Expo 86 put Vancouver on the map, attracting attention from Asia. The main fair site was sold to a Hong Kong developer for $145 million, who turned it into today's forest of tall skinny glass high-rise condo towers. The Hong Kong development of the fair's land paved the way for the Asian money which unmistakably makes its presence known in today's Vancouver. It especially put

Vancouver on the map for those in Hong Kong who were facing the 1997 return of the colony to the People's Republic of China.

Beating forecasted visitor counts by fifty per cent, over 120,000 people on average visited the fair each day, employing a staggering 25,000 local citizens. Visitors spent $20 million on rides and $94 million on food in the fair's seventy restaurants.[810] It was a shot in the arm for Vancouver's economy. It also showed off Vancouver's beauty. Millions of people were now in on Vancouver's secret of stunning scenery. There was an environmental impact too: converting the land from industrial to residential use has greatly reduced the level of pollution in False Creek. Its reputation for being a rainy city was put to the test because of the 172 days the world's fair ran, 130 of them were dry. Today, Vancouver tops many lists of the world's best travel destinations and livability. However, many ask at what cost? Critics argue the city is congested, housing is expensive, retail has been taken over by corporate brands.[811] Many poor people were evicted from residential hotels and rooming houses so landlords could cash in on the millions of tourists expected. When downtown Eastside resident Olaf Solheim committed suicide over his eviction, Pete Seeger came to Vancouver to hold a free concert in his memory. Some believe the Asian money was destined to come eventually anyway, especially since the Canadian government had reformed immigration rules creating an investor category. "Expo was in many ways more of a marker or an accelerator rather than the cause of Vancouver's transition from the old-style Vancouver to a city with a more global metropolitan and cosmopolitan identity," said Kris Olds of the University of Wisconsin.[812]

From the original Transpo theme, some wanted the fair to be heavy on education and content, but others wanted to emphasize having a good time in a celebratory atmosphere with lots of entertainment. With over 43,000 performances in 172 days, it was the largest gathering of entertainment Canada had ever seen. A dizzying number of concerts were held, and some played Point Roberts whilst they were in town.[813]

However, a party environment meant having lots of places to drink beer. British Columbia liquor laws prevented beer from being sold and served on Sundays. With the fair open for five months, and 12.5 million people expected to attend (actual attendance would end up topping twenty-two million because Americans were staying in North America due to overseas terrorism in the news that year, and the Canadian dollar was at an all-time low), it was clear provincial liquor laws would have to change. The year 1986 would see British Columbia liberalize its liquor laws because of Expo 86. Drunken rowdiness increased, and DUIs went up twelve per cent in the first four weeks of the new law, after drunk driving had been declining previously. Public intoxication increased, with Sunday visits to Vancouver's detox center tripling. Despite these drawbacks British Columbians embraced the weekend drinking during the fair and it took hold, as though it was a major thing Vancouverites wanted to hold on to from the fair as much as any of the infrastructure. The temporary drinking laws enacted for the fair took hold and became permanent. This decision would hurt Point Roberts' economy and sharply curtail a half-century tradition of Vancouverites coming to Point Roberts to drink.

The effect of these changes meant the flow of Canadians coming to down to the Point for Sunday drinking dried up overnight. One Sunday the place was packed, and, according to one regular band, the next Sunday, after the B.C. law was changed, they played to two people. Border crossings plummeted from 128,000 in March 1986 to 83,900 in March 1987, and the Breakers had only recently reopened after the fire.

ROCK CONCERTS

The Breakers, and The Reef across the street, had to reinvent their business model after 1986. The taverns diversified from a beer-first model to more diversified weekend spots for fun with beer, rock concerts, bingo and pull-tab gambling. If they couldn't be big sports bars, their large capacities were perfect for resurrection as venues for big rock concerts. A veritable who's who of Canadian rock musicians played each weekend in Point Roberts for most of the 1990s. Big crowds came to tiny Point Roberts to hear big name rock bands, some at the peak of their careers. Let's reminisce about these rock legends, from A to Z.

Canadian female rocker **Lee Aaron**, three-time Toronto Music Award winner for Best Female Vocalist with ten Juno nominations, played Point Roberts in May 1993. Aaron played "Barely Holdin' On" from the 1985 *Call of the Wild* album and "Whatcha Do to My Body" from 1989's *Bodyrock* album, which went double platinum in Canada.

Major Canadian rock band **April Wine** played at least a half-dozen concerts in Point Roberts in the 1990s alone. Concertgoers rocked to hit after hit from April Wine's long discography, which spans from 1971 to 2006. Seven of their albums in a row hit gold or better in Canada, all of their releases between 1975 and 1982 did, and one hit platinum in the U.S. The crowds in Point Roberts thrilled to 1972's "You Could Have Been a Lady" (a number two hit in Canada) and "Bad Side of the Moon" (number sixteen), 1975's "Tonight is a Wonderful Time to Fall in Love" (number five), 1981's "Just Between You and Me" (number six), 1982's "Enough is Enough" (number eight), and other familiar hits like "Roller," "I Like to Rock," and "Sign of the Gypsy Queen." April Wine held concerts at the Breakers in August 1994, July 1995, November 1997, October 1998 and June 1999.

Long John Baldry played the Breakers in April 1992. An English blues singer and voice actor, he sang with Rod Stewart and Elton John, and hit number one in the UK with "Let the Heartaches Begin" in 1967. He moved to Vancouver in 1978, and was known as the voice actor of Dr. Robotnik in *Adventures of Sonic the Hedgehog.*

Barney Bentall and the Legendary Hearts was a Vancouver rock band, whose first album debuted in 1988 and was active through the 1990s. They quickly developed a following, and in 1989 won a Juno Award for most promising group, and several members were nominated for a Genie Award in 1990 for the song "Restless Dreamer" on the *American Boyfriends* soundtrack. They toured extensively in the 1990s, and played Point Roberts more than any other band, over a dozen times between 1991 and 2000. They were the headline act on New Year's Eve 1991 at the Breakers. During these concerts they played their top hits, including "Something to Live For," (a #17 hit in 1987) "Come Back to Me," "Crime Against Love" (#11 in 1990) and "Life Could Be Worse" (#24 in 1991) including tours for their 1992 *Ain't Life Strange* and 1995's *Gin Palace* albums. Bentall's family name is familiar to Vancouverites for several major buildings and construction projects in downtown Vancouver. The group was a regular headlining act in Point Roberts, playing a steady cadence throughout the 1990s, paralleling the height of their active music career: in December 1991, December 1992, April 1993, March 1994, November 1995, September 1996, March 1997, October 1997, April 1998, October 1998 and April 2000.

Chubby Checker not only achieved fame with his 1960 rendition of "The Twist," he singularly made the twist a popular dance style. Checker also popularized the limbo dance. His version of "The Twist" was the most popular single in the history of *Billboard's* Hot 100 singles chart at the time. Checkers had Point Roberts in a twist on May 17, 1980; tickets were $7.50. I'm not sure where Checkers overnighted that evening, but Mount Saint Helens would explode the following morning, sending an ash cloud into the sky visible from Point Roberts.

Canadian rock band **Chilliwack**, from Vancouver, rocked their big hits "My Girl (Gone, Gone, Gone)," a number three hit in Canada, and "Fly At Night," at the Breakers twice toward the end of their career in August 10, 1986 and April 12, 1987.

Bobby Curtola was a Canadian rock and roll singer and teen idol who played the Breakers August 9, 1986. His twenty-five gold singles and twelve gold albums included 1962's big hit "Fortune Teller." By the 1980s he was a well-known regular in Las Vegas, and a big score for Point Roberts.

Grammy-winning American musician **Rick Derringer** played the Breakers in October 1992. Derringer had a number one hit in 1964 as a member of the McCoys with "Hang On Sloopy" and as a solo act with 1973's "Rock & Roll Hoochie Koo." Derringer worked in Steely Dan and with Edgar Winters Group and produced Weird Al Yankovic's first six albums.

Doug and the Slugs, a pop music group from Vancouver, is best remembered for the Canadian Top 40 hits "Too Bad" (1980), "Making It Work" (1983) and "Tomcat Prowl" (1988). They played Point Roberts June 19, 1988, in 1990, and on October 7-8, 1995. "Too Bad" was used as the theme song for *The Norm Show*, a 1999-2001 Canadian sitcom starring Norm Macdonald.

54-40 is a Vancouver-based rock group. Popular on college radio since 1986, they had modest commercial success in the early 1990s. "Baby Ran" from their second album, their third album *Show Me* with its hits "One Day in Your Life" and "One Gun" and 1992's *Dear Dear* stand out from at least six concerts played in Point Roberts. They played the Breakers at least a half-dozen times at the peak of their career, with concerts in February 1992, September 1993, October 1993 and February 1997. It would have been a tragedy had 54-40 never played Point Roberts because the band takes their name from the expansionist vision of U.S. President James Polk, whose slogan was Fifty-Four Forty or Fight! At a time when the U.S. border, and thus Point Roberts, was being defined, many Americans wanted to go big or go home and demand territory up past the fifty-fourth parallel, where Prince Rupert, British Columbia is today. Britain claimed all the way down to California. The compromise created the forty-ninth parallel, and thus Point Roberts, so it's appropriate a band named after the border should play in the town created by the border.

Harlequin is a Winnipeg-based rock band known for many hits including 1982's "Superstitious Feeling." They played Point Roberts January 29, 1994.

Jeff Healey played the Breakers in June 1994, singing his 1989 Billboard number five hit "Angel Eyes." The sight-impaired Canadian musician died of lung cancer in 2008 just a month before the release of his ninth album.

Canadian singer-songwriter, guitarist, and record producer **Colin James** plays a diverse range of blues, rock, and neo-swing music. The six-time Juno award winner's career has spanned from 1988 to the present. He played Point Roberts relatively early in his career, in 1993 during his swing era with the Little Big Band and playing the hit "Surely (I Love You)," and again in 1995 in the lead up to the release of the bluesy *Bad Habits* album. A member of Canadian rock royalty himself, he gave a command performance for Queen Elizabeth II during her royal visit to Saskatchewan in 2005. James' autographed picture greets visitors in the entrance to the Reef Tavern.

Megastars **Jefferson Starship** played Point Roberts February 24, 1996. Their set list included many top Starship songs as well as their earlier Jefferson Airplane-era hits.

Sass Jordan played Point Roberts at the peak of her singing career. Her July 1994 concert promoted the release of her *Rats* album, whose "High Road Easy" peaked at number six in the U.S.

chart, and her two 1998 concerts showcased her *Present* album. Jordan would go on to be a judge on *Canadian Idol* for its entire run.

Portland-based **The Kingsmen** played Point Roberts. Their 1963 version of "Louie Louie" stayed at number two on Billboard charts for six weeks and is the rendition of this classic song most of us know best today.

Buddy Knox played Point Roberts in 1976. The American musician is best-known for his 1957 hit "Party Doll." Knox died in 1999 in the Salish Sea region at Bremerton, Washington of lung cancer.

Vancouver-based **Loverboy** played Point Roberts in 1993, playing their arena rock staples "Working for the Weekend," which hit number two in the U.S. charts in 1981, "Turn Me Loose," a number six hit in the U.S. from 1980, and 1985's "Hot Girls in Love" (number two in the U.S.) and "Lovin' Every Minute of It" (number three in the U.S.).

Canadian rocker **Kim Mitchell** was a frequent draw to Point Roberts, playing his 1984 hit "Go for Soda" in October 1992, March 1995 and November 1998. Mitchell had three platinum, a double-platinum and a triple-platinum album between 1984 and 1995, overlapping the time he was active in Point Roberts.

Alannah Myles rocked her 1989 U.S. number one gold hit "Black Velvet" when she played Point Roberts in March 1996 and in May 1998 when she was promoting her new greatest hits album and celebrating her 1997 induction into the Canadian Association of Broadcasters' Hall of Fame. "Black Velvet" won her the 1990 Grammy for Best Female Rock Vocal Performance and is still a worldwide radio hit to this day. The Canadian singer-songwriter's first album is the only Canadian debut artist to go Diamond with over one million sales in Canada. By the time she played the

Breakers she had won another Best Female Rock Vocal Performance Grammy award.

The **Northern Pikes** rocked their big 1990 hit "She Ain't Pretty" when they played the Breakers in April 1992. The song earned them 1991 Juno nominations for Song of the Year, Best Video and Group of the Year. It headlined the group's 1990 album *Snow in June*, their most successful and only platinum album.

Vancouver-based alternative rockers **The Odds** played the Breakers for the Easter long weekend in April 1993 with Wall Street and She Stole My Beer. They were on tour for their second album *Bedbugs*, which featured their hits "It Falls Apart" and "Heterosexual Man." A year after playing Point Roberts, they earned a 1994 Juno nomination for Best New Group. Their singer now plays with Colin James.

One of the most prolific performers in Point Roberts was Vancouver-based **Powder Blues Band**. Their broad musical style spans blues, pop and jazz and appeals to wide variety of folks, and Powder Blue Band drew crowds at the Breakers at least eight times, with steady billing in May, August and November in 1986, April 1987, June 1988, February 1992 and June 1994. Originating as a Vancouver house band at a Gastown bar, they released five studio albums in the early 1980s alone. Their first album went double platinum in Canada, their second album went platinum and their 1990 greatest hits album went gold. It's no wonder they were one of the first bands brought in to play at the Breakers after Sunday drinking was legalized in British Columbia in 1986.

PRiSM is a Vancouver-based rock band who rocked Point Roberts with four concerts in early 1992 and September 1993. They were 1981 Juno winners for Group of the Year and released big hits like "Don't Let Him Know" and "Spaceship Superstar," which NASA used in March 2011 as the final wakeup song for space shuttle astronauts. Many of their members have gone on to have big careers in the music business as producers, songwriter and song doctor. The incestuous nature of the Vancouver music scene is apparent in PRiSM; various keyboardists have been with Trooper and Colin James Band, including Johnny Ferreira who played a solo concert in Point Roberts in November 1995. PRiSM's 1993 concert at the Breakers promoted their *Jericho* album, their first new album in a decade, which included Bryan Adams as a guest musician.

Vancouver club band **Juan Trak** played Point Roberts for the Canada Day and the U.S. Thanksgiving long weekends in 1993. They had opened for Meatloaf and played Expo 86.

After Barney Bentall, nobody played Point Roberts more than Canadian rock band **Trooper**, who played at least ten concerts over the course of a decade in both the Breakers and the Reef. Trooper was formed by Ra McGuire and Brian Smith, who had previously been together in Winter's Green which became Applejack. It was in Applejack they would perform their original song "Raise a Little Hell," which Trooper reincarnated and would make world famous. They were discovered by Randy Bachman, who produced their first album in 1974. As noted earlier, Bachman was living in Point Roberts, and in 1973 McGuire, Smith and the band were in Point Roberts as they were working with Bachman to release the album. McGuire recalls, "I said 'fuck' through a PA system for the first time. My band mates giggled like girls and flushed with a combination of shame and concern. We were rehearsing, in the afternoon, at the Reef Tavern in Point Roberts, Washington. There was no one else in the room."[814] From that juvenile beginning, Trooper would go on to create four platinum or double platinum albums between 1976 and 1979 and more albums into the early 1990s. They won Group of the Year at the 1980 Juno Awards and in an unusual twist and a testament to their prolific production they had two songs nominated in the Composer of the Year category because the songs were from different albums which were concurrently charting. Trooper and their earlier incarnations held concerts in Point Roberts over a longer span of years – twenty-five, an incredible quarter-century of rocking the Point – more than any other musical group. They played the Breakers as Winter's Green as early as New Year's Eve 1971, and then as Trooper many times over the years. Crowds partied to hits like "Raise a Little Hell," "We're Here for a Good Time (Not a Long Time)," and "The Boys in the Bright White Sportscar" during their concerts in Point Roberts in July 1986, August 1986, May 1987, November 1991, October 1992, December 1994 and March 1996. They were the headline act for the New Year's Eve party at the Breakers in both 1992 and 1993.

Wall Street is a Vancouver area band which played many concerts in Point Roberts, including gigs in the 1980s, April 1992, October 1993, the headline acts for New Year's Eve 1994 and New Year's Eve 1995, and in September 1996. Steve Sukert was the bass player from 1981 to 1987 and recalls life in the band and playing in Point Roberts: "It was quite exciting times playing fifty to ninety nights a year. Most memorable was opening for Doug and the Slugs. We played lots of nights at the Commodore Ballroom, many weekends at the Reef in Point Roberts... After the Breakers burnt down in about 1983, the Reef in Point Roberts was the only place to play. Great room considering it was packed to the rafters most weekends. I recall taking the whole twenty-minute break just to get to the bar and back to the stage again. We would play Friday, Saturday and Sundays there. Even Sundays were good up until the bars in Vancouver opened on Sundays for Expo 86. That killed the band/bar business in Point Roberts. As this piece of USA is only accessible from mainland Canada, the border guards and the RCMP made it difficult for patrons to access the Point and return home after, so there was no incentive to make the trip, despite the great ambiance of Point Roberts."[815]

With all these bands playing, and crowds returning to Point Roberts, beer sales were strong once again. Concertgoers were thirsty, and at one point the Breakers had an incredible 700,000 empty beer bottles piling up. This was enough to lay them end to end around the circumference of Point Roberts ten times.[816] Canada finally gave permission for the bottles to be imported for recycling.

With Canadians staying home on Sundays to drink legal beer, more customers were needed in Point Roberts. Trying to diversify, the Breakers held on for a while with bingo and pull-tab gambling. Known for a while as Breakers Beach Club, the Chippindales all-male revue stripped down in February 1987.[817] All you can eat Dungeness crab as a twelve dollar loss-leader lured Canadian customers. Coin-operated contraptions like pitching machines and jet-ski races were added.

In the mid-1990s there was a crackdown on drunk driving on both sides of the border. When Breakers' customers crossed back into Tsawwassen they were met with Canadian Breathalyzer vans, and with only one road out of the exclave, everybody was caught up in the dragnet. Bars and restaurants began offering shuttle service to homes in Tsawwassen.[818] The Canadian government also gave border staff the power to arrest people for driving under the influence. The Breakers staff, facing nearly one thousand customers on a busy night struggled to monitor who had been served how much to drink so they could be cut off from being served more. The Washington State Liquor Control Board sent a nonstop army of undercover agents into the bar to find any minor slip-up.[819] Breakers eventually closed on May 21, 2001.[820]

THE REEF TAVERN

If all this talk of beer drinking has you thirsty, never fear, across the street is Kiniski's Reef Tavern, owned since July 1988 by former professional wrestler Nick Kiniski. Offering a full bar, The Reef has been a venerable institution on the Point since the 1950s when Ken Waters opened on the site of the Maple Leaf Tavern and the George & Barker salmon cannery. From 1983 to 1986 The Reef picked up the slack for Canadians wanting to drink on Sundays during the time Breakers was being rebuilt from its fire. They were packed in on weekends, as The Reef seats several hundred, an impressive size for sure, but less than half what the Breakers had held.

Figure 101: The Breakers (left) and the Reef (right) at the foot of Gulf Road in 1972 (with the pier not reaching the shore but mostly in tact) at top and in 2017 at bottom. Top photo by *The Point Roberts Guide*. Bottom photo by Mark Swenson.

The Breakers and the Reef diversified their business by offering something else not available in Canada: gambling. In the late 1980s and early 1990s, before the tribal casinos and besides bingo, gambling in Washington meant pull tabs. One of twenty states to allow them, pull tabs are a game of chance in the form of a paper ticket the buyer rips open along a perforated flap. The ticket is compared to a wall poster known as a flare which lists information about prize amounts, the number of prizes available and other pertinent data. If the numbers or slot machine-style images revealed by the ripped-open ticket match the prizes on the flare, the pull tab can be redeemed at the bar, bowling alley, casino or other establishment; better than one in eight tickets wins some sort of prize. In Washington, pull tab tickets cost players, who must be eighteen to play, between ten cents and a dollar each, with prize values ranging as high as five thousand dollars. Some pull tabs feature merchandise, sports memorabilia or tablet computers. The tickets at the Reef cost either twenty-five or fifty cents each, with a top prize of $200. Some players in the Reef sit at the bar tearing open a stack of pull tabs, a bit like one mindlessly eats a whole bowl of potato chips. Those thinking of giving them a try might want to view it as entertainment; on average, only seventy-four per cent of dollars wagered were returned to the players. In 1991 the Reef was the number two seller of pull tabs in all of Washington, at its peak offering over forty different pull tab games. Point Roberts also had large bingo parlors which opened in 1973. Together, these games earned Point Roberts a reputation as a gambling town. In 1992, gamblers wagered over $8.6 million in pull tabs and bingo in Point Roberts.[821]

And just as a change in drinking laws in conjunction with Expo 86 ended the beer-selling heyday in Point Roberts, a change in gambling laws ended the pull-tab heyday. In February 1992, following a 1988 federal ruling which allowed gambling on Indian reservations, the first tribal casino in Washington opened less than thirty-five miles from Point Roberts by the Lummi Nation. The Tulalips followed suit five months later on their land near Marysville, Washington. Eight more would follow in the next five years, including a second tribal casino in Whatcom County and one in northern Skagit County. Casino profits helped the tribes with social services, lifting many out of abject poverty.

Today, The Reef has an outdoor patio right on the beach with tables and a grassy lawn overlooking the Strait of Georgia and the busy Tsawwassen ferry terminal with the huge BC Ferries to the islands coming and going. Orcas are often seen in summer swimming off-shore, commemorated by the orca mural on the east side of the building, painted in August 1993. There are pool tables, darts, big screen TVs, poker tournaments, and their beachside location offers beautiful views and sunsets.

The Reef has the only big piece of neon signage remaining on the Point, lighting up the foot of Gulf Road in a warm red glow at night. It helps set the mood for the rock & roll history made on this block. In the 1950s, several buildings on the Point had neon signage. It was during that decade when the Vancouver metropolitan area had over 19,000 neon signs, at the time one sign for every eighteen residents, the highest number per capita anywhere in the world save Shanghai. Even Las Vegas, known for its garish display of neon couldn't hold a candle to Vancouver, which was North America's capital of neon. Pilots said the neon glow from Vancouver was easy to spot from over a hundred miles away as they approached the airfield.

The retro trend makes folks nostalgic about neon signs today with calls for the preservation of neon, but in the early 1960s outlandish neon signs had been overdone and the times were a-changing. In the United States, the seedy part of town stereotypically had flickering neon, but that's a perspective on neon not found in Canada. Neglected neon signs flicker in the United States because businesses there buy and own their neon signs, and therefore, must maintain them as they're exposed to weather. Less affluent parts of town couldn't afford to get neon maintained and repaired. Neon didn't make their neighborhoods decay, the neighborhood decayed the neon. Vancouver was unique in that neon sign owners did not buy neon, they leased signs from neon manufacturers, who were responsible for maintaining them. Neon manufacturers had steady annuity income from the leases, and the lessee had great-looking neon. And by the early 1960s there was a lot of it. Neon was blamed for what was wrong with Vancouver as it headed into the 1960s at a time when locals wanted the city's reputation to reflect one of outdoor natural beauty. In an effort to clean up the city's view, one local newspaper called for an end to Vancouver's "hideous jungle of signs." Though momentum toward sign control built in the 1960s, a signage bylaw regarding neon signs wouldn't be passed until 1974, when much of Vancouver's neon heritage came down, with the exception of the Granville Street entertainment district, where preserved vintage neon can still be seen.

From babes to beef to beer to bands to betting, for decades Point Roberts was the anything-goes entertainment hub for Vancouver. It suffered its unfair Tijuana image, but it did exploit the difference in laws on the other side of the border to offer British Columbians a forbidden fruit experience they could not get at home.

Our tour ends here at the foot of Gulf Road. Before you take a well-deserved break at one of the Point's restaurants, take a moment to gaze out at the old pier. The Point's original front door refuses to completely wither away, its weathered pilings still standing erect as if to suggest they're ready for duty once more. Standing guard of the Point's rich history, the pier stretches out into the water, hinting with optimism at the potential of Point Roberts, a town like no other.

Figure 102: The old Point Roberts pier in 2017. Photo by Mark Swenson

CHAPTER 9 • HOW DO YOU SOLVE A PROBLEM LIKE POINT ROBERTS?

When governments draw boundary lines, they sometimes create exclaves; all too often exclaves are then left isolated and underserved. Now that you've completed the tour, you can appreciate how Point Roberts benefitted and suffered from its exclave status for years. It had no reliable water source until 1988, only one police officer for decades to manage thousands of rowdy drunk visitors, no harbor until 1977, no bank until 1982, no health clinic until 2003, complicating daily life in a tenuous and highly-seasonal economy. It pays more in taxes than it gets back in services; locals wait in border lineups behind lots of Canadians who spend lots of money on the Point. The taxes earned go to the county, yet the county provides no school on the Point after third grade. Its businesses cater to a transient customer base which at one time gave the Point its unfair Tijuana reputation.

Time and again when it came time to help Point Roberts government agencies passed the buck. The citizens of a unique American town were feeling not merely inconvenienced but actually under threat of being totally assimilated into Canada. Canadians owned nearly all the real estate, had the most-likely source of water and were essentially taking over the town. The U.S. Interior Secretary called the existence of Point Roberts "illogical and anachronistic."[822] The proudly-American locals didn't want to be absorbed, but didn't have the resources to control their destiny. After facing challenge after challenge, after reinventing the town's economy more than a few times after a series of economic setbacks, and after defending against crazy plans by outsiders who didn't realize or care about the impacts of their decisions on Point Roberts, the residents have developed techniques of defending themselves when threatened. Each time, despite internal differences, they band together to take on the latest external menace. This is still a current habit of the population of Point Roberts, as evidenced in recent years by the radio tower fight, the crusade to save Lily Point and fighting proposals for fees to cross the border. At the first sign of peril, the tiny town gets fired up, unites and lobbies to defend its local interests.

After debates in the 1940s about whether to secede and join Canada, attempts to address the problem of Point Roberts became more focused in the 1950s. The Point Roberts Chamber of Commerce was formed in 1951 and quickly organized a formal request to the University of Washington in Seattle to conduct a study of the challenges facing the community. The UW's final report contained recommendations to appoint "a special international commission to make a thorough study of all of the possible solutions to this problem."[823] Washington Senator Scoop Jackson sent a letter to the International Boundary Commission, who maintains the border on the ground including placing markers and clearing vegetation, asking the commission to investigate the Point's challenges.[824] The exasperation of local governments over Point Roberts soon became evident when, in the following year, the Joint Fact-Finding Committee of the Washington Legislature received a brief July 7, 1952 from the Whatcom County Board of Commissioners calling Point Roberts their "orphan problem child."[825] Federal, state and provincial, county and municipality levels of government on both sides of the border all tossed the Point Roberts issue to somebody else like a hot potato. The residents of Point Roberts increasingly demanded to know which level of authority would take responsibility for the survival and interests of the community. One Congressman stated, "If the problems faced by the people of Point Roberts are to be solved, some level of government is going to have to develop a specific proposal and it will have to be backed up with special legislation."[826]

In the early 1960s, residents also looked into getting Point Roberts classified as a development-needy town under the Area Redevelopment Act, which would bring funding for new development projects. The state rejected the Point's application after it was unable to identify specifically how new long-term jobs would be created through detailed economically-justified project proposals, and how this classification would benefit the overall Washington economy, not just the Point's own economic affairs.[827] The Act required a contribution by the community of local funds as earnest money to unlock assistance funds, a sum far too dear for the Point.

In 1962, the Point Roberts Grange organized an appeal to the Washington State Grange to submit a resolution in the United States House of Representatives calling for "all possible federal assistance... be extended to Point Roberts to aid in solving [its] problems, both through the enactment of appropriate legislation by Congress and through the more effective administration of existing laws by the President." Resolution 38 was submitted by Congressman Jack Westland on August 14, 1962 to the 87th Congress. The resolution resulted in some action for once. Funds were allocated for an economic survey called "An Economic Outlook of Point Roberts and Effects of a Proposed Harbor." After three years, the 1965 impact report was finally delivered, but it had made an assumption development was already assured and it was merely extrapolating out the economic impact of development the study assumed was already in the works; it didn't address how to get development plans started in the first place. As such, its recommendations were useless. The silver lining in the report was a validation of several of the community's issues. It concluded the Point Roberts economy was crippled, citing border regulations which limited employment, the difficulties in transporting goods from Canada and the U.S. mainland, and the growing numbers of year-round Canadian residents all as contributing to the Point's instability and preventing investment and long-term planning.[828]

Attempts to reach out to Canadian officials fared even worse. The municipality of Delta and the province of British Columbia routinely rejected pleas from Point Roberts, pointing out it was an American, not Canadian, responsibility to provide water and electricity to towns in the United States. In any case, Canadian law usually prevented the export of utility services. Canadians pointed out their citizens living in Point Roberts paid property taxes to Whatcom County, and couldn't vote in U.S. levies. They were concerned a few hundred Americans could vote to increase taxes on thousands of majority Canadian landowners. The only opening by Canadians in terms of willingness to consider proposals to buy water and other essential resources was immediately cloaked in demands the United States limit the population growth of Point Roberts, exactly the opposite of the locals' objective. Americans felt the Canadians were rigid in their nationalism and Canadians were irked by the gall the Americans had to demand services from a foreign government. Neither side wanted to set a precedent by taking on the Point Roberts situation.[829] A classic stalemate, nobody was going to make the first move.

At the close of the decade the population had doubled since 1960 and problems facing the community were getting worse. The county dissolved the townships in 1969, and the Point Roberts Township – the only official community institution – was no longer an avenue the residents could use to have their voices heard. A formal petition signed by almost all sectors of the town was sent to Washington D.C. asking the federal government "to take whatever action necessary in order to hold a joint conference with the appropriate representatives of Canada in order to discuss the problems of Point Roberts."[830] The goal was to set up a commission with representatives from all levels of government in both the

United States and Canada, and the residents of Point Roberts of course, to work things out.

Progress finally came on April 21, 1971, when the federal governments of both Canada and the United States agreed to put the Point Roberts question once and for all to a joint commission to come up with recommendations on solving the Point's problems. They turned to an institution called the International Joint Commission (IJC). Formed in 1912 as part of the Boundary Waters Treaty of 1909, the IJC is the oldest joint institution working to depoliticize boundary matters between the United States and Canada.[831] The IJC primarily works on matters of boundary waters spanning the United States and Canada, though its remit from the beginning did allow for it to investigate other matters pertaining to the U.S.-Canadian border. In its early days, it was chiefly focused on the Great Lakes and the Saint Lawrence Seaway. There had been dustups between the countries regarding the Lake of the Woods along the Manitoba-Ontario-Minnesota borders, as well as the Saint Mary's, Milk, Sault Sainte Marie and Niagara Rivers.[832] The Saint Mary's and Milk Rivers flow from Montana into Alberta, and the Saint Mary's River flows for 200 miles in Canada before it then re-enters the United States. Irrigation uses of the rivers had been in contention between the nations, and these were key drivers in the establishment of the IJC.[833]

The IJC had worked on issues involving disputes between Washington and British Columbia as well. The mighty Columbia River originates at its headwaters in British Columbia, but most of its length flows through Washington and along its border with Oregon. In the 1950s Washington wanted to build multiple dams along the Columbia, and the IJC performed engineering, technical and economic studies of the potential effects on both countries, which were released in 1959. In 1961 an agreement brokered by the IJC was reached whereby Canada would ensure sufficient water flowed into the United States to fill the dams' reservoirs, and in return the U.S. would compensate Canada with half the downstream power generated.[834]

There have been a small handful of non-water-related cases before the IJC, including one between Washington and British Columbia involving a smelter in Trail, British Columbia. In 1928, the IJC was asked to assess damages from air pollution in Washington emanating from the Trail smelter. The IJC issued its report in 1931 and final settlement came in 1935. Today's "polluter pays" principle results from this case.[835]

Prior to being given the Point Roberts task, the IJC was not unknown in Whatcom County. In the far eastern section of the county, high in the Cascade Mountains, the City of Seattle owns a large dam on the Skagit River. The Ross Dam supplies a good portion of Seattle's electricity, and in 1941 Seattle applied to the IJC to raise the height of the dam, which would enlarge the reservoir behind the dam to the tune of nearly 5500 flooded acres of land in British Columbia. The IJC's handling of this case should have been an omen to the residents of Point Roberts. Seattle's application was approved by the IJC on the condition it compensate the B.C. government who would make whole private landowners from the loss of land due to the flooding.[836] It would take over a quarter century for the compensation to be ironed out, with an agreement finally reached in 1967. Facing protests – political and environmental – the IJC was requested in 1971 to issue an environmental impact report. The results of that report prompted the B.C. government to claim in 1980 the original 1942 order was invalid because it lacked an environmental impact study and the 1967 agreement failed to consider issues later uncovered in the 1971 environmental report. Two score after the process began the issue was still in dispute; it wasn't resolved until 1984.[837] This was the commission which was going to fix Point Roberts.

The Point Roberts issue had been sent to the IJC at a point in time in the early 1970s when the urgency to fix the Point's problems seemed to be reaching critical mass. The community, in its various committees, had been crying for help for two decades. Representatives from Washington's legislature, British Columbia's parliament and the U.S. congressional team in whose district Point Roberts was located began discussing how to address the problem of Point Roberts, leading to the 1971 application to the IJC. Officials at the Canadian federal level were reluctant to go along, and the feds on the American side were very much aware the Ross Dam case was still meandering through the IJC, and the risk of losing their favorable 1942 order was alarming. The two are linked: the compromise was to send both the Ross Dam and Point Roberts cases to the IJC at the same time.[838]

The question the IJC was wading into was what level of government ought to be responsible for the welfare of Point Roberts. The locals had been asking this question for years, and it seemed they were now going to get their answer. The scope of the IJC project was to investigate various problems with which the people of Point Roberts had long been plagued, including customs regulations and laws, the supply of essential services, law enforcement and "any other problem found to exist on account of the unique situation of Point Roberts."[839] This open-ended task went far beyond the IJC's typical boundary waters expertise, so it had its work cut out for it. It was wading into a situation where it would be trying to remedy, and hopefully solve, difficulties caused by a stalemate of regional governmental inaction, patriotic sensitivities and past acrimony across the border.[840] Where the IJC was used to a rational method of technical inquiry, this case was different: it was political. The IJC was going to play as unbiased a role as possible, and in doing so, would likely propose a compromise to placate both American and Canadian interests, each side giving a little bit to meet in the middle. The idea their interests would be the subject of a give and take between outside entities made locals uneasy.

The application to the IJC contained a Terms of Reference the federal officials of the U.S. and Canada wanted studied and for which solutions were sought. The problems were caused and exasperated by the border and Point Roberts' exclave status. The scope set by the Terms of Reference was:

1.   How customs laws and regulations get applied with respect to transporting goods, perishable food, trades tools & equipment in transit through Canada.

2.   Rules covering the ability of Point Roberts residents to work in Canada and for Canadians to work in Point Roberts.

3.   Health and medical care, especially denial of health insurance coverage and compensation, allowing Canadian doctors to practice in Point Roberts.

4.   Review of electricity and phone service.

5.   The issue of law enforcement and the inability to transport suspects in custody through Canada to the U.S. mainland.

6.   "Any other problems found to exist on account of the unique situation of Point Roberts" and to identify solutions "and any other ways of improving the situation."[841]

Initially grateful and relieved serious federal attention was being shone on their community, local residents were at the same time a bit uneasy as few had heard of the IJC. Many wondered if it was yet another sprawling bureaucracy infected with political wrangling, or if it might be an agency which would take their plight seriously and actually reach decisions and get solutions implemented. Yet another shallow survey wouldn't cut it; the locals had already lived through quite a few of those. The issue before the IJC was more profound than daily irritations of life in an exclave. Water, sewers, health care, electricity, and the rest were the face of the problem, but the core issue was residents' ongoing battle to maintain an American identity and to be able to make long-term plans and invite appropriate growth to further their future. The mood in 1971 was the actual existence of the community itself was at risk, and a few bandages on mere inconveniences of living near a border were insufficient. Residents wanted self-determination through long-term, economic transformation by resolving the core issues which impeded revival and growth. They also knew from experience not only could an unknown federal force fail to forge change, it could also enshrine an undesirable outcome based on a misinterpretation of the Point's complex situation. That feeling of vulnerability raised the stakes of the IJC's mission and how it would be interpreted by a people who when threatened could be highly-organized in a frontline of community defense organizations.

The first act of the IJC was to appoint a board. The bureaucratic nature of the IJC showed itself early. After initial excitement over its commencement in April, things went quiet. It would take seven months for anybody to hear anything from the IJC. Finally on November 30, a board was appointed. The International Point Roberts Board (IPRB) would initiate the studies and inquiries, interface with federal departments of both countries, and make the final recommendations back to the IJC.[842] The board had equal numbers of seats from each country; each nation had a chairperson. The Americans on the board were James Scott, a consultant to the U.S. federal government, retired from Foreign Service, who was chair; James Dolliver, Assistant to Washington Governor Dan Evans; and Dr. Manfred Vernon, a political science professor at Western Washington State College (now University) in Bellingham. The Canadian bench included of Dr. Geoffrey Andrew, former Executive Director of the Association of Universities and Colleges, who served as chair; Lloyd Brooks, Deputy Minister of the B.C.

Department of Parks and Recreation; and William Lane, a lawyer for the municipality of Richmond. Conspicuously absent were any representatives from the Canadian federal government, and no seats were held by any member at a county level on the American side, an alarming omission given the role Whatcom County would undoubtedly need to play in any solution.[843] Most glaring of all, nobody on the board was from Point Roberts! The IPRB had no local liaison providing a local perspective as to the nature of the community or its needs. The member of the board physically closest to Point Roberts lived in Vancouver; others resided in Bellingham and Olympia. One member lived in Virginia! Additionally, the IJC gave no funding to the IPRB, expecting the board members to ask the agencies and departments from which they came for resources. This oriented the board toward government entities, not the community. Indeed, no funds were allocated to fund a liaison effort with the community.[844]

Public hearings were conducted in Point Roberts and Vancouver in December 1971, after which the IPRB began its investigation. During the investigation, the residents of Point Roberts had no idea if the IJC was headed in a direction beneficial or harmful to their interests. The IPRB never opened a public-facing office in Point Roberts, so its work was not visible to the community. Although many inquiries are done privately to keep objectivity intact, the IPRB issued no public statements during its investigation. Partially due to the scattered locations of the board members, as late as September 1973 when the IPRB gathered to write their final recommendations it was only their sixth meeting.[845] "To be certain, unless one already knew of the IPRB's investigation, it is probably safe to assume that it would have been difficult to surmise that the IJC had authorized any study of the Point Roberts reference... Too many questions were left unanswered and too many suspicions went unallayed."[846] By not updating the local population as to its progress, concerns grew among the residents. In an editorial which sounded like a Revolutionary War-era declaration of independence, the town newspaper put out a call for the community to organize its own form of governance, "We, the people of Point Roberts asked the International Joint Commission to study our situation and our problems as we saw them, because we recognized the need for international cooperation in helping us find solutions. So, why couldn't we, the people of Point Roberts – rather than just asking each other, "I wonder what the I.J.C. is going to say?" – start thinking now in terms of some type of our own local "International Joint Commission" style of self-government – possibly something along the lines of a "New England Town Meeting" concept of participation in local government, as outlined by Professor Manfred Vernon, Western Washington State College, when he spoke here last year."[847] To the locals all of this was not a good start, triggering its time-tested defense mechanisms when it sensed a threat from the outside.

In the IJC's typical case load of dams, bridges and irrigation projects, technical research is paramount. The Point Roberts project was different, and needed a different approach. The IPRB did not fully appreciate how important it would be to garner community support to address the social nature of the Point Roberts case. By conducting its affairs without community involvement, its technical studies were not grounded in the subjective appreciation required for the unique nature of this project. The IJC's typical methodologies of compiling facts and statistics were insufficient to understand the issues facing Point Roberts; this case required hearing from the residents and having a broad, multi-disciplinary perspective of the complicated and tangled causes of the Point's problems.[848]

The work of the IPRB included contact with government officials, requesting letters of opinion and conducting its own studies. B.C. Hydro was asked to investigate electricity provisioning at the Point. The U.S. Department of Labor was asked to pursue options for allowing Canadians to work in Point Roberts.[849] By exclusively asking outsiders to provide input, the IPRB work veered toward a general approach to the problem. Very early in the process the board solicited a study from the U.S. National Park Service regarding the possibility of creating a national park at Point Roberts. A subsequent study included the national park services of both the U.S. and Canada regarding making Point Roberts the hub of an international park.[850] It is hardly surprising the community had little trust in the IPRB or its work given the board never made attempts to instill trust and basically skipped all liaison work. The very sovereignty of their community was too important to trust an international agency with questionable authority. Before the final report was released, the locals already knew the board's fact-gathering would not be sufficient to identify workable solutions. After two and a half years of silence, the IPRB submitted its conclusions and recommendations to the IJC. The local residents were dismayed and alarmed by the "Report to the International Joint Commission on Solutions to the Problems Facing the Residents of Point Roberts" of October 23, 1973, especially considering IJC has real power whose decisions cannot be appealed by either the U.S. or Canadian governments.

The report was a major disappointment in that it merely described the various problems but inexplicably made no specific resolutions to these challenges. Another white paper waved in the air, it contained no reply to customs regulations, police presence, the sourcing of water or other critical issues which were within the project's scope. After years of work in secrecy, the IPRB actually claimed some of the problems afflicting Point Roberts didn't even exist. The lack of a doctor or clinic in Point Roberts was no issue to the IPRB. Its assumption was Point Roberts is mostly made up of Canadians who generally summer in Point Roberts but reside more than half the year in B.C., so these Canadians could cross the border to see a doctor in British Columbia. Their assumptions about the

Americans were also majorly flawed. It found obscure clauses in the law which allow U.S. citizens to get health insurance to cover admissions to Canadian hospitals if the "hospital was closer to, or substantially more accessible from, the residence of such individual than the nearest hospital in the United States," but ignored the fact not all insurers offer that in their policies, at least affordably. Another reason the IPRB rendered the lack of health care a non-issue was another obscure reference allowing Canadian doctors to respond to emergency calls in Point Roberts. Though true, this covered only emergency situations but not general health care; indeed, Canadian doctors are prohibited from opening a practice in Point Roberts. Besides the fact few people know of such entitlements, they require substantial burden of proof and only covered emergency needs for major incidents, not routine doctor visits. Of course, if a resident had no health insurance none of these remedies were available. These half-hearted dismissals of the health care problem were just one example of the IPRB not fully understanding the gravity of the problem, and thus the IJC could not solve the real issue. The IPRB dismissed other problems in a similar vein.

Its timid "nothing to see here, folks" attitude rendered the findings toothless. For example, the report addressed electricity service for Point Roberts, finding B.C. Hydro would need to be part of the solution. It merely noted B.C. Hydro was hesitant to sign on to any agreement where it would export utilities because it would then, as a provider of utilities to Americans, fall under the U.S. Federal Power Commission regulations. Despite the power the IJC would have to force a resolution, the board passed on a once-in-a-blue-moon opportunity to affect real change by prescribing Canadian utilities work with Point Roberts.

Regarding the crucial issue of water, the IPRB also missed a golden opportunity to deliver help to Point Roberts. The board explored options Point Roberts had already tried and found to be dead ends, such as a pipeline under Boundary Bay from Blaine for which the Department of Agriculture and the state of Washington had already denied funding. Canada would not export water or import sewage to and from Point Roberts and complained Canadian property owners in Point Roberts had to pay property taxes to Whatcom County in the U.S., the IPRB copped out and made an ineffectual lukewarm suggestion the Point Roberts water board and the municipality of Delta conduct a study, as if that hadn't been done before.[851] For the core challenges facing the Point the IPRB failed miserably, squandering its power to make anything of substance happen. This seemed odd until their much bigger ideas for what do with the problem child of Point Roberts became known.

Rather than address specific problems, the board took a more general macro view of how it saw the future of the exclave. It considered four scenarios for the future of Point Roberts: whether Point Roberts should be transferred to Canada, the creation of a large private corporate-owned city on the Point, the creation of a park on Point Roberts, and reclassifying Point Roberts as a conservation area. The first idea explored by the board was whether Point Roberts could or should simply be given, leased or sold to Canada. The United States not being a country known to cede territory lightly, the American members of the board quickly vetoed this notion as politically unacceptable stating "it could not accept such a solution and other solutions should be pursued."[852]

The next scenario evaluated by the IPRB was to let a for-profit corporation develop a regulated private city of 15,000 to 20,000 people on Point Roberts. Pacific & Western Equities Ltd., made up of mostly Canadian executives but incorporated in Washington, put forth a $200 million proposal to develop the self-contained private city they described as a "recreational-retirement community." Envisaging a Golden Girls version of Celebration, a family-centric city of seven thousand built in Florida by Disney Corporation, Pacific & Western painted a vision of transforming much of Point

Roberts into a private city of up to 22,000 people with master-planned neighborhoods of new single family homes and condominiums connected by private roads. All undeveloped land in Point Roberts would have become one of the master planned neighborhoods, with treed buffer areas surrounding each residential area to serve as paths and bridle trails. Amenities would include all beaches made public, two golf courses, a 500-berth marina, a 100-room resort hotel, a thirty acre commercial village and conservation areas. The developers' proposal called for them to provide roads and utilities including electricity, water and sewers to all homes on the Point.[853] The business case calculated a population of fifteen to twenty thousand Canadian and American residents was the break-even point to fund the development of services and utilities and to build an economic base, and would justify major infrastructure projects such as that long-desired water pipeline under Boundary Bay from Blaine.[854] Privately-funded development was attractive to the IPRB since it did not rely upon public taxes as a cost center. Generating a significant new tax base as a profit center, Point Roberts would become Whatcom County's second-largest city, six times as large as Lynden, the next-largest city in the county after Bellingham. News reports noted Point Roberts would become denser than East Chicago, its beaches akin to Coney Island.[855]

The board was concerned about private corporate-run cities, and insisted the proposal would only work if there were tight regulations on the corporation, and if the county zoned the town appropriately.[856] The Canadians on the board were attracted to the idea; for once Point Roberts wouldn't be looking to them to provide utilities though there was distrust the developers could pull it off and would in the end still look to Canada for the sourcing of utilities. Canadians were troubled by the doubling of the population living on the Roberts peninsula, which would put pressure on Canadian infrastructure leading to the Point,[857] and a significantly larger Canadian population on Point Roberts would steal business from businesses in Tsawwassen, which would suddenly have a town of equal size sharing the Roberts peninsula. Perhaps most importantly Canadian residents would be paying property taxes to Whatcom County but would be ineligible to vote on legislation impacting their taxes or provisioning of services, though that was already true.[858] In its final report, the IPRB did not recommend the private corporate-run city solution to the IJC, but the proposal came closer to reality than many realize. Pacific & Western had quietly been "assembling sufficient land" by buying property on Point Roberts.[859] By 1973 they owned or had interest in a full fifty-six per cent of the land on the Point, with options to buy hundreds more acres.[860] Pacific & Western also held a supportive petition signed by 109 U.S. voters living at Point Roberts.[861]

The next proposal considered was turning Point Roberts into a national or state park. The U.S. National Park Service quickly put a stop to any discussion of a national park when it contacted the IPRB and informed them Point Roberts didn't qualify according to their strict criteria and rules and would benefit more Canadians than Americans, saying, "Although there are some historic values present, these are not deemed to be of national significance. In addition much of the story which might be told here can be better told at the nearby proposed San Juan Island National Historical Park. Recreation values exist and expansion of existing public parks may be advisable but potential users are almost all Canadian due to the physical location of the peninsula. Similar nearby areas, some perhaps with greater potential are more easily accessible to United States citizens."[862] Locating a state park at Point Roberts, which would come along with water, police and fire services, fared no better. State parks must be served by state highways, and without ferry service or a bridge, Point Roberts wasn't an eligible site.[863] It was added even if ferry service could be established, Washington would not fund a state park in a remote corner of the state which would benefit far more Canadians than Americans.

Point Roberts was again deceived by the politics of its exclave status, this time by state-level government.[864]

The last solution evaluated by the IPRB was to turn Point Roberts into an international conservation area, and this was the proposal toward which the board leaned; indeed, the idea of turning Point Roberts into an international park was approved unanimously by the IPRB. This notion started from a joint feasibility study presented by the U.S. National Park Service and the Canadian National and Historic Parks Branch in March 1973 entitled "An Inventory of International Parks Possibilities: Point Roberts, Boundary Bay, San Juan and Gulf Islands Archipelago."[865] The proposal called for the establishment of a 3000 square mile (half of it water) bi-national park spanning from Gabriola to Whidbey Island, swallowing many towns and communities, ninety public parks and fifteen wildlife refuges. It would provide marinas, beaches and even underwater parks.[866] A board called the "bi-national forum," similar to the IPRB with three Americans and three Canadians, would make policy and legislative recommendations for the park to all levels of government in both countries regarding water, wildlife, land use, transportation and the like. The park was to have a hub called the "headquarters" where officials would be based. Recreational infrastructure would be planned and developed from this hub. The bi-national forum would become the governing authority of the headquarters, with special powers to obtain land; regulate development; provide water, sewers, fire, police and transportation within the headquarters zone. The IPRB decided the Roberts peninsula and a portion of South Delta would be the headquarters zone and Point Roberts would become the capital of the park.[867] The inspiration and model for an international park at Point Roberts came from its sister city at the other end of the U.S.-Canadian border. An international park had been established in 1964 on Campobello Island, with the United States and Canada splitting evenly the cost of developing, operating and maintaining it. The IPRB didn't bother to specify how costs for the Point Roberts headquarters would be paid or how the forum would interface with various levels of government in each country.

Ironically, the favored solution did the least in solving the core issues facing Point Roberts. There were vague references to the providing water and sewers required by the headquarters area, with an assumption Canada would be providing it, despite Canada's assurances this was not only illegal under Canadian law but politically D.O.A. The board envisaged the forum would have wide powers, writing in its report, "it should be possible to alleviate Point Roberts' water shortages and to provide an adequate waste disposal system within a reasonable period of time ... even if this ... would require amendment to existing British Columbia legislation regarding the export of water."[868] Most of the urgent needs of Point Roberts, the reason for the report in the first place, were not addressed at all. The report to the IJC was predominantly about a park at Point Roberts, not the people of Point Roberts. It assumed the problems of the Point would just get sorted out as the park was established. Locals were too savvy to trust this kind of wishful thinking.[869]

Many groups, including organizations, government agencies and elected officials, expressed concern they had not been contacted or consulted by the IPRB for their input. Many entities which would be within the park spoke up to voice their opposition to the plan, including the San Juan County Planning Department, the Landowners and Taxpayers Association of San Juan County, the San Juan County Commissioners, the Lummi Nation, Whatcom County Commissioners Chairman Johnson, whose constituency included Point Roberts, and the U.S. Navy.[870]

The impact of the designation of its land as a park would have been profound for Point Roberts. What the proposal essentially called for was to transfer responsibility for not only Point Roberts but also all of the San Juan Islands in San Juan County and

Whidbey and Camano Islands in Island County and the Canadian Southern Gulf Islands to the bi-national forum. Thousands of Americans relatively far from the border would be living under an extra-constitutional board, half of whom would be Canadian. Still nominally in the United States, thousands of Americans would be living under a non-American jurisdiction. Nominally part of Whatcom County, Point Roberts would be in the international park's headquarters area, meaning the bi-national forum would run local affairs. Some saw it as streamlining, others as a new layer of control, and some saw it as nothing less than a foreign takeover.[871] From the IPRB's perspective they were offering the people of Point Roberts utilities and the chance to live in a cool park. The park concept sidestepped the legal intricacies from the Point's geography and exclave status. The idea of an international park was meant to tame nationalistic feelings with a common project cloaked in an aura of cooperation.[872] The board also solved the problem of Canadians paying taxes to a government with whom they had no voting rights, as they would be controlled by a half-Canadian board.

Although some felt the park proposal was the best chance for the Point's treasured shorelines to remain undeveloped and natural, other Americans in Point Roberts freaked out, seeing it as ceding their town to an unelected half-Canadian board. Whatcom County commissioners issued a statement in opposition. It said giving "this six-man body the control over zoning and all other matters in such a large area is... government without representation and a basic violation of citizens' rights." Committees formed with names like "U.S. Citizens of Point Roberts" opposing what they viewed as transfer of sovereignty to Canada.[873] The Point Roberts community wasn't looking to change their political status; indeed it was the threat of being swallowed up by Canada which started the petition to the IJC in the first place. Proudly American, they were prepared to fight to keep the rights of self-determination and freedom from foreign interference.[874]

The expectation going in was significant de-population of Point Roberts would occur as a result of the plan. When residents moved away or died, they would be forced to sell their property to the park; they couldn't pass it down to their heirs or sell it to a private buyer. If your home burned down, you couldn't rebuild it; it had to be sold to the park.[875] This fact wasn't hidden; the IPRB came right out and depicted in its report to the IJC, the "gradual reduction of the resident population of Point Roberts," and without pesky people, the perpetual problems of the Point would wither away. The de-populated Point "would, in and of itself, reduce" the Point's problems, according to the IPRB report.[876] The plan called for no new permits to be issued for building on any undeveloped lot. Residents could be the last of their family to live in the park or leave right away; either way they had to sell their property to the park. Paul Muldoon writes, "It may be argued that while no formal transfer of territory was specified, there were to be substantial property 'sales' as well as jurisdictional surrender to the 'headquarters area' that included Point Roberts."[877]

From the release of the report October 23 to the initial public hearings in December of 1973, the IPRB did nothing to educate the locals about the proposal. They did not launch any public relations or media campaign to sell the idea. It offered neither details nor data to dismiss the rumors which were running wild.[878] The board failed to appreciate the people were expecting relief from daily challenges and a more promising future for their unique community, but the IPRB was instead advocating a very different preordained "master plan" to create a very different Point Roberts.

Correspondence between the IPRB and the IJC indicates the international park proposal was prominent in the board's thinking from the very beginning.[879] As early as April 1971 one British Columbia Member of Parliament already had the IJC case on his radar in advocating for a Campobello-style international park on the Roberts peninsula, actually predicting the IPRB would advocate for a Campobello-style international park.[880]   Doubts were raised whether the board's preoccupation with the international park idea clouded their objective assessment of the other options. Regardless, since the park idea trumped real solutions for Point Roberts' problems, the IPRB had veered away from its core mission and scope from the get-go.

Not surprisingly, when the IJC held public hearings in Point Roberts about the IPRB recommendations, the reaction of the local community was overwhelmingly negative. In a pre-Internet era, it was difficult for the average citizen to get information about the IJC plan. A *Vancouver Sun* article at the time called the international park at Point Roberts "perhaps the most misunderstood issue of the decade," citing the challenges of getting access to reliable information about the proposal: "Copies of its report and many details had to be written away for or examined at a library. Therefore, many people got their information from skimpy newspaper stories. It was inevitable that by the time the public hearings began on December 3, minds had been made up before the facts were made clear."[881]

Those who could access the report found there were scant specifics about exactly how Point Roberts being the headquarters area of the park would impact the community.   Details were nowhere to be found. There were unanswered questions whether commercial businesses, and thus jobs, would be allowed in the park, how infrastructure improvements would improve access and how the expected sharp increase in traffic would be handled. Locals were disappointed to not find any details about how they would be compensated for their homes and land if Point Roberts was to be repurposed as the park headquarters. The Point Roberts Grange Society, the Maple Beach Property Owners Association of Vancouver, the Canadian Property Owners Association of Point Roberts and the Point Roberts Planning Committee all voiced concern about the lack of information about the process by which property would be transferred from its owners in Point Roberts.[882] These groups argued in the public hearings the unelected bi-national forum was unconstitutional, as it was responsible to both national governments, not to the people living within the headquarters area. The community stood united in its defense of self-determination. In June 1971 a meeting was held of forty-eight American citizens. A committee which promised "no recommendation will be made regarding secession... The association will not initiate or support any discussion regarding change of sovereignty of Point Roberts."[883] This group would in 1972 go on to become the Point Roberts Voters Association, specifically to unite the community in response to the IPRB study.

The Canadian view was to make sure the park blocked large-scale growth in Point Roberts, preventing demand for Canadian services. D.J. Morrison, mayor of Delta, issued two ultimatums for support: a condition all undeveloped land in Point Roberts be acquired for the park, and all further development limit the population of the Roberts peninsula south of the 49th Parallel to current population levels. He reiterated Delta's long-standing opposition to legitimize the usage of Canadian utilities or services to drive growth in Point Roberts.[884] Higher levels of the government and environmental organizations were generally in support of the plan. The Governor of Washington and the Premier of British Columbia were both on board, as were the Sierra Club, the Audubon Society, the National Seashore Alliance, the B.C. Wildlife Federation and the Federal Minister for the Environment in Ottawa.[885] Local Delta business owners signaled a more cautionary tone; in one Tsawwassen retail shop's ad in the Point Roberts paper the owner added the phrase, "We are Behind Autonomy for Point Roberts and Tsawwassen. We Have Grown Up with These Twin Communities."[886]

One reason the board didn't launch a PR campaign in Point Roberts for their proposal was because they didn't anticipate there would be a community any longer at Point Roberts. The IPRB viewed the Point's laundry list of problems as evidence the town was beyond hope and in any case was naturally declining. "The Board report expected the community to wither away in the wake of the international park, and this would in course resolve the problems at the Point. This expectation showed how far the board strayed from its original purpose to remedy the plight of Point Roberts. The IPRB believed the community was dying anyway, and decided to focus on the grand scheme of the international park and conveniently assume that nature would take its course and Point Roberts would no longer be a problem for the authorities. Under this view, there was no need to recommend specific solutions to the Point's problems."[887]

After the public hearings, the IJC knew the IPRB proposal was not only unpopular but was actually vehemently opposed by the community. The IJC, which had failed to anticipate the prospect of a negative reaction from Point Roberts, chalked up the negativity to the intangible nature of the park and rampant misinformation among the public.[888] After an awkward moment where it wasn't clear what the IJC would do in the face of strenuous opposition heard in the public hearings, the IJC asked the IPRB to create a task force to make a decision as to whether there was enough cooperation and agreement among stakeholders for the international park to be feasible. The task force would investigate the impact of the board's park proposal and related recommendations, but the board could not find enough people willing to cooperate.[889] In June 1974, the IJC asked the board to write a supplemental report focused specifically on Point Roberts, with a more issue-oriented approach, which it delivered on September 15. Not surprisingly, the Supplemental Report came to the same conclusion as the original report. In the introduction the board stated "the problems initially identified by the two governments were minor when compared to a number of other more fundamental problems facing the existing population." It also recognized a U.S.-only solution was problematic, and accepted involvement of Canadian governments was contingent on Canadians having a voice in growth in Point Roberts.[890] The board wrote, "... it is necessary that the United States citizens on the Point and local and state legislators should come to recognize that the local and provincial governments in Canada are entitled to have a view of the population" density of Point Roberts, if Canada is to be expected to provide road access to the Point and other services.[891] Indeed, it concluded by stating until all levels of government in both countries agreed to bilateral cooperation, it could not meet its objectives. As a result, the IPRB recommended the IJC not adopt the international park proposal.[892] The IJC announced the international park proposal was officially dead in October 1974. The IJC's final report to the national governments in August 1977 concluded its international park recommendation was rejected primarily due to opposition by the people of Point Roberts. In it the IJC stated "until such time as the local jurisdictions have reached some sort of accommodation concerning the Point Roberts question, there is little the Commission can do in this matter."[893] The local residents had blocked the threat to their sovereignty and national identity, but six years after the IJC case was opened, no progress had been made on the Point's problems, and no viable solutions on the horizon. The IJC left Point Roberts' problems unsolved, with antagonized neighbors in a stalemate.[894]

The board did suggest in the Supplemental Report a new idea: that Point Roberts be named a "free zone" by the U.S. government to alleviate customs issues governing transportation, admissibility and use of trades professionals, and imports of perishable foods. However, this was a minor point in the report, easily overlooked.[895]

A Washington State Senate memorandum in February 1974 requested the IJC study of Point Roberts be abandoned until a Select Committee could make its own recommendations about Point Roberts. It did not endorse the park proposal, instead suggesting local solutions in combination with cooperation between Washington and British Columbia.[896]

Although the case was complex, the IJC failed because of the approach it and its board took. The board took a narrow technical focus consistent with past IJC cases, did not liaise with the community and was preoccupied with a preordained international park solution for Point Roberts. Its "grand solution," designed to deliver a dazzling park concept to distract from local antagonisms, failed to solve specific problems specified in the project scope.[897] Looking back it seems ridiculous a three thousand square mile park was the proposed solution to a 4.9 square mile exclave's problems. It was supposed to overcome national antagonisms core to the issue, but ended up not only not using its power to solve them, but actually making them worse. Unanimously viewed as a big failure, the IJC experience did succeed in showing locals and other Point Roberts stakeholders what an outside solution looked like, reinforcing calls for local cooperation on the problem child.[898]

Few residents of Point Roberts today remember the IJC, but the IJC remembers Point Roberts. "Point Roberts was more than a mere anomaly in the case history of the Commission; rather, the reference represents one of the few 'black marks' on the otherwise impeccable record of the IJC."[899] It was a rare case of the Commission not being able to make a recommendation to the national governments. The failure of the IJC to adjust its methodologies and techniques for a new type of case like the one at Point Roberts caused experts to reevaluate whether the IJC should be used for cases beyond boundary waters issues. Muldoon concludes, "Stripped of its traditional technical basis for resolving disputes, the IJC was asked to play a role more closely akin to that of a political body rather than that of an administrative agency. At the time of the reference, the Commission was neither prepared nor equipped to meet the challenges of the case."[900] The Point Roberts case is significant in helping experts to realize a formal institutional process has limitations when utilized for dispute settlement. Bi-national agencies like the IJC are not a substitute for diplomacy and political negotiations at a local level. The learning from Point Roberts is to not expect too much from bilateral agencies. They excel at implementing a common empirical basis for negotiations and institutional processes, but when the task diverges from its traditional framework, they aren't in their sweet spot.

Point Roberts had been in limbo for six years. Major development had been put on hold in the early 1970s as a result of the town's future being up-in-the-air. With the cloud of the IJC's international park proposal lifted in the mid-1970s, several development projects, including the marina, began immediately.

CHAPTER 10 • POINTED IN THE RIGHT DIRECTION

Perched at the end of a Canadian peninsula sticking out into the Salish Sea, Point Roberts, home to barely a thousand people, played an oversized role in the history of the region. Tiny Point Roberts was significant to the Coast Salish people, early white settlers and European immigrants, the salmon fishing industry, seaside fun and the Canadian leisure class, alcohol and smuggling. It's a microcosm of Pacific Northwest and Salish Sea history, all conveniently located in one tidy package. Point Roberts' history is representative of the history of the Salish Sea, home to over eight million people making up over three per cent of the U.S. population and seven per cent of Canada's population. The Salish Sea region is the ninth-largest megalopolis in the United States and third-largest in Canada. Point Roberts sits at the center of the densely-populated major urban centers in the region at a time when the concept of a unifed Salish Sea ecosystem is solidifying. As the region is seen as one entity, Point Roberts has much to offer from its strategically central location where Canada and the United States come together.

Ounce for ounce, or as a local is more likely to say, gram for gram, no city of its size can match Point Roberts when it comes to scenery, history, culture, things to do, and international intrigue. It's all here: centuries-old aboriginal culture; activism for the protection of endangered species; squatters, pirates and smuggling; Daniel and Goliath battles against government bureaucracy and greedy corporations; global crime sprees; and even good old sex, drugs and rock n' roll. Sure, big cities have all of that, but in the case of Point Roberts we're talking about all of that happening in an isolated 4.9 square mile inconvenient asterisk of America.

Yet for all that concentrated history there is no museum and the obelisk is the only significant historical monument. The unique and instrumental Icelandic heritage is barely visible anymore. There is no Icelandic-themed gift shop, no parade on Iceland's national day (June 17), no Icelandic memorial other than the cemetery plaque. Some information and historical photos of the Coast Salish people, the canneries and fish traps have been placed in parks and are brought out during special events, but there's no museum to display the local historical society's impressive collection. There are no replicas of a Coast Salish long house or the salmon drying racks after which the Point earned its original name, Cheltenem. An artificial display of Coast Salish culture is likely not the best way to understand it anyway. Stuart Christie wrote about the Coast Salish during the 1993 Resort at Lily Point proposal, "No doubt turning Chelh-ten-em away from salmon culture toward a more artifactual rendering of Lummi sovereignty, as with a tribal museum, could have nearly as deleterious effects as the proposed golf courses. The imperative remains, instead, to keep a functioning and productive site of Lummi salmon culture and its sovereignty alive to an ongoing process of community definition."[901] Perhaps a joint outreach project between a local group and the Lummi Nation could help bring this history to life. Groups in Point Roberts could provide supplies and resources for Coast Salish youth to experience the building of traditional salmon drying racks as their ancestors did on their sovereign land. A demonstration and solemn ceremony could be organized at Cheltenem, showing how reef net-caught sockeye are prepared and tied to the frames for drying – what the word "cheltenem" means – as the Coast Salish people did for thousands of years right here. This could help everybody appreciate and experience Cheltenem in a more authentic way, and come together to share an understanding of this special place.

Public infrastructure for tourism would pay for itself. The tourism potential of Point Roberts is exceptional, offering its slow pace, relaxed atmosphere, recreation, beaches, sunny warm weather, views and yes, history. There are 2.4 million residents in Metro Vancouver, which receives over 12 million tourists per year. Over 2.7 million cars drive by on Highway 17 each year going to and from the ferries in Tsawwassen, coming within three miles of Point Roberts. The Point is a ten minute drive from Tsawwassen Mills, one of the 100 largest malls in the world, the fourteenth-largest in Canada and the third-largest in British Columbia. Over 1.1 million Washingtonians live north of Seattle and well within range of the Point. Point Roberts is a great day trip for all these people who are tantalizingly close. Most of them have no idea Point Roberts exists, let alone consider it for a weekend getaway.

Even if they make it here, it's not immediately obvious what there is to do. There's no clear focal point of the community to encapsulate the potential experience. If visitors stay long enough to poke around, after a lovely forested canopy first impression, the main drag opens up into a commercial strip. There is almost no lodging, so unless you've planned the trip in advance and booked a private home online, the Point is a day trip. But forget overnight; little suggests to the visitor how they would even spend a couple of hours here. With a large plurality of visitors spending only fifteen minutes here, and most spending less than an hour, Point Roberts must offer a suggestion to these fleeting visitors why they should, indeed how they could, spend just another hour: where they could have a meal, poke in some cute shops, walk a beach, hike in George Vancouver's footsteps, learn about real Salish Sea pirates, maybe see some wildlife and spend a few Loonies. The border crossing survey revealed recreation was the third-most popular reason for visiting Point Roberts[902] and there is much which could be done to capitalize on this potential. Just as one tries to spot the Big 5 animals on an African safari, the Point could promote its connection to nature in the midst of an urban ecosystem. Come to Point Roberts, play on the beach and try to spot the Big 4: orcas, bald eagles, great blue herons and Icelandic horses (or deer or Dungeness crabs, etc.). You'd never know any of this was possible from how the Point presents itself to the outsiders upon whom the community is dependent. I've lost count how many cars have flagged me down as I walked or biked along the street, asking me if there is a village center, what there is to do, if there is anywhere to eat or what I recommend they see. Imagine how many don't bother to ask. Better sign-posting is needed for trails, parks and beach access. Marketing campaigns at the Tsawwassen Mills mall, B.C. Ferries, Vancouver International Airport, in addition to digital ads and social media marketing of course, would drive awareness. Like the "pork, the other white meat" campaign, Point Roberts could launch a campaign to "visit the other San Juan Island," where smugglers and pirates once thrived. Without a focal center, Point Roberts will be stuck in a public perception which dates back to at least 1894 when the *Victoria Colonist* wrote of the Point, "The land at the end of the promontory is completely isolated. It is in the United States but not

Figure 103: "Welcome to Little America" chamber of commerce sign at the entrance to Point Roberts. Photo by Mark Swenson.

of it. Its value to the American government is infinitesimal. As a piece of territory, it is really not worth considering."[903]

Protruding into the center of the Salish Sea, tiny Point Roberts is at the intersection of major metropolitan areas: Vancouver to the north, Bellingham to the southeast, Seattle to the south and Victoria to the southwest. Having a collective name for the Salish Sea region recognizes the interconnectedness of everybody sharing this maritime resource. That's the dichotomy of Point Roberts. When viewed as a central hub location within the Salish Sea, it has enormous potential; when viewed as an isolated exclave outpost, it retains its charm. Point Roberts has been trying to balance this for decades. The Point's location at the tip of the Roberts peninsula, connected to the mainland but near the idyllic islands offshore, could be the basis of a strategic regional transportation hub. The idea of a ferry to the mainland has been kicked around for a long time. There are few options for where a car ferry landing could be located; the Gulf Road pier would need complete overhaul, the marina entrance is narrow and environmental and governmental regulations would be onerous, though not impossible. A car ferry connection would make the Point a little bit less of an exclave than it is today, eliminating the requirement of traveling through Canada to get to the Point by car. But it would also provide a vital transportation link with its compatriots on the mainland and open up tourism potential. Ferry service could be thought of as a continuation of Washington State Highway 548 from Blaine. With ferry service, Point Roberts could be an alternative route to Vancouver from the U.S. mainland. This route could be a contingency should any national security issue develop at the Peace Arch. As a hub, Point Roberts could connect the Salish Sea in ways not currently served. A passenger ferry link between Metro Vancouver and the San Juan Islands could be based in Point Roberts. Point Roberts is a handy launching point to reach three of Washington's best state parks: Sucia, Matia and Patos Islands, just twelve miles off shore and currently only served by private boat.

Point Roberts could connect the Salish Sea: the U.S. mainland, the San Juan Islands, Metro Vancouver, with quick connections from a Point Roberts ferry hub to the Tsawwassen ferry terminal for easy continuing service further into British Columbia. Instead of the IJC's idea of a park headquarters, Point Roberts could be a transportation hub and a convenient place from which visitors can base a trip to the Salish Sea region.

To some, however, talk of a transportation hub and the border lineups it would create is abhorrent no matter the number of jobs it might generate. For them, the slow-paced rural character, the woodsy environment, the wildlife (including just seventy-six remaining local orcas), the peace and quiet, the emptiness within view of metropolitan infrastructure is the essence of Point Roberts, and development and growth should be subservient to maintaining a cohesive rural small-town charm – a sense of community. Like many towns, Point Roberts struggles finding the right balance, but has lots of experience in trying. The exploitation of the salmon runs in the fish traps and canneries was a Point Roberts out of balance with treaty obligations and nature, spawning (sorry) the ensuing piracy for which the Point is known. The community struggled to find that balance during the dance between development and the heron rookery, gas station moratoriums, permits for adult entertainment, the Character Plan, tree retention bylaws and the fight for water.

Perhaps the greatest and most permanent balancing act is the Point's relationship with Canada, a complex subject felt every day by the international boundary. John F. Kennedy said of the U.S.-Canadian border, "Geography has made us neighbors, economy has made us partners, history has made us friends."[904] As the lifeblood of the local economy, Canadians need a compelling reason to visit Point Roberts beyond filling up the tank. They're here anyway; there must be a focus on leveraging that presence with some a clear reason to check out what the Point has to offer. What is the macro-level growth path from the current offering of cheap gas and parcel pickup? The parcel services in Point Roberts represent a need by Canadian consumers to be part of, and have access to, the U.S. economy. Having a presence in the United States goes beyond an address: it offers access to digital technologies and services not yet fully available or optimized in Canada. U.S. consumers enjoy a wider range of content available sooner. Having a U.S. presence dramatically expands ecommerce options; a U.S.-based IP address unlocks content and services. Services to help Canadians have a digital fingerprint based in the U.S. will be a growth area for border towns in the future and as the closest piece of the United States to millions of Vancouverites, Point Roberts is ideally-situated to lead this trend. Duty-free merchandise would attract shoppers who might also spend at other local shops. It's fun to watch Canadian visitors shop in the Point's supermarket. The awe and amazement at the variety and selection, low prices, huge lotteries and exotic candy bars is an opportunity to market goods to Canadians specifically for their novelty value. A retail experience with innovative products unavailable in Canada would make Point Roberts a showcase for the newest U.S. tech or boutique craft offerings. Repeat traffic could be generated by a treasure hunt mentality from a continually-updated offering of new products. How many towns have no chain stores? Point Roberts could play up a "buy local" theme. A "best of Whatcom County" retail offering could attract Canadians who appreciate locally-sourced goods, perhaps a pairing of a Bellingham craft beer with a pinkish burger at one of the Point's restaurants would be a novel, slightly taboo experience. In a nod to the Point's past with selling forbidden fruit – beer on Sundays, pull tabs, the burgers – a trip to Point Roberts could be positioned as a chance to indulge (like pirates?), which drives impulsive spending.

To generate these cross-border shoppers, Point Roberts needs greater visibility. First, Vancouverites have to know Point Roberts is their closest, easiest and quickest way to get to the U.S. economy. Advertising and digital marketing could generate top-of-mind awareness of the Point as an option for accessing the U.S. market. It's become fashionable for districts of cities to come up with a shortened name. San Francisco has "SoMa" for South of Market Street, and Denver has "LoDo" for Lower Downtown. To tap into how convenient its shops and restaurants are to Metro Vancouver, Point Roberts could capitalize on this modern trend by positioning itself as the hip PoRo.[905]

As Point Roberts is the third-busiest border crossing on the 49th parallel, it deserves web cameras and digital highway signage displaying wait times as are done for all the other crossings in the county, two of which process less traffic. But these data are only provided for crossings served by state highways, and Tyee Drive is not a state highway. Designation as an extension of State Highway 548 would open up state-level infrastructure possibilities, from digital highway signage to state parks to ferry service.

Additionally, visitors have to get here. Jitneys picked up visitors at the Ladner ferry in the old days to bring Canadians to Point Roberts; the need for them hasn't gone away. Border logistics make cross-border transportation challenging, but a shuttle bus to Tsawwassen Mills mall or Metro Vancouver transit bus 601 and the Canada Line metro system would enable seamless travel from the Point to downtown Vancouver for Canadians who don't want to make the drive and sit in border lineups, or who wish to enjoy an adult beverage or two whilst here.

It's important to know your customer. When visitors do make their way here, it should be intuitive how to have a good experience for somebody who has just crossed the border. Signage is lacking and inconsistent. Every non-American visitor to Point Roberts uses the metric system, but the Point offers little to help. Much of the growth and capital in greater Vancouver is driven by Asian investors, but there are no businesses or signage directed at this market segment. When viewed from the perspective of a visitor who has just crossed the border knowing nothing about Point Roberts, it's no wonder most will have left the Point in less time than it takes to drink a latte. An extra Twoonie from each one would mean millions to the local economy.

The border is often cited for Point Roberts' stunted growth; however you see that, either good or bad; it certainly has had a monumental impact on the Point's history and economy. It is through the border Point Roberts creates a handshake to British Columbia. It is due to the border the Point has been able to benefit in many ways. Rather than be victimized by it, as much as possible the Point should own its border town uniqueness. The border keeps the Point safe and creates market opportunities it can exploit.

From a business development and marketing view, Point Roberts makes an ideal incubator and test market. Once you enter by land, you're a captive audience. Its isolation enables new products and concepts to be tested with a minimum of market noise. The steady and dynamic flow of Canadian visitors who would be exposed to ideas being tested in Point Roberts provides a useful degree of randomness. The Point offers a desirable blend of Baby Boomer retirees and young affluent tech-savvy professionals. Whatcom County and the state of Washington could also use Point Roberts do conduct isolated tests of innovative legislation and service-provisioning logistics within a relatively contained area, including the usage of smart identification and new procedures in state fishing and shellfish licensing. Despite the market segmentation models depicting the Point as a technology backwater, Point Roberts is a perfect proving ground for emerging technology. To help address the challenges of providing services to the remote exclave, Point Roberts could pioneer regular drone service to bring goods to and from the mainland, alleviating the need to involve Canadian customs. It could then sell its model to other communities where location presents access challenges. The Point's quiet rural roads could be used to test alternatives to gasoline-powered cars and self-driving technology. Virtual reality could help transcend the Point's remote location. Instead of waiting for legislative representatives to visit, Point Roberts could pioneer the usage of virtual reality technology for civic involvement with government officials on the mainland. Some local residents cannot cross the border and are thus captive on the Point. The community could showcase using virtual reality technology to participate in events held on the mainland as a model to other remote communities. An augmented reality app could drive high-tech tourism by superimposing history on physical landmarks around the Point; imagine walking the Lily Point lowlands in the footsteps of George Vancouver, alongside a hologram George Vancouver in your augmented reality glasses. Necessity is the mother of invention and the Point's unique situation has given it plenty of opportunities to innovate throughout its history; there's no reason it couldn't lead the Salish Sea, indeed the world, in virtual reality and high-tech tourism, especially situated conveniently between the software hubs of Seattle and Vancouver. This could drive high-paying jobs with light environmental impact.

Height restrictions, the lack of sewers and other building constraints means businesses which are small, agile and even temporary could do well in Point Roberts. The trend toward popup retail stores could be used to offer a short-term, better-get-to-Point Roberts-to-see-it-before-it's-gone treasure hunt experience of finding something novel. During the IJC study, the IPRB suggestion of having Washington's trade fair exhibition hall at Point Roberts is one of the few sensible ideas produced. An event space at Point Roberts could offer a unique experience in a beautiful location, competing with Vancouver-area venues struggling under B.C.'s draconian alcohol laws. Virtual workspace for innovation labs and software hackathons could attract high-tech Canadian talent to plug in and incubate their projects in a cool setting with a beach fire in the evening. With ecommerce sales expected to keep doubling, Point Roberts is well-poised to continue to exploit its chasm-crossing digital divide as Canada lags in retail digitalization. The Point offers the "last mile" (or kilometer as it were) between the Canadian consumer and the U.S. market, a physical connection to a digital experience which will take forms we can only imagine today. Perhaps no town on the Salish Sea has a wider gulf between its potential and its limitations. Business development processes are essential for taking action to operationalize the use cases which have the highest potential, helping Point Roberts get ideas identified, funded, tested and realized.

To underpin all of this, Point Roberts needs a crisper brand. Its current brand image has improved from the Tijuana of the North days, but it is still fuzzy. Is it a seaside resort? A rural enclave within a big metro area? A place for cheap commodities for Canadians? I'd suggest these are not truly differentiated. Birch Bay is a seaside resort; most of the county is also rural and the border crossing at Blaine and Sumas also offer cheap beer. Some towns encapsulate a brand using a symbol or mascot, along the lines of the consistent lighthouse theme on Campobello Island. When Forks, Washington began capitalizing on the *Twilight* books set in the town the number of visitors mushroomed from 10,000 per year to 73,000. Point Roberts has several potential options for an icon. The smuggling and pirate theme could be fun, though nearby Friday Harbor started a pirate festival in 2017. Perhaps a mascot could be named Bob, from Point Bob.

With potential town themes and icons being claimed by others, the one truly unique attribute of Point Roberts is the fact it is an exclave. There are only four of these in America, and they ain't making more. In a country of homogenized corporate sameness, anything unique and authentic has market potential. It is the isolation of being an exclave which makes Point Roberts utterly unique in the U.S. market. Some people travel to Point Roberts specifically as a geographic oddity bucket list task. Drawn to the novelty of an exclave, they want to say they've been there, and experience going through the borders and looking out at America and Canada from offshore. Since Point Roberts is a quirk of geography, its brand could play up the exclave with an overlay of quirkiness. The local saying, "We're all here because we're not all there" wears this quirkiness as a badge of honor. There are all manner of amazing superlatives and novel experiences just waiting to be packaged up into a unique destination with a quirky brand. Visiting Point Roberts must be on your bucket list! Come see for yourself the daily logistical obstacles Point Roberts residents face which most Americans can't imagine! Try buying gas by the liter in the USA and paying for it with plastic Canadian money! See orcas, eagles or all Big 4! The more people who experience Point Roberts not only shop and eat and contribute to the economy, but they talk about it when they get home and post about it on social media, thus creating more demand to visit.

Point Roberts could own its exclave status in a fun, quirky way which would cut through the clutter in the marketplace and stand out as a unique Salish Sea destination and experience. Instead of apologizing for the border, why not play up the border crossing and make it fun at the same time? Crossing the border is part of the iconic Point Roberts experience, but they generally don't stamp your passport at the border crossing anymore. One form of gamification could be a welcome kiosk selling a souvenir Point Roberts passport – with the Stars and Stripes and a Maple Leaf on the cover. Visitors could stamp their "passport" themselves with commemorative rubber stamps or "visa" stickers (think pirates, salmon, Icelandic flags, the obelisk, eagles, orcas, beaches). There could be a series of commemorative stamps at the public parks and participating businesses; visitors are meant to explore the Point (read: go beyond Tyee Drive) to collect them all to fill up their souvenir passport, each stamp reinforcing the unique exclave experience. Where else do you get to do that? A mobile app version of the same idea could get visitors to take pictures at the

Point's landmarks to fill spaces in a virtual photo album – try to collect the whole set to earn badges and share socially, creating viral buzz about Point Bob. Visitors could also use a printer to create a postcard from a photo on their phone (or buy a ready-made Point Roberts postcard at the welcome kiosk) and have it mailed to friends (or themselves back home) with a Point Roberts commemorative postmark to prove they've been to this amazing town, mixing the digital and physical into a unique exclave experience available only here.

Those who take time to explore Point Roberts will love it (they always do) and come to realize Point Roberts shouldn't only be defined by the border, or its exclave status, or its beaches individually. Its breathtaking views and wildlife, multi-disciplinary history, colorful characters and strategic location together offer a unique Salish Sea experience in a convenient quirky package available nowhere else. Point Roberts has a fascinating history, but the potential for its future is equally alluring.

ROUTE SUMMARY

Here is a summary of the route followed in this book, with tour highlights, organized by chapters in the book.

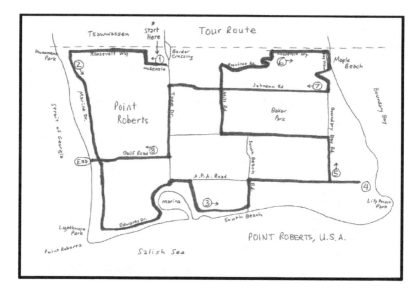

1. Enter Point Roberts at the border station, and once on Tyee Drive, turn onto Mackenzie Way. Turn left on Roosevelt Way. Stop at Monument Park and hike to the beach.
2. Travel south on Marine Drive past the golf course, Freeman Beach (the approximate location of the original Roberts Town) and Lighthouse Cannery. Stop at Lighthouse Marine Park and follow the shoreline trail to the *Sunsweep* monument and the light at Point Roberts. Look for orcas. From the park, continue east on Edwards Drive and encircle the marina. Turn right at A.P.A. Road and again on Simondson Road. Park at the marina and check out the boats along the harborside path, restaurant and public beach.
3. Simondson Road becomes Edwards Drive. At its eastern end, park as it curves to become South Beach Road. Explore

South Beach and the narrow lanes of cute summer cabins. Go north on South Beach road, jog quickly to the left on A.P.A. Road to see the town's church. Turn around and go east on A.P.A. Road to Pauls Road. Park at the top of Pauls Road, explore the trail through the forest and descend the grand staircase to the beach. Continue on A.P.A. Road to the top of the hill and check out the Icelandic monument in the cemetery.

4. Park at Lily Point Marine Park and follow the mail trail; descend the trail to the beach and check out the aboriginal and fishing history of Point Roberts.

5. Leave Lily Point by going west on A.P.A. Road. Turn right on Boundary Bay Road, and left on Benson Road. Park at Baker Community Field and hike across the field and check out the school, old water towers and public forest trails. Return to the car and continue west on Benson Road, past the fire station and clinic. A quick jog to the left on South Beach Road reveals the local jail. Return to Benson Road and turn left, then right on Mill Road. Turn right on Province Road and right on Roosevelt Way.

6. Turn right on Derby Street, then left on Maple Street. Check out the midden sites on this street. Turn left on Meadow Lane and note the Lower Port border crossing where *American Boyfriends* was filmed. Turn right on Roosevelt Way and go to its end at the beach. Park in the public parking spots at the base of Roosevelt Way or the "tree streets," and explore Maple Beach. Leave by going south on Bay View Drive, noting where the original stores and resort businesses were. Turn right on Elm Street and go up the hill on Goodman Road.

7. Turn right on Johnson Road. Turn left on Tyee Drive and note the gas stations selling gas by the liter. Pop into the supermarket to get a copy of the local newspaper and check today's tides. Turn right on Gulf Road.

8. Park at the Community Center and see the community garden, playground and rusting automated salmon processing machine. The library, outdoor market or visitor information booth may be open. Continue on Gulf Road to Whale Bay Village and patronize the local shops and restaurants. Continue down to the water's edge. Watch for orcas offshore over a beer in the Reef, reflecting on the decades of rock concerts performed on this street. Reflect on the old pier reaching out into the Salish Sea.

PLANNING A VISIT

GETTING TO POINT ROBERTS

Point Roberts is located off British Columbia Highway 17, just south of the Tsawwassen community of Delta. From the United States, cross the border into Canada at either of Blaine's border crossings, and continue north on B.C. Highway 99 to exit 26. From Vancouver, travel south on B.C. Highway 99 to exit 26. Once on Highway 17 go west toward Tsawwassen and the ferries. Turn left at the stoplight at 56th Street. From the Tsawwassen ferry terminal, turn right on 56th Street. Stay on 56th Street until you get to the Point Roberts border crossing.

WHEN TO VISIT

The best season to visit Point Roberts is in July and August. The weather is nice, with daytime highs averaging in the 60s Fahrenheit. These months offer the best chance of seeing orcas from Lighthouse Park and there are more businesses open. It's more likely a festival or community event will be taking place. There are also very low minus tides during the summer. If at all possible, time your visit when there is a minus tide. Select a day with the lowest tide possible. A minus tide allows you to get the most from the Point's beaches. If the tide is minus two or more, explore the Seabright Farms beach or the public tidelands north of Lily Point. A minus three foot tide should be spent walking out to the boundary marker at Maple Beach. If the tide is minus 3.5 feet or more, consider walking on the reef at Lily Point. The shoulder seasons before and after the summer peak season are also good times to visit. The Point is quiet in the winter, most seasonal businesses are closed, it gets dark early and the weather can be crummy, but the almost-spooky emptiness of the exclave is a unique experience too.

WHAT TO BRING

Because it is an exclave, unless you're arriving by boat or plane from the U.S. mainland, you will need to have proof of citizenship to enter and exit Point Roberts. For adults, that means a passport, a trusted traveler card (NEXUS or Global Entry to enter Point Roberts. Note: unlike the NEXUS program which is jointly operated by the U.S. and Canada, Global Entry is a U.S. program, not a Canadian one, so it can't be used to leave Point Roberts and enter Canada; have a second form of proof of citizenship to leave if you enter Point Roberts using a Global Entry card) or one of the enhanced drivers licenses where proof of citizenship is validated. Kids need one of those or a certified copy of a birth certificate. To bring in somebody else's kid(s) you'll need a notarized letter from their parents indicating they know their kids are with you and that you have their permission to cross the international border with their kids. Do not bring prohibited goods (in either country, such as firearms into Canada) over the border; websites like www.cbp.gov have current information.

Any time of year, plan to visit the Point's beaches, and bring an extra pair of footwear which can be worn in salt water. You'll need the footwear as you walk over rocky tidal zones until you get to the sandbars, where you can take them off and go barefoot. They're also handy to wade through eelgrass in the tide pools when you can't see where you're stepping. It's also fun to hike in the wooded trails crisscrossing the Point, so a pair of footwear for hiking on trails with occasional muddy sections is a good idea.

A pair of field glasses will help you view wildlife and the views from the beaches and cliffs ringing the peninsula. Don't forget a camera.

It can be windy on the beach, so dress in layers or a grab a windbreaker jacket.

Even if it's raining in Seattle and Vancouver, there's a good chance it's sunny in Point Roberts, so you'll need sunglasses and sunscreen. Evenings on the beach can be buggy, so grab insect repellant.

Verizon is the only U.S. mobile carrier in Point Roberts, so if you're on another American network, you will likely not have coverage or you will roam onto a Canadian network. The best place to try to get a U.S. signal is at Lily Point Park. Canadian mobile carriers generally have good coverage in Point Roberts. Wifi is available at the library and some of the restaurants.

The Point is great for biking, so consider bringing bicycles (a folding bike is ideal), or rent a bike on Gulf Road during your visit. Point Roberts is a great place for beach activities like skim boarding, surfing, stand-up paddle boarding and kayaking, so it's worth bringing that gear if you're here during a minus tide. Don't forget a beach towel.

ITINERARIES

Here are some suggested itineraries for checking out Point Roberts, depending on how much time you have to spend on the Point.

An Hour or Two

If you just have an hour or two, drive the route in this book, making three stops: at Monument Park, at Lighthouse Park, and at Lily Point to see the main viewpoint from the back of the parking lot. Have a meal or drink at one of the water-view restaurants or bars at the marina or on Gulf Road.

A Day

If you have most of a day, drive the route in this book. Check out the public stairs at Seabright Farms. Stop at Lily Point and walk the loop trail and the stairs and path down to the beach. If there's a minus tide, coincide your beach time during the hour on either side of low tide. Have lunch at a restaurant or self-cater a beach picnic from the supermarket. After lunch check out the shops on Gulf Road, hike the switchback trail to the beach at Monument Park to stand in the northwesternmost point in the United States. After dinner at one of the Point's eateries, don't miss Lighthouse Park, perhaps for a sunset stroll.

A Weekend

If you have a second day, hike the forest trails behind Baker Community Field or Lily Point's secondary trails, walk the seawall at Maple Beach and stroll quayside at the marina. Rent a bike and follow chapters 2, 3 and 8 in this book.

THINGS TO DO
See the "Having Fun" section in Chapter 6.

Shopping and Eating

Visit the Point's shops and restaurants. Most are along Tyee Drive and Gulf Road, and a couple are at South Beach and the marina.

Hiking

It's easy to commune with nature on the many hiking trails in the forests on Point Roberts. Use a GPS device to find hidden geocaches. Monument Park has a switchback trail down the bluff to the beach. Lily Point Park has gravel primary and dirt secondary trails in the forest. The forest behind Baker Field and west of the cell phone tower have extensive hiking trails. The public can use the path around Seabright Farms including its grand staircase to Crystal Water Beach. Less arduous is the accessible brick path around the marina basin. Capture and share photos of the Point's community art project, its colorfully-painted fire hydrants.

Biking

Bring your bikes or rent them on Gulf Road. Bike the loop of Marine Drive to Lighthouse Park, along Edwards Drive around the marina to South Beach. Return via APA Road, Tyee Drive and Gulf Road.

Wildlife Viewing and Birding

Bald eagles and great blue herons are easy to spot any time of year. Maple Beach and Lily Point have shoreline on Boundary Bay which is on the Pacific Flyway, home to thousands of birds. Always keep an eye (and ear) out for orcas and other marine mammals (tip: you may hear an orca before you see it), especially off Lighthouse Park. Have your field glasses and camera handy.

Beach Fun

As a peninsula, the Point is ringed with beaches; public beaches and water access points can be found on all 3 sides of the Point. The beaches on the western and southern shores have ample driftwood for forts. Check the tide charts to take advantage of low tides which expose miles of sandbars. Tide pools offer a glimpse into the marine life.

Sports

The golf course offers a chance to get out on the links. There's a skate park on Benson Road. Water sports of all kinds are possible at Point Roberts. Kayaks, canoes, stand-up paddleboards, skim boards, surfboards, rowboats, motorized water craft are all fun ways to get on the water. A boat launch is available at Lighthouse Park and the marina. Catch your own dinner; fishing, crabbing and clamming are possible in season.

Experience the Novelty of an Exclave

Stand on the northwestern most point in the lower 48 states. Visit Boundary Marker #1. Drive Roosevelt Way where the homes on either side of the street are in different countries. Trace the border to the mainland and see the border cutout on the mountains to the east. View Canada offshore to the south from the *north*. Locate the reef buoy offshore to identify where the fish traps – and fish pirates – once made Point Roberts famous. Send a postcard with a Point Roberts postmark to prove you've been here! Retrace the footsteps of George Vancouver's Expedition and the Coast Salish people and connect to the history of the Salish Sea in a physical way.

Kid Fun

There are playgrounds at the Community Center on Gulf Road, Maple Beach Park on Maple Street, and the school on Benson Road. Kids can run off all their energy at Baker Field on Benson Road, along with the Point's skate park. All four corners of the Point are parks. The southwestern corner of the Point is flat and great for biking. Stay overnight in the campground at Lighthouse Park and cook up some s'mores. Build a driftwood fort. Try an American candy bar. Go blackberry picking in August and September.

Accessible Touring

Portions of the trail at Monument Park, Lighthouse Park and Lily Point are flat gravel and accessible-friendly. The brick path around the marina basin is a lovely spot, with benches to stop and soak in the quayside charm. The Community Center has a senior's program including meals on Wednesdays and Fridays.

POINT ROBERTS TIMELINE

BCE	2450	Earliest Coast Salish settlement in Pt Roberts
BCE	2400	Roberts peninsula connects to mainland, no longer a San Juan island
~	1017	Coast Salish invent reef net fishing method at Point Roberts
January 26	1700	strongest earthquake to hit Pt Roberts, measuring 8.7-9.2
	1772	George Vancouver and Henry Roberts meet on Captain Cook's second voyage
	1776	Vancouver and Roberts work together again on Captain Cook's third voyage
February	1779	Vancouver and Roberts witness Cook's murder and fail in attempt to rescue Cook's remains from Hawaiians
	1783	In Treaty of Paris Benjamin Franklin establishes U.S.-Canadian border at northwesternmost point of U.S. at that time, leading to the 49th parallel as the western boundary
	1784	Henry Roberts' maps published in Cook's atlas
December 15	1790	Captain for *Discovery* switches from Henry Roberts to George Vancouver
June	1791	Francisco de Eliza Expedition first Europeans to see Point Roberts, naming it Cepeda Island
Spring	1792	Smallpox takes heavy toll on Lummis
June 12	1792	Capt Vancouver names Point Roberts and comes ashore at Lily Point
June 22	1792	Capt Vancouver stays overnight at Point Roberts on his way back to Birch Bay
October 15	1795	George Vancouver Expedition arrives back in England
February 9	1796	Henry Roberts leaves England to take Guiana from the Dutch
April 22	1796	Henry Roberts takes 3 colonies from the Dutch
August 25	1796	Henry Roberts dies at age 40 in the

		Caribbean of yellow fever
May 12	1798	George Vancouver dies at age 40 in Petersham, England
August 15	1803	Sir James Douglas, future blockader of Point Roberts, born in Demarara, liberated by Henry Roberts
	1818	Border drawn on 49th parallel between Lake of the Woods & the Rocky Mountains
	1819	Spain relinquishes claims to Point Roberts in treaty with U.S.
August	1825	British botanist finds hundreds of snakes at South Beach
August	1827	HBC reports Coast Salish "chief of Point Roberts" traded salmon at Fort Langley
December	1827	McMillan stays at Point Roberts escorting HBC Chief Trader Mackenzie who was later murdered by Coast Salish after leaving Point Roberts
June 15	1846	Treaty of Washington establishes border on 49th parallel, creating Point Roberts; mainland British Columbia named New Caledonia
	1851	Colony of Vancouver Island established
December 15	1852	Henry Roeder is first white settler in Whatcom County
September 10	1853	First reports of white men fishing at Point Roberts
	1855	Point Elliott Treaty signed at Mukilteo exchanging land for rights to fish at "usual & accustomed places"
June 27	1857	Boundary Commission engineers begin marking the border at Point Roberts
November	1857	News of the discovery of gold, leading to the Fraser Gold Rush, initiated based on arrest at Point Roberts
November	1857	First post-contact settlement on Point Roberts, Roberts Town, runs for 2 years
December	1857	Stalemate in negotiations to draw boundary through San Juan Islands
May	1858	Gov. Douglas requires gold miners to register at Victoria; Roberts Town thrives as smuggling alternative

May 21 - Jun 26	1858	*Otter* and *Satellite* blockade Point Roberts to prevent miners from evading registration at Victoria
August 1	1858	Gov. Douglas overnights in Roberts Town on his way to be sworn in as Governor or newly-created colony of British Columbia
August 13	1858	Campbell & Hawkins meet each other at Camp Semiahmoo to organize boundary survey work
August 30	1858	Gov. Douglas overnights in Roberts Town on his way to Fort Langley
November 18	1858	Several British dignitaries overnight in Roberts Town
June	1859	Engineers actively surveying Point Roberts
June 15	1859	Pig shot on San Juan Island, leading to the Pig War; many boundary surveyors go to war
July 18	1859	Fire destroys several Roberts Town buildings
September 13	1859	Point Roberts becomes a military reservation
	1865	Obelisk placed in Monument Park
October 21	1872	Kaiser Wilhelm I resolves Pig War
	1873	John Harris becomes first permanent white settler on Point Roberts
July	1873	Coast Salish harass John Harris over his fishing at Point Roberts reef
	1875	John Elwood moves to Point Roberts
	1877	John Waller moves to Point Roberts
	1878	John Waller tears down Coast Salish camp at Lily Point and installs the first fish trap in Salish Sea
	1878	Joseph Goodfellow moves to Point Roberts & opens a saltery & fish traps
	1879	Delta becomes a municipality
	1880	Mount Baker's last eruption
	1883	John Harris murdered
	1883	Fish piracy first reported at Point Roberts
July 5	1884	Point Roberts military reservation status ends, but federal government retains ownership of the land
September	1885	John Waller drowns
	1886	First school formed
	1889	Crab meat cannery operates at South Beach,

		first cannery at Point Roberts
	1890	U.S. Government vacates Point Roberts
	1890	E A Wadhams moves to Lily Point & sets up fish traps
	1891	P J Whalen squats at Maple Beach
	1892	Fish traps extend beyond Point Roberts reef
December 17	1892	E A Wadhams opens cannery at Lily Point (fourth salmon cannery in the U.S. Salish Sea)
February	1893	25 canneries merge to become Alaska Packers Association
March 7	1893	First Icelander settles in Point Roberts
	1893	Washington requires licenses to operate fish traps
summer	1893	Goodfellow sues Wadhams over trap placement
early	1894	Wadhams sells cannery at Lily Point to APA
June 15	1894	Large group of Icelanders arrive from Victoria to squat at Point Roberts
	1894	First post office, under name Brewster, WA
	1895	Two thirds of all Washington fish traps are at Point Roberts; less than 4% of sockeye salmon making it thru fish taps to Coast Salish reef nets
	1895	Coast Salish Lummis sue APA for interfering on their treaty-protected fishing rights
	1890s	Brewster parcels out his land for a downtown at foot of Gulf Road
	1896	Waters Mercantile opens
	1897	Post office renamed Point Roberts, WA
	1898	Equality Colony socialist commune fishes at Point Roberts
May 22	1899	Coast Salish Lummis' case against APA reaches U.S. Supreme Court but is dismissed
	1899	George & Barker cannery first opened by Leonard Pike
	1899	Whalens offer tent camping in Maple Beach
	1900	Ferry service from Seattle to Point Roberts with continuing service to Alaska; runs until 1904

May	1900	Hotel at base of Gulf Road burns down
	1900	White schoolhouse opens on Gulf Road
	1901	Harlan Smith publishes paper about his excavation of Maple Beach middens
	1901	Immigration raids at APA cannery
	1902	A reported 500 fish pirates targeting fish traps at Point Roberts
	1902	Grange Hall built
	1903	"Iron Chink" automates cannery process, eliminating jobs
	1903	Point Roberts fish traps blamed for collapsing sockeye runs by BC Fisheries
	1903	Smuggling of Japanese workers through Point Roberts at its peak
	1904	Population reaches 100
	1904	Half the squatter population is now Icelandic
	1905	Ah Fat opens restaurant
May	1908	President Roosevelt grants squatters rights to stay on and own their land
	1908	Fish pirates conduct brazen armed robbery of fish traps
August	1908	Worst wildfire in known history, much of south & east Point Roberts burns
	1909	Forty armed fish pirates attack Point Roberts fish traps
	1910	Few Chinese workers remain in Point Roberts canneries
	1910	Ferry service between Ladner & Richmond begins
	1911	Point Roberts Township organized
	1911	Building at 1379 Gulf Road built, restaurant in recent times
	1912	Whalens sell lots for cabins in Maple Beach, including beach rights
	1913	Building at 1385 Gulf Road built, originally sheriff's office
	1914	Sea entrance to Tule filled in & drained to create polders
	1914	First roads within Point Roberts built
	1915	Lutheran congregation formed
November	1915	Cemetery opens

	1915	Ah Fat, long time accepted & respected Chinese man, dies
	1915	Fish piracy made illegal
	1916	Prohibition begins in Washington
	1916	Land for a church is donated
	1916	Waters opens Maple Beach store at 63 Bay View
	1917	APA cannery at Lily Point closes
	1917	Slavonians dominate salmon purse seining industry at Point Roberts
	1919	First road built to Point Roberts
	1919	First border station
	1919	Glenfield hunting lodge opens in Maple Beach
	1920	Largaud mill opens
	1920	Whalen's first store at 43 Bay View
	1921	Trinity Lutheran Church built
	1921	Prohibition ends in Canada
	1922	Jitney service between Ladner ferry and Maple Beach begins
	1926	Biplane lands on Maple Beach & gives rides to local children
	1928	Whalen opens mini-golf course in Maple Beach
	1928	Ben's Store opens
	1929	Grange Society takes over grange building
	1929	S. S. *Riverton* runs into Point Roberts pier
	1930	George & Barker cannery closes
	1931	Electricity service begins
	1931	Freeman Beach cottage community built
	1931	First Maple Beach gas station at Whalen's
	1932	Maples Store opens at 81 Bay View
December 23	1932	Major storm floods southwestern corner of Point Roberts
	1933	White House built at South Beach
	1933	Several of first bars in Washington to open after Prohibition open in Point Roberts
	1934	First wooden border station building
	1934	Dike Road (Edwards Drive) constructed as dike and southern shore road

	1934	Point Roberts egg producers join poultry cooperative
	1930s	Point Roberts farmers form the Point Roberts Potato Growers Association
	1934	Lighthouse Cannery opens
	1934	Washington Initiative 77 bans fish traps
	1934	Point Roberts USA billboard placed on King George Highway
	1935	Maple Leaf tavern opens
	1935	*Tulip*'s last year in operation
	1930s	Bay View Hotel at base of Gulf Road burns down
	1936	Lower port border crossing opens
	1936	Waters' Maple Beach store burns down
	1937	New school built by WPA opens on Gulf Road
	1937	fire destroys buildings at end of Gulf Road pier
	1938	Outdoor roller skating rink opens in Maple Beach
	1939	Point Roberts Auto Freight develops process to seal trucks for transit to U.S. mainland
	1940	Iwersens buy Lighthouse cannery; can salmon & later refit as a clam cannery
	1940s	Eighteen local young men serve in World War II
	1940s	Boundary Bay Air Force Base activity a constant presence
	1942	Residents protest 8pm border closing time
July 27	1943	Airplane crash just off the beach at Lighthouse Park
	1944	Stafholt Icelandic retirement home opens in Blaine
December 15	1944	3 die in air force bombing practice accident at Point Roberts
January 9	1945	3 die in air force bombing practice accident at Point Roberts
January 10	1945	4 parachute to safety in air force bombing practice accident at Point Roberts
	1945	First paved roads
June 26	1945	Final WWII plane crash at Point Roberts

	1948	Metcalfe's opens on Canadian side with door to Maple Beach
	1948	Fellowship Camp opens
	1949	Border stations open until midnight
summer	1949	Charles Borden excavates middens at Maple Beach
	1949	The Freeze opens at 43 Bay View
August	1950	BC business magnate killed in plane crash at Point Roberts
July	1951	Horse race track opens in Maple Beach
	1951	Chamber of commerce forms
July 7	1952	Whatcom County calls Point Roberts its "orphan problem child"
	1952	Santa Ship visits Point Roberts
	1953	Last cattle herd leaves, ending an agricultural era of Point Roberts
	1953	Change in state law allows Canadians to own property in Washington
	1953	Fire district formed
	1955	Residential phone service begins
	1950s	The Reef opens
	1950s	Original homesteads broken up into small cottage lots
August	1956	First fire truck
December	1956	Water district formed
	1957	Margaret Laurence moves to Point Roberts for 5 years, writing the *Stone Angel* here
	1957	Maples Store becomes Clark's
January	1958	Gulf Road fire hall opens
	1958	Roof House restaurant opens
	1958	Whalen roller skating rink at Maple Beach closes
November	1958	Point Roberts Harbor Committee organizes
	1959	Canadian homeowner donates 10 feet of land to Monument Park so all of obelisk is in park
	1959	Tsawwassen ferry terminal opens
	1959	Massey Tunnel, originally Deas Is. Tunnel, opens, making Point Roberts more accessible
	1959	Gulf Road pier closes for good
	1959	Border stations open 16 hours a day

	1961	Border stations open 24 hours a day
	1961	Governor Rosellini is first Governor to visit Point Roberts
	1961	Lighthouse Cannery closes
	1962	Highway 99 opens as new main highway from Peace Arch to Vancouver bringing traffic closer to Point Roberts
October	1962	Typhoon Freda causes major damage at Point Roberts & across Pacific Northwest
	1963	School closes due to low enrolment; all kids must go to school in Blaine
	1963	Nielson's Hardware store opens
	1963	Point Roberts assigned ZIP code 98281
January	1964	Monument Park opens
	1964	Jail opens
January	1964	USCGC *Point Roberts* christened by U.S. Coast Guard
	1964	Proposals floated to make Point Roberts a duty free zone port
	1968	New US border station opens
	1969	Washington state rules road ends which abut a beach are public access points to water
	1969	County dissolves Point Roberts Township; township property transferred to parks district
	1969	Proposal to move the Washington Trade Fair from Seattle Center to Point Roberts
December	1969	Canadian officials view in-transit goods as importation, cracking down on Point Roberts
	1970	Canada bans capture of orcas
June 22	1970	Battle of Point Roberts, grader tears up road after he wasn't paid, low speed chase to border with shots fired
August 8	1970	Seven orcas who frequented Point Roberts captured in Penn Cove and sold to corporate parks like SeaWorld
	1970	Roberts Bank Superport opens, dominating the northwest view from Point Roberts
	1971	Delta Cable begins cable TV service
April 21	1971	US & Canada federal gov't put Point Roberts question to IJC

	1971	X-rated theatre opens on Gulf Road
	1971	Great blue herons move from Tsawwassen to Point Roberts and establish large rookery
December	1971	Public hearings in Point Roberts for the IJC
	1972	Ranulph Fiennes ends his Headless Valley expedition getting lost at Point Roberts
	1972	Trinity Lutheran Church reformed as Trinity Community Church
	1972	Point Roberts Air Park opens
	1972	The Cannery nightclub opens in old Lighthouse Cannery on Marine Drive
	1972	Brian Seymour, Simon Fraser Univ., excavates middens in Maple Beach
	1972	Bachman Turner Overdrive live in Point Roberts
	1972	Border crossings top 500,000 for first time
April 9	1973	Point Roberts Voters' Association forms
June 16	1973	Lighthouse Marine Park opens
August 9	1973	John Meier held in Point Roberts jail
	1973	Severe drought requires water to be trucked in from Blaine
October 23	1973	IJC International Park proposal could have forced locals off Point Roberts
	1973	Heart writes "Crazy On You" in Point Roberts
February	1974	Boldt Decision restores treaty-protected fishing rights, awarding 50% of catch to Coast Salish
	1974	Medium rare hamburgers banned in Canada
October	1974	International Park proposal officially dead
	1975	Public park and beach created at marina in exchange for cutting through Edwards Drive
Spring	1976	Lower Port border crossing closes
	1976	*Ocean Star* newspaper begins publishing
	1976	Last orca captured in Washington; SeaWorld banned from capturing orcas in Washington
	1976	Voter initiative to build sewer system fails
November	1976	Clinic wing of fire hall added

December 28	1976	Entire water board recalled in vote, first successful recall election in Whatcom County history
	1977	Driving range opens on Benson Road & Tyee Drive
	1977	Point Roberts Marina opens
August	1977	Steeple added to church
	1977	Point Roberts Historical Society has first meeting
summer	1977	Efforts to close X-rated theatre fail
August	1977	IJC final report to federal government admits failure to help
December 28	1977	Tsawwassen adds second lane on 56th St. leading to Point Roberts border station
	1978	Icelandic share of Point Roberts population drops to 14%
February	1978	Lily Point fenced to keep public out
October 9	1978	Float plane crashes on take-off at South Beach
December 29	1978	Hang glider crashes into Lily Point cliffs
	1979	US border station expands, adding 3rd lane for vehicles
May	1979	*Huck Finn & Friends* TV series filmed at Point Roberts
	1979	Point Roberts Plan approved
	1979	Benson Road fire hall opens
	1979	Adult book store opens across the street from the X-rated theatre on Gulf Road
summer	1979	Portion of Lily Point is logged as first phase of development for Seacliffe Development
	1980	South Beach Store becomes a restaurant
	1980	Popular *Vancouver Sun* columnist Penny Wise retires & moves to Point Roberts & writes Penny Wise column for local paper
	1980	Screenplay for Canadian film *Out of the Blue* written in Point Roberts
April	1980	Well levels at record low, water usage restrictions begin
	1980	Richard Clark book published and his interviews with long-time residents air on Delta Cable local access channel
December	1980	Proposal to rename APA Road to Fernwood

		Road
March	1981	Water district travels to Hong Kong studying desalinization plant options
May	1981	Whalen installs chain link fence along Maple Beach to keep it for private use only
	1981	First formal proposal to Delta to buy water
	1981	Point Roberts Theatre is most-profitable X-rated theatre in United States
	1981	Five acres in Lily Point lowlands burn
	1981	Ballot measure to incorporate fails
	1982	Point Roberts Airpark hosts first fly-in
September 1	1982	First supermarket at Point Roberts opens
September 1	1982	First bank at Point Roberts opens
October 3	1982	*Seattle Post-Intelligencer* article labels Point Roberts "Tijuana of the North"
December 16	1982	Extensive storm damage and flooding; Maple Beach sea wall washed away for 18 months
	1983	Border crossings into Point Roberts surpass 1 million in 1 year
March	1983	New well fails
	1983	Public officials plead with homeowners to post house numbers; 911 calls can't be found
May	1983	Top speed limit on Point Roberts lowered to 30 miles per hour
June	1983	Oldest currently-operated gas station opens
August 16	1983	SeaWorld asks a federal hearing to overrule state law & allow it to capture all remaining Salish Sea orcas for their profit
November 21	1983	Breakers burns down
	1984	Current post office opens
	1984	Orca 'museum' opens in Lighthouse Marine Park, operates until 2014
July	1984	Undersea water pipeline from Blaine formally proposed
	1984	New porn megastore proposed for Point Roberts is not approved
summer	1984	Concrete seawall at Maple Beach constructed
December	1984	Seacliffe's expired approval is re-approved to develop Lily Point
May	1985	Local newspaper, *All Point Bulletin*, begins publication

June	1985	Shell station opens
June	1985	Can-Am station opens
September 3	1985	Breakers reopens
	1985	Airpark closes
	1985	60 gas pumps added in 2 years
	1985	It's discovered BC Tel was not a legal phone provider for Point Roberts
November 2	1985	*Sunsweep* art monument placed in Lighthouse Marine Park as part of an international exclave art project
February 24	1986	Owners of Point Roberts X-rated Theatre lose case at U.S. Supreme Court, allowing cities to regulate porn zoning
	1986	George Reifel revitalizes Point Roberts chamber of commerce
May	1986	British Columbia legalizes alcohol sales on Sundays, ending Point Roberts' monopoly
June 30	1986	Washington Utility Commission rules Point Roberts is unassigned phone territory
April	1987	Current Canadian Boundary Bay border station opens
May	1987	Gulf Road widened
August	1987	Simundson Road connects with Edwards Drive
September 24	1987	Filming begins in Point Roberts of *Beyond the Stars*
autumn	1987	Marjorie Mann, University of Victoria, conducts language survey which identifies a Point Roberts accent
March	1988	Whidbey Telecom office opens on Johnson Road
April 19	1988	Agreement signed with Greater Vancouver to buy water
May	1988	Solomon well, which had provided 35% of Point Roberts' water, goes dry
May 7	1988	Dead grey whale washes up on shore at Point Roberts
June 4	1988	Phone service switches to Whidbey Telecom, free local calls to Vancouver end, switch from area code 604 to 206
August	1988	Reservoir on Roosevelt Way built
October 22	1988	Iceland's president, Vigdis Finnbogadottir

		visits Point Roberts
November	1988	Heron rookery benefit concerts
December 1	1988	*American Boyfriends* filmed in Point Roberts
	1989	Flashing red light at Tyee & Gulf installed
February	1989	Chevron station opens
February	1989	Moratorium on gas stations passed
February	1989	Mailbox rentals (other than Ben's) opens
February	1989	Grange Hall sold to private owners
	1989	X-rated cinema on Gulf Road closes
	1989	Roosevelt Way water reservoir constructed
July 4	1989	Airplane being filmed in a Disney movie lands at Point Roberts Air Park after refused entry to Canada
	1989	Border crossings top 2 million
	1989	Salish Sea term coined
January	1990	Point Roberts Subarea Comprehensive Plan adopts goals
January	1990	Landslide at Lily Point
	1990	Development banned near heron rookery
February	1991	Private Resort at Lily Point proposed with 200 condos, 200 hotel rooms, golf course, <20% trees to be kept
February	1991	CNN added to Delta Cable service
May	1991	Benson Road dump closes
July	1991	Johnson Road extension between Mill Road and Tyee Drive opens
August	1991	Arrival of the World Wide Web enables living at the Point without having a job here
September 16	1991	Mandatory garbage collection service begins
October	1991	Marketplace supermarket expansion
October 10	1991	Car crashes into Ben's Store for 2nd time
	1991	British Columbia GST introduction spikes traffic to Point Roberts
	1991	First parcel receiving businesses
December	1991	Local gas tax approved
	1992	Border crossings into Point Roberts peak at 2.65 million in 1 year
	1992	Restaurant at marina opens
March	1992	Ben's Store closes
December	1992	Construction begins on golf course

January	1993	Point Roberts Character Plan Group given mandate
April	1993	Residents-only border lane proposal rejected
	1993	Cascade Marine Trail opens, with Point Roberts as its northernmost point
September	1993	Current school built on Benson Road
February	1994	Tyee Drive widened between border & Gulf Road
September 13	1994	Coast Salish stage major protest at Point Roberts over early closure of salmon season
	1994	Character Plan approved by Whatcom County
November	1994	PACE "Trusted traveler program" lane opens
January	1995	Area code changes to 360
February	1995	Bill moves through Congress to create $3 fee to cross border
February	1995	Proposed ferry service to Bellingham advances
April	1995	Fistfight at water board meeting
May	1995	Garbage service in Point Roberts privatized
December	1996	Fifteen homes washed away in major storm
June 26	1997	Resort at Lily Point not approved
July 21	1998	Current Point Roberts border station opens
December	1998	National Public Radio airs segment on Point Roberts including local interviews
	1999	Point Roberts Garden Tour begins
	1999	Point Roberts Airpark reopens after several year closure
March	1999	Major sloughing in Lily Point landslide
spring	1999	Whalen farm windmill installed
	1999	Board game Dao invented in Point Roberts
January	2000	Whalens donate Maple Beach as public park
	2000	Point Roberts Lighthouse Society formed
	2001	Golf course & country club opens
May 21	2001	Breakers closes
September 11	2001	Border closes for several hours; nobody can enter by land
November 26	2001	CNN profiles Point Roberts due to continuing post-9/11 long border lineups
	2002	NEXUS program opens, replacing PACE

May	2002	New border markers installed along Roosevelt Way
May 15	2002	Governor Gary Locke visits Point Roberts
	2003	Clinic opens
June	2004	Great blue herons abandon rookery & move to Tsawwassen
August	2004	Point Roberts featured in *National Geographic*'s ZIP code series
September	2004	NEXUS lane opens at Point Roberts
	2004	*Golf Digest* rates Point Roberts Country Club #8 in Best New Affordable Golf Courses
February	2005	Point Roberts Hospital District approved
	2005	Skate park opens
May	2006	Clark's store in Maple Beach torn down
	2006	Lighthouse Park entrance fee eliminated
August	2006	Three acres of Lily Point lowlands burn
June	2008	Whatcom Land Trust buys Lily Point to establish a park
	2008	Whalen RV park closes
June	2009	Monument Park switchback trail to beach opens
August 19	2009	Ryan Jenkins comes through Point Roberts
August	2009	Garbage service interrupted for 6 months between change in providers
September	2009	Tsunami warning system installed
September	2009	Barefoot Bandit burgles several homes in Point Roberts during 18 months on the lam
October	2009	The term "Salish Sea" formally adopted in Washington
	2009	Local airline begins 4x/week regularly-scheduled commercial air service between Point Roberts & Bellingham
February 10	2010	Both U.S. & Canada officially recognize term Salish Sea
	2010	Point Roberts Community Advisory Committee organized
May	2012	KRPI applies to build 5 150-ft radio towers
December	2012	Japanese ship crashes into Superport causeway, spilling 30 tons of coal into waters just north of Point Roberts
April 30	2013	Cell phone coverage by a U.S. carrier begins

	2013	Roberts peninsula herons subject of ground-breaking study of their symbiotic relationship with bald eagles
July	2013	Border Policy Research Institute surveys 1,871 people in Point Roberts border study
	2013	Fire chief invites community to paint fire hydrants
	2014	Scenic loop created
March	2014	Rhino horn smuggling operation busted
January	2015	Seabright Staircase opens
March	2015	KRPI radio towers blocked
Autumn	2016	Metcalfe's torn down
May	2017	Becomes sister city with Campobello Island
August	2017	Golf and country club changes hands & renamed Bald Eagle Golf Club

TABLE OF FIGURES

ENDNOTES

CHAPTER 1 ENDNOTES

[1] Sandor Gyarmati, "Point Roberts dulled by sagging Loonie: Merchants in American peninsula feeling the pinch as trips across the line are on the decline," *Delta Optimist*, February 17, 2016.

[2] Steven Beningo, "Trends in Border Crossing Volumes 1994-2005," Bureau of Transportation Statistics, Research and Innovative Technology Administration, U.S. Department of Transportation, October 23, 2006 PowerPoint presentation to the Transportation Border Working Group.

[3] *All Point Bulletin*, April 1992.

[4] *Ocean Star*, December 1979.

[5] *Ocean Star*, July 1982.

[6] *All Point Bulletin,* February 1993.

[7] *All Point Bulletin*, March 1995.

[8] *All Point Bulletin*, March 1996.

[9] Gwen Szychter, *Chewassen, Tsawwassen or Chiltinm: The Land Facing the Sea* (Delta, 2007), 13.

[10] *All Point Bulletin*, April 1987.

[11] *All Point Bulletin*, April 1993.

[12] *All Point Bulletin*, July 1991.

[13] *All Point Bulletin*, November 1994.

[14] Whatcom County of Governments. *International Mobility and Trade Corridor Program.* http://theimtc.com/pace/ (accessed November 29, 2016).

[15] *All Point Bulletin*, December 2001.

[16] Jay Mayfield, "Pacific partners," *Frontline,* Winter 2011: 18.

[17] Christopher Dingman and Daniel Edge, "Monetizing some benefits of participation in NEXUS," Border Policy Brief, Border Policy Research Institute, Summer 2015, Volume 10, Number 3, page 2. http://ww.wwu.edu/bpri/files/2015_SummerBorderBrief.pdf

[18] Meg Olson, *All Point Bulletin*, December 2013.

[19] Alton Lee, *The Bizarre Careers of John R. Brinkley* (Lexington, KY: University Press of Kentucky, 2002), 11-12.

[20] Ibid, 20-22.

[21] Pope Brock, *Charlatan: America's Most Dangerous Huckster, the Man Who Pursued Him, and the Age of Flimflam* (New York: Crown Publishing, 2008), 24.

[22] Gene Fowler and Bill Crawford, *Border Radio: Quacks, yodelers, pitchmen, psychics, and other amazing broadcasters of the American airwaves* (Austin: Texas Monthly Press, 1987).

[23] Lee, *Bizarre Careers*, 219.

[24] Brock, *Charlatan*, 41.

[25] John Belton, "Awkward Transitions: Hitchcock's Blackmail and the Dynamics of Early Film Sound," *The Musical Quarterly* 83, no. 2 (Summer 1999): 227-246.

[26] Brock, *Charlatan*, 43-44.

[27] Ibid, 41.

[28] Ibid, 47-48.

[29] Ibid, 56-59.

[30] KFKB is today the call letters of a station in Forks, WA, the west-northwesternmost town in United States, the opposite of Point Roberts, which is the north-northwesternmost U.S. town.

[31] Fowler, *Border Radio*.

[32] Brock, *Charlatan*, 122-124.

[33] Ibid, 89-90.

[34] Fowler, *Border Radio*.

[35] Brock, *Charlatan*, 155.

[36] Lee, *Bizarre Carrers*, 127-129.

[37] Steven Simmons, ed., *Fairness Doctrine and the Media* (Berkeley, CA: University of California Press, 1978), 33–35.

[38] Fowler, *Border Radio*.

[39] Brock, *Charlatan*, 168.

[40] Ibid, 175-176.

[41] Lee, *Bizarre Careers*, 173.

[42] Ibid, 147.

[43] Brock, Charlatan, 208-209.

[44] Ibid, 177-178.

[45] Ibid, 199-200.

[46] Ibid, 264.

[47] *All Point Bulletin*, June 2002.

[48] *All Point Bulletin*, October 1986.

[49] *Westside Record-Journal*, October 4, 1989.

[50] *Ocean Star*, September 1984, 4.

[51] Eric de Place, "Are Coal Export Terminals Good Neighbors? A Closer Look at Coal Dust," Sightline, March 15, 2011, http://www.sightline.org/2011/03/15/are-coal-export-terminals-good-neighbors (accessed July 29, 2016).

[52] Erik Olson, "Westshore provides glimpse of Longview's potential future with coal," (Longview) *Daily News*, February 12, 2011

[53] Delta is the name of the municipality which today contains both Tsawwassen and Ladner.

[54] Olson, "Westshore."

[55] I.M. Jones, R.W. Butler, R.C. Ydenberg, "Recent switch by the Great Blue Heron *Ardea herodias fannini* in the Pacific northwest to associative nesting with Bald Eagles (*Haliaeetus leucocephalus*) to gain predator protection," Centre for Wildlife Ecology, Department of Biological Sciences, Simon Fraser University, Burnaby, BC, *Canadian Journal of Zoology*, NCR Research Press, July 2013.

[56] *All Point Bulletin*, April 1988.

[57] *All Point Bulletin*, July 1993.

[58] Alec McEwen, "A Guardian of the Boundary," *British Columbia Historical News*, Vol. 19, No. 2, 1986, 5.

[59] Ibid.

[60] John Davis, "The Unguarded Boundary," *The Geographical Review*, vol. 12, no. 4, October 1922, 600.

[61] Szychter, *Chewassen*, 62-3.

[62] Murray, Anne, *Tracing Our Past: A Heritage Guide to Boundary Bay* (Delta, BC: Nature Guides BC, 2009), 54.

[63] Fort Langley Journals, British Columbia Archives, Royal B.C. Museum, Victoria, B.C., 1827-30.

[64] Knick and Lyn Pyles, "Looking Back at Point Roberts' Maritime History," 18.

[65] Though Oregon does appear in the official British title of the same treaty: "Treaty between Her Majesty and the United States of America, for the Settlement of the Oregon Boundary."

[66] Samuel Anderson, British Surveyor, papers, Peace Arch State Park, 74.

[67] Ibid.

[68] W. W. Hastings papers, Report of Inspector Joseph Mansfield at Camp Semiahmoo, December 1858. surreyhistory.ca/campsemi.html, 2014.

[69] McEwen, 6.

[70] *All Point Bulletin*, April 1996.

[71] McEwen, 7.

[72] *Ocean Star*, February 1979.

[73] Szychter, 160.

[74] *All Point Bulletin*, July 2001.

[75] Harry Thompson, "Point Pioneers in Review: Jeppe Thompson," *Point Roberts Guide*, August 1972, 13.

[76] Szychter, 160.

[77] Christopher Rocchio, "Ryan Jenkins' Dad Reiterates Son's Innocence, Questions Investigation," RealityTVWorld.com, September 1, 2009.

[78] Michael Platt, "Jenkins' Dad Says Son Died Terrified and Alone," *Vancouver Sun*, August 24, 2009.

[79] The spelling Zepeda is also used.

[80] Richard Blumenthal, *The Early Exploration of Inland Washington Waters: Journals and Logs from Six Expeditions, 1786–1792* (Jefferson NC: McFarland, 2004), 67.

[81] *The Edinburgh Review*, Volume 78, 185.

[82] John Naish, *The Interwoven Lives of George Vancouver, Archibald Menzies, Joseph Whidbey, and Peter Puget: Exploring the Pacific Northwest Coast* (Lewiston, New York: Edwin Mellen Printers, 1996), 31.

[83] Ibid, 29.

[84] Samantha Cavell, *Playing at Command: Midshipmen and Quarterdeck Boys In the Royal Navy, 1793-1815* (Brisbane Australia: Bachelor of Business Thesis, Queensland University of Technology, May 2006) 23-4.

[85] Jonathan Raban, *Passage to Juneau: A Sea and its Meaning* (New York: Vintage Departures, 1999), 134.

[86] Ibid, 196.

[87] Naish, *Interwoven Lives*, 33.

[88] Ibid, 7.

[89] Ibid, 37.

[90] Ibid.

[91] Ibid, 43.

[92] Ibid, 79.

[93] Ibid, 15.

[94] Ibid, 39.

[95] Ibid, 16.

[96] William Blake, *The American Encyclopedia of History, Biography and Travel, Comprising Ancient and Modern History: The Biography of the*

Eminent Men of Europe and America, and the Lives of Distinguished Travelers (New York: J. H. Miller, 1856), 892.
[97] Naish, 39.
[98] Raban, *Passage*, 138.
[99] Ibid, 50-1.
[100] Naish, 80.
[101] Raban, *Passage*, 134.
[102] Cummins Speakman and Rhoda Hackler, "Vancouver in Hawaii," *Hawaiian Journal of History* (Honolulu: Hawaiian Historical Society, 1989) 23.
[103] Naish, *Interwoven Lives*, 136.
[104] Ibid, 152.
[105] Ibid, 155.
[106] Ibid, 157.
[107] Ibid, 163.
[108] George Vancouver, *A Voyage of Discovery to the North Pacific Ocean: And Round Theworld; in which the Coast of North-west America Has Been Carefully Examined and Accurately Surveyed, Volume 1*, 1798, 298.
[109] Naish, *Interwoven Lives*, 164.
[110] John Kendrick, *The Men with Wood Feet: The Spanish Exploration of the Pacific Northwest* (Toronto: NC Press, 1985), 112.
[111] Raban, *Passage*, 195.
[112] Naish, *Interwoven Lives*, 3.
[113] Raban, *Passage*, 195.
[114] Naish, *Interwoven Lives*, 165.
[115] Stephen Hume, "The Birth of Modern British Columbia Part 7," *Vancouver Sun*, November 17, 2007, D9.
[116] Naish, *Interwoven Lives*, 7.
[117] *All Point Bulletin*, June 1992.
[118] Point Roberts Golf & Country Club, pointrobertsgolfcourse.com
[119] *Ocean Star*, August 1977.
[120] *All Point Bulletin*, February 1993.
[121] *All Point Bulletin*, March 1993.
[122] *All Point Bulletin*, December 2002.
[123] *All Point Bulletin*, January 2004, 13.
[124] *Ocean Star*, February 1979.
[125] Personal interview with author, 2016.
[126] *All Point Bulletin*, November 1991.

127 *All Point Bulletin*, November 1987.

CHAPTER 2 ENDNOTES

128 *Point Roberts Guide*, June 1972, 2.

129 Western Washington University, Salish Sea Center, website, http://www.wwu.edu/salishsea/history.shtml (accessed Nov 30 2016).

130 Ibid.

131 *Ocean Star*, July 1980.

132 Ruth Kirk and Carmela Alexander, *Exploring Washington's Past: A Road Guide to History* (Seattle: University of Washington Press, 1990), 230.

133 *Ocean Star*, May 1977.

134 Daniel Boxberger, *To Fish In Common: The Ethnohistory of Lummi Indian Salmon Fishing* (Seattle: University of Washington Press, 2000), 27.

135 *Victoria Colonist*, July 22, 1859.

136 Queensborough Revenue Station, website, https://queenboroughrevenuestation.wordpress.com/ (accessed February 4, 2017)

137 Ibid.

138 Ibid.

139 Ibid.

140 *Point Roberts Guide*, "Point Pioneers in Review: Portrait of the Freemans," April 1972, 3.

141 *Ocean Star*, August 1978.

142 *Point Roberts Guide*, August 1972, 21.

143 *Ocean Star*, July 1982.

144 *All Point Bulletin*, September 1989.

145 *All Point Bulletin*, October 1996.

146 *Ocean Star*, Summer 1978.

147 *Ocean Star*, October 1978.

148 *All Point Bulletin*, June 1994.

149 *All Point Bulletin*, June 1988.

150 Personal interview, March 2017.

151 *All Point Bulletin*, September 1989.

152 *Ocean Star*, July 1977.

153 Amelia Hill, "Fiennes: No more polar expeditions," *The Guardian*, October 29, 2000.

[154] Ranulph Fiennes, *The Headless Valley* (London: Hodder and Stoughton, 1973), 206.

[155] Ibid.

[156] Hill, *Fiennes.*

[157] *Point Roberts Guide*, "Chairman of the Board – and Rock Hound," June 1972, 15.

[158] *Point Roberts Guide*, May 1972, 7.

[159] *Point Roberts Guide*, "Fee Schedules for Lighthouse Park," June 1972, 22.

[160] *All Point Bulletin*, October 1995.

[161] *All Point Bulletin*, June 2006.

[162] *Ocean Star*, March 1981.

[163] *All Point Bulletin*, April 1993.

[164] *Point Roberts Guide*, "Lighthouse Marine Park and Its Manager," May 1972, 9.

[165] Hickman, Matt, "11 American geographic anomalies", MNN.com, May 27, 2016, http://www.mnn.com/lifestyle/eco-tourism/stories/11-american-geographic-anomalies (accessed August, 7, 2016)

[166] *All Point Bulletin*, November 1985.

[167] *All Point Bulletin*, August 1985.

[168] *Ocean Star*, January 1977.

[169] Ibid.

[170] Ibid.

[171] *Ocean Star*, October 1976.

[172] USCGC Point Roberts Historian's Office, website, http://www.uscg.mil/history/webcutters/Point_Roberts.pdf (accessed November 4, 2016).

[173] National Recreation Trails Database, website, http://www.americantrails.org/NRTDatabase/trailDetail.php?recordID=655 (accessed 2-08-16).

[174] Sandra Pollard, *Puget Sound Whales For Sale: The Fight to End Orca Hunting* (Charleston, SC: History Press, 2014), 24.

[175] *Blackfish*, Gabriela Cowperthwaite, Magnolia Pictures, 2013.

[176] Erik Lacitis, "Remembering Namu: An Ex-Hunter Looks Back, No Regrets In His Wake," *The Seattle Times*, November 23, 1997.

[177] Federal Register, "Endangered and Threatened Wildlife and Plants: Endangered Status for Southern Resident Killer Whales," National Marine Fisheries Service (NMFS), National Oceanic and Atmospheric

Administration (NOAA), Commerce Department, Vol. 70, No. 222, November 18, 2005.

[178] Erich Hoyt, *Orca: The Whale Called Killer* (Rochester, NY: Camden House, 1990).

[179] Pollard, *Puget Sound Whales*, 33.

[180] Ibid, 43.

[181] Ibid, 48.

[182] Ibid, 120.

[183] *Ocean Star*, August 1983, "Hearing Set On Plan To Capture Whales," 2.

[184] Whale & Dolphin Conservation, whales.org, "Wild and Free Solo Ride," accessed April 2, 2017.

[185] Pollard, *Puget Sound Whales*, 99.

[186] Neate, Rupert, "SeaWorld sees profits plunge 84% as customers desert controversial park," *The Guardian*, August 6, 2015.

[187] Ibid.

[188] Whale & Dolphin Conservation, "Action Alert: Corky Serves 30 Years," December 9, 1999.

[189] Personal interview, March 2017.

[190] Lottie Roeder Roth, *History of Whatcom County Volume 1* (Chicago: Pioneer Historical Publishing Company, 1926).

[191] *All Point Bulletin*, January 1982.

[192] *All Point Bulletin*, February 1997.

[193] *Ocean Star*, March 1977.

[194] *All Point Bulletin*, October 2009.

[195] *All Point Bulletin*, April 2008.

[196] Arthur Finch, Secretary, Point Roberts Harbor Committee, "Point Roberts: Washington: A Look at the Past with a View to the Future," Point Roberts, November, 1971, 17.

[197] Paul Muldoon, *International Joint Commission and Point Roberts: A Venture into a New Area of Concern* (Hamilton: McMaster University, September 1983), 114.

[198] Ibid.

[199] *Point Roberts Guide*, "Stormy Weather," March 1972, 14.

[200] *Ocean Star*, August 1977.

[201] *Ocean Star*, July 1991, "Marina Shoreline Permit Approved, With Conditions", 3.

[202] *Ocean Star*, February 1982.

[203] Tristan Hopper, "Point Roberts, Washington: A Little Slice of The U.S., Only Accessible Through Canada," *National Post*, February 27, 2012.
[204] *All Point Bulletin*, January 2004.
[205] *All Point Bulletin*, November 2007.
[206] *All Point Bulletin*, April 1995.
[207] *All Point Bulletin*, September 1995.
[208] *All Point Bulletin*, October 1998.
[209] *All Point Bulletin*, April 1997.
[210] *Ocean Star*, March 1977.
[211] *Westside Record-Journal*, July 12, 1989.
[212] *All Point Bulletin*, September 1987.

CHAPTER 3 ENDNOTES

[213] Jill Foran, *Vancouver's Old-Time Scoundrels: Gassy Jack's Exploits and Other Skulduggery* (Victoria: Heritage House, 2003), 46-7.
[214] *The Blaine Journal*, "As They Found It," December 12, 1889.
[215] Lottie Roeder Roth, *History of Whatcom County Volume 1* (Chicago: Pioneer Historical Publishing Company, 1926), 242.
[216] Roth, 215.
[217] Ibid, 242.
[218] Ibid.
[219] *All Point Bulletin*, October 1989.
[220] Don Meikle, *Point Roberts Cemetery 1914 – 2006* (Point Roberts, WA, 2006), 3.
[221] *Ocean Star*, November 6, 1980.
[222] Phil Dougherty, "Point Roberts – Thumbnail History," Essay 9158, Historylink.org, September 15, 2009.
[223] *The Bellingham Bay Evening Express*, "Squatters," Vol. 5, No. 6, April 7, 1893, 1.
[224] George Orwell, *Homage to Catalonia* (London: Heinemann Octopus, 1938), ch. 1.
[225] Jose Peirats, *Anarchists in the Spanish Revolution* (London: Freedom Press, 1990), 117-21.
[226] Frank Mintz, *Anarchism and Workers' Self-Management in Revolutionary Spain* (Oakland: AK Press, 2013), ch. 2.
[227] Personal interview, March 2017.

[228] Robert Neuwirth, *Shadow Cities: A Billion Squatters, A New Urban World* (London: Routledge, 2004).
[229] Kesia Reeve, "Squatting Since 1945: The enduring relevance of material need," in Peter Somerville and Nigel Sprigings, *Housing and Social Policy,* London: Routledge, 197–216.
[230] Runa Thordarson, *Echoes from the Past* (Point Roberts, 1975), 16.
[231] A significant portion of the souls living on Point Roberts between 1892 and 1940 were transient cannery workers. We'll investigate the Point Roberts canneries in detail in chapter 4, but in terms of eras of settlement on Point Roberts, they were an important part of the local economy. Hidden from view as they worked from dawn to dusk inside the canneries, they lived in dormitories or outdoor camps adjacent to the canneries. They lived here only during the summer months and were not counted in the local population.
[232] Richard Clark, *Point Roberts, USA: the History of a Canadian Enclave* (Bellingham: Textype Publishing, 1980), 53.
[233] Personal interview, April 2017.
[234] Ibid.
[235] *Ocean Star*, June 1980.
[236] Personal interview, April 2017.
[237] *Ocean Star*, February 1980.
[238] Personal interview, July 2017.
[239] *Ocean Star*, June 1980.
[240] Paul Muldoon, *International Joint Commission and Point Roberts: A Venture into a New Area of Concern* (Hamilton: McMaster University, September 1983), 102.
[241] *Point Roberts Guide*, 1972.
[242] *All Point Bulletin*, January 2004.
[243] *Ocean Star*, July 1978.
[244] *All Point Bulletin*, June 1991.
[245] Funbeach, website, "Public Beach Access: What's Legal, What's Not," Funbeach.org (accessed Aug 28, 2016).
[246] Brian Kelly, "Beach Rights: This Sand is Your Sand, This Sand is My Sand," *The South Whidbey Record*, August 26, 2009, http://www.southwhidbeyrecord.com/news/54854032.html# (accessed May 18, 2016).
[247] Ibid.

[248] (US v Winans 198 US 371 1905), Daniel Boxberger, *To Fish In Common: The Ethnohistory of Lummi Indian Salmon Fishing* (Seattle: University of Washington Press, 2000), 88.

[249] Ibid.

[250] Christopher Dunagan, "The Legal Dilemma of Beach Walking," *Kitsap Sun*, July 5, 2010. http://www.kitsapsun.com/news/local/the-legal-dilemma-of-beach-walking-ep-419637973-357591681.html (accessed May 18, 2016).

[251] Kelly.

[252] Dunagan.

[253] Ibid.

[254] Funbeach.

[255] Dunagan.

[256] Ibid.

[257] Ibid.

[258] Ibid.

[259] WAC 173-26-201(3)(c)(vi) and RCW 35.79.035, "Shoreline Public Access," Shoreline Master Program, Department of Ecology, State of Washington, January 6, 2011, chapter 9, 5-7.

[260] Ibid, 7.

[261] Dunagan.

[262] *Ocean Star*, October 1984.

[263] Drew Pettus, "Problems in Administrating Point Roberts, Washington," report to county government, December 31, 1969, 18.

[264] Personal interview, April 2017.

[265] *Ocean Star*, August 1977.

[266] *All Point Bulletin*, July 2011.

[267] Stefan Einarsson, *A History of Icelandic Literature* (New York: Johns Hopkins for the American Scandinavian Foundation, 1957), 263.

[268] Muldoon, 97.

[269] Personal interview, April 2017.

[270] *Ocean Star*, May 1982.

[271] *Bellingham Herald*, "Is U.S. to Lose Point Roberts?," December 3, 1950, 9.

[272] Muldoon, 107.

[273] Ibid.

[274] *Bellingham Herald*, April 13, 1952.

[275] Ibid, 116.

276 Moira Farrow, "What Point Roberts Scheme 'Really' Means", *Vancouver Sun*, 26 January 1974, 6.

277 *Bellingham Herald*, "Is U.S. to Lose Point Roberts?," December 3, 1950, 9.

278 *Ocean Star*, October 1980.

279 Donez Xiques, *Margaret Laurence: The Making of a Writer* (Toronto: Dundurn, 2005) 270.

280 *Ocean Star*, May 1980.

281 BCLocalNews.com, "George C. Reifel: Beer baron, rumrunner, and conservationist," February 15, 2013. www.bclocalnews.com/news/191251391.html (accessed Feb 4, 2017).

282 Ibid.

283 Ibid.

284 *All Point Bulletin*, April 1988.

285 *All Point Bulletin*, April 1992.

286 *All Point Bulletin*, November 1995.

287 Personal interview, July 2017.

288 Gwen Szychter, *Chewassen, Tsawwassen or Chiltinm: The Land Facing the Sea* (Delta, 2007), 28-9.

289 Movoto.com.

290 *All Point Bulletin*, February 1993.

291 *All Point Bulletin*, April 2001.

292 Ibid.

293 http://segmentationsolutions.nielsen.com/mybestsegments, accessed August 2017.

294 KUOW-FM, "Do Pacific Northwesterners have an accent?" http://kuow.org/post/do-pacific-northwesterners-have-accent

295 Marjorie Mann, "Dialect Contact and Dialect Transition: A Case Study (of Point Roberts USA)," Working Papers of the Linguistics Circle of the University of Victoria, Vol. 8, Nr. 1 (1989), 60.

296 Ibid.

297 Ibid, 61.

298 Ibid, 62.

299 Ibid.

300 Ibid, 71.

301 Ibid, 69.

302 Ibid, 59.

303 Ibid, 64.

[304] Ibid, 69.

[305] Ibid, 66.

[306] Eagleskyenet.com, Eagle Nest Map, eagleskyenet.com/eagle-nest-map/, accessed May 20, 2017.

[307] Personal interview, April 2017.

[308] Phuong Le, "Lucrative Dungeness crab fishery faces threat from acidic oceans," *Bellingham Herald*, September 22, 2016.

[309] Kie Relyea, "Lost Nets, Crab Post Pulled from Whatcom County Waters," *Bellingham Herald*, May 27, 2015.

[310] Washington Deptartment of Fish & Wildlife, "History of Puget Sound Commercial Dungeness Crab Fishery," accessed May 1, 2017.

[311] "Pacific Coast News," *Spokane Spokesman-Review*, August 15, 1897.

[312] *All Point Bulletin*, September 1987.

[313] *Ocean Star*, June 1988.

[314] *All Point Bulletin*, July 1999.

[315] *Ocean Star*, April 1984.

[316] Anne Murray, "Anne Murray: From snakes to spawn, wildlife congregations show richness of local habitat," *The Georgia Straight*, March 31, 2015.

[317] Personal interview, April 2017.

[318] Murray, "Anne Murray."

[319] *Ocean Star*, November 1983.

[320] *Point Roberts Guide*, "Deer Extinction Feared," July 1971, 10.

[321] *Point Roberts Guide*, "Social Notes," August 1971, 15.

[322] *All Point Bulletin*, November 2005.

[323] *All Point Bulletin*, December 1999.

[324] *All Point Bulletin*, June 2002.

[325] *All Point Bulletin*, April 1993.

[326] *All Point Bulletin*, November 1988.

[327] *All Point Bulletin*, December 1998.

[328] Ibid.

CHAPTER 4 ENDNOTES

[329] Mark Robbins and Steve Wolff, "Defining Lily Point," Sept 14, 2010, www.ross-park.net/apamaples/docs/defining_lily_point_v3_final (accessed February 4, 2017), 11; Personal interview, April 2017.

[330] *Ocean Star*, February 1979.

331 *Ocean Star*, April 1982.

332 *All Point Bulletin*, June 1988.

333 *All Point Bulletin*, July 2001.

334 *All Point Bulletin*, November 2007.

335 Earth Observatory at NASA, "Closeup on Forests of the Pacific Northwest," February 17, 2012, https://earthobservatory.nasa.gov/IOTD//view.php?id=76699

336 Personal interview, March 2017.

337 Personal interview, April 2017.

338 Maclachlan, Morag, ed. *The Fort Langley Journals, 1827-1830* (Vancouver: University of British Columbia Press, 1998), 123.

339 C. P. Newcombe, ed., *Menzies – Journal of Vancouver's Voyages April to October, 1792* (Victoria, BC: Archives of British Columbia Memoir, 5), 60.

340 Jonathan Raban, *Passage to Juneau: A Sea and its Meanings* (New York: Vintage Departures, 1999) 78.

341 Daniel Boxberger, *To Fish In Common: The Ethnohistory of Lummi Indian Salmon Fishing* (Seattle: University of Washington Press, 2000), 21.

342 Lissa Wadewitz, *The Nature of Borders: Salmon, Boundaries and Bandits on the Salish Sea* (Seattle: Center for the Study of the Pacific Northwest and University of Washington Press, 2012), 27.

343 Ibid, 6.

344 Ibid, 7.

345 Raban, 105.

346 Ibid, 103.

347 Over a dozen spellings of Cheltenem were encountered during research.

348 Boxberger, *To Fish in Common*, 13.

349 Wadewitz, *Nature of Borders*, 22.

350 Wadewitz, *Nature of Borders*, 28.

351 Boxberger, *To Fish in Common*, 13.

352 Wadewitz, *Nature of Borders*, 22.

353 Boxberger, *To Fish in Common*, 15.

354 Wadewitz, *Nature of Borders*, 59.

355 Ibid, 57.

356 Ibid, 61.

357 Ibid, 64-5.

358 Ibid, 64.

[359] Boxberger, *To Fish in Common*, 29.

[360] Richard Clark, *Point Roberts, USA: The History of a Canaidan Exclave* (Bellingham: Textype Publishing, 1980), 80.

[361] *The Bellingham Bay Mail*, April 6, 1878, 3.

[362] Lottie Roeder Roth, *History of Whatcom County Volume 1* (Chicago: Pioneer Historical Publishing Company, 1926), 431.

[363] Ibid.

[364] Wadewitz, *Nature of Borders*, 159.

[365] Laugi Thorstenson, *A Short Story of a Long Life: Eight Decades of Memories* (Point Roberts: self-published, 1987), 40.

[366] Boxberger, *To Fish in Common*, 53.

[367] Frances Herring, *Among the People of British Columbia* (London: T. Fisher Unwin, 1903), 280.

[368] *Point Roberts Guide*, August 1971, 15.

[369] Runa Thordarson, "Echoes from the Past," 1975, 19.

[370] Thorstenson, "A Short Story," 11.

[371] Point Roberts Historical Society sign, Lily Point Park.

[372] Ella Van Oosten, *Point Roberts Guide*, "Point Pioneers in Review: Jesse Thompson," August 1972, 15.

[373] *Point Roberts Guide*, "Point Pioneers in Review: Portrait of Laugi and Jonas Thorstenson," August 1971, 3.

[374] Boxberger, *To Fish in Common*, 49.

[375] Yelm History Project, "Usual & Accustomed Places I – The Medicine Creek Treaty," May 7, 2010, www.yelmhistoryproject.com/?p=907, accessed July 13, 2017.

[376] Boxberger, *To Fish in Common*, 44.

[377] Wadewitz, *Nature of Borders*, 133.

[378] Ibid, 159.

[379] Boxberger, *To Fish in Common*, 77.

[380] *All Point Bulletin*, July 1999.

[381] Boxberger, *To Fish in Common*, 77.

[382] Ibid, 73.

[383] Joshua Stilts, *Whatcom Fish Tales: A Historical Look at the County's Seafood Industry* (Bellingham: Village Books, 2016), 13.

[384] Roth, 666.

[385] Stilts, *Whatcom Fish Tales*, 16.

[386] Latte Republic, website, "A Working Day in a Cannery," April 22, 2008 http://latterepublic1.blogspot.com/2008/04/working-day-in-cannery.html

[387] Wadewitz, *Nature of Borders*, 129.
[388] Ibid, 156.
[389] Stilts, *Whatcom Fish Tales*, 12.
[390] Murray, Anne, *Tracing Our Past: A Heritage Guide to Boundary Bay* (Delta, BC: Nature Guides BC, 2009), 126.
[391] Wadewitz, 152.
[392] Murray, *Tracing Our Past*, 125.
[393] Clark, *Point Roberts, USA*, 81.
[394] Ibid, 51-52.
[395] Alaska Packers Association records 1841-1989, Center for Pacific Northwest Studies, Heritage Resources, Western Washington University, Bellingham WA.
[396] Point Roberts Historical Society.
[397] Thorstenson, "A Short Story," 17.
[398] Boxberger, *To Fish in Common*, 53.
[399] Wadewitz, *Nature of Borders*, 75.
[400] Stilts, *Whatcom Fish Tales*, 43.
[401] Wadewitz, *Nature of Borders*, 118.
[402] Stilts, *Whatcom Fish Tales*, 43.
[403] Wadewitz, *Nature of Borders*, 145.
[404] Wadewitz, *Nature of Borders*, 97.
[405] *Blaine Journal*, May 17, 1895.
[406] Wadewitz, *Nature of Borders*, 100.
[407] Boxberger, *To Fish in Common*, 83.
[408] Kris Lomedico, personal interview.
[409] Boxberger, *To Fish in Common*, 86.
[410] *Ocean Star*, March 1979.
[411] "Northwest Corner of the U.S.," *The Blaine Journal, Homeseeker's Edition*, April 1909, 8.
[412] *All Point Bulletin*, October 2003.
[413] Point Roberts Historical Society, "This Old House" lecture series, July 16, 2016.
[414] Boxberger, *To Fish in Common*, 63.
[415] Wadewitz, *Nature of Borders*, 104.
[416] *Point Roberts Guide*, July 1971, 6.
[417] Thorstenson, "A Short Story," 5.
[418] Bill Olson, "Point Pioneers in Review: A Portrait of the Olsons," *Point Roberts Guide*, July 1972, 3.

[419] Thorstenson, "A Short Story," 13.

[420] Charles Pierce Le Warne, *Utopias on Puget Sound 1885-1915* (Seattle: University of Washington Press, 1975), 3.

[421] Ibid, 3.

[422] Ibid, 84-85.

[423] John Sabella, "Sockeye and the Age of Sail: the Story of the Alaska Packers Association," video, April 22, 2011, https://www.youtube.com/watch?v=qN55l8ejhdU

[424] Wadewitz, *Nature of Borders*, 108.

[425] Ibid, 113.

[426] *Ocean Star*, November 1981.

[427] Wadewitz, *Nature of Borders*, 71.

[428] Ibid, 89.

[429] Ibid, 122.

[430] Ibid, 128.

[431] Ibid, 124.

[432] Ibid, 131.

[433] Ibid, 132.

[434] Ibid, 130.

[435] Ibid, 124.

[436] Ibid, 127.

[437] Ibid, 130.

[438] Ibid, 125.

[439] Ibid, 126.

[440] Ibid, 134.

[441] Ibid, 135.

[442] Ibid, 142.

[443] Ibid, 148.

[444] Ibid, 149.

[445] Ibid, 142.

[446] Thorstenson, "A Short Story," 45.

[447] Wilson Criscione, "Nearly 700 illegal crab pots seized in waters near Blaine," *Bellingham Herald*, September 24, 2015, www.bellinghamherald.com/news/local/crime/article36471936.html (accessed August 11, 2016).

[448] Boxberger, *To Fish in Common*, 67.

[449] Richard Clark, *Social Change in an American Exclave Community* (Bellingham, 1969).

[450] George Moskovita, *Living Off the Pacific Ocean Floor* (Corvallis, OR: Oregon State University Press, 2015), 21-22.
[451] Ibid, 12.
[452] Ibid, 26-27.
[453] Ibid, 14.
[454] Ibid, 133.
[455] Personal interview, December 2015.
[456] Moskovita, *Living Off the Pacific Ocean Floor*, 128.
[457] Personal interview, March 2017.
[458] Robert Ruby and John Brown, *Esther Ross: Stillaguamish Champion* (Norman OK: University of Oklahoma Press, 2001), 103. Based on interviews with Georgene Swenson on December 15, 1995 and January 3, 1996.
[459] Personal interview, March 2017.
[460] *Ocean Star*, January 1977.
[461] *All Point Bulletin*, October 1994.
[462] *Ocean Star*, April 1982.
[463] *All Point Roberts*, October 2006.
[464] *Ocean Star*, February 1978.
[465] *Ocean Star*, July 1979.
[466] *Ocean Star*, March 1980.
[467] *Ocean Star*, February 1984, 1.
[468] *Ocean Star*, May 1984.
[469] *Ocean Star*, August 1984.
[470] *Ocean Star*, December 1984.
[471] *Ocean Star*, October 1984, 4.
[472] *All Point Bulletin*, March 1991.
[473] *All Point Bulletin*, August 1994, September 1994.
[474] Kenneth Cooper, Address to Whatcom County Council Planning Commission, "Partial Lily Point Re-Zoning Hearing," Bellingham, March 24, 1993.
[475] *All Point Bulletin*, August 1997.
[476] *All Point Bulletin*, November 2003.
[477] *All Point Bulletin*, December 2004.
[478] *All Point Bulletin*, July 2007.
[479] All Point Bulletin, July 2008.
[480] Ibid.
[481] *Ocean Star*, December 1980.

482 *Ocean Star*, October 1980.

CHAPTER 5 ENDNOTES

483 *Ocean Star*, March 1981.

484 Richard Clark, *Point Roberts, USA: The History of a Canadian Enclave* (Bellingham: Textype Publishing, 1980), 104.

485 *Point Roberts Guide*, "Point Roberts Community Association," June 1971, 6.

486 *All Point Bulletin*, February 1993.

487 *All Point Bulletin*, March 1993.

488 *All Point Bulletin*, January 1995.

489 *All Point Bulletin*, May 1999.

490 *All Point Bulletin*, July 2002.

491 *All Point Bulletin*, September 2002.

492 *All Point Bulletin*, August 1995.

493 *All Point Bulletin*, December 1992.

494 Paul Muldoon, *International Joint Commission and Point Roberts: A Venture into a New Area of Concern* (Hamilton: McMaster University, September 1983), 103.

495 *Ocean Star*, December 1979.

496 *All Point Bulletin*, April 1988.

497 Linda Allen, editor, *The Rainy Day Song Book: Traditional and Contemporary Songs of the Northwest* (Bellingham: Whatcom Museum & Fairhaven Press, 1980).

498 Paddy Graber, "The Re-Grading Tale of 1970," song, 1978.

499 Ibid.

500 *Ocean Star*, August 1983.

501 *Ocean Star*, June 1983.

502 *All Point Bulletin*, June 2004.

503 *Ocean Star*, June 1980.

504 *All Point Bulletin*, August 1994.

505 Laugi Thorstenson, *A Short Story of a Long Life: Eight Decades of Memories* (Point Roberts, self-published, 1987), 51.

506 *Ocean Star*, July 1978.

507 Personal interview, June 2016.

508 *Point Roberts Guide*, "Report: Annual Meeting, Point Roberts Community Association," June 1972, 5.

[509] *Point Roberts Guide*, "Plans to Develop Local Park," September 1972, 3.

[510] *Point Roberts Guide*, "Point Roberts Community Park," December 1972, 12.

[511] *All Point Bulletin*, June 1988.

[512] George Elsner, "Point Pioneers in Review: A Portrait of the Elsners," *Point Roberts Guide*, June 1972, 3.

[513] Margret Thordarson Kragnes and Shannon Tomsen, *The Story of Ben's Daughter: Margret Thordarson Kragnes* (Point Roberts: self-published, 2011), 14.

[514] *Ocean Star*, February 1978.

[515] *All Point Bulletin*, October 1993.

[516] *All Point Bulletin*, February 2005.

[517] Thorstenson, *A Short Story*, 4.

[518] Ron Rockey, Master Warrant Officer, MMM CD, Retired; "A Dry Land Sailor Comes of Age," http://firehouse651.com/anedrylandsailor.htm (accessed February 4, 2017).

[519] Carl Julius, "Point Pioneers in Review: Portrait of the Juliuses," *Point Roberts Guide*, May 1972, 3.

[520] *Ocean Star*, October 1976.

[521] *All Point Roberts*, November 2007.

[522] Paul Muldoon, *International Joint Commission and Point Roberts: A Venture into a New Area of Concern* (Hamilton: McMaster University, September 1983), 104.

[523] *Bellingham Herald*, "Is U.S. to Lose Point Roberts?," December 3, 1950, 9.

[524] *All Point Bulletin*, April 1995.

[525] *All Point Bulletin*, February 2007.

[526] *All Point Bulletin*, March 2005.

[527] *All Point Bulletin*, October 2015.

[528] *Ocean Star*, April 1981.

[529] Areavibes, http://www.areavibes.com/point+roberts-wa/crime/ (accessed July 2016).

[530] Personal interview, June 2016.

[531] Gerald Bellett, *Age of Secrets: The Conspiracy that Toppled Richard Nixon and the Hidden Death of Howard Hughes* (Minneapolis: Voyageur Press, 1995), chapter 4.

[532] Ibid.

[533] Ibid, chapter 9.

534 Ibid, chapter 8.

535 Ibid, chapter 10.

536 Ibid.

537 Larry DuBois and Laurence Gonzales, "Hughes, Nixon and the CIA: The Watergate Conspiracy Woodward and Bernstein Missed," *Playboy*, September 1976.

538 Bellett, *Age of Secrets*, chapter 11.

539 Ibid.

540 Ibid.

541 Ibid.

542 Ibid, chapter 14.

543 Ibid, chapter 13.

544 Ibid, chapter 15.

545 Ibid.

546 Ibid, chapter 18.

547 Ibid, chapter 15.

548 Ibid, chapter 5.

549 *Point Roberts Guide*, "Gravel Pit Management explains excavation operation," August 3, 1973, 4.

CHAPTER 6 ENDNOTES

550 *All Point Bulletin*, March 2000.

551 Point Roberts Historical Society library archives.

552 *All Point Bulletin*, February 2009.

553 Susan Roy, *These Mysterious People Shaping History and Archaeology in a Northwest Coast Community* (Montreal: McGill/Queen's University Press, October 2010), 240.

554 Ibid.

555 Susan Roy, ""Who Were These Mysterious People?" -- çc̓sna:m, the Marpole Midden, and the Dispossession of Aboriginal Lands in British Columbia," *British Columbia Studies* (152, Winter 2006–2007): 67–95.

556 Anne Murray, *Tracing Our Past: A Heritage Guide to Boundary Bay* (Delta BC: NatureGuides BC, 2008), 6.

557 Brian Thom, "The Whalen Farm Site," University of Victoria, May 1997), http://www.web.uvic.ca/~bthom1/Media/pdfs/archaeology/whalen-new.htm (accessed 27 January 2016).

558 Ibid.

559 *All Point Bulletin*, July 2001.
560 Point Roberts Historical Society library archives.
561 Thom.
562 Murray, *Tracing Our Past*, 25.
563 Ibid.
564 Ibid.
565 Ibid.
566 Ibid, 33.
567 Mark Robbins and Steve Wolff, "Defining Lily Point," Sept 14, 2010, 6. http://www.ross-park.net/apamaples/docs/ defining_lily_point_v3_final.pdf
568 *All Point Bulletin*, October 2002
569 Personal interview, April 2017.
570 Personal interview, March 2017.
571 Ibid.
572 *Ocean Star*, March 1977.
573 Gwen Szychter, *Chewassen, Tsawwassen or Chiltinm: The Land Facing the Sea* (Delta, 2007), 13.
574 *Westside Record-Journal,* December 7, 1988.
575 Point Roberts Historical Society library archives.
576 Ibid.
577 Ibid.
578 *All Point Bulletin*, July 1999.
579 Point Roberts Historical Society library archives.
580 Ibid.
581 *All Point Bulletin*, July 1999.
582 Point Roberts Historical Society, library archives.
583 Ibid.
584 Point Roberts Historical Society, "This Old House" lecture series, July 9, 2016.
585 Point Roberts Historical Society, library archives.
586 *All Point Bulletin*, November 2000.
587 Point Roberts Historical Society, "This Old House" lecture series, July 9, 2016.
588 *All Point Bulletin*, November 2000.
589 Point Roberts Historical Society, library archives.
590 *Ocean Star*, October 1979.
591 Point Roberts Historical Society, library archives.

[592] Not to be confused with Waters' larger store on the west side of Point Roberts, which we'll discuss in Chapter 8.

[593] Point Roberts Historical Society, library archives.

[594] Ibid.

[595] *All Point Bulletin*, September 1997.

[596] *All Point Bulletin*, June 1992.

[597] *All Point Bulletin*, January 2007.

[598] *Ocean Star*, June 1981.

[599] Ibid.

[600] *Ocean Star*, January 1983.

[601] *Ocean Star*, September 1983.

[602] *Ocean Star*, July 1984.

[603] *All Point Bulletin*, May 2000.

[604] *Westside Record-Journal*, January 25, 1989.

[605] *All Point Bulletin*, July 1999.

[606] *All Point Bulletin*, August 1987.

[607] *All Point Bulletin*, June 1986.

[608] *Ocean Star*, December 1977.

[609] Robert Gray, "The Santa Ship," *Scouting*, November-December 1990, 27.

[610] Ibid, 51.

[611] Ibid.

[612] *Ocean Star*, December 1977.

[613] Al Booze, "Santa Claus, Ahoy!" *Eugene Register-Guard*, Decmeber 15, 1968, 11.

[614] Gray, *Santa Ship*, 50.

[615] *All Point Bulletin*, October 2009.

[616] Jason Kersten, "The Airplane Thief," *Rolling Stone*, 1104, May 13, 2010.

[617] Ibid.

[618] Ibid.

[619] Ibid.

[620] *All Point Bulletin*, November 2004.

[621] Dora Thompson, "Point Pioneers in Review: Jeppe Thompson," *Point Roberts Guide*, August 1972, 11.

[622] Ibid.

[623] *All Point Bulletin*, May 2009.

[624] *All Point Bulletin*, May 1999.

[625] *Ocean Star*, May 1979.

CHAPTER 7 ENDNOTES

[626] *Ocean Star*, June 1981.
[627] Drew Pettus, "Problems in Administering Point Roberts, Washington," report to county, December 31, 1969, 22.
[628] *All Point Bulletin*, January 1986.
[629] *All Point Bulletin*, May 1991.
[630] *Ocean Star*, July 1982.
[631] *All Point Bulletin*, August 1991.
[632] *All Point Bulletin*, February 1995.
[633] *All Point Bulletin*, January 2009.
[634] Point Roberts Historical Society, "This Old House" lecture series, July 23, 2016.
[635] Pettus, "Problems," 23.
[636] *Ocean Star*, February 1987.
[637] *Ocean Star*, September 1985.
[638] *All Point Bulletin*, August 1986.
[639] *All Point Bulletin*, July 1987.
[640] *All Point Bulletin*, May 1988.
[641] Gwen Szychter, *Chewassen, Tsawwassen or Chiltinm: The Land Facing the Sea* (Delta, 2007), 160.
[642] *Ocean Star*, June 1981.
[643] *All Point Bulletin*, February 2013.
[644] Point Roberts Historical Society library archives.
[645] Pettus, "Problems," 24.
[646] *Vancouver Sun*, "Hearings on Point Roberts Set by Border Corrmission," May 28, 1971.
[647] Carol Woodman, "Point Roberts a Unique Place to Reside," Carol Woodman's Adventures, http://carolwoodman.blogspot.com, September 14, 2008.
[648] Ibid.
[649] *Ocean Star*, December 1976.
[650] *Ocean Star*, October 1981.
[651] *Ocean Star*, September 1984.
[652] Sonja Nelson, "Water Trade Talks Resume in January," *Ocean Star*, January 1982.
[653] Carolyn Price, "There is Water," *Ocean Star*, December 1982.

654 *Ocean Star*, September 1984.

655 *All Point Bulletin*, "Water Pact Sealed," May 1988, 1.

656 *All Point Bulletin*, June 1991.

657 *All Point Bulletin*, May 1988.

658 *All Point Bulletin*, June 1988.

659 *Westside Record-Journal*, August 9, 1989.

660 Point Roberts Water District notes, Western Washington University Archives, Bellingham, Washington.

661 *All Point Bulletin*, August 1990.

662 *All Point Bulletin*, January 2004.

663 *All Point Bulletin*, July 1991.

664 *Ocean Star*, March 1977.

665 James Hughes, "Point Roberts Could be State's Top Attraction: Freeport or Another Monaco Suggested for Orphaned Area," *Seattle Argus*, October 23, 1964.

666 Decker, "Economic Otltlook for Point Roberts and Effects of a Proposed Harbour," 1965.

667 Dan Coughlin, "Point Roberts as Trade Site," *Seattle Post-Intelligencer*, March 23, 1969.

668 *All Point Bulletin*, August 2002.

669 *All Point Bulletin*, February 2002.

670 *All Point Bulletin*, January 2004.

671 *All Point Bulletin*, February 2002.

672 *All Point Bulletin*, February 2004.

673 Meg Olson, *All Point Bulletin*, December 2013.

674 Ibid.

675 *Ocean Star*, April 1983.

676 *Ocean Star*, June 1983.

677 *All Point Bulletin*, March 1994.

678 *All Point Bulletin*, March 1989.

679 *All Point Bulletin*, March 1992.

680 *All Point Bulletin*, May 1985.

681 *Ocean Star*, September 1982.

682 *All Point Bulletin*, November 1985.

683 *All Point Bulletin*, September 1991.

684 *All Point Bulletin*, November 1991.

685 *All Point Bulletin*, June 1995.

686 *All Point Bulletin*, July 1991.

687 All Point Bulletin, September 2011, 8.
688 *All Point Bulletin*, February 1989.
689 *All Point Bulletin*, July 1998.
690 Point Roberts Historical Society, "This Old House" lecture series, August 27, 2016.
691 *All Point Bulletin*, September 1992.
692 *Ocean Star*, March 1979.
693 Margret Thordarson Kragnes and Shannon Tomsen, The Story of Ben's Daughter: Margret Thordarson Kragnes (Point Roberts: self-published, 2011), 17.
694 Point Roberts Historical Society, "This Old House" lecture series, August 27, 2016.
695 *Ocean Star*, March 1983.
696 *All Point Bulletin*, November 1987.
697 *All Point Bulletin*, December 1991.
698 *All Point Bulletin*, March 1992.
699 *All Point Bulletin*, September 1992.
700 Sandor Gyarmati, "Point Roberts dulled by sagging Loonie: Merchants in American peninsula feeling the pinch as trips across the line are on the decline," *Delta Optimist*, February 17, 2016.
701 *Ocean Star*, June 1979.
702 *Montreal Gazette*, "B.C. Digs in for 1980 beer drought," July 29, 1980, 6.
703 *Ocean Star*, October 1980.
704 *Ocean Star*, December 1983.
705 *All Point Bulletin*, April 1992.
706 *Ocean Star*, June 1979.
707 *Ocean Star*, June 1979.
708 *Ocean Star*, February 1982.
709 *Canadian Shipper*, "Navigating the Digital Divide: Survey examines challenges of retail logistics," May 20, 2016.
710 Ibid.
711 Ibid.
712 Pat Grubb, "Waiting to get into Canada," *All Point Bulletin*, September 2009.
713 Olson, *All Point Bulletin*, December 2015.
714 *All Point Bulletin*, March 1989.
715 *All Point Bulletin*, February 1987.

[716] Gyarmati.

[717] Dave Gallagher, "Online sales slow in Whatcom border towns as loonie falters," *Bellingham Herald*, March 27, 2016.

[718] Michael Doyle, "Canadian who smuggled rhino horns via Point Roberts gets gored with stiff sentence," *Bellingham Herald*, March 25, 2015.

CHAPTER 8 ENDNOTES

[719] Well, *working* sewers. Technically, Tijuana does have a dated sewer system but it routinely leaks millions of gallons of sewage onto California beaches near the Mexican border.

[720] "Canadians Go South for Fun," *Billboard*, May 8 1943, 58.

[721] William Borders, "Canada's Nationalism Hits an Isolated U.S. Town," *The New York Times*, October 5, 1973, 8.

[722] "Water is Not for Sale," *Globe & Mail*, August 16, 1973.

[723] "The Point Strikes Back!" *Point Roberts Guide*, May 1971, 13.

[724] *Ocean Star*, March 1981.

[725] Kathy McCarthy, "A Bit of U.S. Clinging to Canada, Point Roberts Waits for Boom," *Los Angeles Times*, October 5, 1986. http://articles.latimes.com/1986-10-05/news/mn-4587_1_point-roberts

[726] *Los Angeles Times*, "A woodsy Northwest retreat gets the water it wanted, with a flood of development," November 13, 1989.

[727] Paul Nussbaum, "It's Just A Little Bit Of Canada Cut Off From Mainland, U.S. Town Leads Dual Life," *Philadelphia Inquirer*, December 5, 1988.

[728] *The Seattle Times*, "Point Roberts: Foot In State, Heart In Canada," September 15, 1991.

[729] *Christian Science Monitor*, "As U.S. cracks down on its borders, Canada records a rise in illegal migrants," December 11, 1994.

[730] *All Point Bulletin*, May 2010.

[731] *All Point Bulletin*, December 1998.

[732] Erla Zwingle, "ZIP USA: 98281: Almost Heaven, Almost Canada: What's life like on a five-square-mile (thirteen-square-kilometer) patch of U.S. soil at the tip of a Canadian peninsula?" *National Geographic*, August 2004.

[733] John Pomfret, "The Border's Right Here, but the Debate Is Many Miles Away," *Washington Post*, July 20, 2006.

[734] Tristan Hopper, "Point Roberts, Washington: A Little Slice of The U.S., Only Accessible Through Canada," *National Post*, February 27, 2012.

[735] Larry Pynn, "Point Roberts Feels the Squeeze of the Low Loonie," *Vancouver Sun*, January 15, 2016.

[736] Ken Jennings, "Driving to Point Roberts, Washington? Don't Forget Your Passport," *Conde Nast Traveler*, October 15, 2012.

[737] *Ocean Star*, September 1979.

[738] Charles Hillinger, "Getting to the Point: Canadians Like to Hang Out Where the U.S. Hangs On," *Louisville Courier-Journal*, May 31, 1981.

[739] *Ocean Star*, July 1984.

[740] *Ocean Star*, November 1984, 1.

[741] *Ocean Star*, February 1985.

[742] *Ocean Star*, March 1985.

[743] *All Point Bulletin*, March 2015.

[744] *Ocean Star*, August 1977.

[745] Charles Hillinger, "Getting to the Point, Canadians like to hang out where the U.S. hangs on," *Louisville Courier-Journal*, May 31, 1981

[746] Ibid.

[747] *Ocean Star*, August 1977.

[748] *Ocean Star*, June 1982.

[749] *Ocean Star*, September 1984.

[750] *Ocean Star*, March 1985.

[751] Hillinger, "Getting to the Point."

[752] *Ocean Star*, October 1984.

[753] *Westside Record-Journal*, October 4, 1989.

[754] *Ocean Star*, October 1979.

[755] *Ocean Star*, February 1980.

[756] *Ocean Star*, July 1980.

[757] *Ocean Star*, December 1977.

[758] *Point Roberts Guide*, 1972.

[759] *All Point Bulletin*, April 2005.

[760] *Ocean Star*, July 1980.

[761] *All Point Bulletin*, May 1996.

[762] *Ocean Star*, December 1979.

[763] *All Point Bulletin*, July 2002.

[764] *Ocean Star*, December 1979.

[765] *All Point Bulletin*, July 2001.

[766] Personal interview, March 2017.

[767] *Ocean Star*, May 1977.

[768] *All Point Bulletin*, March 1989.

[769] Point Roberts Historical Society, library archives.

[770] Ibid.

[771] Ibid.

[772] Laugi Thorstenson, *A Short Story of a Long Life: Eight Decades of Memories* (Point Roberts, self-published, 1987), 12.

[773] *All Point Bulletin*, September 1994.

[774] George Moskovita, *Living Off the Pacific Ocean Floor* (Corvallis, OR: Oregon State University Press, 2015), 26.

[775] Point Roberts Historical Society, library archives.

[776] Tristin Hopper, "Medium-rare burgers are taboo in Canada but may not be as perilous as thought," *National Post*, March 2, 2012.

[777] Harry Thompson, "Point Pioneers in Review: Jeppe Thompson," *Point Roberts Guide*, August 1972, 13.

[778] Norman Clark, *The Dry Years: Prohibition and Social Change in Washington* (Seattle: University of Washington Press, 1988), xi.

[779] Ibid.

[780] Personal interview, April 2017.

[781] Point Roberts Historical Society, library archives.

[782] *Ocean Star*, March 1982.

[783] Kenneth Chan, "Tie for B. C. to end its draconian laws on alcohol," VanCityBuzz.com, August 25, 2012.

[784] Sarah Berman, "BC's Five Looniest Liquor Laws: Raise a glass to our lush province's most outlandish legal hangovers," TheTyee.ca, December 30, 2011.

[785] Chan.

[786] Berman.

[787] Chan.

[788] Chan.

[789] *All Point Bulletin*, June 2001.

[790] *Billboard*, "Canadians Go South for Fun," May 8 1943, 58.

[791] Ibid.

[792] *Ocean Star*, February 1983.

[793] Hillinger, Getting to the Point.

[794] Ibid.

[795] Ibid.

[796] *All Point Bulletin*, June 2001.

[797] *Ocean Star*, January 1977.

[798] *Ocean Star*, August 1977.

[799] Richbienstock, "Nancy Wilson Recalls the Making of Heart's "Crazy on You"," Guitar World Acoustic Nation Blog, guitarworld.com, August 17, 2015.

[800] Ray Shasho, "Interview: Heart Original Guitarist Roger Fisher "Getting Voted Out Saved My Life!"," Classicrockhereandnow.com, Feb 14, 2012.

[801] Ann & Nancy Wilson, *Kicking & Dreaming: A Story of Heart, Soul, and Rock and Roll* (New York: HarperCollins, 2012), 90.

[802] Richbienstock.

[803] *Ocean Star*, December 1983.

[804] *Ocean Star*, July 1984.

[805] *All Point Bulletin*, November 1995.

[806] *Ocean Star*, November 1980.

[807] John Mackie, "Expo 86: The biggest single catalyst for dramatic change in Vancouver," *Vancouver Sun*, May 6, 2011.

[808] bobbea.com/expo-86/history.html

[809] Ibid.

[810] Doug Ward, "Expo 86: The city opened its door and became more livable, more sophisticated and a lot more interesting," *Vancouver Sun*, April 29, 2006.

[811] Ibid.

[812] Ibid.

[813] Concerts were held at Expo 86 by Harry Belafonte, Anne Murray, Bruce Cockburn, Miles Davis, Wynton Marsalis, Annie Lennox & the Eurythmics, Julio Iglesias, Amy Grant, Loverboy, Liberace, the Mormon Tabernacle Choir, Joan Baez with Don McLean, Kenny Loggins, Lou Rawls & The 5th Dimension, Kim Mitchell, Johnny Cash, Depeche Mode, Joe Jackson, George Thorogood & the Delaware Destroyers, Smokey Robinson, John Denver, The Beach Boys, Air Supply, Peter Paul & Mary, The Manhattan Transfer, The Temptations, k.d. lang, Sheena Easton, Trooper, Bryan Adams, Kool & The Gang, Roy Orbison, Fats Domino and Jerry Lee Lewis. The fair brought comedians including Bill Cosby, Bob Newhart, Bob Hope, Red Skelton, Joan Rivers, Howie Mandel and George Burns.

[814] Ra McGuire, "My Life with the F-Word," The Loop, August 15, 2013, issue 8. www.loopinsight.com

[815] http://pnwbands.com/reef.html

[816] *All Point Bulletin*, March 1993.

[817] *All Point Bulletin*, February 1987.

[818] *All Point Bulletin*, February 2002.

[819] http://pnwbands.com/breakersthe.html

[820] *All Point Bulletin*, June 2001.

[821] *All Point Bulletin*, April 1993.

CHAPTER 9 ENDNOTES

[822] *Vancouver Sun*, "Joint Park Studied for Point Roberts," March 26, 1965.

[823] Paul Muldoon, *International Joint Commission and Point Roberts: A Venture into a New Area of Concern* (Hamilton: McMaster University, September 1983), 106.

[824] Ibid.

[825] Ibid.

[826] Ibid, 118.

[827] Ibid, 115.

[828] John Decker, "A Study Prepared for the Whatcom County Planning Commission," Bellingham, Washington, 1965.

[829] Muldoon, 119-20.

[830] Richard Clark, *Social Change in an American Exclave Community*, thesis, Bellingham, 1969, 113.

[831] Muldoon, 5.

[832] Ibid, 27.

[833] Ibid, 32.

[834] Ibid, 52.

[835] Ibid, 70-71.

[836] Ibid, 36.

[837] Ibid, 37.

[838] *Edmonton Journal*, "'No Man's Land' Probe Continues," April 24, 1971.

[839] *International Joint Commission Terms of Reference*, 1.

[840] Muldoon, 75-76.

[841] Ibid, 139-140.

[842] Ibid, 141.

[843] Ibid, 143.

[844] Ibid, 146.

[845] *Victoria Daily Colonist*, "Canada, U.S. Pondering Roberts," September 6, 1973.

[846] Muldoon, 148.

[847] *Point Roberts Guide*, July 1972, 2.

[848] Muldoon, 150-151.

[849] Ibid, 147.
[850] International Point Roberts Board, "Report to the International Joint Commission on Solutions to the Problems Facing the Residents of Point Roberts," October 23, 1973, 37.
[851] Muldoon, 154.
[852] IPRB, 1, 13. *Vancouver Sun*, "Committee Works Out Plan to Deal with Point Roberts," September 6, 1973.
[853] Muldoon, 156.
[854] Ibid, 157.
[855] Moria Farrow, "What Point Roberts Scheme 'Really' Means," *Vancouver Sun,* January 26, 1974, 6.
[856] Muldoon, 157.
[857] IPRB, 2.
[858] Muldoon, 158.
[859] *Vancouver Sun*, "Point Roberts Plan Supported," July 17, 1972.
[860] Muldoon, 159.
[861] *Point Roberts Guide*, "Decision Making," August 3, 1973, 2.
[862] IPRB, 37-38.
[863] Ibid, 39.
[864] Muldoon, 160.
[865] Ibid, 161.
[866] IPRB, 3-7, 43-50.
[867] Ibid, 45-46.
[868] Ibid, 52.
[869] Muldoon, 165.
[870] IJC Public Hearings, 77, 250-252, 264-265.
[871] Muldoon, 165.
[872] Ibid, 199-200.
[873] *Vancouver Sun*, "U.S. Officials, Point Roberts' Residents Take Firm Stand Against I.J.C. Park Plan," November 5, 1973.
[874] Muldoon, 204.
[875] Richard Clark, interview with Poul Neilsen, "History and Social Structure of Point Roberts Episode 10," Delta BC: Delta Cable 10, 1980.
[876] IPRB, 10.
[877] Muldoon, 166.
[878] Ibid, 167.
[879] Ibid, 168.

[880] Peter Calamai, "No Man's Land Probe Continues," *Edmonton Journal*, April 24, 1971.

[881] Farrow.

[882] Public Hearings, 163-166, 196-197, 241.

[883] *Point Roberts Guide*, "American Citizens Meet," July 1971, 2.

[884] Ibid, 362-365.

[885] Muldoon, 179.

[886] *Point Roberts Guide*, May 1972, 15.

[887] Muldoon, 176.

[888] IJC Annual Report 1974, Ottawa & Washington, May 1975, 20.

[889] Muldoon, 179-180.

[890] IPRB Supplemental Report, 2.

[891] Ibid, 31.

[892] Ibid, 33.

[893] Muldoon, 183-184.

[894] Ibid, 136.

[895] IPRB Supplemental Report, 10-14.

[896] *Vancouver Sun*, "International Body Shelves Point Roberts Park Plan," October 7, 1974.

[897] Muldoon, 184-185.

[898] Ibid, 185-186.

[899] Ibid, 195.

[900] Ibid, 215-216.

CHAPTER 10 ENDNOTES

[901] Stuart Christie, *Plural Sovereignties and Contemporary Indigenous Literature* (New York: Palgrave Macmillan, 2009), 126.

[902] Olson, *All Point Bulletin*, December 2013.

[903] *Ocean Star*, November 1981.

[904] *All Point Bulletin*, April 1988.

[905] Not that Point Roberts needs another nickname, though "the Point" isn't the most intuitive name – which point?

INDEX

CPSIA information can be obtained
at www.ICGtesting.com
Printed in the USA
FSHW010253160920
73454FS